The Financial Controller and CFO's Toolkit

The Financial Controller and CFO's Toolkit

Lean Practices to Transform Your Finance Team

Third Edition

DAVID PARMENTER

WILEY

Published by John Wiley & Sons, Inc., Hoboken, New Jersey.

The second edition of this book was published in 2011 under the title *Winning CFOs: Implementing and Applying Better Practices*. The first edition was published in 2007 under the title *Pareto's 80/20 Rule for Corporate Accountants*.

Published simultaneously in Canada.

For general information on our other products and services or for technical support, please contact our Customer Care Department within the United States at (800) 762-2974, outside the United States at (317) 572-3993 or fax (317) 572-4002.

Wiley publishes in a variety of print and electronic formats and by print-on-demand. Some material included with standard print versions of this book may not be included in e-books or in print-on-demand. If this book refers to media such as a CD or DVD that is not included in the version you purchased, you may download this material at http://booksupport.wiley.com. For more information about Wiley products, visit www.wiley.com.

Library of Congress Cataloging-in-Publication Data is available:
ISBN 978-1-119-28654-7 (Hardcover)
ISBN 978-1-119-29131-2 (ePDF)
ISBN 978-1-119-29132-9 (ePub)

Cover Design: Wiley
Cover Image: © Kamaga/iStockphoto

Printed in the United States of America

10 9 8 7 6 5 4 3 2 1

Contents

About the Author   ix

Testimonials   xi

Introduction   xiii

Acknowledgments   xxi

PART I: CHANGE—WHY THE NEED AND HOW TO LEAD

Chapter 1: Getting Your Finance Team Future Ready   3

Chapter 2: Leading and Selling the Change   17

PART II: TO BE COMPLETED BEFORE THE NEXT MONTH-END

Chapter 3: Rapid Month-End Reporting: By Working Day Three or Less   29

PART III: TECHNOLOGIES TO ADOPT

Chapter 4: Future-Ready Technologies   49

PART IV: PROGRESS YOU NEED TO MAKE WITHIN THE NEXT SIX MONTHS

Chapter 5: Reduce Accounts Payable Volumes by 60 Percent   77

Chapter 6: Month-End Reporting Refinements   91

Chapter 7: Lean Reporting—Informatively
and Error Free   101

Chapter 8: Lean Board Reporting   135

Chapter 9: A Lean Annual Planning Process—Ten Working
Days or Less!   149

Chapter 10: Lean and Smarter Work Methods   177

Chapter 11: Effective Leadership, Growing
and Retaining Talent   199

Chapter 12: Quick Annual Reporting: Within 15 Working
Days Post Year-End   225

Chapter 13: Managing Your Accounts Receivable   245

Chapter 14: Attracting and Recruiting Talent   249

Chapter 15: Lean Accounting   265

PART V: HOW FINANCE TEAMS CAN HELP THEIR
ORGANIZATIONS GET FUTURE READY
Chapter 16: Implementing Quarterly Rolling Forecasting
and Planning   281

Chapter 17: Finding Your Organization's Operational
Critical Success Factors   315

Chapter 18: Getting Your KPIs to Work   327

Chapter 19: Reporting Performance Measures   351

PART VI: AREAS WHERE COSTLY MISTAKES
CAN BE MADE
Chapter 20: Performance Bonus Schemes   371

Chapter 21: Takeovers and Mergers   387

Chapter 22: The Hidden Costs of Reorganizations and Downsizing   399

Appendix A: Useful Letters and Memos   409

Appendix B: Rules for a Bulletproof Presentation   419

Appendix C: Satisfaction Survey for a Finance Team   427

Index   435

About the Author

David Parmenter is an international writer and speaker who is known for his engaging presentations and practical and informative books. His workshops have created substantial change in many attendees' organizations. David is a leading expert on lean finance team practices, rolling forecasting and planning, and the development of winning key performance indicators (KPIs). His work on KPIs is recognized internationally as a breakthrough in understanding how to make performance measures work. He has delivered interactive workshops in 31 countries over the last 20 years. David has worked for Ernst & Young, BP Oil Ltd., Arthur Andersen, and PricewaterhouseCoopers, and is a fellow of the Institute of Chartered Accountants in England and Wales. He is a regular writer for professional and business journals.

This book is a follow-on from *Pareto's 80/20 Rule for Corporate Accountants* and *Winning CFOs—Implementing and Applying Better Practices*. He is also the author of *Key Performance Indicators: Developing, Implementing and Using Winning KPIs, Key Performance Indicators for Government and Non Profit Agencies: Implementing Winning KPIs*, and *The Leading-Edge Manager's Guide to Success* (all from Wiley).

David Parmenter can be contacted via parmenter@waymark.co.nz or on +64 4 499 0007. His website, www.davidparmenter.com, contains many white papers, articles, and freeware that will be useful to readers to implement change.

Testimonials

What can you expect from this book? Why not read these testimonials on David Parmenter's previous edition of this book and on his workshops and key note addresses.

Praise for the book "Winning CFOs" (the second edition)

Mr. Parmenter has created yet another fine management reference tool with his Winning CFOs book. It reveals how a CFO can be a better manager, and run an accounting and finance function that delivers world-class results. Highly recommended reading for the CFO who is committed to self-improvement. Steven M. Bragg, author of *Accounting Best Practices*

In this timely book, David Parmenter provides CFOs and their finance colleagues with a number of practical guidelines that will enable them to spend less time on the basic accounting routines and more time adding value and becoming a valued business partner. Jeremy Hope, author of *Reinventing the CFO*

The CFO can make a major contribution to value creation by the use of information focusing on the critical value drivers in the business. These practical tools and techniques will be invaluable to the busy CFO.
Ken Lever, CFO, Xchanging plc

Praise for the "Lean Finance Team Processes" workshop

We attended David's course on "Winning Finance Teams" and we have had instant success with our Flash report. My Accounting team managed to get the flash report for November completed by 4.00pm on the second day. The workshop gave us the tools and the mindset to achieve this result. Ron Milne, General Manager Finance, Enware Australia Pty Ltd

The three main highlights for me from attending David Parmenter's "Winning CFO" were; David's tight and punchy delivery style, access to soft copy templates to customise and implement in my organisation, and breakout sessions at the end of each

section. Amanda McPherson, Director of Finance, Melbourne Convention Exhibition Centre

One of our team members attended your lean finance team processes one-day workshop in Sydney and from that we have: reduced our monthly management report (approximately 30 pages) to the A3 report template from the course, shortened our month end process, run daily stand -up meetings (scrums) for those still involved in the month-end process. Kelly Simpson, Australian Financial Controller, Harcourts

These workshops are now available as recorded webinars, see www.davidparmenter.com for details.

Praise for David Parmenter's key note addresses

David Parmenter held a keynote speech and an in-depth session at our two main events (Copenhagen & Tampa, USA). He is a very inspiring speaker with some interesting topics on his agenda. He delivers his messages in a controversial and humoristic way. His session rated as number one among all speakers. Maj Nedergaard, Research & Campaign Manager, Targit

David Parmenter gave a key note address at our one-day Management Accounting Conference. The audience gave him the highest ratings with comments such as "Best speaker ever, thoroughly enjoyed it." Jess Vailima, Conference Coordinator, New Zealand Institute of Chartered Accountants

The two presentations delivered at our annual conference were superb with a high degree of satisfaction from the attendees. Not only were the sessions entertaining they contained profound messages. The electronic templates that David provided attendees have been worth the attendee's conference fee! Carolyn Campbell-Wood, Chief Financial Officer, Australian Medicare Local Alliance

Introduction

I am convinced that corporate accountants, as professionals, want to leave a legacy before they move on. To be remembered they need to have made a permanent improvement to the organization.

Many finance teams are merely processing machines, moving from one deadline to the next, having too little time to invest in being a business partner to budget holders and senior management.

I know this from observation and my own personal experience.

 ## THE THIRD VERSION

This book is a third version, as it follows on from *Pareto's 80/20 Rule for Corporate Accountants* and *Winning CFOs: Implementing and Applying Better Practices*. The book has been restructured to facilitate easier implementation and is accompanied with a 100-page toolkit. The reader can access, free of charge, a PDF of the suggested templates, checklists and templates from www.davidparmenter.com/The_Financial_Controller_and_CFO's_Toolkit.

The better practices in this book are ignored at your peril, as they are based on the wisdom and better practices of over 5,000 accountants whom I have met through delivering my workshops and webcasts around the world.

I would like to add that few, if any, of these practices were used by me when I was a corporate accountant; thus senior management did not shed a tear when I left the organization. It is my mission to ensure CFOs, financial controllers, and management accountants leave a legacy that remains long after they have left the organization.

> *David Parmenter*
> *Writer, Speaker, Facilitator*
> *Helping organizations measure, report, and improve performance*
> Waymark House, 20 John Street, Titahi Bay,
> New Zealand (+ 64 4) 499 0007
> parmenter@waymark.co.nz   www.davidparmenter.com
>
> 15 September 2016
>
> Dear CFO and Financial Controller,
>
> **Invitation to leave a profound legacy in your organization**
>
> This book will cover the better practices that will have a profound impact on the way your finance team functions and help you make a difference as a **leader** and **business partner**. Do you find yourself and your team locked up in the past as historians, still trapped by the archaic annual planning process, constantly fighting fires, and unappreciated by the organization at large? If so, the panacea for you is here.
>
> This book is written from the standpoint of an accountant and observer. It is a book that you need to read before you pass it down to your direct reports. Far too many CFOs have passed on the responsibility of keeping abreast of 21st century lean finance team methods to their younger accounting staff. While the detail is the domain of the younger corporate accountants, continuing learning is a duty that all of us need to shoulder.
>
> This book is designed to transform your contribution, increase your job satisfaction and profile in the organization, and help you leave a legacy in every organization you work for. Please, would you at least read the following chapters:
>
> - Chapter 1 Getting Your Finance Team Future Ready
> - Chapter 2 Leading and Selling the Change
> - Chapter 10 Lean and Smarter Work Methods
> - Chapter 11 Effective Leadership—Growing and Retaining Talent
> - Chapter 16 Implementing Quarterly Rolling Forecasting and Planning
> - Chapters 17 Finding Your Organization's Operational Critical Success Factors

- Chapters 18 Getting Your KPIs to Work
- Chapter 20 Performance Bonus Schemes

Invest 45 minutes of your time to make use of the support materials (webcasts, electronic templates) on www. davidparmenter.com.

I am hopeful that someday in the future we will meet, whether it is at a course or over a coffee. It is my fervent wish that you will be able to say, "I used this book to make a difference." It will mean that both you and I will have left a legacy.

Kind regards,

David Parmenter

HOW TO USE THE BOOK

This book is divided into six parts and appendices. Exhibit I.1 explains the purpose of each section.

THE PDF TOOLKIT

With all my books there is a heavy focus on implementation. The purpose is to prepare the route forward. To second guess the problems the finance team will need to address and set out the major tasks they will need to undertake. Naturally, each implementation will reflect the organization's culture, future-ready status, and the level of commitment from the CFO and his or her direct reports.

The PDF toolkit is to be read and used in conjunction with *The Financial Controller and CFO's Toolkit—Lean Finance Teams' Best Practices*. The location of the templates is indicated in the relevant chapters.

To support your implementing the strategies and best practices in this book, the following electronic media are available:

- Webcasts and recorded presentations (see www.davidparmenter.com/ webcasts). Some of these are free to everyone and some are accessed via a third party for a fee.

EXHIBIT I.1 Book Outline

Section	Outline	Significance
Part I: Change—why the need and how to lead	Covers why there is a need to change and move away from the existing practices. Includes how to sell change to management and staff and lead the change in the organization.	Far too often, change initiatives fail. By following the leading thinkers in this space, John Kotter and Zaffron and Logan, you will be successful in leading the change.
Part II: To be completed before the next month-end	How you can save days out of the month-end close process.	A fast month-end is the first step on the journey to adopting lean finance team practices.
Part III: Technologies to adopt	Focuses on the technologies you need to implement to achieve efficiency and accuracy.	Removing the reliance on Excel spreadsheets that are unsuitable, in order to move forward with appropriate solutions.
Part IV: Progress you need to make within the next six months	Focuses on the areas where the finance team can score the easy goals in the next six months.	The better practices here, if implemented, will free up time so more strategic initiatives can be executed successfully.
Part V: How finance teams can help their organizations get future ready	Focuses on more wide-ranging changes, such as introducing winning key performance indicators and quarterly rolling planning, which will require a heavy investment of time from the finance team.	These modern initiatives will have a profound impact on your organization, with the finance team as the driver of change.
Part VI: Areas where costly mistakes can be made	Focuses on areas where the CFO can and should save the organization from making costly mistakes, such as performance bonus schemes, takeovers, reorganizations, and downsizing.	The CFO's involvement in these strategic issues will have an extensive positive effect on the organization as a whole.
Appendices and the PDF toolkit	The appendices include useful letters and rules for a bulletproof presentation. The companion PDF toolkit is filled with templates and checklists.	These templates, guidelines and diagrams will kick start the implementation process.

- A PDF download of the checklists, draft agendas, questionnaires, and worksheets referred to in the chapters are available from www.davidparmen ter.com/The_Financial_Controller_and_CFO's_Toolkit. The website will refer to a word from a specific page in this book that you need to use as a password to access these free.
- The electronic versions of all the templates and most of the report formats, featured in the book, can be purchased from www.davidparmenter.com.

 ## REPORTING HISTORY OR MAKING IT

The impact of the efficient and effective practices listed in the book will, if implemented, make a major change to the nature of work performed by the accounting team. There will be a migration away from low-value processing activities into the more value-added areas such as advisory, being a business partner with budget holders, and implementing new systems.

As Exhibit I.2 shows, the change in focus should mean we are working smarter, not harder. This change in workload will, over time, lead to the

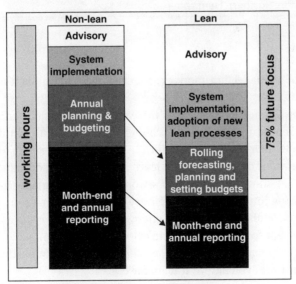

EXHIBIT I.2 Impact of Working Smarter, Not Harder

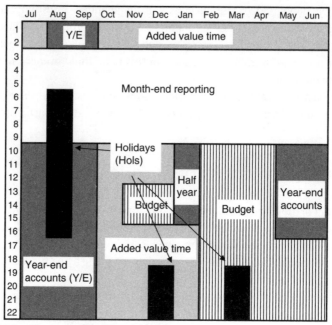

EXHIBIT I.3 The Year's Workload of a Non-Lean Finance Team (Based on a June year-end in the Northern Hemisphere)

formation of a smaller but more experienced accounting team and a better work–life balance.

In many finance teams around the world, far too much time is spent in month-end reporting, the annual accounts, and the annual planning process, as shown in Exhibit I.3. I call these three activities the trifecta of lost opportunities for the accounting team. They leave so little time to add value.

Exhibit I.4 shows how the year's workload will change with shift away from processing into more service delivery work (based on a June year-end in the Northern Hemisphere). The key change is to radically reduce the time the accounting team spends in the trifecta of lost opportunities.

The better practices in this book will approximately double the amount of "added value time" you and your team have.

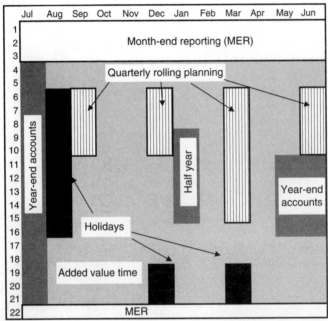

EXHIBIT I.4 The Year's Workload of a Lean Finance Team (Based on a June year-end in the Northern Hemisphere)

Acknowledgments

would like to acknowledge all those accountants who have shared their better practices with me during workshops I have delivered around the world. This book is about their successes; I am merely the communicator.

This book has been influenced by the great writers who have led my thinking. I would especially like to acknowledge the late Jeremy Hope, who was an invaluable mentor for over 10 years, and the finance teams whom I have worked with.

A big thank you to all those who have collaborated on this book and my colleagues (Jennifer and Francesca). A special thanks goes to my wife, Jennifer, who proofread the original submission.

To all of the abovementioned people and all the other people who have been a direction in my life, I say thank you for providing me with the launching pad for the journey I am now on.

PART ONE

Change—Why the Need and How to Lead

1

Getting Your Finance Team Future Ready

OVERVIEW

Many finance teams are far from being future ready. They spend long, frustrated hours working with antiquated error-prone systems—and to make it worse, they follow procedures because they were carried out last month. This chapter will take a brief look at areas the finance team can focus on to become future ready. It also explores how the lean movement affects modern accounting, the importance of Peter Drucker's abandonment, and why we should take Steve Jobs' advice and challenge the status quo.

This book outlines how finance teams can help their organizations by getting their team future ready. By *future ready*, I mean a finance team that is fast and light on its feet and able to react quickly to events as they unfold. A finance team that is nimble through utilizing world best practices, and is an advanced adopter of leading-edge technologies. Finally, a future-ready finance team embraces modern people practices, abandons the ill-conceived management practices of the past, and is thus able to retain its talented staff.

Many finance teams are far from being future ready. How many finance teams today have:

- Fully embraced all the lean finance team practices?
- An annual planning process that helps their organization prepare for the unexpected?
- Successfully adopted the tried and tested leading-edge technologies available in the twenty-first century?

A BURNING PLATFORM?

Many finance teams spend long frustrated hours working with antiquated, error-prone systems—and to make it worse, they follow procedures because they were carried out last month.

Yes, indeed the platform is on fire, and we need to jump off right now. Many performance management processes that I used during my brief time with BP Oil, and helped support as a consultant for Ernst & Whinney, are well and truly broken. I am talking about key performance indicators (KPIs), the annual planning process, forecasting, using outdated technology, and, to round it off, slow month-end and year-end reporting.

These processes have not worked for years—and possibly never worked. The finance teams have presided over an annual planning process where management and the board are told the lies they wanted to hear. The finance teams have issued reports that often end up in an executive's briefcase, which, on their third return journey back to the office, are deemed as read.

There are now significant performance gaps between what CFOs see as important and their current proficiency in that area. In the 2015 IBM Global C-suite study,[1] CFOs were saying that the two most important areas for them were "Identify and track new revenue growth opportunities" and "Develop talent in the finance organization". However, the biggest skill gap was with the integration of information across the enterprise, as shown in Exhibit 1.1.

REPORTING HISTORY OR MAKING IT

When Henry Ford said "You can have any color you like as long as it is black," the world of commerce was a simpler place. The Ford company only had to work

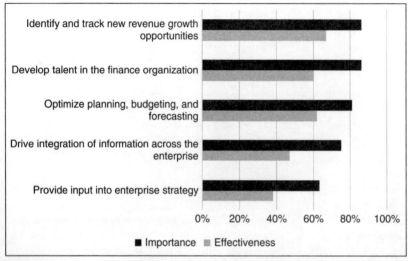

EXHIBIT 1.1 The biggest performance gaps in finance teams *Source:* IBM Global C-Suite Study 2015 based on approximately 600 CFO interviews.

out its production capacity in a year and it could then estimate sales, having backed out the expected movement in inventory.

Large production runs, lengthy month-end processes, were the order of the day. Charles Horngren's "Cost Accounting: A Managerial Emphasis" and books like it were locked into detail and a view into costing, budgeting, and allocation of overheads that is directly opposed to the lean movement.

When I was studying commerce at Liverpool University I was taught well to deliver services that Ford might have needed when building the model T Ford. The accounting profession has learned many bad habits:

Area	Bad habit
Direct labor costs are variable	Treating direct labor costs as variable, yet we cannot go back to the Victorian times and hire staff on a daily basis.
Transferring operating costs to the balance sheet	Absorbing as many fixed costs into WIP and closing stock as possible, thereby transferring costs from the current period to subsequent periods.
Wedded to complexity	Installing one complex system after another (e.g., timesheets, work orders, detailed inventory tracking systems, and activity based costing).
Detail is good	Having a large chart of accounts with 200+ account codes for the P/L.

(continued)

Area	Bad habit
Slow month-ends	Overseeing a slow month-end reporting process as finance teams pursue the perfect number. Yet we are only required to get to a true and fair number, and the "right" month-end number does not exist.
Slow year-ends	Signing up with the auditors for a slow year-end accounts exercise with most of the finance team's time in the first quarter being spent endlessly adjusting the month 12 number. The final audited numbers often being within 5% of those reported at month 12. In other words, we have in reality come full circle.
Spreadsheet epidemic	A spreadsheet for everything, and most certainly, multiple versions of the truth.
Maintaining an annual planning process	Managing the annual planning process, believing that it must be of some use. Each year, thinking that this time the annual planning process will be better, quicker, and easier than last year's disaster.
Generating unread reports	Generating reports that will not be read.
Reporting on a calendar month-end	Blindly following Julius Caesar's calendar, rather than explore the many benefits of reporting with four- or five week months that end on the same day each month.

Maybe It Is Time for Therapy

Two hundred years ago, when the Napoleonic Wars were raging, the English Navy had a device for retribution. It was called the cat o' nine tails. The English Navy stopped using this multi-tailed whip a long, long time ago, so why do so many accountants pick up the cat o' nine tails and whip themselves time and time again?

If it is not the cat o' nine tails, it is shooting ourselves in the foot. This book is about stopping this self-inflicted punishment and changing our ways.

Escaping the Catch-22

Joseph Heller's iconic 1961 book, *Catch 22*,[2] introduced a new term to popular culture. The *Oxford English Dictionary* defined "Catch 22" as "*a situation or predicament characterized by absurdity or senselessness.*"

I see many finance teams in this situation. The slow month-end reporting, the never ending annual planning process, and the long, drawn-out annual reporting cycle are both beautifully summed up by the above Catch 22 definition. How do we get out of this Catch 22? The finance team needs to create time for change, to have more time to act. Where do we find this time? We find it by aiming for these lean finance team benchmarks:

Area	Lean finance team benchmarks
Month-end accounts	Fast month-end by day three or less (by next month-end); reporting by the close of the first working day within 12 to 18 months and being able to report net profit intra-month (virtual reporting) inside of three years.
Year-end accounts	Commit the auditors, your finance team, your board and executives to a 15-working-day signed set of annual accounts.
Annual planning	Produce the annual plan in less than two weeks from the rolling planning exercises. Eventually, the annual plan will be dropped in favor of a quarterly rolling planning process.
Key performance indicators (KPIs)	Work with no more than 10 KPIs in the organization. The other operational measures that are not key to operational performance should number less than 80 and be renamed (see the 10/80/10 rule in Chapter 18).
Excel ad hoc systems	All spreadsheets over 100 rows are replaced with a robust solution e.g., for forecasting using one of the modern planning and reporting tools.
Streamlining the chart of accounts	Having less than 50 account codes for profit and loss. Any more is unnecessary and leads to miscoding.

LEAN MOVEMENT

The finance team needs to embrace the lean movement to slim down all of its processes so it can be less locked in to the past. This change will have an impact on the workload of the team, as shown in Exhibit 1.2, which compares an antiquated team and a lean finance team.

The significant increase in advisory time will lead to:

- Adding more value to the business units the finance team supports
- Selling and leading change, in particular with regard to new systems
- Leading the battle against waste as Jeremy Hope has suggested[3]
- Having time to adopt the profound lean practices such as Post-it reengineering, Scrum, Kanban, and action meetings

The end result will be participating in more rewarding work and a happy and more fulfilled finance team.

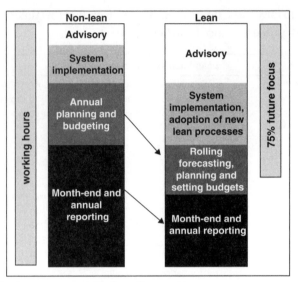

EXHIBIT 1.2   Lean versus a non-lean finance team

Background to the Lean Movement

The lean movement is largely credited as a Japanese process that was responsible for the meteoric rise of the Japanese multinationals over the period 1960 to 2000. However, when you look at its origins, you see the influence of American writers such as Edwards Deming. Over the years, there have been many institutes and consultancy methodologies that make up the lean movement as we see it today.

The lean movement has been part of workshops for more than 20 years, but lean accounting has been a much more recent phenomenon lead by a series of thinkers and dates back to roughly 2004. The key players include:

- Jeremy Hope[4]
- Brian Maskell[5]
- Jean Cunningham[6]
- Frances Kennedy[7]

Although most corporate accountants are aware of the revolution of *lean* and its positive impact on private, government, and nonprofit sectors, few have realized the profound impact it has on the accounting function. The pioneers of lean accounting have now blazed a pathway that all corporate accountants need to walk along.

Indeed, the *lean accounting* movement has been gaining momentum around the world. Thus, it will not be long before CEOs start asking questions about this hot topic. It is imperative that corporate accountants, sooner rather than later, understand the concepts of lean accounting and its implications for their finance team and organization.

In fact, the movement has progressed to such an extent that there is now an annual lean accounting summit, which can be found easily on the Internet.

Lean Is About Eliminating the Eight Wastes

In lean there are eight types of waste. These wastes are seen within the whole organization and within the accounting function. I have outlined the eight wastes below:

Eight types of waste	Within the accounting function
1. **Over-production:** Having long production runs that produce more product than the current customers' immediate demand. This is done to reduce downtime.	Our reports are too large and go into too much detail.
2. **Waiting:** Production operators waiting because a machine has gone down or a component is not available.	The processing of batches of AP or AR transactions where these batches wait for hours or days before processing. Also the month-end, year-end, annual planning processes have too much waiting time.
3. **Transportation:** Moving materials around the factory. Buying raw materials and components from distant suppliers.	The finance team is always shuffling information around team members.
4. **Extra processing:** Processes that appear productive but are unimportant to the customer. Painting and finishing components that are not seen. Designing additional features into a product that the customers do not use (e.g., the many features in Excel that are heralded each upgrade but in reality hardly used).	The chart of accounts, the month-end, year-end, annual planning processes all have extra processing within them.

(continued)

5. **Excess inventory:** Having materials, components, work-in-process, and finished goods levels above the immediate need.	The way we have transferred this period's sunk costs into next period production costs has created a blowout in inventory.
6. **Waste of motion:** Having to search for tools, parts, or forms.	The finance function needs a make-over in time and motion. We all need to know where everything is filed and be disciplined in maintaining this.
7. **Defects, scrap, and rework in production:** Complex inspection steps to overcome poor processes or poor design.	Accounting function generates many spread sheets that have a dubious function. They are completed because they were completed last month.
8. **Unused employee creativity:** Employee ideas having to jump over many obstacles before adoption.	Based on Toyota, we would need to have 10 innovations implemented per team member per year within the finance function.

"Most businesses processes are 90% waste and 10% value-added work."

—Dr. Jeffrey Liker

Liker points out that Boeing reduced over a trillion internal transactions through adopting lean.

Toyota's 14 Lean Management Principles and Their Relevance

I believe Toyota to be possibly the greatest company in the world. It has 14 lean management principles which are the backbone to its culture and Toyota can embed these principles in all countries it operates within. Its Kentucky plant in the USA exceeded all Toyota expectations with its acceptance of the Toyota Way. To understand the Toyota principles one needs to read Jeffrey Liker's book *The Toyota Way*. He has broken them down into four categories as set out in Exhibit 1.3.

I believe that Toyota's 14 principles should be embedded in all private, government, and non-profit agencies as best they can. They would make a profound impact on the organizations, benefiting the staff, management, board, and customers. I have included an overview of Toyota's 14 management principles in the attached electronic media.

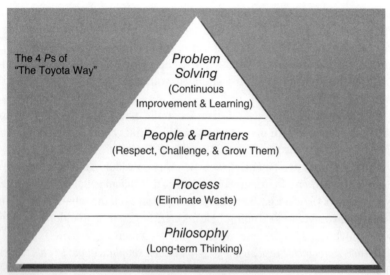

The 4 Ps of
"The Toyota Way"

Problem Solving
(Continuous
Improvement & Learning)

People & Partners
(Respect, Challenge, & Grow Them)

Process
(Eliminate Waste)

Philosophy
(Long-term Thinking)

EXHIBIT 1.3   Jeffrey Liker's analysis of Toyota's 14 principles
Source: www.jeffliker.com

 IMPORTANCE OF ABANDONMENT

From the time we were at kindergarten we have had a fear of ever admitting we were wrong. In our personal lives we have, in some cases, held onto an abusive relationship for too long because we were scared to admit, to the world at large, we had made a mistake. The longer the relationship goes on we hold onto the hope that it will come right and we can always then say to our family,

"I told you so." In reality this does not happen. If I was to go into a reader's garage, what would I find? Maybe an exercise machine that started off life in great excitement as we envisaged a leaner self. After a couple of weeks in the lounge it started its inexorable journey to the garage, there to rest under the dust cover for a day in the future when we would use it again so we could say "I told you so."

In the world of commerce this trait is equally damaging. We will hold onto systems, keep going with projects, keep writing that report that nobody reads because to remove it would mean a loss of face. Let's get over it.

Management guru Peter Drucker,[8] whom I consider to be the Leonardo da Vinci of management, frequently used the word *abandonment*. I think it is one of the top 10 gifts Drucker gave us all. He said, "Don't tell me what you're doing, tell me what you've stopped doing." He frequently said that abandonment is the key to innovation. He left some rather telling statements.

If leaders are unable to abandon yesterday, they simply will not be able to create tomorrow.

Without systematic and purposeful abandonment, an organization will be overtaken by events. It will squander its best resources on things it should never have been doing or should no longer do. As a result, it will lack the resources needed to exploit the opportunities that arise.

In finance, many processes are followed, year-in and year-out, because "it's the way things have always been done." When staff question, "Why do we do this?" the CFO or financial controller will often answer, "There must be a reason; so please do it." In order for the better practices in this book to work, there must be an adoption of:

▪ An abandonment of processes and procedures that are broken
▪ A letting go of the past
▪ A commitment to challenge the rules of the past

An organization that embraced Peter Drucker's abandonment earmarked the first Monday of every month for "abandonment meetings at every management level." Each session targets a different area, so that over the course of a year, everything is given the once-over. This process would work well in the finance team, except we should meet once a week to discuss at least two abandonments.

Every organization I have come across should have an abandonment KPI measuring the number of abandonments that have been made around the organization last week. Teams that were no embracing the concept would soon want to get the CEO's attention and acclaim by embracing the concept.

The act of abandonment gives a tremendous sense of relief to the finance team, for it stops the past from haunting the future. It takes courage and conviction from the CFO. Knowing when to abandon and having the courage to do so are important leadership attributes.

I have included in the electronic media a book review of Elizabeth Haas Edersheim's *The Definitive Drucker*.[9] Read the book for more on abandonment and his other great advice. I consider this book one of the top 10 management books I have read. I hope, like me, you will become a follower of the great Peter Drucker.

THE IMPORTANCE OF CHALLENGING THE STATUS QUO

Far too often, we have accepted antiquated and anti-lean practices within the corporate accounting repertoire as the status quo. If the medical profession used our approach, it would probably still be using leeches. (Well, actually, I understand that leeches are still used in special cases.) The medical profession has breakthrough conferences on a regular basis, and all the practicing surgeons in that field attend and adopt the new procedure. This should be the corporate finance model. The problem with corporate finance is that the "surgeon," the CFO, is often too busy to attend, caught in the aforementioned Catch-22.

In an interview, called "The Lost Interview," Steve Jobs was asked, "As a 22-year-old worth $10 million, and a 25-year-old worth $100 million, how did you get your business acumen?" He said that over time, he realized that most business was pretty straightforward. He talked about when Apple had its first computerized manufacturing plant for the Apple II and the accountant sent Steve Jobs his first standard costing report. Jobs asked, "Why do we have a standard cost and not an actual cost?" The response was, "That is the way it's done." He soon realized that the reason was the accounting system could not record an actual cost quick enough. When that was fixed, standard costing reports vanished.

In business, Jobs believed that few in management thought deeply about why things were done. He came up with this quote I want to share with you. I believe this quote should be on every wall and in front of every work station in the finance team work area.

"Your time is limited, so don't waste it living someone else's life. Don't be trapped into living with the results of other people's thinking. Don't let the noise of others' opinions drown your own inner voice."

—*Steve Jobs*

 PDF DOWNLOAD

To assist the finance team on the journey, templates, checklists, and book reviews have been provided. The reader can access, free of charge, a PDF of the following material from www.davidparmenter.com/The_Financial_Controller_and_CFO's_Toolkit.

The templates include:

- A book review of Elizabeth Haas Edersheim's *The Definitive Drucker*
- The Toyota 14 management principles
- My analysis of Drucker's top 10 gifts

NOTES

1. Joseph Heller's iconic 1961 book, *Catch 22* (New York: Simon & Schuster; 50th Anniversary edition, 2011).
2. Ibid.
3. Jeremy Hope, "Reinventing the CFO: How Financial Managers Can Transform Their Roles and Add Greater Value," *Harvard Business Press* (2006).
4. Ibid.
5. Frances Kennedy with Brian Maskell, "Why Do We Need Lean Accounting and How Does It Work?" *Journal of Corporate Accounting & Finance* (March/April 2007).
6. Jean Cunningham, "The Lean vs. Standard Costing Accounting Conundrum," *Finance & Management Faculty Journal, ICAEW* (June 2012).
7. Kennedy and Maskell.
8. To understand Peter Drucker's work, read Elizabeth Haas Edersheim, *The Definitive Drucker: Challenges for Tomorrow's Executives—Final Advice from the Father of Modern Management* (New York: McGraw-Hill, 2006).
9. Ibid.

CHAPTER TWO

Leading and Selling the Change

OVERVIEW

Far too many well-meaning initiatives fail because we have not understood the psychology behind getting change to work. This chapter explores the work of Steve Zaffron and Dave Logan in *The Three Laws of Performance* and John Kotter's *Leading Change*. It covers the importance of Harry Mills' *"self-persuasion,"* sets out an eight-stage process that will help you implement the practices in this book, and offers guidance on delivering persuasive presentations.

B efore we venture on to the process of implementation, we need first to address selling the change within our organization. Finance teams around the world have wanted to embrace lean practices but are weary because many initiatives both inside the finance team and in other teams fail far too often.

As we will know from past experiences, this sales process is not easy and can be prone to failure. I would argue that more than half the initiatives that are declined at the concept stage were undersold. In other words, given the right approach, the initiative would have gone ahead.

If you are not prepared to learn the skills to cover the common deficiencies in a *selling change* process, I would argue that you are resigning yourself to providing the same service level for years to come. Selling change requires a special set of skills and we all can, and should, get better at it.

Three books have opened up the way for us to rethink change and to apply techniques that will get change over the line.

 ## STEVE ZAFFRON AND DAVE LOGAN

Steve Zaffron and Dave Logan have written a compelling book, *The Three Laws of Performance*,[1] that explains why so many change initiatives have failed. The first law is "How people perform correlates to how situations occur to them." The writers point out that the organization's "default future," which, we as individuals just know in our bones, will happen—will be made to happen. Thus, in an organization with a systemic problem, the organization's staff will be driven to make initiatives fail so that the default future prevails.

They went on to say that is why the more you change the more you stay the same. The key to change is to recreate, in the organization's staff minds, a new vision of the future—let's call it an *invented future*.

Zaffron and Logan signal the importance of language (the second law), without language we would not have a past or a future. It is the ability to use language that enables us to categorize thoughts as either the past or the future. Without language we would be like the cat on the mat, sunning itself for yet another afternoon, thinking about the next meal but without the ability to process complex thought.

They then say in order to make change, we need to use a future-based language (the third law). It is interesting; if you listen to the outstanding orators of the past such as Sir Winston Churchill, you will hear future-based language at work. These great speakers knew, intuitively, about the power of future-based language.

We shall fight on the beaches, we shall fight on the landing grounds, we shall fight in the fields and in the streets, we shall fight in the hills; we shall never surrender.

HARRY MILLS

Harry Mills, a multiple business book author, has written extensively about persuasion.[2] In his recent work, *The Aha! Advantage*,[3] he talks about the significance of self-persuasion.

> *"Self-persuasion is fundamentally more powerful than direct persuasion essentially because of the way it reduces resistance."*

Mills talks about the four faces of the *Aha!* moment, as shown in Exhibit 2.1, the point when your audience gets the message and now persuades itself to adopt the message as if it was their own.

Mills' work is very consistent with Zaffron and Logan. We need to get the staff in the organization to have for themselves that *Aha!* moment, that "Hell, no! We do not want the default future." When the staff come to this point, change is inevitable.

The Anatomy of an *Aha!* Moment

IMPASSE
"I'm stuck"

REFLECTION
"I need to clear my mind"

INSIGHT
"Aha!"

MOTIVATION
"Let's go for it!"

EXHIBIT 2.1 The four faces of the *Aha!* moment *Source:* The Mills Group

This means we need to structure our workshops so there is more involvement, more chance for staff to have that *Aha!* moment, and less dogmatic rhetoric about the facts.

JOHN KOTTER

In 1996, John Kotter published *Leading Change*,[4] which quickly became the seminal work in the field of change management. He pointed out that effecting change—real, transformative change—is hard. Kotter proposed an eight-stage process for creating major change, a clear map to follow when persuading an organization to move. I will discuss each Kotter stage while at the same time embedding Saffron & Logan and Harry Mills' thinking. If you follow these stages, you will increase the chances of change projects many fold.

Establish a sense of urgency—Here we need to appeal both to the intellectual and the emotional sides of the executive team. There are two stages. First, ambush the CEO with a compelling elevator pitch so you get to stage two. Second, deliver a masterful sales presentation of around 15 to 20 minutes, aimed at obtaining permission to run a focus group to assess, validate, and scope the proposed initiative.

Create a guiding coalition—In every organization you have oracles, those individuals everyone refers you to when you need something answered (e.g., "You need to talk to Pat"). These oracles exist right across the organization and might hold seemingly unimportant positions. Do not be fooled.

An investment at this stage is paramount. In one case study, an organization held three two-week workshops that were designed to progress their planning tool implementation. Yes, that is six weeks of workshops. The CEO was present for part of each of the workshops and the wisdom from the oracles was channeled by an expert facilitator into a successful blueprint for the project.

No project will ever succeed without a guiding coalition of oracles behind it. In *The Three Laws of Performance*, Zaffron and Logan point out that when you present the "burning platform" you are aiming for an overwhelming "Hell, no!" response upon asking the question, "Do you want the default future?" The oracles want the alternative future, which you have also articulated.

However, Mills has warned us to be patient, give time for the staff to discuss, think, and mull over the content. In most cases a two day workshop will be more beneficial in giving staff time to let self-persuasion work.

Develop a vision and strategy—In order for the journey to be seen and resources made available, we must master future-based language that is compelling and motivational. As mentioned, Zaffron and Logan have signified the importance of language (the second law) and that it is crucial that you talk using a future-based language (the third law).

Communicate the change vision—Kotter emphasized that it's not likely that you will under-communicate a little bit; you will probably under-communicate a lot, by a factor of 10 to 100 times. This will undermine your initiative, no matter how well planned. During a project, the project leader needs to obtain permission from the CEO to gate crash any gathering in the organization and have a 10-minute slot to outline the project and progress to date. One surefire way to failure is to believe that staff will read your project newsletters and emails.

Empower broad-based action—Early on the need for change and the right to change must be handed over to teams within the organization. Zaffron and Logan concur with this view. Once the invented future is set in the minds of the organization's staff, the staff will march toward this future. All the great writers have emphasized that some chaos is good, so let teams embrace the project in their own way.

Generate quick wins—Obvious to us all but frequently missed. Always remember that senior management is, on occasion, inflicted by attention deficit disorder. Progress in a methodical and introverted way at your peril. We need easy wins, celebrated extrovertly, and we need to ensure we set up the CEO to score the easy goals.

Consolidate gains and produce more change—This is the flywheel affect so well put by Jim Collins in his books, *Built to Last*[5] and *Good to Great*.[6] When the staff are working in unison the flywheel of change will turn quicker and quicker. This was very evident in the planning tool implementation case study featured in Chapter 4.

Anchor new approaches in the culture—Make heroes of the change agents, make sure their values are embedded in the corporate values, and now ensure you weed out those in management who have not embraced the change and who, over time, will be dowsing the fire at night when nobody is looking.

SELLING TO THE SENIOR MANAGEMENT TEAM

The process of getting the senior management team (SMT) on board requires an understanding of the need to sell through the buyer's emotional drivers, a well-prepared elevator pitch, and a masterful sales presentation. The object of the sales pitch is to obtain permission to run a focus group to assess, validate, and scope the proposed initiative.

Learn to Sell by Using the Emotional Drivers of the Buyer

It is through your audience's emotional drivers, and not through logic, that a story is sold. Failure to appreciate this has undermined many an accountant's pitch to the board.

All major projects need a public relations machine behind them. No presentation, email, memo, or paper related to a major change should go out unless it has been vetted by your PR expert. Do not get offended when they rewrite most of your content. Just admire their genius and claim the credit when the PR process works—that's what everybody else does.

SELLING BY EMOTIONAL DRIVERS: HOW A CAR SALE IS MADE

Three customers arrive on the same day to look at a car that has been featured in the local newspaper. The first person is a young IT professional, generation Y, and wearing latest designer clothing. The salesperson slowly walks up and assesses the emotional drivers of this potential buyer. Having ascertained that the young man is an IT guru, working for a major search engine organization, the salesperson says, "I hope you have some track racing experience. You need to be a Lewis Hamilton to handle this beast. This car has 320 BHP, a twin turbo, and corners like it's on railway tracks. Only a top driver can handle this beast. It's a real driver's car." SOLD.

The second person could be me, with my gray hair visible. The salesperson might say, "This car is five-star rated for safety, with eight air bags, enough power to get you out of trouble, unbelievable braking when you have to avoid the idiots on the road, and tires that will never fail you." SOLD.

The third person is wearing stylish clothing and is impeccably well groomed. The opening sales line might be, "This car has won many awards for its design. Sit in the driver's seat and see the quality of the finish. Everything is in the right place. You look a million dollars in that outfit you are wearing and every time you drive this car you will feel like a million dollars!" SOLD.

The Elevator Speech

Having now understood why prior initiatives have failed through poor selling let us now look at how we get the SMT motivated. The key is to have a 30-second elevator speech that is designed to capture their attention. It must be ready so that when we next bump into the decision makers, we are practiced and ready.

The 30-second elevator speech is designed to capture their attention. The term came about in management books describing how you need to be able to get a point across in an elevator ride, as sometimes this is the only chance you may have to have a one on one with the decision maker. The aim is, as they walk away, that they ask you to come to their office in the next few days to discuss this further.

An elevator interaction might go like this.

In answer to the question, "How are you?" you might say, "I am troubled." "Why is that?" being the natural response from the CEO. To which you reply, "I have just been looking at _____ and I have estimated that over the next 10 years, we will be spending $__M and $__M on this if we do nothing. I have been researching a new approach, tried and tested elsewhere, that would save much of this cost. I just need 15 minutes of your time to explain this."

The key is to fine-tune the elevator speech so that it is compelling. I recommend you practice your elevator speech at least 10 times so that it is focused and no longer than 30 seconds. As Kotter, says we need to create a sense of urgency and connect both intellectually and emotionally.

Deliver a Compelling Burning Platform Presentation

Assuming the elevator speech has given us an audience, we need to prepare and deliver a presentation that will get the senior management team to agree to holding a focus group workshop with the organization's "oracles."

A sales pitch to the senior management team and the board should go as follows:

- Make sure you have a good proposal and one with a sound focus on the emotional drivers that will matter to your audience.
- Focus on selling to the thought leader on the senior management team and board before presenting your proposal. This may take weeks of informal meetings, sending copies of articles, telling better practice stories, and so on, to awaken interest. Remember that the thought leader may not be the CEO or board chairperson.
- Make sure you prime the thought leader to speak first after your presentation has been delivered. This gives your proposal the best chance of a positive vote.
- Go for an easy next step, the running of a one day focus group with the organization's oracles.[7] You state, "If I can convince the oracles that this project will work, and get their involvement in the project plan, I will be able to present to you a project that has a greater chance of success."

It's important to get this presentation right, because you will probably not get a second chance. Thus one needs to embrace the better practices around delivering "killer" presentations. I have recently read *The Presentation Secrets of Steve Jobs: How to Be Insanely Great in Front of Any Audience* by Carmine Gallo.[8] It is a compelling read. I have incorporated his work along with the work of Nancy Duarte's *Slide:ology: The Art and Science of Creating Great Presentations*[9] and Garr Reynolds' *Presentation Zen: Simple Ideas on Presentation Design and Delivery*[10] in creating a list of the top tips to deliver compelling presentations. This checklist is included in Appendix B.

THE POWER OF THE FOCUS GROUP

I have found holding a one-day focus group meeting is a superb way to get a coalition of oracles behind the project. This focus group meeting would be attended by a cross section of 15 to 30 experienced staff, covering the business units, teams, area offices, and head office, and covering the different roles from administrators to senior management team members.

This focus group meeting should discuss the existing issues with performance measures, expose the attendees to the new thinking, outline the intended approach, and seek their advice to decide if the project is viable, and if so what lessons could be learned from past projects.

The aim of this workshop is to get the green light and secure the full support of the attendees. The next step is to develop a robust blueprint that sets out the direction and the requirements, using some of the oracles who have attended the focus group workshop.

I have prepared agendas for the focus group workshops to re-engineer month-end reporting, annual planning, and the annual accounts. These are available in the PDF download.

 PDF DOWNLOAD

To assist the finance team on the journey, templates, checklists, and book reviews have been provided. The reader can access, free of charge, a PDF of the following material from www.davidparmenter.com/The_Financial_Controller_and_CFO's_Toolkit.

The PDF download for this chapter includes:

- A book review of *The Three Laws of Performance*
- A book review of *Leading Change*
- Selling pitch PowerPoint presentations

 NOTES

1. Steve Zaffron and Dave Logan, *The Three Laws of Performance* (San Francisco: Jossey-Bass, 2011).
2. Harry Mills, *Artful Persuasion: How to Command Attention, Change Minds, and Influence People* (New York: AMACOM, 2000).
3. Harry Mills, *The Aha! Advantage* (The Mills Group, 2015).

4. John Kotter, *"Leading Change,"* Harvard Business Review Press (2012).

5. Jim Collins, Jerry Porras, *Built to Last: Successful Habits of Visionary Companies* (New York: Harper Business Essentials, 2004).

6. Jim Collins, *Good to Great: Why Some Companies Make the Leap ... And Others Don't* (New York: HarperBusiness, 2001).

7. The organization's "oracles" being those "go to" individuals everyone refers you to when you need to get something done.

8. Carmine Gallo, *The Presentation Secrets of Steve Jobs: How to Be Insanely Great in Front of Any Audience* (New York: McGraw-Hill Education, 2009).

9. Nancy Duarte, *Slide:ology: The Art and Science of Creating Great Presentations* (Sabastopol, CA: O'Reilly Media, 2008).

10. Garr Reynolds, *Presentation Zen: Simple Ideas on Presentation Design and Delivery* (Berkeley, CA: New Riders, 2nd ed., 2011).

PART TWO

To be Completed Before the Next Month-End

CHAPTER THREE

Rapid Month-End Reporting:
By Working Day Three or Less

OVERVIEW

Although many large organizations have made massive inroads into fast and accurate month-end reporting the vast majority of finance teams around the world have month-end processes that are career limiting, to say the least.

This chapter explores the processes you can abandon, those you need to bring forward, and when the cutoffs should occur. All these changes can occur before your next month-end. Many of these practices are common sense; however, common sense is not always evident.

Many large organizations have made massive inroads into fast and accurate month-end reporting. I say to them, "Celebrate your achievement," but still read this chapter as you may be able to achieve a quicker month-end close. However, the vast majority of finance teams around the world have month-end processes that are career limiting.

This chapter is an extract from my white paper, "Reporting rapidly, informatively and error free."[1]

When I was a corporate accountant, each month-end had a life of its own. You never knew when and where the next problem was going to come from. Two or three days away, we always appeared to have it under control, and yet each month we were faxing (email was not on the scene then) the result five minutes before the deadline. Our fingers were crossed as a series of late adjustments had meant that the quality assurance (QA) work we had done was invalid and we did not have the luxury of doing the QA again. Does this sound familiar?

CEOs need to demand a complete and radical change if they are to free management and accountants from the shackles of a zero-sum process—reporting last month's results halfway through the following month. Here are the facts:

- Leading finance teams are now providing commentary and numbers by the first working day.
- Companies are migrating to closing the month on the same day each month (i.e., months are either four or five weeks).
- In leading organizations, the senior management team (SMT) is letting go of report writing—SMT members are no longer rewriting reports. They have informed the board that they concur with the writer's findings but it is a delegated report.

See the attached electronic media for a checklist of implementation steps to reduce month-end reporting time frames and for the common bottlenecks in month-end reporting and techniques to get around them.

RATING SCALE FOR MONTH-END REPORTING

The following rating scale, see Exhibit 3.1, shows the time frames of month-end reporting across the 5,000 corporate accountants I have presented to in the past 20 years.

EXHIBIT 3.1 Speed of Month-End Reporting Ranking

Exceptional	Outstanding	Above Average	Average
One working day	Two to three working days	Four working days	Five working days

BENEFITS OF QUICK MONTH-END REPORTING

As a CFO of a tertiary institution said, "Every day spent producing reports is a day less spent on analysis and projects." There are a larger number of benefits to management and the finance team of quick reporting, and these are set out in Exhibit 3.2.

 ## IMPACT OF A QUICK MONTH-END ON THE FINANCE TEAM WORKLOAD

The impact of quick month-end reporting is a redistribution of work moving out of the low value processing activities of month-end annual accounts to the more future focused activities such as rolling forecasting, systems implementation, and advisory, as shown in Exhibit 3.3. This is often accompanied by a

EXHIBIT 3.2 Table of Benefits of Quick Reporting

Benefits to Management	Benefits to the Finance Team
1. Reporting plays a bigger part in the decision-making process. 2. Reduction in detail and length of reports. 3. Reduced cost to organization of month-end reporting. 4. More time spent analyzing trends. 5. More time spent on achieving results. 6. Greater budget holder ownership (accruals, variance analysis, coding, corrections during month, better understanding, etc.). 7. Less senior management time invested in month-end.	1. Staff are more productive as efficiencies are locked in and bottlenecks are tackled. 2. Removal of out of date and inefficient processes. 3. Happier staff with higher morale and increased job satisfaction. 4. Finance staff focus is now on being a business partner to the budget holder, helping them to shape the future. 5. The team has more time to be involved in rewarding activities, such as quarterly rolling forecasts, project work, and so forth. 6. Greater proportion of qualified finance staff. 7. Less senior finance team time invested in month-end; the change also leads to a very quick year-end

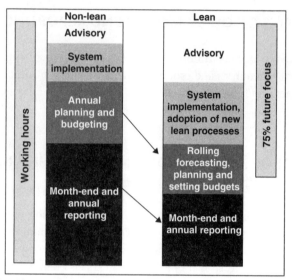

EXHIBIT 3.3   Changing the focus of our work

change in the mix of the finance team, which results in a higher percentage of qualified staff.

A rapid month-end gives the finance team more time for the future. There are, on average, 22 working days a month. For a day one reporting entity, the finance team has 21 days allocated to the current month and beyond. A finance team taking 9 days to report has only 13 days left, a 40 percent reduction.

It is important to cost out to management and the board the month-end reporting process. When doing this exercise, remember that senior management barely has 32 weeks of productive time when you remove holidays, sick leave, travel time, and routine management meetings. Thus, a cost of $1,000 per day is not unrealistic. Based on an organization with 40 budget holders, with around 500 full-time staff, I believe the cost estimate is between $0.9 million and $1.5 million.

Such an analysis can be easily performed by your accounting team in 30 minutes, and will be valuable in the sale process of changing month-end reporting time frames.

I have included a costing template in the reader download as a guide to this exercise.

MAJOR STEPS YOU CAN DO BEFORE YOUR NEXT MONTH-END

Set out next are the major steps you can achieve within the month you are currently in.

Establish Reporting Rules within the Finance Team

Members of the finance team have to realize that they are sculptors, not scientists. There needs to be recognition that the monthly accounts are not precise documents. Assessments need to be made, and the monthly accounts will never be right; they can only be a true and fair view. We could hold the accounts payable open for six months after month-end and still not have the plumber's invoice that arrives when the plumber's company is doing its year-end and realizes that it has forgotten to invoice for work done.

We therefore need some rules about the month-end reporting process which need to be signed off by all the accountants. The month-end financial report should:

- Not be delayed for detail.
- Be consistent—between months, judgment calls, and format.
- Be a true and fair view and error free.
- Be concise—less than 10 pages (include the major business units' one-page reports but exclude minor units reports. These are shown as a consolidated number in the consolidated P/L).
- Be a merging of numbers, graphs, and comments on one page.
- Not be changed for adjustments that are likely to be set off by others yet to be found—instead all adjustments are to be offset against each other on an "overs and unders" schedule.
- Be based on an agreed corporate view of materiality. Materiality will not be set at a different level for each budget holder. If materiality is set at $20,000 for a P/L item consolidated result, then this amount is set for adjustments, variance reporting, and accruals across all entities.

I have included a draft set of rules for the finance team in the reader download.

Catch All Adjustments in an "Overs and Unders" Schedule

Month-end reporting is not the time for spring cleaning, no matter how tempting it can be. This requires a re-education within the finance team and with budget holders.

All miscodings, unless resulting in a material misstatement of the P/L, are processed during the following month. Budget holders are educated to review their cost center numbers via online access to the G/L during the month and are requested to highlight any discrepancies immediately with the finance team.

We want to have a regime where we catch all material adjustments and see the net result of them before any decision is made to adjust (e.g., only a material month-end misstatement will result in processing an adjustment). The first time you do this, set up two overs and unders spreadsheets, see Exhibit 3.4, at the close of the last working day.

One spreadsheet is to trap major adjustments. If materiality is set at $40,000 for a P/L adjustment, I would recommend setting the threshold for the over and unders schedule at around 40–50%. In this case it would be between $16,000 and $20,000, so I would go for $20,000. The other overs and unders schedule is to trap minor adjustments between $5,000 and $19,000.

If they find adjustments, the accountants will enter them on the appropriate spreadsheets that reside on a shared drive on the local area network. More

Source	Raised by	JV #	Adjustment		P/L impact		B/S impact	
					Dr	Cr	Dr	Cr
Budget holder	Pat	1	Dr	Consultancy Fees (Dept 10)	45			
			Cr	Consultancy Fees (Dept 12)		45		
Budget holder	John	2	Dr	Training courses (Dept 6)	10			
			Cr	Training courses (Dept 16)		10		
Debtors review	Jean	3	Dr	Bad debts write-off (ABC in liquidation)	25			
			Cr	Provision for doubtful debts				25
_____	Dave	4	Dr	_____			15	
			Cr	_____		15		
		etc						
					80	70		
					−70			
			Net impact on P/L		10			

EXHIBIT 3.4 Maintaining an "overs and unders" schedule

often than not, you will note that adjustments have a tendency to net each other off.

If there is a material misstatement of the net result, we will process one or two appropriate adjustments and then remove them from this schedule. This will bring the total of the overs and unders to an acceptable figure. We then process all the other adjustments during the quiet time in the following mid-month. In the quiet of mid-month, the minor adjustments are reviewed for their causes and work done to fix the problems. This minor schedule is now no longer continued.

Avoid a Huge Wave of Accounts Payable Invoices at Month-End

The last thing the accounts payable (AP) team needs is to receive a tsunami of invoices on the last day of cutoff, as shown in Exhibit 3.5. It is important to push processing back from month-end by avoiding a payment run at month-end. It is a better practice to have weekly or daily direct credit payment runs with none happening within the last and first two days of month-end.

Change invoicing cycles on all monthly accounts such as utilities, credit cards, stationery, and so on (e.g., invoice cycle including transactions from May 28 to June 27 and being received electronically by June 28). Since you are looking at one month's activity it is not worth preparing accruals for these suppliers as the previous month's reversing accrual will make any difference immaterial.

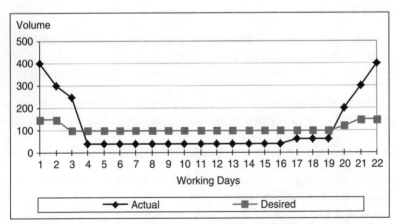

EXHIBIT 3.5 Accounts payable invoice processing volumes during month

EXHIBIT 3.6 Month-End Timings Explanation

Day −2	Day −1	Day +1	Day +2
Second to last working day	Last working day	First working day of new month	Second working day of new month

Early Closing of the Accounts Payable Ledger

I have not come across an organization that can justify closing off accounts payable after the last day of the month. Whatever date you pick to close AP, you will never trap all the invoices. Remember, we are after a true and fair view; we are sculptors rather than scientists.

If accounts payable is held open after month-end, you will find it difficult to complete prompt month-end reporting. What benefit does holding open the accounts payable for one or two days have? We could hold the accounts payable open for six months after month-end and still not get the plumber's invoice that arrives when they are doing their year-end and realize they have forgotten to invoice for work done on the refit.

Better practice is to cut off accounts payable at noon on the last working day. In my workshops, I have come across organizations that cut off accounts payable even earlier, on day 2 and day 3 (see Exhibit 3.6). They manage this by more reliance on recurring reversing accruals, supplemented by budget holders accruals for the larger one-off amounts. They place timeliness above preciseness. This requires good communication to budget holders and suppliers, with the latter sending their invoices earlier through changing the billing timings, as already mentioned.

> "Your month-end result doesn't become more accurate the longer you leave it. It just becomes more expensive to produce."
> —*Quote from a CFO with international blue chip experience*

In order to lock in this change you may need to run a workshop with the budget holders and follow up with one-to-one educational support, as required.

Close Accruals before the Accounts Payable Cutoff

The accruals cutoff does not need to be after the accounts payable (AP) cutoff; it can and should be before. Let me explain.

One smart accountant I have come across worked out that budget holders know little more about month-end purchase invoices at day+2 than at day 2. So, the accountant introduced accrual cutoff on day 2, the day before month-end. Budget holders were required to send their last invoices for processing to meet the month-end AP cutoff by noon day–2, which gave AP 24 hours to process them before the day 1 AP cutoff. He also told them to prepare their accruals in the afternoon of day–2, directly into the G/L.

All that is required is a guarantee that all invoices approved for payment by budget holders within the deadline will in fact be processed prior to the AP cutoff, or accrued directly by the AP team.

Cutting off accruals early recognizes that month-end invoices will not arrive miraculously by day+1 or day+2 so staff will need to phone some key suppliers to get accrual information regardless of when the cutoff is.

Set a Materiality Rule for Accruals

We need to set a materiality rule for accruals. If materiality is set at $40,000 for a P/L item, I would recommend setting the threshold for the minimum department accrual at around 40–50% of this number. In this case it would be between $16,000 and $20,000, so I would go for $20,000. If a department is too small to have $20,000 worth of accruals, then it does not need to do accruals.

If materiality is set at $20,000 for a P/L item, then we might set the minimum threshold for accrual total for each business unit between say $8,000–$10,000 (using the 40–50% rule). In this case I would set it at $10,000. If a department is too small to have $10,000 worth of accruals, then it does not need to do accruals. This should limit accruals to less than half the budget holders in the organization. If a manager of a small budget complains, point out that they will be able to accrue when they get promoted. We should set limits on the individual debit items in the accruals to somewhere around a quarter of the accrual threshold. If departmental accruals must be greater than $20,000, each debit must be greater than $5,000.

Avoid Inter company Adjustments

To stop the politics of intercompany disagreements at month-end instigate a simple rule that the accounts payable (AP) or accounts receivable (AR) ledger is always right, and the other party has to adjust accordingly. Leave the intercompany parties to sort the issues out in the following month. I have included a draft memo in Appendix A that the CEO would be advised to send out.

Resourceful organizations use intercompany software, where the transaction is entered by the selling party, and the software simultaneously posts the transactions in the buyer's and seller's general ledgers. They also only amend for major internal profit adjustments.

These tools are priced to be available for the SME market. To source this software, simply use one of these searches in your preferred search engine ("intercompany + software," "intercompany accounting + software").

Early Closing-Off of Accounts Receivable

Close off accounts receivable immediately on the last working day. If you have high last-day transaction volumes, it is better to go for a cutoff at noon on the last working day with transactions in the afternoon being carried forward to the first day of the new month. Closing off earlier is more important if you have an organization where the sales representatives make a lot of sales on the last working day of the month (e.g., car dealers). You simply say to them, "All sales made on the last day of the month will now be in the following month." This will start their game a little earlier.

Remember that training will be required in dispatch and accounts receivable to ensure cutoff is clean each month-end.

Early Capital Expenditure Cutoff

Why are you performing depreciation calculations at month-end when inventive organizations have this already done much earlier? They close off capital projects at least one week before month-end. Any equipment arriving in the last week is therefore treated as if it arrived next month. It still can be unwrapped and plugged in or driven.

The depreciation is calculated and posted by day 3. In my workshops, I have found accountants, with organizations where depreciation is not significant, who use the depreciation calculations from the annual plan and correct to actual at month 12.

Early Inventory Cutoff

Sophisticated organizations can get their month-end inventory cutoff immediately at close of business on the last working day (day 1). However, some manufacturing organizations take a day or two into the next month to manage this process. This creates an unnecessary delay in month-end accounts.

If your systems are not state of the art, make the inventory cutoff at the close of business on day 2 with all production on the last day being carried forward to the next month. This gives one day to check the valuation and records. The close-off transfer of work in progress to finished goods also is done on day 2, with day 1 production treated as belonging to the next month.

These early cutoffs will require cooperation between accounts payable and inventory staff to ensure raw materials arriving on the last day and the matching liability are treated as the next month's transaction or accrued.

Always avoid a month-end stock count, as these should be done on a rolling basis and be held no nearer to month-end than the third week of the month (e.g., one jewelry chain I know counts watches one month, gold chains the next month at a quiet time during the month).

From 5 p.m. Last Day to 5 p.m. First Working Day

What happens in the next 24 hours is critical to the success of month-end reporting. At 5 p.m. on the last working day all the cutoffs should be done. We can print off the first cut of the numbers. This report would be designed for a detailed review and would contain the last three months' numbers and the months' numbers from last year in a series of columns. All the reporting and management accountants should take a copy home and look for areas where they think the numbers could be wrong.

Budget holders should be sent their accounts and they should be given until noon day+1 to complete their commentary on major variances. The variance must be over \$___ (based on materiality level for whole organization) and >10 percent of budget before a comment is required.

At 9 a.m. the following day, all the accountants meet to discuss the areas where further work is needed to be sure that the numbers are "true and fair." At the meeting, "Who is reviewing what?" is decided and a time is set to meet again before the flash report numbers are finalized that day.

Between 3 and 4 p.m. on the first day, you call all the accountants back and ask, "What did you find?" and then look at the net effect of all adjustments on the overs and unders schedule. More often than not, you will note that adjustments have a tendency to net each other off. Book only the adjustments required to restate the numbers as "true and fair." You are now in a position to prepare the one-page flash report for the CEO.

Deliver a Flash Report at the End of Day 1

Issuing a flash report on the (P & L) bottom line to the CEO stating a level of accuracy of, say, $+/-5\%$ or $+/-10$ by the close of business on the first day is a very important practice. There is not a CEO on this planet who would not welcome a heads-up number on such a timely basis. See Exhibit 3.7 for an example of a flash report.

Flash Report for the Month Ending 31 December 20__

	This month $000s			>$100K
	Actual	Target	Variance	
Revenue				
Revenue 1	5,550	5,650	(100)	⇔
Revenue 2	3,550	3,450	100	⇔
Revenue 3	2,450	2,200	250	✓
Other revenue	2,250	2,350	(100)	⇔
Total Revenue	13,800	13,650	150	⇔
Less: Cost of sales	(11,500)	(11,280)	(220)	⇔
Gross Profit	2,300	2,370	(70)	
Expenses				
Expense 1	1,280	1,260	(20)	
Expense 2	340	320	(20)	
Expense 3	220	200	(20)	
Expense 4	180	160	(20)	
Other expenses	170	110	(60)	
Total Expenses	2,190	2,050	(140)	⇔
Surplus/(Deficit)	110	320	(210)	✗

✓	Major positive variance, comment required
✗	Major negative variance, comment required
⇔	Within expectations, no comment required

Areas to Note

1. _____

_____

2. _____

_____

3. _____

_____

4. _____

_____

EXHIBIT 3.7 Flash report to CEO at end of day one

It is important not to provide too many lines because you may find yourself with another variance report on your hands if you have a CEO who fails to look at the big picture. Never attempt a flash report until the AP, AR, and accrual cutoffs have been successfully moved back to the last working day of the month. Otherwise, you will be using the accruals to change final numbers so they can closely match your flash numbers, a practice I would not recommend.

The flash result will act like a great appetizer, and the CEO's appetite for month-end information will be largely satisfied. This creates a great opportunity to reduce the CEO final report to an A3 page, as shown in Chapter 7.

 ## MAJOR QUALITY ASSURANCE TASKS AFTER DAY 1

When the flash report is done and has been discussed with the CEO, we need to focus on the reporting pack. The important issue to remember here is that the month-end can never be right; it can only be a true and fair view.

Ban All Late Changes to the Month-End Report

Once the flash report has been issued, at the close of business on the first working day, teams should continue with recording any adjustment found in the relevant overs and unders spreadsheet.

No changes are permitted to the numbers reported in the flash report until the entire review has been completed. The accounting team can then assess which adjustments are worthy of processing. As many have no P & L impact, they would be held back for adjustment in the following month.

Once the reporting pack is prepared, no adjustments are allowed unless they are very material. There is nothing worse for the finance team than to submit a finance report to the CEO that is inconsistent. This is frequently caused by a late change not being processed properly through the report. As night follows day, the CEO will be sure to find it. I am sure many readers have been guilty of this one.

It is far better to hold back the adjustments. If the CEO says to you, "I thought the sales were higher," you can say, "Pat, it is a pleasure working for such an astute CEO. You are right, the sales are understated by $30,000; however, there are adjustments adding up to $27,000 going the opposite way, so I have not booked the adjustments, as the net difference is immaterial. I am booking these through this month. However, if you like, I will adjust this month's report." Most CEOs will feel pleased with themselves for spotting the shortfall and then move on to another issue.

Stop Variance Reporting at Account Code

This month-end we need to stop reporting variances at account code level. We should report at a higher level. I call this a category level, which is discussed in Chapters 9 and 16 on annual planning and rolling forecasting.

We also need to establish some rules for variance reporting. If materiality is set at $40,000 for a P/L item, then this amount should also be incorporated in the variance reporting rules: A variance has to be the greater of 10% of budget and over $_____ ($40,000 in the above example).

Stop Monthly Reforecasting of Year-End

One process that corporate accountants have done without really thinking about it has been the monthly reforecasting of the year-end position.

Reforecasting the year-end position monthly is wrong on many counts:

- The task is done after the month-end numbers are known, and it now delays the month-end results. It produces a number that, due to time constraints, has little input and no buy-in from the budget holders. I call these forecasts *top–top forecasts*, where the finance team members talk among themselves and with senior management.
- Why should one bad month or one good month translate into a change of the year-end position? We gain and lose major customers and key products rise and wane. This is the life cycle we have witnessed many times. Besides, if you change your forecast each month, management and the board know whatever number you have told them is wrong—you will change it next month, as shown in Exhibit 3.8.
- Reforecasting should occur only four times a year, using a bottom-up process and a proper planning tool, as explained in Chapter 16 on rolling forecasting. Only businesses that are in a volatile sector would need to forecast parts of their operations monthly (e.g., the airline industry would update exchange rates, passenger volume predictions, and aviation fuel costs).

Key Month-End Activities after Reengineering

The key activities in a day 3 month-end are set out in the Exhibit 3.9.

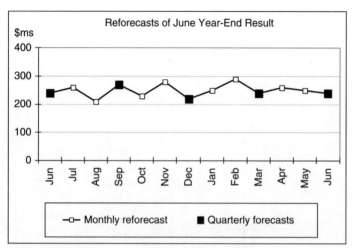

EXHIBIT 3.8 Replacing the number noise of monthly reforecasts with quarterly rolling forecasts

PDF DOWNLOAD

To assist the finance team on the journey, templates, checklists, and book reviews have been provided. The reader can access, free of charge, a PDF of the following material from www.davidparmenter.com/The_Financial_ Controller_and_CFO's_Toolkit.

The PDF download for this chapter includes:

- Template for costing the month-end processes
- Draft set of month-end rules for the finance team

EXHIBIT 3.9 Key Activities of a Day Three Month-End

Day –3 & earlier	Day –2	Day –1	Day +1	Day +2 & +3
▪ Payroll accrual finalized ▪ Depreciation finalized ▪ Balance sheet G/L a/cs reviewed for reasonable ▪ Daily bank a/c reconciliation (DBR)	▪ Close-off accruals ▪ DBR	▪ Close-off AP, AR, work in progress (WIP), WIP to finished goods, production for last day, time sheets, noon ▪ First close of G/L ▪ Numbers available to budget holders by 5 p.m. ▪ DBR	▪ Flash report by 5 p.m. to CEO ▪ Second close of G/L ▪ Budget holders complete their two-page report ▪ DBR	▪ Report preparation ▪ Quality assurance procedures ▪ Report preparation ▪ Issue report ▪ DBR

- Month-end reporting checklist
- Month-end bottlenecks and techniques to get around them
- Implementation plan for an organization with over 600 FTEs

 NOTE

1. David Parmenter, "Rapid Reporting in Three Days or Less and Error Free," www.davidparmenter.com 2015.

PART THREE

III

Technologies to Adopt

CHAPTER FOUR

Future-Ready Technologies

OVERVIEW

Many finance teams have underinvested in twenty-first-century systems and relied too heavily on spreadsheets. Far too much time and money has been reinvested in upgrading the general ledger (G/L) and far too little on monthly reporting, forecasting, budgeting, accounts payable, drill-down, and consolidation software. This chapter answers the questions *"Which systems should I invest in?"* and *"How should I go about it?"*

Far too much money is reinvested in upgrading the general ledger (G/L). In a modern company, the G/L only does the basic task of holding the financial numbers for the year. Monthly reporting, latest forecast numbers, budget numbers, and even the drill-down facility available to budget holders often reside outside the G/L package, so why reinvest?

BAN SPREADSHEETS FROM CORE FINANCE ROUTINES

Spreadsheets have no place in forecasting, budgeting, and many other core financial routines. Spreadsheets were not designed for many of the tasks they are currently used to accomplish. In fact, at workshops I often remark in jest that many people, if they worked at NASA, would try to use Microsoft Excel for the US space program, and many would believe that it would be appropriate to do so.

A spreadsheet is a great tool for creating static graphs for a report or designing and testing a reporting template. It is not, and never should have been, a building block for your company's finance systems. Two accounting firms have pointed out that there is approximately a 90 percent chance of a logic error for every 150 rows in an Excel workbook.[1]

Some of the common problems with spreadsheets are:

Broken links or formulas. An individual might add or eliminate a row or column so that, when a group of spreadsheets is rolled up, the master spreadsheet is taking the wrong number from the one that was modified.

Consolidation errors. Often, a spreadsheet will lock up or show a screen full of "REF," "REF," "REF" errors, because it was not designed to be a tool for handling a rollup of dozens of different worksheets.

Input of the wrong numbers. Entering the wrong number can happen in any process, but spreadsheet-based systems often require rekeying of information, which can produce data inconsistencies. A spreadsheet might use a look-up table that is out of date or an entry might have been inadvertently or mistakenly overwritten.

Incorrect formulas. A subtotal might omit one or more rows, columns, or both. An individual might overwrite a formula because he or she believes the replacement is more accurate. Or, someone might use an outdated spreadsheet. Another problem that arises with spreadsheets is that allocation models might not allocate 100 percent of the costs. Allocation methods might also be inconsistent.

No proper version control. Using an outdated version of a spreadsheet is very common.

Lack of robustness. Confidence in the number a spreadsheet churns out is not assured. Many times, you cannot check all the formulas because they can be found in any cell of the spreadsheet.

Inability to accommodate changes to assumptions quickly. What would you do if your CEO asked, "If we stopped production of computer printers, what would be the financial impact? I need the answer at the close of play today." Your spreadsheets are not able to provide that quick answer.

Design is by accounting staff who are not programmers. Most accounting staff have not been trained in system documentation and quality assurance, which you would expect from a designer of a core company system.

Multiple versions of the truth. Many people in a business can use spreadsheets to create their own view to a ridiculous level of detail. This can lead, as a friend once said to me, "to the march of a million spreadsheets."

Jeremy Hope[2] of *Beyond Budgeting* fame and more recently author of the groundbreaking book *Reinventing the CFO* points out that Sarbanes-Oxley may be the sword that finally removes the spreadsheet from key financial monthly routines: "In theory at least, every change to a formula or even a change to the number of rows needs to be documented."

Rule of 100 Rows

I believe you can build a model in a spreadsheet application and can keep it within 100 rows without much risk. Pass this threshold and you expose yourself, your finance team, and the organization.

Finance teams require a robust tool, not a spreadsheet that was built by an innovative accountant and that, now, no one can understand. I always ask in workshops, "Who has a massive spreadsheet written by someone else that you have to pray before you use it?" You can see the pain in the instant response. Most people know that the person who built the spreadsheet certainly was not trained in operational systems design. The workbook will be a collage of evolving logic that only the originator has a chance to understand. Often, the main hurdle is the finance team's reluctance to divorce itself from the spreadsheet program. It has been a long and comfortable marriage, albeit one that has limited the finance team's performance.

NEW CFO FINDS AN ERROR

A financial controller came to me with a great tale. He had just completed the annual budget that his team had been working on for many weeks, long into the night and on weekends. Proudly, one Friday

(continued)

(continued)

afternoon, he walked into the office of the recently appointed CFO and announced the first cut of the annual plan. The CFO spent five minutes looking at the plan and after quickly calculating some numbers said, "This annual plan is wrong; the numbers do not make sense."

The financial controller was taken aback, because he had made a special effort to conduct quality assurance on the numbers, and he had done comparisons to last year's plan, along with a few other things. He had wanted to make the best impression.

The CFO called him over to look at his brief calculation, "Pat, we know the planned sales have been signed off already, gross profit margin historically has been around __ percent, overheads are roughly $__, and thus, I am expecting a number around $__ to $__." The financial controller could only agree.

That weekend, the team poured over the spreadsheet, which was enormous and included the consolidation of many worksheets from many sources. Late on Sunday, team members experienced a "eureka" moment. An error was found and the news was rushed to the financial controller. As they processed the correction, they looked with disbelief because the new number was within the outline the CFO had suggested. "We have a pretty smart CFO; let's see how long this error has been around. Please look at the last two years' annual plan models," Pat requested.

As the financial controller recalled to me, with a wry smile, the error had been in the plans for the previous two years and had gone completely undetected.

Career Limiting

As a corporate accountant, being an expert at Excel will show you are a technical dinosaur, one who has not embraced modern tools and does not understand the inherent risks in running core financial systems with a high-risk tool.

To those readers who believe spreadsheets are still appropriate for financial systems, I say to them, why not build your general ledger in a spreadsheet program, and while you are at it, all your operational systems? Try explaining to the CEO that only one person knows how these systems work, and he or she left four years ago. You might as well clear your desk now.

SEVEN TECHNOLOGIES TO UNDERSTAND AND EVALUATE

Instead of changing your G/L, I believe the CFO and the finance team have better investment opportunities elsewhere, which will turn the accounting function into a paperless office. The order of priority should be:

- Implement a planning and forecasting tool and migrate all forecasting and budgeting processes onto it.
- Upgrade accounts payable systems (e.g., accounts payable automation and electronic expense claim systems).
- Acquire a reporting tool and migrate all reporting onto it (e.g., Tableau, Qlikview, Dundas, Targit).
- Add a drill-down front end to the G/L if it is not already part of your G/L (e.g., PowerPlay and Crystal Reporting).
- Install consolidation and intercompany software.
- Acquire a collaborative disclosure management application.
- Implement a electronic board paper application.

Upgrade the G/L only after you have acquired the above systems and maximized the existing G/L.

PLANNING AND FORECASTING TOOLS

A decade ago, the electronic spreadsheet was still state-of-the-art for the budgeting process and the only practical option for most midsize companies. However, what might have started as a simple budget model often grew into a spreadsheet that soon got out of control. Moreover, considering the time and effort required to turn that mass of spreadsheets into a coherent budget, that should not have been considered "inexpensive." With the introduction of dedicated planning tool software for all sizes of organizations, spreadsheets are not the optimal approach any longer.

I have written a detailed paper, "Why You Need a Planning Tool and How to Sell the Concept to the Senior Management Team,"[3] which you can access from the IBM Library on www.ibm.com search "Parmenter." In my white paper,

I have outlined how you can learn how to get management to understand why an investment in a planning tool is essential. The paper covers:

- Making the planning tool sale to your senior management team
- Getting the green light from influential sages in your business
- Evaluating potential planning tools
- Selecting a planning tool

A CASE STUDY IN SELECTING AND IMPLEMENTING A PLANNING TOOL

Ballance Agri-Nuturients Ltd. (Ballance) is a farmer-owned cooperative with 700 employees. Ballance has one of New Zealand's largest SAP software implementations, including SAP applications for business intelligence (BI), supply chain management, finance, and process integration.

Ballance's Finance Team

The finance team members in Ballance knew they had to move on from their Excel forecasting model, as not only was it unable to deliver the decision-based information required but it had become a monstrosity with many additions over its 15-year life. The Excel model had grown to 254 separate workbooks that had to be manually consolidated in a five-hour nerve-wracking consolidation. Staff dreaded the possible appearance of the "REF," "REF," "REF" across their screens.

They needed a tool that could help their dynamic organization focus on the future opportunities and threats.

They also needed to migrate away from the annual planning process where budgets were prepared between 3 and 15 months prior to that period starting. Each month the Ballance finance team was tied in the circle of chasing their tail to explain why a forecast made so long ago was wrong.

Scoping the Needs and Planning Tool Selection

As an organization with a "thinking approach" to management, Ballance set about assessing which planning tools could deliver its requirements. They used a consultancy firm to ascertain that there were two options for them, the planning tool linked to their GL provider and a tier-one standalone planning product.

They then hired a planning tool developer to be a facilitator during the blueprint design, making it clear that the blueprint must be capable of "going to market" and be implemented by another planning tool provider. In fact, the facilitator's organization lost out, albeit, they were paid for all their facilitation work.

Implementation of the Planning Tool

The blueprint design process was based on the Toyota principle, "Make decisions slowly by consensus, thoroughly considering all options, and then implement the decisions rapidly." They held three two-week workshops. Yes, that is six weeks of workshops. This incredible upfront investment ensured they had a clear understanding of their needs from the model, how the model should work, that every process in the model was using well-thought-out logic, and that wherever possible a "helicopter" big picture view was retained.

An important feature was that the implementation was a business rather than finance owned. It was foremost a tool for the business, implemented by the business, for the business. System testers came from the business, not the system provider. This had mutual benefits in that the business had users who understood the system prior to launch and the provider had testers who could ask questions with industry insights.

The first forecast was produced a month earlier than previously. This helped cement in the staffs' minds that the new TM1 system was better and worth supporting.

Rolling Forecasts

The rolling forecasting system Ballance developed had the following features:

- Forecasts now belong to the business.
- Forecasts are a rolling, business view and not tied to the financial year.
- Forecasts are for a specific period, 18 months ahead in detail and in summary level 36 months ahead.
- Forecasts are updated every month with inventory planning data.
- They are updated quarterly with financial numbers.
- Assumptions are detailed, monitored, and reviewed.
- The forecasting system is linked into its ERP (enterprise resource planning) system.
- The forecasting system is linked with the sales and operational planning.

(continued)

(continued)

Although the forecast is owned by the business, this does not mean Finance are sitting in the grandstand watching the process. The finance team tests the process to ensure the right questions were being asked. They test the "What ifs?" and understand what the key result indicators are. For Ballance, the input ensured that the company's impressive record on reducing costs and increasing revenue would continue to be supported by this development.

Benefits to Ballance from the Rolling Planning

The benefits of the model have been profound. After two years, the organization has:

■ Saved money through better understanding of bank facilities' requirements
■ Achieved more accurate predictions of profitability and dividend payments
■ Been able to pay rebates to shareholders six weeks earlier, improving shareholders' (farmers') cash flow
■ Become more future focused
■ Improved the recovery of raw material cost fluctuations

There is a detailed review of this case study in the electronic media attached to this book.

New planning tools are being built all the time, and Exhibit 4.1 will certainly be out of date by the time you are reading it.

I have made an attempt to categorize the tools into three tiers. Tier 1 represents major systems where an investment will be substantial and is best suited to larger organizations, say over 750 employees. Tier 3 is more an entry level tool suitable for SMEs below 250 employees. Some tools scale better than others and offer cheaper entry through a cut down version or you pay by your usage.

Exhibit 4.1 is not intended to be a comprehensive list, as this would be a book in itself. The following search strings will help unearth many applications:

■ "Planning tools"
■ "Quarterly rolling forecasting" + "applications"
■ "Forecasting tools" + "rolling"

EXHIBIT 4.1 Analysis of Planning Tools

Tier	Package Name	Website	Cloud Option	Free Trial / Demo
3	A3 Modeling	www.a3solutions.com	Yes	Free model
3	Active Planner	www.epicor.com	No	Demo, webinars
1,2,3	Adaptive Planning	www.adaptiveinsights.com	Yes	Free trial
2,3,	Alight Planning	www.alightplanning.com	No	Demos
3	Big Boss	www.bigbosssoft.com	No	Free trial
3	BizBudg Online	www.bizbudg.com	No	Free trial
1,2,3	BOARD International	www.board.com	No	Demo, webinars
2,3	Budget Maestro	www.centage.com	Yes	Free trial
3	Calxa Premier	www.calxa.com	Yes	Guarantee
3	Castaway	www.castawayforecasting.com	No	Demo
1,2	Cognos TM1	www-03.ibm.com	Yes	Demo only
2,3	Budget Maestro	www.centage.com	No	Free trial.
2,3	Forecast5	www.forecast5.com/	No	Free trial, webinars
2,3	4cast Pro	4Castsolutions.net	No	Free trial
2,3	GIDE Financial Modelling Suite	www.capterra.com/budgeting-software	No	Free trial for 30 days
1,2	Host Analytics EPM Suite	www.hostanalytics.com	Yes	Demo only
1	Hyperion Planning	www.oracle.com	Yes	Video, pod, and on line chat
2	Infor CPM Planning and Budgeting	www.infor.com	No	Demo only
3	Invest for Excel	www.datapartner.fi/en	No	Free trial

(continued)

57

EXHIBIT 4.1 (Continued)

Tier	Package Name	Website	Cloud Option	Free Trial / Demo
2,3	Jedox	www.jedox.com	Yes	Free trial
2,3	Maxiplan	www.maxiplan.com.au	No	No
2,3	Mondelio 6.3	www.mondelio.com	Next version	No
2,3	Planguru	www.planguru.com	Yes	Free trial
2,3	PowerBudget	www.chameleon.com.au	No	Demo
2,3	PowerPlan	www.powerplan.com	Yes	Whitepapers
1,2,3	Prophix11	www.prophix.com	No	Demo, webinars
2,3	Questica Budget	www.questica.com	Yes	Demo
2,3	Quantrix	www.quantrix.com	Yes	Free trial
2,3	Rocket CorPlanning	www.rocketsoftware.com	No	Videos
2,3	Sage 50 Forecasting	www.sage.co.uk/sage-50-forecasting	No	Free trial
1, 2,3	SAS Financial Management	www.sas.com	No	Whitepapers
2,3	Tagetik 4	www.tagetik.com	Yes	Demo only
2,3	Vanguard Financial Forecasting	www.vanguardsw.com	No	Webinar
2,3	Visual cash Focus	http://www.cashfocus.com	No	Free trial
2,3	Whitebirchs	www.whitebirchsoftware.com	Yes	Demo

Examples of some G/L software providers that have their own planning tools:

SAP	SAP Business Objects, InfiniteInsight Solution	www.SAP.com
JD Edwards	Insight for JD Edwards	www.insightsoftware.com/
Microsoft Dynamics GP & Azure	Microsoft Forecaster Microsoft Dynamics AX	www.microsoft.com
Sage		Sage 50 Forecasting

 ## UPGRADE ACCOUNTS PAYABLE SYSTEMS

Finance teams need to invest in accounts payable (AP) to reduce transaction volumes and make the AP operation paperless. For the finance team, the best return on your dollar investment is going to be in AP.

There have been major advancements in technology for AP teams. The return on investment from using AP technology is greater than any other equivalent investment in other service departments within a business. Why, then, are some AP teams so underinvested? This is due to:

- Lack of understanding by the CFO of the technologies and their benefits
- The AP team not researching the technologies
- Insufficient selling of these technologies by application suppliers

It is safe to say that there is a technology suitable for SMEs and large enterprises that will make them paperless. A recent study showed the winds of change (see Exhibit 4.2). As can be seen, if you are not using electronic payments and purchasing cards, you are already behind the eight ball. The extent of automated payables options is extensive, as shown in Exhibit 4.3.

In their paper, Paystream Advisors point out:

Once invoice or other payables data are captured electronically, the question to ask is: Does this invoice need to be approved? The ability to derive an automated answer by using business rules, which, in turn, trigger appropriate workflows, is the centerpiece of an automated AP environment. If the answer to the question is no, the system will move the invoice into the payment process. If the answer is yes, the system will route it to the approving party, along with any necessary decision support documents and information. Business rules, flexible workflow, and transactional transparency are essential.

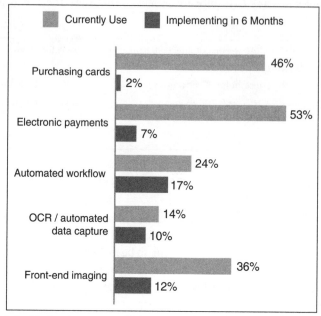

EXHIBIT 4.2 Technology currently in use or planned to be implemented in next six months. *Source: AP Automation for Small to Medium Enterprises,* PayStream Advisors, 2015

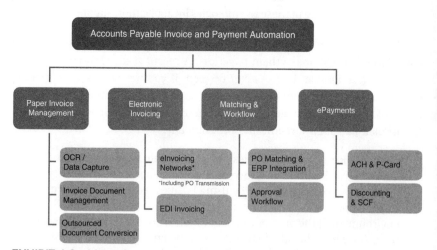

EXHIBIT 4.3 Major Components of Payables Automation *Source: AP Automation for Small to Medium Enterprises,* PayStream Advisors, 2015

Make the Best Use of Your AP System

Most accounting systems come with an integrated purchase order system. Some even enable orders to be sent automatically to preferred suppliers, whose price list has been reviewed via the system by the budget holder. This is a major exercise, and one that should be researched immediately. There will be an organization near your locality that has your accounting system where the purchase order system is working successfully. Visit that company and learn how to implement the purchase system.

Review of Software Solutions

In Exhibit 4.4, I have outlined some solutions offered by application providers. Your best solution is to access the G/L networks offered by your accounting software provider or through Linked-in. All you need to ask is:

- What systems are you using?
- How do you rate them out of one to five (five being a ground changer)?

Investigate all those applications that work with your accounting software scoring four or more.

USING A REPORTING TOOL

The advancement of reporting tools has meant that the G/L is used merely as a collecting area for financial data for the month. A better practice is to have a reporting tool collect this data from the G/L overnight, or in some cases weekly, so that the budget holders can drill into their revenues and costs during the month. Management accountants also will use this reporting tool when analyzing costs because it contains prior months' figures in a continuous stream, enabling them to do cross-year financial comparisons seamlessly. Exhibit 4.5 outlines some reporting tools offered by application providers.

Excel has no place as a reporting tool. Again, it is too prone to disaster. There is no problem where the system automatically downloads to Excel, with all the programming logic being resident in the system and basically bombproof. The problem arises when the system has been built in-house, often by someone who has now left the company, with the accuracy of formatting the G/L download relying on Excel formulas reading the imported file. This is simply a disaster waiting to happen.

EXHIBIT 4.4 Some Accounts Payable Providers and Their Applications

Supplier	Website	Background Information Found on Their Website	Free Trial / Demo
Anybill	www.anybill.com	An end-to-end accounts payable automation solution streamlines your accounts payable workflow process, from invoice capture to approval to payment. It has 24/7 access over the Internet, clear approval authority, and improved reporting.	Video, webinars
Basware	www.basware.co.nz	Basware provides open, secure, cloud-based purchase-to-pay and e-invoicing solutions to organizations of all sizes, resulting in greater efficiencies in procurement, accounts payable, and accounts receivable.	Videos, papers, etc.
Concur	www.concur.co.uk	An integrated, mobile T&E solution, which enables employees to quickly and easily submit their trips and expenses. This gives organizations visibility into spend to ensure travel and expenses are compliant and to find opportunities to save costs.	Demo
Cvision	www.cvisiontech.com	Offers an advanced, automated solution for invoice processing. Capable of recognizing and extracting relevant information within each invoice. After extracting information from incoming invoices, it can automatically reconcile the invoice information with the corresponding data in the AP system.	Free evaluation
Direct Insite	www.directinsite.com	Direct Insite's Invoices On-Line e-invoicing platform transforms complex accounts payable (AP) and procure-to-pay processes.	Whitepapers
Ferret Software	www.ferretsoftware.co.nz	Provides document management technologies that will assist with bulk scanning paper AP invoices directly into your financial system, electronic routing of AP invoices for approval, and automated invoice data entry.	Videos, etc.
Kofax	www.kofax.com	Provides information capture and automates invoice processing and data entry. It includes workflows for discrepancy processing, resolution and accounting details, as well as real-time ERP integration for SAP and Oracle E-Business Suite, a self-service supplier portal, and an AP process optimization dashboard.	Webinar, whitepapers
ReadSoft	www.readsoft.com	Accounts payable (AP) automation with ReadSoft enables control of received and invoiced goods, automatic purchase order matching, optional automatic posting of invoices, enhanced security, and early notification of errors.	Free 2013 AP Automation Study

EXHIBIT 4.5 Reporting Tools Offered by Application Providers

Reporting Tool Suppliers	Website
Caspio	www.caspio.com
Combit Software	www.combit.net
Devexpress	www.devexpress.com
Dundas Data Visualization	www.dundas.com
Megalytic	www.megalytic.com
SAP BusinessObjects	www.sap.com
SAP Crystal Reports	www.sap.com
Sisense.com	www.sisense.com
Spotlightreporting.com/	www.spotlightreporting.com
SQL Server Reporting Services	www.msdn.microsoft.com
Tableau	www.tableau.com
Targit.com	www.targit.com

TURBO YOUR G/L WITH A FRIENDLY FRONT END

It is important that budget holders take ownership of their part of the G/L. To this end, we need to offer them a user-friendly interface to their part of the G/L. There are a number of tools that can make an old G/L feel like a twenty-first-century version. Exhibit 4.6 outlines some front-end tools for general ledgers.

EXHIBIT 4.6 Front-End Tools for General Ledgers

Supplier	Website
AccountMate Software Corporation	www.accountmate.com/source.asp
Combit	www.combit.net
Infor F9	www.infor.com
Praxinet Drillanywhere	www.praxinet.com
SQL Power Group	www.sqlpower.ca/

Companies are reporting that they have had great success by downloading transactions (daily or weekly) from the G/L into these drill-down tools, allowing read-only access to budget holders.

With a drill-down tool, budget holders never look at the G/L. Management accountants and budget holders also will use this reporting tool when analyzing costs. The drill-down tool offers trend analysis that transcends the year-end, enabling budget holders to look at the last 18- or 24-month trend seamlessly.

A by-product of these reporting tools is that CFOs are now questioning why they need to invest in the first-tier accounting systems. In Australia, one CFO is running the G/L of an organization with 400 full-time employees on the mind-your-own-business (MYOB) accounting G/L. As he said, "Why invest thousands when all the G/L does is to hold the historic numbers and only a couple of accountants access it? In our company, all the reporting against budget and drill-down access used by budget holders is performed in auxiliary systems."

CONSOLIDATION AND INTERCOMPANY SOFTWARE

Performing a consolidation in a spreadsheet is inappropriate—or, put more bluntly, is stupid. There are now excellent systems that organize this for you and enable the subsidiaries to have their own general ledger and account code structure. Their trial balance is simply mapped into the consolidated entity's account codes. An exploration of any search engine will also find some freeware, robust older versions available at no cost. Try this search: consolidation+software+freeware. Using this search, I soon found the solutions listed in Exhibit 4.7.

Larger conglomerates need to have a sophisticated communication system between them. Far too many finance teams are conned into thinking that they need to standardize the G/Ls for this. Yes, it will do the job, but at what cost? The primary beneficiaries are the G/L providers and the associated consultants, who no doubt can now buy that second summerhouse by their favorite lake.

The answer lies with accessing sophisticated intercompany software that enables an automatic interface for intergroup transactions where one party to the transaction does the entry for both G/Ls. This software, like the consolidation software, allows subsidiaries to keep their own G/L and account codes. In a brief search I found the intercompany software set out in Exhibit 4.8.

At the time of writing this edition a useful forum to seek answers from is supported by www.proformative.com.

EXHIBIT 4.7 Consolidation Tool Offerings

Supplier	Website
Adaptive Consolidation	www.adaptiveinsights.com
BlackLine Consolidation Integrity Manager	www.blackline.com
Board International	www.board.com
Host Analytics Inc.	hwww.hostanalytics.com
Hyperion Financial Management	www.oracle.com
Intacct	www.intacct.com
Mona Group Reporting	www.sigmaconso.com
Netsuite	www.netsuite.com
OneStream XF	www.onestreamsoftware.com
Tagetik	www.tagetik.com
Tensoft Multi-National Consolidation	www.Tensoft.com
Tidemark	www.tidemark.com

EXHIBIT 4.8 Intercompany Software Offerings

Supplier	Website
Coprocess SA	www.coprocess.com
Intercompany Hub	www.blackline.com
IQMS	www.iqms.com

COLLABORATIVE DISCLOSURE MANAGEMENT

This software ensures that you have one database that is the sole source of the truth. All reports, presentations, and public documents are automatically updated from this software if the numbers have changed. It even recalculates any disclosed variances.

To produce external and internal reports, one needs to gather data across systems and across Microsoft Word, Microsoft Excel, and Microsoft PowerPoint files. Much information is passed back and forth over insecure channels, such as email, until the report is complete.

EXHIBIT 4.9   Collaborative Disclosure Management Software Offerings

Supplier	Website
Tagetik	www.tagetik.com
IBM Cognos	www.ibm.com
Hyperion	www.oracle.com
SAP BusinessObjects	www.sap.com

Disclosure management software will help you:

- Have one version of the truth so that if sales year to date is being reported it will be the same whether it is the Sales & Marketing report or the Finance report.
- Harness the "wisdom of the crowd."
- Provide commentary and numbers which are all internally consistent.
- Speed up year-end accounts, planning and forecasting, board presentations, and reports.

I consider it unprofessional for a finance team, in an organization with over 400 FTEs, to report to a board and shareholders in any other way. Insert into your search engine "Collaborative Disclosure Management +YouTube" and listen to some talks on the topic. In a brief search I found the CDM software set out in Exhibit 4.9

 ## PAPERLESS BOARD MEETING

Many of the procedures that support a board meeting have changed little since Charles Dickens's time. Board members receive large board papers that they have difficulty finding the time to read. In the twenty-first-century we should be using technology.

The board members should receive all board papers via specialized board paper software. They can make their notes on the system and when the board members arrive at the meeting they are directed to the relevant section by a screen that emerges out of the board table just in front of them. No papers are allowed in the boardroom, as this would delay proceedings. The chairperson, with the help of the CEO executive assistant, loads the relevant paper onto the screen and each member can see the points they have made on the screen in front of them.

Electronic board paper systems offer many features including:

- Access to papers from anywhere, anytime, as soon as they are available
- Intuitive and simple to use
- Notes easily attached to pages
- Instantaneous edits, page numbering, and so on
- Absolute security of board papers

A search using "electronic board papers + systems" found the following on the first two search engine pages.

Supplier of electronic board software
www.azeusconvene.com
www.boardadvantage.com
www.boardeffect.com
www.boardpacks.com
www.boardpad.com
www.boardtrac.com.au
www.cgsboardworks.com
www.diligent.com (Diligent boardbooks)
www.pervasent.com (board-papers)

Designing your own in-house system using SharePoint or simply lodging the board papers as PDFs in a secure area of the website, which the board members can access from their office, is an option that should be treated as a holding option only as it is deficient on a number of counts, including lack of automating page numbering, poor security, and PDFs can get disorganized by board members.

The key to both these options is that the board financial report is made available as soon as it has been completed. Other board papers likewise can be read as and when they are ready, instead of the last paper determining when the board report is sent out by courier.

The executive information system (EIS) can also be made available to board members who can examine those areas of particular interest before the board meeting.

MAXIMIZE THE USE OF THE EXISTING G/L

You are most likely using only 30 to 40 percent of your G/L's features or capability. Some better practices to maximize the value of your existing G/L are:

- Train, and train again, your budget holders on how to use the G/L. Delegate the responsibility of maintaining their part of the G/L to budget holders.
- Invest in a G/L upgrade only if you already have a procurement system and a planning tool.
- Get your G/L consultant in next week for a day to see where you can better use your G/L's built-in features—you will be pleasantly surprised.

One CFO receives a visit three to four times a year from the G/L consultant, who reviews what the finance team is doing and then reminds them of other processing features within the G/L that will save them time. These processing features would have been covered in the training but have been forgotten as they have not been put into regular use.

 ## AVOIDING THE HARD SELL TO UPGRADE YOUR G/L

The impression I have is that all the major general ledger (G/L) systems are designed by freshly minted MBAs who have never been a CFO in their lives. This is the only explanation I can think of for the unnecessary complexity that is embedded in most of the major G/L applications. The major G/L systems, like SAP, have now made implementing a G/L as complex as setting off to the moon. You need truckloads of consultants to implement the systems.

If you are ever in a hotel lobby and you see a team arrive, smiling, looking refreshed, beautifully dressed, with very expensive shoes and of course scratch-free leather briefcases (as the team members have always flown business class), and you happen to follow them to the elevator, when they press the executive floor button, ask, "By chance, are you SAP implementers?"

It is important for the CFO to avoid the hard sell that the G/L providers make. They are experts at selling the systems through your emotional drivers. The Sarbanes–Oxley Act of 2002 has made millions for their bottom line. Instead, the CFO has to look carefully at the options that are available if you want to keep complexity out of the G/L.

Besides investing in an overly complex G/L, many CFOs are party to a huge investment in other systems that serve to lock in analysis at the micro level (e.g., activity-based costing applications). Jeremy Hope of *Beyond Budgeting* fame points out in his book *Reinventing the CFO*[4] that many such systems are dubious.

I firmly believe that if CFOs visited more sites that are using their intended new applications, they might think twice before going ahead. Some of the large G/L applications are so complex that only rocket scientists can implement them, and thus the organization and their bank account are now taken hostage for the foreseeable future.

 ## IMPLEMENTING A NEW SYSTEM

As discussed in Chapter 2, leading and selling change is a far more complex process than one would first believe. The extra time dedicated to embracing Kotter's eight stages with Kaffron and Logan's work is well worth doing. It is far better than spending time fixing the carnage at the base of the cliff.

Appraising the Options

Limit your choice to three. With clever use of the search engine and word of mouth, you should be able to reduce your choice to three options.

Avoid doing a request for information. One sure way to bury yourself in detail is to put out a request for information. You will get too many responses. Every provider under the sun will send you brochures and then inundate you with follow-up phone calls. You have just become the newest hot sales prospect. I have a better solution for you, and it involves the following actions:

Ask users of your G/L. Contact your general ledger supplier and ask, "Who is a very sophisticated user of this general ledger, and who uses a _____tool?" Alternatively, ask your general ledger supplier for the contact details of the three most sophisticated users of your G/L. You will find that they have also made progress with many of the systems you have identified. Arrange to visit at least three who are using these tools, and see how they have linked the two systems. Put their chosen system into the mix.

Internet search. Search the Internet for the _____ tool that has a local support provider. The last thing you need is a team being flown in each week that stays at five-star hotels.

Visit three to four sites. Select between three and four providers who can deliver the solution and visit the different sites where they are using the preferred tools. You will gain further insight into the operations of the tools.

Many large accounting applications have a suite of tools. Before you short-list them, check out all the standalone tools that work with your general ledger because:

- The tools packaged with general ledgers seldom are the best in their field.
- All tools can accept data from any general ledger.
- A tool independent from the general ledger provider might be a cheaper and better option.

Set out in Exhibit 4.10 is a suggested checklist to use when evaluating the planning tool providers you have short-listed. There is a column for each of the short-listed suppliers.

Seek Approval for Proposal Process

At this stage, a presentation is prepared for the senior management team. The focus of the presentation is:

- The current annual planning process "pain points"
- The status of the current spreadsheet application
- The focus group findings
- The recommended shortlist of the planning tool providers
- The likely costs

The goal is a recommendation to commence a request for proposal process.

Test the Best Applications and Close the Deal

After you have reduced the number of providers to the best three applications, request from the providers that they demonstrate how their application can operate with your organization. Agree to pay two to three days of consultancy fees to each provider and evaluate results. Paying the fees enables you to retain copies of the work. In reality, you will get a bargain, as the providers will be putting in much more than time.

Nothing is more frustrating to a provider who has worked hard on the proposal than not to be given the courtesy of a fair hearing. Frequently, in proposal situations, one party is on the inside track, usually someone who might have

EXHIBIT 4.10 "Planner Tool Provider" Evaluation Checklist

Ratings of planning tool providers against key requirements:

The supplier has an agent who is local.	☐ Yes ☐ No	☐ Yes ☐ No	☐ Yes ☐ No
They are skilled trainers.	☐ Yes ☐ No	☐ Yes ☐ No	☐ Yes ☐ No
They have worked with our G/L.	☐ Yes ☐ No	☐ Yes ☐ No	☐ Yes ☐ No
The tool is easy to use.	☐ Yes ☐ No	☐ Yes ☐ No	☐ Yes ☐ No
License costs are reasonable.	☐ Yes ☐ No	☐ Yes ☐ No	☐ Yes ☐ No
The supplier's key consultants are available for this project.	☐ Yes ☐ No	☐ Yes ☐ No	☐ Yes ☐ No
Demonstration shows that they understand our requirements.	☐ Yes ☐ No	☐ Yes ☐ No	☐ Yes ☐ No
Good feedback from 1st reference site.	☐ Yes ☐ No	☐ Yes ☐ No	☐ Yes ☐ No
Good feedback from 2nd reference site.	☐ Yes ☐ No	☐ Yes ☐ No	☐ Yes ☐ No

already completed an assignment for the client. Make it a level playing field and listen to the other proposals for the following reasons:

* You can gain insight into how the model can work.
* Other applications may have better local support. Any tool that requires consultant's visiting from overseas should only be selected after extra reference checks.
* You want to select consultants who can present a complex message simply. You want to avoid dealing with consultants who should have been rocket scientists as they see complexity in everything.
* One team will be much better at understanding your needs. These should be rated accordingly.

Contractual Process

Often, too little time or mental horsepower is invested in the contracting process. To avoid pitfalls, you should:

* Ensure that the key consultants you have identified on the vendor's team are contracted for a certain number of days because they are often over-committed.
* Write into the contract that the interim payments are tied to deliveries to keep everyone focused.
* Make sure it is clear in the contract that the building of the model will be done largely by in-house staff, who will be trained and mentored by the provider. The skilled in-house staff will always understand the issues of the organization better than any external consultant.

Training of In-House Experts

Select at least four in-house staff to become experts on the new tool. Over time you will find these staff will be head hunted so always maintain this level of in-house competence. Not only will this save you money in the long run, but you will have the system you need.

Have Three Pilots

Pilot the application on three business units (BUs), as advised by Peter Drucker. Drucker pointed out that one pilot will never be enough, as all the employees will point out that the pilot was not representative. Two pilots are better, but why not three? The greatest management thinker of all time is seldom wrong.

You want to pilot in BUs who have a good relationship with the implementation team, have a BU leader who is supportive of the project, and has used technology well in the past.

It is important to fine tune the tool on this run before the rollout to all other business units.

PDF DOWNLOAD

To assist the finance team on the journey, templates and checklists have been provided. The reader can access, free of charge, a PDF of the suggested worksheets, checklists, and templates from www.davidparmenter.com/The_Financial_Controller_and_CFO's_Toolkit.

The PDF download for this chapter includes:

- The full Ballance Nutrients case study into selecting and implementing a planning tool
- An updated list of available planning tools
- An updated list of accounts payable providers and their applications
- An updated list of available reporting tools
- A 15 step program on implementing a planning tool

NOTES

1. Coopers and Lybrand found 90 percent of all spreadsheets composed of more than 150 rows contained errors (*Journal of Accountancy*, "How to Make Spreadsheets Error-Proof") and KPMG found 91 percent of 22 spreadsheets taken from an industry sample contained errors (KPMG Management

Consulting, "Supporting the Decision Maker: A Guide to the Value of Business Modeling").

2. Jeremy Hope, *Reinventing the CFO: How Financial Managers Can Transform Their Roles and Add Greater Value* (Boston: Harvard Business Press, 2006).

3. David Parmenter, "Why You Need a Planning Tool and How to Sell the Concept to the Senior Management Team," IBM whitepapers 2015. You can access from www.ibm.com search "Parmenter."

4. Hope.

PART FOUR

IV

Progress You Need to Make within the Next Six Months

5

Reduce Accounts Payable Volumes by 60 Percent

OVERVIEW

The accounts payable team is the center of an accounting function, for without its smooth operation, the finance team can never move forward. This chapter explores the better practices adopted by leading-edge accounts payable teams.

Many large organizations have made massive inroads into accounts payable and, quite frankly, will find this chapter rather basic. To those I say simply, move to the next chapter. However, many finance teams are wedded to Charles Dickens processes and procedures. This chapter is an extract from my white paper "50 + Ways to Improve Your Accounts Payable Function."[1]

REMOVAL OF ALL CHARLES DICKENS PROCESSES

I believe the accounts payable team is the center of an accounting function, for without its smooth operation:

- Monthly accounts cannot be prepared promptly.
- The company does not, at any point in time, know its total liabilities.
- Budget holders spend too much of their valuable time processing orders and approving invoices for payment.
- There is a low level of accuracy in the monthly accounts due to missed liabilities and posting errors.
- The processing procedures are more akin to the Charles Dickens era than to the twenty-first century (after all, Charles Dickens had a checkbook and received paper-based invoices).
- Suppliers are forever on the phone querying payments.
- Expense claims are a nightmare for claimants and the accounts payable team.

The key twenty-first-century AP better practices are investing in AP technology, see Chapter 4, eliminating the receipt of paper based invoices, and moving the AP workload away from processing into the more value-added areas, as shown in Exhibit 5.1. This move, at the same time, will increase AP team job satisfaction and appreciation from budget holders.

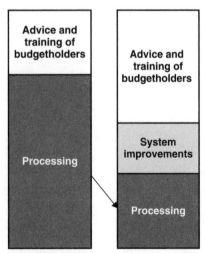

EXHIBIT 5.1 Changes in the balance of work

MOVE TO A PAPERLESS ACCOUNTS PAYABLE FUNCTION

Why do we go from an electronic transaction in the supplier's accounting system to a paper-based invoice? Surely we should be able to change this easily with our major suppliers. Many U.S. multinationals have achieved this already. It requires an investment, skilled AP staff, and retraining of the budget holders. The rewards are immense.

To appreciate the benefits, the AP team should regularly visit the website for Accounts Payable and Procure-to-Pay professionals (www.theaccounts payablenetwork.com).

The various ways to make this move into the twenty-first-century AP paperless procedures include:

System	Description
▪ Electronic ordering system	▪ Invest in an electronic ordering system (procurement system) so control is at the order stage, receipting is electronic, and supplier invoices can be automatically matched to orders and paid. See "Get Your Electronic Ordering System to Work" section in this chapter.
▪ Purchase card	▪ Introduce the purchase card to all staff with delegated authority so all small-value items can be purchased through the purchase card, thereby saving thousands of hours of processing time by both budget holders and the accounts payable teams. See "Get a Purchase Card System Implemented as Soon as Possible" section in this chapter.
▪ Electronic supplier feeds	▪ Invest in liaison time with all major suppliers to organize electronic feeds of the invoices which will include the general ledger account codes—this requires liaison between the two IT teams, yours and the suppliers!
▪ Web based expense claim	▪ Acquire an integrated web based expense claim system so employees, wherever they are, can process their claims. These systems are now linked to the user's mobile phone so pictures of the transaction dockets are photographed and uploaded into the system, doing away with the requirement that all expense receipts are to be sent to, and stored by, the AP team. Some purchase cards can also accommodate cash expense items.

(continued)

System	Description
▪ Eliminate all checks	▪ Eliminate all check payments, framing the last check on the CEO's office wall; see "Mount the Last Signed Check on the CEO's Wall" later in the chapter.
▪ Scanning	▪ Set up an email address for the AP team so that all invoices have to be sent electronically to accountspayable@_____.com. This ensures you already have an image and thus reduces the need for scanning. Scanning should be used while paper based invoices are being received without orders, or including amounts which are different to their corresponding order. The scanned image is sent to the originator for approval with the original always held by the AP team.
▪ Load remittances onto your website	▪ Post remittances electronically onto your website in a secure area so that suppliers with passwords can download them. This removes the need to send remittances by email or post.
▪ Key suppliers online access	▪ Allow your key suppliers online read only access, through password access, to their account in the AP so they can reconcile their ledger.

GET YOUR ELECTRONIC ORDERING SYSTEM TO WORK

Most accounting systems come with an integrated purchase order system. The more sophisticated systems give 24/7 access to the designated supplier's online price list and then email automatically the order onto the supplier, providing the order is within the budget holder's delegated authority.

These systems should be purchased and fully implemented before the accounting team ever considers upgrading the general ledger (G/L). Getting the electronic ordering system to work effectively is a major exercise, and one that should be researched immediately. There will be an organization that uses the same accounting system and where the purchase order system is working well. Visit that organization and learn how to implement the system.

GET A PURCHASING CARD SYSTEM IMPLEMENTED AS SOON AS POSSIBLE

A purchasing card card is a free AP system, run by your card provider, financed by your suppliers. Using these cards in all organizations from the private to government and nonprofit sectors is a no-brainer. It just needs to be researched and sold properly. Never, never call it a credit card; call it a free accounts payable system. Please reread my chapter on selling change before you promote this invaluable tool.

I estimate that the full cost from ordering, receipting, paying and filing, including time spent handling supplier queries is between $35 and $55 per transaction. That's pretty horrific when you realize that a high portion of your transactions are for minor amounts. Exhibit 5.2 shows a typical profile of AP invoices. The bulk of invoices coming to the accounts payable team may be for low-value amounts, especially if consolidation invoices have not yet been organized.

Remember that it costs the same to process a $10 transaction as it does a $100,000 transaction. In addition, is it appropriate to request budget holders to raise an order in your purchase order system for a $20 transaction? Surely the AP system is designed around 100 percent compliance of major invoices,

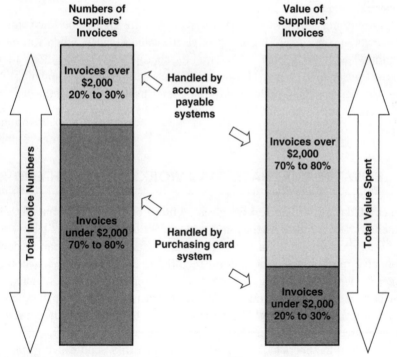

EXHIBIT 5.2 AP invoices that a purchasing card is targeting

EXHIBIT 5.3   Example of a purchase card

say over $2,000, $3,000, or $5,000, depending on your size. Purchasing cards (see Exhibit 5.3) are different from a credit card and are here to stay.

Most organizations are happy with this level of control and will accept the sole liability for the card expenditure. However, the ever-cautious organization can have the liability rest with the staffperson, who must be reimbursed before the payment is due. This involves more processing steps so it is not the preferred option.

Purchasing cards work particularly well with high-value/low-volume items where you are purchasing through the same suppliers when you have organized, with the supplier, to also enter the appropriate G/L code information on the transaction. The two IT functions just need to get together and map out the G/L codes for the supplies and the card informs the supplier of the department code. This is not difficult, as most suppliers will not affect more than three G/L codes!

HOW THE PURCHASE CARD WORKS AT MONTH-END

On cutoff day all card holders are given 24 hours or so to ensure that all their expenditures are coded. All the purchasing cards holder has to do is access, via the web, the bank's purchasing cards system (which, of course, can be done from an airport lounge) and enter the required security details to get access to the statement. If the card holder has purchased from a designated supplier, all will be coded, thus underpinning national contracts. It will only be the one-off purchases that need coding. The card system can be preset with the most frequently used purchasing card G/L codes to aid efficiency.

AP team members look at the status of statements, send warning emails ("Please code your expenditure by 5 p.m. tomorrow"), and, where necessary, code all uncoded expenditure. *Shame and name* lists and the odd phone call from the CEO saying, "What do you not understand about the importance of this system?" will ensure that card holders realize that any breach of compliance is seen as career limiting!

AP can simply upload all the expenditure straight into the G/L, and all the purchasing cards can be paid by one—yes, one—direct debit payment. Now I am sure can you understand why most US organizations use a purchasing card.

 ## THE BETTER PRACTICES WITH PURCHASE CARDS

The better practices with purchase cards include:

- A minimum amount is set before accounts payable will process a one-off supplier's invoice through the AP system. As a minimum, I would suggest $2,000. The only exception is you will always process you main suppliers' transactions through the AP system, regardless of how small the invoice. You need to look at the profile of your expenditure. You want at least 50 percent of the volume to be caught by the purchase card system.
- All employees who make regular purchases are given a purchase card.
- Employees who make only one-off payments do so through their own credit card and claim back or use their manager's purchase card.
- Corporate credit cards are recalled, as they represent a duplication.
- You never take purchase cards away from staff who are not coding their expenditure—you simply set the hounds on them!
- Pick the purchase card that offers the easiest system, which links well with your G/L, permits supplier to code, and has a cash expense claim add-on.
- For suppliers who are reluctant to lose the 2 to 3 percent, reimburse this fee based on the actual annual spend, which is easily sourced from the purchase card system.

For more information, search the web for "purchasing card" + " name of your bank." All you need to do is contact your bank, which will have many better practice examples.

> My financial controller lobbied hard for a purchase card for all staff with all expenditure under $2,000 being processed via the card. The staff entered coding for purchases that were not already recoded by the supplier, and the approval process was online. Thousands of transactions were replaced by one electronic feed and one direct debit.
> —*CFO with blue chip experience*

CUT OFF ACCOUNTS PAYABLE ON THE LAST WORKING DAY

Better practice is to cut off AP at noon on the last working day. If AP is held open, you will find it difficult to complete prompt month-end reporting. What benefit does holding open AP for one or two days have? Chapter 3 covers cutting off accounts payables on the last working day and how to limit accruals and bring them forward. Please reread this for more information.

 ## MOUNT THE LAST SIGNED CHECK ON THE CEO'S WALL

In all workshops, I find leading-edge organizations that do not have a checkbook. However, for many organizations, some suppliers still request checks. The question is, how do you get the reluctant suppliers to give you their bank details?

Some progressive companies have given up mailing letters to suppliers requesting the move to electronic payment, and have instead hired temporary staff to call suppliers. One company with 99 percent of accounts paying by direct debit (and still not happy) calls suppliers and says, "We would like to pay you, but we cannot. [Pause.] We are a modern company and pay all our accounts electronically. We have thrown away the checkbook and are at a loss as to how we can pay you, as you have ignored our requests for your bank account details!" One company canceled its check payment run and was able to obtain 120 suppliers' bank details within four hours of phoning them to say, "We cannot pay you!"

I recommend that the last check be written payable to "A.N. Other" for 99 cents. This check is then ceremoniously mounted in a golden frame with a plaque saying, "This is the last check and is a symbol of our drive to end all Charles Dickens processes." The framed check is then mounted in the CEO's office. The CEO will get much pleasure in answering visitors when they ask, "What is that check doing in a frame?"

The benefits from using electronic funds transfers as a payment method include lower costs, predictable cash flows, and fewer supplier phone calls over late payment.

PERFORM FREQUENT DIRECT CREDIT PAYMENT RUNS

It is a better practice to perform frequent direct credit payment runs, in fact treating this as a normal day-to-day activity. In organizations doing frequent runs, an invoice is received directly by AP from the supplier, and the details are matched to the electronic order and the electronic receipting flag that says "goods/services have been received in full." Once order, invoice, and receipting match one another, a payment is processed on the agreed future payment date.

IMPROVE BUDGET HOLDERS' COOPERATION

There are many ways to improve budget holders' cooperation:

- Increase budget holder turnaround on purchase invoice approval by linking performance to their bonus element.
- Establish account management within the finance team (e.g., Sarah looks after budget holders A, B, and C; Ted looks after budget holders D, E, and F).
- Send a "welcome letter" to new budget holders to train them from the beginning and eliminate potential bad habits before they have a chance to become permanent.
- Hold workshops outlining how budget holders, and their relevant staff, should work with the finance systems (AP, reporting system, G/L, completion of expense claims, use of the purchasing card, etc.).
- Reward and recognize good budget holder behavior.
- Make budget holders aware of all their errors.

SPEED UP BUDGET HOLDERS' CORRECTION OF OMISSIONS

One company reports that it now has a 24-hour turnaround for all branches to approve all invoices that cannot be matched to orders and that have not been electronically receipted. If a branch manager does not achieve this on one single day in the month, he or she loses one month's performance bonus. The CEO was

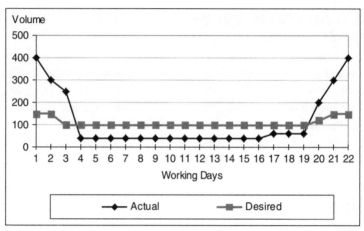

EXHIBIT 5.4   AP invoice processing volumes during month

approached and got behind this initiative. This takes clever marketing, and is well worth the effort. This change, along with streamlining of supplier invoice timings, will have a profound impact on processing volumes, helping to smooth out the workload, as shown in Exhibit 5.4.

 ## A WELCOME LETTER TO ALL NEW BUDGET HOLDERS

Imagine the goodwill created when a new employee receives a welcome letter from the AP department asking for a slot to deliver a 20-minute training session for the individual within the next few weeks. Why wait until new employees are educated by the uneducated (budget holders who do not know or do not comply with the AP procedures)? Get in there first. Deliver a brief training presentation, including:

- Procedures
- Forms
- Problems we have, and why they create a lot of wasted time
- How budget holders and the AP team can work most effectively together
- The presence of *shame and name* lists—you point out, "But this, of course, will not affect you!"

This presentation is best delivered in a casual format, on a laptop, placed in front of the new budget holder. See Appendix A for a draft welcome letter.

INTRODUCE "SHAME AND NAME" LISTS

If you want to change human behavior, you need to work on it for a duration of 12 weeks, and during this time, the penny will drop. If you create a number of *shame and name* lists and ask the CEO and the senior management team (SMT), to phone a few culprits each week you will, over 12 weeks, create change. I would recommend preparing a laminated card with all the league tables (i.e., lists of the culprits with the highest number of errors, exceptions, etc.), cut to fit the inside pocket of the SMT members' jackets. All the SMT need to do is discuss the matter with the budget holders with enough firmness that the budget holder understands that repetition will be career limiting. The suggested lists are:

- Budget holders with the most purchase invoices without a corresponding order
- Employees with late expense claims
- Budget holders with purchase invoices awaiting approval that are already outside the set approval turnaround time
- Budget holders who have missed deadlines

Remember, you will never want to invite all the budget holders to your Sunday afternoon barbeque, so do not worry about being unpopular with a noncompliant budget holder. You need to make one thing clear: Not complying with the accounting system requirements is going to prevent any chance of climbing the corporate ladder. In other words, there are three options open to these nonconforming budget holders: You leave the organization, they leave the organization, or they change. You might, as one attendee pointed out, want to call these lists "budget holders requiring further training."

REWARD GOOD BUDGET HOLDER BEHAVIOR

One accounting team gives a bottle of wine a month to the budget holder who provides the first complete month-end submission. This simple acknowledgment has provided the appropriate environment for timely submissions from budget holders. It is also important to record the "winner " on the finance team home page on the organization's intranet so the relevant budget holder gets the recognition, which is the main reward.

HAVE A CLOSER RELATIONSHIP WITH YOUR MAIN SUPPLIERS

There are a number of ways a closer relationship with suppliers can improve processing. The more your key suppliers' systems are linked to yours, the better. It is simply an issue of getting the two IT departments together around the same table. Better practices include:

- Having all major suppliers link their systems with yours and having the supplier provide consolidated electronic invoices that are already G/L coded. Set a target of getting your top five suppliers all electronic within the next three months. You will need to get on the phone today to talk to your counterpart in the supplier organization (the CFO or management accountant). Do not leave this to the IT department to organize, as they might find this type of exercise personally challenging. Where have you seen an IT department full of extroverts and great communicators?
- Have one stationery supplier and introduce consignment stationery cupboards on all floors in the organization. Staff then can take out what stationery they need. At first, this will lead to some waste. You simply chart usage and compare average usage per employee per floor. The stationer then invoices you monthly, in a consolidated invoice, sent electronically with floor-by-floor usage.

    The consignment stock is replenished each week. During these visits, the stationer brings in the one-off items that have been ordered in the last two days, thus avoiding the courier charges.
- Bring the invoicing of all monthly accounts, such as utilities, credit cards, and so on, earlier in the month (e.g., invoice cycle including transactions from May 28 to June 27 and being received by June 28). You still have a month's transactions, and thus, many finance teams would avoid accruing the remaining business days to month-end, as there is a set-off from the previous month.
- Ask major suppliers to request an order from your budget holders; support this by not paying supplier invoices unless there is a purchase order. Simply return the invoices to suppliers and ask them to attach the purchase order (they will not want to repeat this activity more than once!).
- Require suppliers to enter their transactions into your system. When I work for IBM, I enter my invoice against a particular order. No order number means there is no chance to enter the transaction.
- Ask large-volume, small-dollar suppliers to accept your purchasing card.

SELF-GENERATED INVOICES (BUYER-CREATED INVOICES)

Where a supplier invoice will be received too late, where some product may be missing (raw material blown out of the truck), or where your systems are so sophisticated that you have no need for a supplier's paperwork, a *buyer-created invoice* will aid efficiency.

The supplier's shipping document is used to determine the quantity of goods supplied or, in the case of a weigh-bridge process, the actual weight, measured by the weigh bridge. The agreed weight is then multiplied by the agreed purchase contract price to calculate the amount owed. The customer then direct credits the supplier, who also is sent an electronic invoice. The invoice contains all required details, such as quantity, date of service, taxes, value, total payable, and a unique invoice number using, say, the first three letters of your company, two letters of theirs, and four numbers (e.g., invoice #dsbbd1234).

The benefits of this process include:

- Reduced data entry costs
- Elimination of duplicate and lost invoice condition
- Reduction in processing steps
- Reduction in queries arising from invoice and delivery mismatches
- Minimization of clerical error

PDF DOWNLOAD

To assist the finance team on the journey, templates, checklists, and book reviews have been provided. The reader can access, free of charge, a PDF of the following material from www.davidparmenter.com/The_Financial_ Controller_and_CFO's_Toolkit.

The PDF download for this chapter includes:

- Copy of some purchase card instructions
- Draft welcome letter to new budget holders

 NOTE

1. David Parmenter, "50+ Ways to Improve Your Accounts Payable Function," www.davidparmenter.com, 2015.

CHAPTER SIX

Month-End Reporting Refinements

OVERVIEW

When the first month-end has been reengineered, there are some other changes that will make a substantial difference to how fast your month-end can be. This chapter explores the other changes that you need to make, Day 1 and virtual reporting case studies, and why 4,4,5 week period reporting suits all organizations.

Once you have achieved a much faster month-end, you will have the time to implement some further refinements covered in this chapter. This chapter is an extract from my white paper, "Rapid Reporting in Three Days or Less and Error Free."[1]

AVOID LATE TIMESHEETS

I personally believe timesheets are only required if they are used for revenue generation, and even that is debatable. One accounting firm in the United Kingdom has dispensed with timesheets as it correctly pointed out, "We spent a lot of time filling out timesheets only to invoice the client a different amount of time in most cases." The accounting firm now agrees on a fee range and discusses with the client where the fee should be on the scale. Their staff turnover has dropped dramatically and they estimated up to six percent of time was invested, by all staff filling out timesheets in six-minute units.

Get staff to complete non-revenue-generating time sheets by day −3 and to include their best guess for the remaining two days. You could even get them to project forward for the full week. Even if the estimates were 100 percent wrong, there would not be a material misstatement.

Ask all relevant staff to complete revenue-generating timesheets by noon on the last working day, with a best guess for the afternoon and corrections processed on the next weeks' timesheet. If by lunchtime staff members do not know what they are doing that afternoon, maybe they should be working for your competition.

MINIMIZE BUDGET HOLDERS' MONTH-END REPORTING

Budget holders' reports should be limited to half an hour of preparation. A one-page report should suffice, or two pages if you are using performance indicators. I once saw a pile of reports on a finance manager's desk. When I asked what they were, he said they were the budget holders' month-end reports. "What do you use them for?" I asked. "I do not use them; I call the budget holders if I need an explanation of a major variance," he replied. Hundreds of hours of budget holder time were wasted each month that could have been better spent getting home at a reasonable hour. A good starting point is to cost out the monthly report preparation, as described in Chapter 3.

AVOID THE REWRITING OF REPORTS

Some organizations have made a major cultural change to report writing, committing the board, CEO, and the SMT to avoid rewrites at all costs, saving thousands of dollars a month of management time. The board no longer considers the quality of the board papers a reflection of the CEO's performance. The organizations have learned to delegate and empower their staff so that the SMT and board papers are being written with limited input from senior managers and are being tabled with few amendments, provided that the SMT agrees with the recommendations. The CFO can choose to put a caveat on each finance report: "While I concur with the recommendations, the report was written by _____."

The SMT and board understand that the report is not written in SMT-speak. Board members are encouraged to comment directly to the writer about strengths and areas for improvement in report writing. Where necessary, the writers are also the presenters. The organization thus has a much more relaxed week leading up to the board meeting, having largely delegated the report writing and the associated stress. The rewards include motivated and more competent staff and general managers being free to spend more time contributing to the bottom line.

 ## REPORTING BASED ON 4 OR 5 WEEKS

Julius Caesar gave us the calendar we use today. It is not a good business tool because it creates 12 dramas a year for the finance team and budget holders, with each month being slightly different.

Between three and five months every year will end on a weekend, and finance teams often find that the month-end processes are smoother for these months. Why not close off on the nearest Friday/Saturday/Sunday to month end, as many U.S. companies do? This is sometimes called 4, 4, 5 reporting (see Exhibit 6.1 for the timings). The benefits of this include precise four- or

Dates for a Friday close (nearest to calendar month-end) *					A/P close	A/R close	FA close	Stock close
	2016		2017					
	No. of week		No. of week					
May	4	Friday, May 27, 2016	4	Friday, May 26, 2017	Noon Fri	5 P.M.	Noon Fri	5 P.M. Fri
June	5	Friday, July 01, 2016	5	Friday, June 30, 2017	"-"	"-"	"-"	"-"
July	4	Friday, July 29, 2016	4	Friday, July 28, 2017	"-"	"-"	"-"	"-"
August	4	Friday, August 26, 2016	4	Friday, August 25, 2017	"-"	"-"	"-"	"-"
September	5	Friday, September 30, 2016	5	Friday, September 29, 2017	"-"	"-"	"-"	"-"

EXHIBIT 6.1 Closing on the same day each month (4, 4, 5 accounting)

five-week months, which make comparisons more meaningful, and there is less impact on the workweek as the systems are rolled over at the weekend.

Otherwise, every month is a drama because we close on a different calendar day. Every month we have to issue detailed instructions that effectively say, "The tasks you did on Wednesday last month please complete on Thursday this month. The tasks you did on Thursday last month please complete on Friday" and so on.

Closing off at the weekend can be done for all sectors; some will require more liaison than others. It also would make a big difference in the public and not-for-profit sectors. You simply present to the board June's results and balance sheet. You do not need to highlight the July close. At year-end, the missing two or extra two days of income and balance sheet movement will be taken up in the auditor's "overs and unders" schedule.

You need to choose whether it is to be the last Saturday or the nearest Saturday, last Sunday or nearest Sunday to month-end, and so on. The last Saturday can have you closing six days before month-end, whereas the preferred option of the nearest Saturday will be a maximum of only two working days out.

By making this change, you are beginning to create 12 nonevents a year, the ultimate goal for all corporate accountants.

To make progress in this area, I would recommend the following:

- Contact your general ledger supplier and ask, "Who uses our G/L and closes on a set day each month?" They will link you to them and you will see first-hand the benefits of 4, 4, 5 accounting periods. Ask them, "Would you go back to regular calendar reporting?" Most are likely to give you a look that says, "Are you crazy?"
- Choose which day. It is best to be the nearest rather than the last "Friday", "Saturday", "Tuesday" to month end, etc. The last Saturday can have you closing six days before month-end, whereas the preferred option of nearest Saturday will only be a maximum of two working days out.
- Talk through the audit ramifications with the auditors, as they will have handled it before. At year-end, the missing day of income (two days on leap year) and balance sheet movement will be taken up in the auditor's "overs and unders" schedule. You simply close on December 29 but call the year to the December 31. The misstatement will be lost in the roundings.
- I would not inform the board. You simply present to the board December's result and balance sheet. You do not need to highlight the December 29 close.

DELAY CHANGING YOUR ACCOUNTING SYSTEM

Companies should be able to achieve day 3 reporting, no matter how antiquated their accounting system is. Much can be achieved with an old system. An old G/L is not an excuse for not reaching day 3 reporting! If you still believe the G/L is the problem, you need a paradigm shift in your thinking.

Many CFOs in large organizations are misled into making a huge investment in large G/Ls that serve to lock in analysis at the micro level. Jeremy Hope, of *Beyond Budgeting* fame, points out in his recent book[2] that many such systems are dubious. I concur, for these systems often are designed by the people who always wanted to be NASA scientists and who have never run a finance team in their life.

> "Business upgrades to G/L and other core systems often simply replicate existing processes and do not take the opportunity to redesign those processes into new systems. There are many tools in modern systems that are never used!"
> —CFO *with international blue chip experience*

Most accounting systems come with an integrated purchase order system. Some systems enable the order to be priced using the supplier's online price list and then emailed automatically to the preferred supplier, provided the order is within the budget holder's delegated authority. These systems should be purchased and implemented before the accounting team ever considers upgrading the G/L.

REMOVING SPREADSHEETS FROM THE MONTH-END ROUTINES

Excel has no place as a reporting or consolidation tool as it is too prone to disaster. This was explained in Chapter 4 on technology. It would be worth another read now to reiterate the dangers of relying on Excel as a reporting tool.

There is no problem when a system automatically downloads to Excel, with all the programming logic being resident in the system and thus bomb-proof. The problem arises when the system has been built in-house, often by someone who has left the company. Now the accuracy of reports relies on Excel formulas reading the imported G/L download. This is, as you may have personally experienced, a calamity waiting to happen.

DAY ONE REPORTING AND VIRTUAL CLOSING

Quick month-end reporting has been around since the early 1990s, when far-sighted CFOs starting looking at the concept of day one reporting (DOR).

What Is Day One Reporting?

DOR is the condensing down of the monthly reporting process so that the month-end processes are completed and management reports are issued all within Day One, the first day after the previous month-end. Organizations that are achieving DOR complete all of the next tasks by 5 P.M. on Day One:

- Transaction information processed
- Accruals raised
- Consolidations complete
- Reports prepared
- Commentary/analysis added
- Reports issued to CEO

The introduction of DOR has created a precedent that means that reporting five, six, seven, or eight working days after month-end will soon be a perilous activity for the CFO. How will you explain this time wasting to a CEO who was used to Day One reporting in his or her previous employment?

In other words, soon it will not be acceptable for organizations and will be career limiting for CFOs to be responsible for time-consuming and costly month-end processes.

Case Study: Johnson & Johnson Vision Products USA

Around 1980, the first articles about DOR started to appear, and one of the first companies to put this into practice was Johnson & Johnson Vision Products USA, the makers of Acuvue soft contact lenses. The company had not realized there was a real problem until it benchmarked against other companies. It found, to its horror, that its two weeks to close was resulting in the company "paying more to have monthly reports ready later." In other words, the quicker companies had fewer accounting resources. Johnson & Johnson quickly got to Day Three reporting by following these steps:

- All management was made aware of the problem.
- Buy-in was obtained from management.
- A multifunctional project team was set up (reporting, marketing, operations, information technology [IT], production planning).
- The project team was empowered to make decisions.
- The focus was on continuous improvement and teamwork.
- Deadlines were adhered to.

At Day Three, the company hit the wall; improvement now required a complete paradigm shift by the finance group. The group needed to reengineer the process, so it:

- Identified nonvalue tasks, such as: posting of automated journals on Day One, journals having to be reviewed before entry into system, period production not finalized until Day Two, allocations not made until end of Day Two, inventory movement entries not made until Day Three.
- Applied the Pareto principle (80/20) rigorously, focusing on the big numbers. Materiality levels were established—manual journal entry line items were reduced by 80 percent.
- Eliminated all interdepartmental corrections at month-end.
- Eliminated management review, as budget holders now had responsibility to resolve issues.
- Condensed the management report into one page of key indicators plus one page on the business unit's performance.
- Used estimates to avoid slowing down the process. (The difference between estimate and actual was found never to be significant.)
- Communicated changes to month-end reports far in advance.
- Ensured that budget holders tracked activity throughout the month, eliminating the usual surprises found during the closing process.
- Processed allocations without reviewing departmental spending.
- Moved preparations for month-end close to before period-end instead of after.
- Replaced reconciled accounts in Days One and Two with variance analysis.
- Manually entered the last day's debtors and cash receipts as total, and the details were handled later.

EXHIBIT 6.2   Johnson & Johnson Time Frames

Original Johnson & Johnson Time Frames	Suggested Targets for the Reader
At start—8 days	Immediately go to 3 day close
6 months later—3 days	6 months later—2 days
12 months from start—2 days	12 months from start—1 day
24 months from start—1 day	24 months from start—virtual close

See Exhibit 6.2 for the Johnson & Johnson time frame. I suggest the same for your organization.

Johnson & Johnson streamlined all processes by following three principles: (1) eliminate what you can, (2) simplify what is left, and (3) consolidate similar activities or information—and in so doing reached the El Dorado of accounting Day One reporting.

Case Study: Motorola—12 Nonevents a Year

In the 1990s, Motorola had six operating sectors each containing multiple divisions over 30 nations with over 40 balance sheets. It moved from an eight-day close to a two-day close quickly by following these steps:

- Adopt world-class "better practices."
- Look for ways to change; don't say, "No, it can't be done."
- Allow natural competition between sectors to reduce errors (nobody likes being on the bottom).
- Count the processing errors, which moved from 10,000 errors for every 700,000 transactions to 1,000 errors per 2 million transactions (Five Sigma) with a target of only three errors per million (Six Sigma).
- Eliminate time costly errors.
- Use "Post-it" reengineering (see section in Chapter 10, "Lean and Smarter Work Methods").
- Allow sectors to have their own accounting systems.
- Look for hundreds of small (1 percent) improvements.

The financial impact of this change was amazing, with the worldwide finance costs falling from 2.4 percent of annual revenue to about 1 percent (a reported savings of greater than $10 million per year). Motorola found that its final reports were virtually error free. In other words, by being quicker, the company also successfully tackled the error rate. The month-ends were drama free, with less anxiety and higher morale in the accounting team. What was also unbelievable was that the company stated that the finance team managers even had more time for analysis within this Day One reporting regime than they had previously in the error-prone, eight-day close.

These two case studies had a profound impact on my appreciation of how a month-end could be reengineered and led me to developing the "Post-it reengineering" process featured in Chapter 10.

Day One Reporting Has Been Superseded by Virtual Closing

Day One reporting has been superseded by those who have developed systems capable of giving the CFO a full accrual net result at any time during the month. The *virtual close*, as it is called, is performed by CISCO, Motorola, Oracle, Dell, Wells Fargo, Citigroup, JP Morgan Chase, and Alcoa.

Research on Quick Month-Ends

There has been much research on quick month-ends, and an Internet search using the string "month-end" + "quick" + "reporting" will find further information.

 PDF DOWNLOAD

To assist the finance team on the journey, I have included some articles. The reader can access, free of charge, a PDF of the following material from www .davidparmenter.com/The_Financial_Controller_and_CFO's_Toolkit.

The PDF download for this chapter includes:

- Articles on 4 or 5 week reporting periods
- Articles on virtual reporting

 NOTES

1. David Parmenter, "Rapid Reporting in Three Days or Less and Error Free," www.davidparmenter.com 2015.
2. Jeremy Hope, *Reinventing the CFO: How Financial Managers Can Transform Their Roles and Add Greater Value* (Boston: Harvard Business School Press, 2006).

CHAPTER SEVEN

Lean Reporting—Informatively and Error Free

OVERVIEW

Many management reports are merely memorandums of information. They arrive too late and are error prone and too detailed. This chapter explores the foundation stones to reporting; one-page formats that will make a difference. It also refers to the work of data visualization expert, Stephen Few, and the quality control steps you should take to make sure all your reports are error free.

Many management reports are not management tools; they are merely memorandums of information. They arrive too late, well after the horse has bolted, and contain errors due to quality assurance steps being undermined by late adjustments. They also contain far too much detail and are produced just because we did it last month. As management tools, management reports should encourage timely action in the right direction by reporting on those activities the board and management need the staff to focus on.

THE FOUNDATION STONES OF REPORTING

Board members and the senior management team have complained for years that they are sent too much information, yet we still insist on preparing a large month-end finance report. The cost of preparing, analyzing, and checking this information is a major burden on the accounting function, creating significant time delays and consequently minimizing the information's value.

Over the years of studying reporting I have developed some foundation stones for reporting:

- Reports should be completed quickly on a true and fair view basis avoiding unnecessary detail. For example, is it necessary to report Sales of $23,456,327? Surely $23.5 million is much easier to read and relate to.
- Where possible, limit the report to one page, albeit sometimes a fanfold page (A3). This forces one to be concise by keeping it to commentary to highlight points and inserting only graphs that really matter.
- Have a comprehensive quality assurance process so the reports are totally consistent internally and agree to the source numbers every time.
- Use best-practice graphics—following the guidelines of Stephen Few, an expert on data visualization. Incorporate trend analysis on key lines going back at least 15 months so that you have a direct comparison to last year.
- Utilize twenty-first-century reporting tools so managers can see their reports on their tablet.
- Reports need to be completed quickly on a true and fair view basis as discussed in Chapter 3. This requires that at all times we reflect on materiality at a group level and ensure that the numbers agree to source, are prepared using robust systems (that excludes spreadsheets), and have been reviewed for reasonableness.

CONCISE, ONE-PAGE FORMATS

The following formats comply with the reporting rules and only show a line if it represents over 10 percent of the total revenue or expenditure. Thus, reporting by account code is a thing of the past. Managers can do this by reviewing their unit's numbers in the drill-down reporting tool. Variances are only highlighted by an automatic icon if they are over a threshold and over 10 percent of the budget.

Reporting a Business Unit's Performance

A business unit's report should be limited to one page and should be completed in 20 to 30 minutes. Nobody wants a dissertation, and nobody will read it. If the business unit manager is having problems, it is far too late to bring them up in the monthly report. The finance team should have alerted senior management during the month, and discussions should have been held then on what best to do.

Exhibit 7.1 is an example of a monthly business unit's report. The profit and loss statement (P & L) is summarized in 10 to 15 lines. Two graphs are shown; one looks at the trend of the major expenditure items and the other looks at revenue if a profit center, or a graph may contrast financial and nonfinancial numbers—in this case, tourist numbers against personnel costs.

An icon system has been established to highlight variances, as shown in Exhibit 7.1. A suggested way is to ignore all variances less than a certain amount. For all variances over this amount, allow a tolerance of, say, plus or minus 10 percent and show an icon for this, and then show as a positive or negative any variance over 10 percent. In this example the monthly variances threshold is $20,000, the year to date and year-end threshold are set at $100,000. For variances over these figures but within 10 percent, we show a "within tolerance" icon < > and no comment is required.

The notes are the main highlights and action steps to take. No other commentary is provided on the business unit's P & L. The business unit manager can discuss other issues in person with the CEO. Each business unit may have up to five different graphs, and the two that show the most pertinent information are shown in that month's report. Each business unit report will look slightly different. The titles of the key lines and graphs may be different.

Note the use of the graph titles to say something meaningful, treat them like a journalist treats the titles to their articles.

Value Stream Reporting

A new form of accounting has emerged, known as *lean accounting*. It is based on the lean concepts that first emerged within the Japanese multinational manufacturers.

Operating Statement for the Period Ending 31 January 20__

Month $000s Actual	Budget	Variance			Year-to-date $000s Actual	Budget	Variance		Full Year $000s Budget	Forecast	Variance	
				Revenue								
1,430	1,380	50	⇔	Revenue 1	5,720	5,520	200	⇔	17,200	16,600	600	⇔
1,430	1,380	50	⇔	**Total Revenue**	5,720	5,520	200	⇔	17,200	16,600	600	⇔
				Less								
267	220	(47)	✗	Commissions	1,068	880	(188)	✗	3,200	2,600	(600)	✗
1,163	1,160	3		**Gross Profit**	4,652	4,640	12		14,000	14,000	0	
				Expenses								
278	260	(18)		Expense 1	1,240	1,040	(200)	✗	3,300	3,100	(200)	⇔
218	210	(8)		Expense 2	672	840	168	✓	2,600	2,500	(100)	⇔
188	180	(8)		Expense 3	752	720	(32)		2,300	2,200	(100)	⇔
158	150	(8)		Expense 4	632	600	(32)		1,900	1,800	(100)	⇔
128	120	(8)		Expense 5	512	480	(32)		1,500	1,400	(100)	⇔
50	70	20	✓	Expense 6	672	680	8		1,000	1,300	300	✓
1,020	990	(30)	⇔	**Total Expenses**	4,080	3,960	(120)	⇔	12,200	11,900	(300)	⇔
143	170	(27)	✗	**Surplus/(Deficit)**	572	680	(108)	✗	1,800	2,100	(300)	✗

Major Costs are Rising — $000s (bar chart, Nov–Jan)
Legend: □ Commissions ▨ Expense 1 ■ Expense 2 ■ Expense 3

Operational Wages Under Control (line chart, Nov–Jan)
Legend: —■— Visitor numbers —◆— Operational wages (exc. HQ)

Areas to Note:

1. _____

2. _____

3. _____

4. _____

EXHIBIT 7.1   Example of a business unit's report

If you are a manufacturing entity, then you need to explore this immediately. Value streams are a collection of products that share the same processes and include the costs from all people and resources involved in value stream. Brian Maskell said, "A value stream is a sequence of steps both value adding and non–value adding required to complete a product or service from beginning to end."[1]

Instead of looking at departments, business units, or product costs, we look at the value streams. These value streams can be one product or a cluster of products that go through a similar process. In Exhibit 7.2, we are looking at a company that makes only two products, a truck and a car.

Value Stream Income Statement				
	Car	Truck	Sustaining	Total Plant
Sales	60,000	40,000		100,000
Material costs of goods sold	-20,000	-15,000		-35,000
Employee costs	-9,000	-8,000	-5,000	-22,000
Machine costs	-10,000	-5,000		-15,000
Occupancy costs	-6,000	-4,000	-5,000	-15,000
Other costs	-1,000	-1,000		-2,000
Value stream costs	-46,000	-33,000	-10,000	-89,000
Value stream profit	14,000	7,000	-10,000	11,000
Inventory reduction (labor and overhead from prior periods)				0
Inventory increase (labor and overhead carried forward)				3,000
Plant profit				14,000
Corporate allocation				-12,000
Net operating income				2,000

EXHIBIT 7.2   Reporting using value streams

Value stream accounting has come out of the lean movement with writers such as Brian Maskell and Frances Kennedy[2] who point out that accounting, control, and measurement methods need to change substantially.

Here are the main differences:

- Labor and machine costs are assigned directly to value streams using some simple cost driver, but such allocations are held to a minimum, certainly not using activity-based costing models. The existing labor force is not treated as variable unless you need to employ extra staff.
- Sustaining costs, which are necessary costs that support the entire facility but cannot be directly associated with particular value streams, are not allocated to value streams, but are shown in a separate column. Sustaining costs include management and support, facility costs, information technology, and human resource management costs that are not associated directly with a value stream.
- Inventory changes are reported separately as below-the-line adjustments and reported for the entire entity, not the separate value streams. This allows the value stream managers to assess their individual value streams without the complexities of the inventory changes affecting the value stream profit. If the company succeeds in adopting just-in-time inventory methods, the issue would largely disappear. Consequently, the motivation for manipulating inventory values also disappears.
- Under lean accounting, occupancy costs are actually assigned to value streams according to the amount of space used. Assignment of these costs provides motivation for the value stream teams to reduce occupancy costs. However, no attempt to absorb all of the occupancy costs is required. Space not used by a value stream is charged to sustaining costs. As a result, occupancy costs are handled in a similar manner to traditional accounting, but they are assigned to value streams instead of other cost objects such as products or divisions.
- Standard costs and price and volume variances—a backbone of classical management accounting—is abandoned.
- Very few allocations are used other than allocation of occupancy costs.
- Costing of a product is not related to the amount of labor or machine time expended. It is based on the rate of flow through the value stream. This issue is explored in more detail in Chapter 15.

Reporting Consolidated Profit and Loss

Exhibit 7.3 is an example of reporting a consolidated P & L account. This report summarizes the P & L in 10 to 15 lines. Instead of looking at consolidated costs, such as personnel, premises, and so forth, the report summarizes the expenditures of the divisions/business units. The two graphs shown in the exhibit look

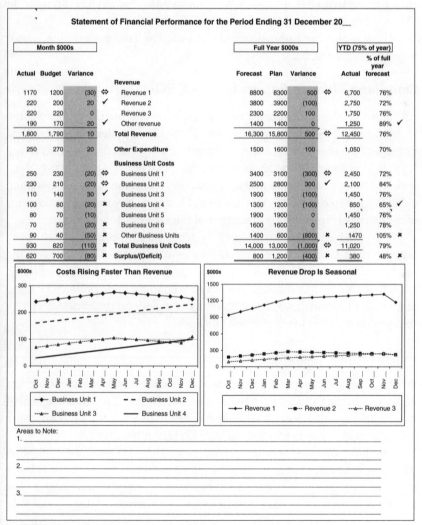

EXHIBIT 7.3   Example of a consolidated profit and loss report

at the trends in major revenue and expenditure and a banner headline is used for the graph title.

A number of different graphs will be maintained and the most pertinent ones will be shown. The notes are the main highlights and action steps to take. The YTD budget is not shown, as this is by now wildly out of date. Instead, we show YTD as a percentage of the most recent year-end forecast, highlighting where the forecast might be too optimistic or too pessimistic. This forecast would be revised once a quarter, and not monthly, as already discussed in Chapter 3 on month-end reporting.

There is no other commentary on the P&L. The icons are fully automated based on preset criteria.

One-Page Finance Report for the CEO

All CEOs like a great summary page where they can see the whole picture. In my research I came across this one-pager that I believe is an excellent example of clever reporting. On one A3 page (U.S. standard fanfold), the finance team has summarized the areas to note, financial performance year to date, reviewed the major business units, and commented on the summary P & L and balance sheet (see Exhibit 7.4). The concept here is to give the CEO a summary of the financial report that is easier to read than the full finance report.

Once you have designed this carefully, you will find, I am sure, that this page becomes the main report. Both sides of the page can be used. The back side of the page could include summary business unit performance, or ranking tables for retail branches, or a dashboard summarizing financial and nonfinancial information, as shown in Chapter 8. Whatever you include on the back side, ensure that you do not go below a 10-point font size.

Reporting the Balance Sheet

Exhibit 7.5 is an example of a summary balance sheet with rounded numbers in millions, more rounded than the numbers in the P/L (e.g., tell management that debtors owe just under $3.2 million rather than $3,189,235; I can assure you, most will remember $3 million but forget the other number).

The balance sheet should have no more than 10 categories following the 10 percent rule discussed earlier. Each additional category in the balance sheet serves to confuse management and benefits only the accountants. The graphs focus on main balance sheet issues such as debtors' aging, stock levels, aging of key operational assets (e.g., average age of different types of planes), and cash levels.

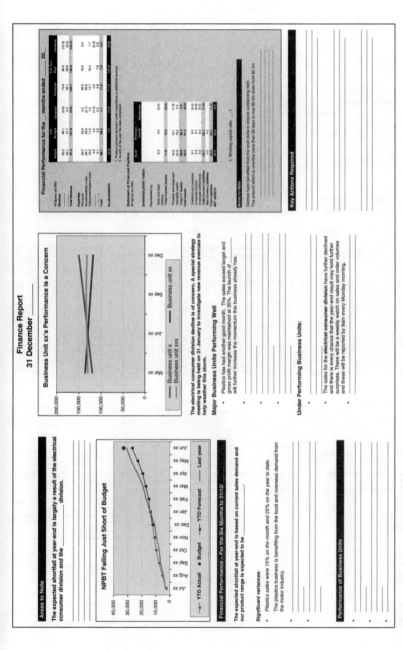

EXHIBIT 7.4 A3 (fanfold) CEO's finance report

Statement of Financial position as at 30 April 20___
$Ms

	Month-End Actual	Last Month Actual
Bank and Cash	10.2	10.3
Debtors	3.2	3.0
Stock	2.5	2.2
Fixed Assets	9.0	9.1
Other Assets	1.1	1.2
Total Assets	26.0	25.8
Accounts Payable	(4.0)	(3.0)
Other Liabilities	(1.0)	(1.0)
Net Assets	21.0	21.8
Funded by		
Current Year Profit	2.7	3.3
Accumulated Funds	18.3	18.5
Total Equity	21.0	21.8

Areas to Note:

1. _____

2. _____

3. _____

4. _____

EXHIBIT 7.5 Example of a summary balance sheet

Reporting a Quarterly Rolling Accrual Forecast

The update of the year-end forecast should occur once a quarter, as explained in Chapter 16. Exhibit 7.6 shows a number of features worth discussing:

■ Only show monthly data for the next six months. After that, quarterly is sufficient.

Summary of Forecast Profit & Loss for the period ending _____

* includes estimate for December

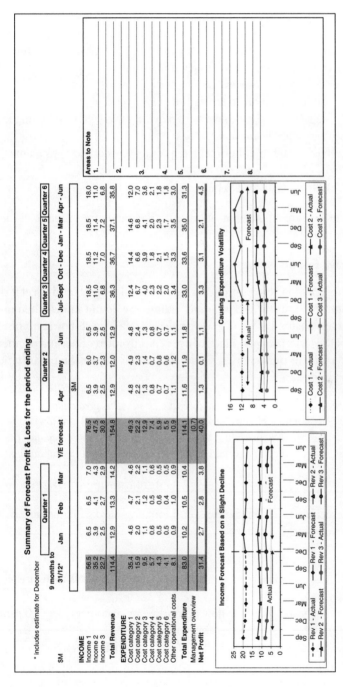

$M	9 months to 31/12*	Quarter 1			Y/E forecast	Quarter 2			Quarter 3	Quarter 4	Quarter 5	Quarter 6
		Jan	Feb	Mar		Apr	May	Jun	Jul-Sept	Oct-Dec	Jan-Mar	Apr-Jun
					$M							
INCOME												
Income 1	56.5	6.5	6.5	7.0	76.5	6.5	6.0	6.5	18.5	18.5	18.5	18.0
Income 2	35.2	3.9	4.1	4.3	47.5	3.9	3.7	3.9	11.0	11.2	11.4	11.0
Income 3	22.7	2.5	2.7	2.9	30.8	2.5	2.3	2.5	6.8	7.0	7.2	6.8
Total Revenue	114.4	12.9	13.3	14.2	154.8	12.9	12.0	12.9	36.3	36.7	37.1	35.8
EXPENDITURE												
Cost category 1	35.4	4.6	4.7	4.6	49.3	4.8	4.9	4.8	12.4	14.4	14.6	12.0
Cost category 2	15.9	2.0	2.1	2.2	22.2	2.2	2.3	2.4	6.7	6.6	6.8	7.0
Cost category 3	9.5	1.1	1.2	1.1	12.9	1.3	1.4	1.3	4.0	3.9	4.1	3.6
Cost category 4	5.7	0.6	0.5	0.6	7.4	0.8	0.7	0.8	2.3	1.8	2.0	2.1
Cost category 5	4.3	0.5	0.6	0.5	5.9	0.7	0.8	0.7	2.2	2.1	2.3	1.8
Cost category 6	4.1	0.5	0.4	0.5	5.5	0.7	0.6	0.7	2.0	1.5	1.7	1.8
Other operational costs	8.1	0.9	1.0	0.9	10.9	1.1	1.2	1.1	3.4	3.3	3.5	3.0
Total Expenditure	83.0	10.2	10.5	10.4	114.1	11.6	11.9	11.8	33.0	33.6	35.0	31.3
Management overview					(0.7)							
Net Profit	31.4	2.7	2.8	3.8	40.0	1.3	0.1	1.1	3.3	3.1	2.1	4.5

Income Forecast Based on a Slight Decline

25
20
15
10
5
0

Sep Dec Mar Jun Sep Dec Mar Jun

Actual

Forecast

- Rev 1 - Actual
- Rev 1 - Forecast
- Rev 2 - Actual
- Rev 2 - Forecast
- Rev 3 - Actual
- Rev 3 - Forecast

Causing Expenditure Volatility

16
12
8
4
0

Sep Dec Mar Jun Sep Dec Mar Jun Sep Dec Mar Jun

Actual

Forecast

- Cost 1 - Actual
- Cost 1 - Forecast
- Cost 2 - Actual
- Cost 2 - Forecast
- Cost 3 - Actual
- Cost 3 - Forecast

Areas to Note

1.

2.

3.

4.

5.

6.

7.

8.

EXHIBIT 7.6 Example of a quarterly rolling accrual forecast report

111

- Only forecast at category status, never at account code level.
- Forecast each category line to the level of accuracy the CEO would expect; for example, top line of revenue in Exhibit 7.5 is forecast to nearest $0.5 million, other revenue lines to nearest $0.1 million.
- Forecast 18 months forward.
- The expenditure graph looks at the three main expenditure lines and highlights where budget holders are playing the old game of hiding funds in case they might be needed.
- The revenue graph highlights the reasonableness of the sales teams' projections.
- Commentary is restricted to bullet points.

Chapter 16 explains the reasoning and the foundation stones of a rolling forecasting process.

Cash Flow Forecasting

Cash flow forecasting is error prone for many of us. It is very hard to get it right for the following reasons: lack of information—we do not know when major customers are paying us; no historic analysis of daily cash flows; no historic tracking of the large receipts; a lack of use of electronic receipts and payments; and often a lack of understanding and coordination with the organization's buyers and sales staff.

> *"The most important part of a forecast is not the prediction of what is likely to happen, but the strength of the logic behind the forecast— even a broken clock is right twice a day. The best way to gauge the present against the future changes is to look back twice as far as you look forward."*
> —Paul Saffo, Institute of the Future

The forecast process includes several building blocks of a better-practice daily cash flow.

Enter the certain figures first

- Rent, rates, leases, loan repayments, loan interest, payroll, taxes are all certain payments.
- Identify separately the cash flow of your major customers (over 10 percent of sales) as they are more certain.
- On one line, identify the cash flow of all other customers who have signed up for a direct debit (DD)—it is a good idea to offer continuing discounts to customers to accept direct debiting onto their bank account.

- Identify payments to your major suppliers (over 10 percent of total spend) paid by DD or by direct credit (DC) initiated by the supplier.
- On one line, identify the payment to all minor suppliers paid by DC.

Trap the history of your daily cash flows

- You will need at least the last 24 months of cash flows data in the same categories that you are forecasting in—the best place for storing this historic data is in a forecasting application.
- Use trend graphs in your forecasting application to help understand seasonal fluctuations—remember, you need to go back twice as far as you look forward.

Use appropriate time frame

- Look forward at least to week 5 in working days and to week 13 in weeks—the month-end is irrelevant for cash flow forecasting, as a cash flow crisis comes at any time.
- It is normally okay to cash flow model in months from month 4 onward—this modeling can be automated from the accrual forecasting model. In some cases, a cash flow is projected out two financial years or for a rolling 24-month period.

Use automatic feeds to the cash forecasting application

- Use daily major receipts from accounts receivable.
- Tax payment calculations can be automated.
- For key customers, cash flows can be accurately predicted in the short term.

Do cash flow forecast on a planning application, not Excel

- Put the cash flow on an appropriate forecasting application—Excel is best left to noncore activities such as designing a report template or one-off diagrams. See Chapter 4 for the reasoning behind this statement.

Exhibits 7.7 and 7.8 show the short-term cash flow predicted by day and the longer-range one going out in months, which typically would be generated from the accrual forecast via standard timing amendments.

Monthly Sales Report from Stephen Few

Sales reports can be very detailed covering many pages or screens, or you can follow the reporting rules and get a summary report on a page or on a smart phone's screen.

Summary of cashflow for the next 13 weeks

	Day 1	Day 2	Day 3	Day 4	Day 5	Day 6	etc	Day 25 last day of the 5th week	Week 6	Wk 7 to 12	Week #13	Last week Actual	Last week Cash Forecast	Last week Variance
Revenues														
Key customer (over 10% of total revenue) cashflows														
Customer #1			340				etc			etc		340	280	60 ✓
Customer #2	280	240	250	210			etc			etc		735	570	165 ✓
Customer #3					400		etc		690	etc	1,500	550	490	60 ✓
Other customers - paying by EFT (DC and DD)	405	230	250	180	210	230	etc	405	580	etc	800			
Other customers - check payments	2,550	1,800	1,900	1,800	1,750	1,900	etc	2,000	10,200	etc	10,200	13,700	13,550	150
Revenue cashflows	3,235	2,270	2,490	2,190	2,360	2,360	etc	2,405	12,960	etc	12,500	15,325	14,890	435
Known Expenditure														
Major suppliers on EFT	(250)	(350)	(450)	(460)	(380)	(600)	etc	(550)	(3,050)	etc	(3,050)	(4,040)	(2,940)	(1,100) ✗
Minor suppliers on EFT	(110)	(120)	(220)	(110)	(120)	(220)	etc	(320)	(1,500)	etc	(1,500)	(720)	(1,120)	400 ✓
Taxes paid		(450)					etc		(450)	etc	(450)	(350)	(450)	100
Payroll			(1,700)				etc	(1,700)	(1,700)	etc	(1,700)	(3,400)	(3,500)	100
Other operating costs - check payments	(180)	(190)	(200)	(180)	(190)	(200)	etc	(210)	(6,500)	etc	(6,500)	(1,350)	(1,250)	(100)
Operating free cash flow	2,695	1,160	(80)	1,440	1,670	1,340	etc	(375)	760	etc	300	5,465	5,730	(265)
Interest expense	(240)						etc	(240)	(240)	etc	(240)	(480)	(480)	-
Loan & dividends	2,000	(100)					etc			etc		1,700	1,700	-
Capital expenditure	(400)			(100)	(200)		etc			etc	(1,200)	(600)	(600)	-
Other items e.g. proceeds, other income			20			20	etc			etc		40	40	-
Total cash flow	4,055	1,060	(60)	1,340	1,470	1,280	etc	(615)	520	etc	(1,140)	6,125	6,390	(265)
Closing Bank Balance	(2,500) 1,555	2,615	2,555	3,895	5,365	6,625	etc	1,940	2,460	etc	1,320	(2,500)	(2,750)	(265)

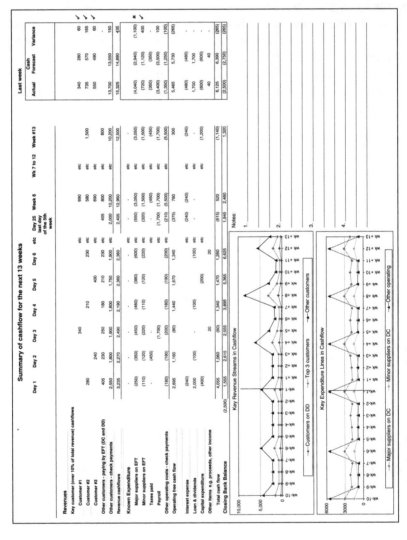

Key Revenue Streams in Cashflow
— Customers on DD — Top 3 customers — Other customers
(wk -10 … wk +13)

Key Expenditure Lines in Cashflow
— Major suppliers on DC — Minor suppliers on DC — Other operating
(wk -10 … wk +13)

Notes:
1.
2.
3.
4.

EXHIBIT 7.7 Example of a short range cash flow report

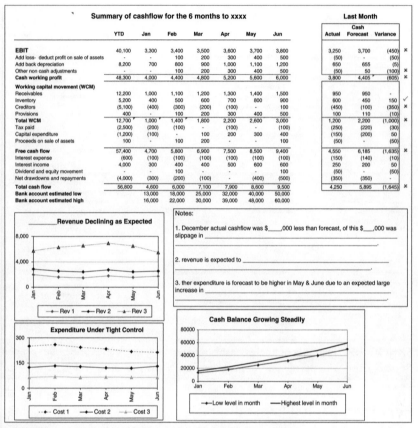

Summary of cashflow for the 6 months to xxxx | **Last Month**

	YTD	Jan	Feb	Mar	Apr	May	Jun	Actual	Forecast	Variance	
EBIT	40,100	3,300	3,400	3,500	3,600	3,700	3,800	3,250	3,700	(450)	x
Add loss- deduct profit on sale of assets	-	-	100	200	300	400	500	(50)	-	(50)	
Add back depreciation	8,200	700	800	900	1,000	1,100	1,200	650	655	(5)	
Other non cash adjustments	-	-	100	200	300	400	500	(50)	50	(100)	x
Cash working profit	48,300	4,000	4,400	4,800	5,200	5,600	6,000	3,800	4,405	(605)	x
Working capital movement (WCM)											
Receivables	12,200	1,000	1,100	1,200	1,300	1,400	1,500	950	950	-	
Inventory	5,200	400	500	600	700	800	900	600	450	150	✓
Creditors	(5,100)	(400)	(300)	(200)	(100)	-	100	(450)	(100)	(350)	x
Provisions	400	-	100	200	300	400	500	100	110	(10)	
Total WCM	12,700	1,000	1,400	1,800	2,200	2,600	3,000	1,200	2,200	(1,000)	x
Tax paid	(2,500)	(200)	(100)	-	(100)	-	(100)	(250)	(220)	(30)	
Capital expenditure	(1,200)	(100)	-	100	200	300	400	(150)	(200)	50	
Proceeds on sale of assets	100	-	100	200	-	-	100	(50)	-	(50)	
Free cash flow	57,400	4,700	5,800	6,900	7,500	8,500	9,400	4,550	6,185	(1,635)	x
Interest expense	(600)	(100)	(100)	(100)	(100)	(100)	(100)	(150)	(140)	(10)	
Interest income	4,000	300	400	400	500	600	600	250	200	50	
Dividend and equity movement	-	-	100	-	-	-	100	(50)	-	(50)	
Net drawdowns and repayments	(4,000)	(300)	(200)	(100)	-	(400)	(500)	(350)	(350)	-	
Total cash flow	56,800	4,600	6,000	7,100	7,900	8,600	9,500	4,250	5,895	(1,645)	x
Bank account estimated low		13,000	18,000	25,000	32,000	40,000	50,000				
Bank account estimated high		16,000	22,000	30,000	39,000	48,000	60,000				

Notes:

1. December actual cashflow was $____,000 less than forecast, of this $____,000 was slippage in _____.

2. revenue is expected to _____.

3. ther expenditure is forecast to be higher in May & June due to an expected large increase in _____.

Revenue Declining as Expected — Rev 1, Rev 2, Rev 3

Expenditure Under Tight Control — Cost 1, Cost 2, Cost 3

Cash Balance Growing Steadily — Low level in month, Highest level in month

EXHIBIT 7.8 Example of a longer range cash flow report

Stephen Few[3] has introduced a new concept that is well worth understanding—a combination of a spark line and bullet graphs (see Exhibit 7.9). A spark line graph looks like a line graph without the axes. Even with this truncated diagram you can still see the trend. The bullet graph shows different detail about current performance. The shades are good to poor performance, and the dark vertical line indicates the target.

Stephen Few is very cautious about the use of color. He points out that many readers will have some form of color blindness. In Exhibit 7.9, the only use of color would be red bullet points indicating the exceptions that need investigation and follow-up.

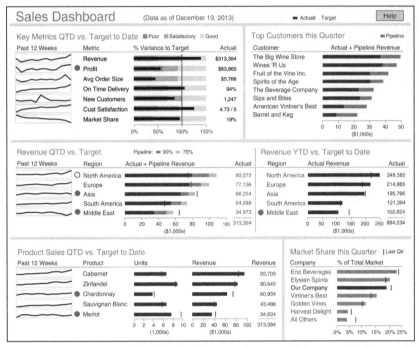

EXHIBIT 7.9   Example of a sales dashboard utilizing spark lines and bullet graphs
Source: Used with permission of Stephen Few, www.perceptualedge.com

Reporting Capital Expenditure

There are two main issues with reporting capital expenditure (CAPEX). First and most important, there will be CAPEX slippage. Worse still is the fact that the aim of CAPEX was to improve working conditions, improve quality of products/services, increase profitability, and so on. If an office renovation has been approved, why is it completed in the last month of the year? Surely it would have been better for it to have been completed in the first couple of months, as the staff would have the benefit of it. We therefore need a report (see Exhibit 7.10) that contrasts the percentage of capital spent on key projects against the percentage of the year gone. The aim is for status of the CAPEX projects to beat the year-gone progress bar.

Second, it is important to control the CAPEX approval process. During the life of a CAPEX project, there might be signs that it is going over budget. Normally, this is hidden from the board until management is sure there is a problem. If you have a process whereby the board is informed about the possibility of CAPEX exceeding the budget as soon as it is recognized the board

Capital Expenditure for the Period Ending 31 December 20__

	% spent	YTD Actual	Annual Budget	Outstanding
Div 1	50%	45	90	45
Div 2	31%	25	80	55
Div 3	70%	63	90	27
Div 4	72%	93	130	37
Div 5	56%	25	45	20
Other Divs	58%	105	180	75
Average	56%			
% of Year gone	75%			
Total		356	615	259

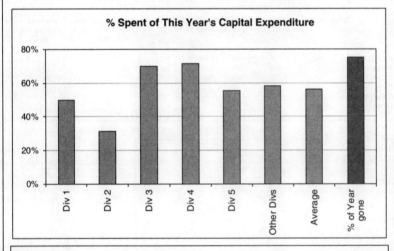

Areas to note:

1. _____

2. _____

3. _____

4. _____

EXHIBIT 7.10   Example of a simple CAPEX slippage report

has time to act. The board can make the decision whether to require a formal application for the additional expenditure or defer until more information is known about the magnitude of the over expenditure. In Exhibit 7.11, the board would hold off as there is still half the project to go so the over expenditure might not eventuate. The board might flag that a progress brief is required by the project manager for the next meeting or request a new CAPEX approval application.

Capital Expenditure For the Period Ending 31 December _____

$000s

	Unspent CAPEX b/f	Current Year Budget	Approved Changes	Total Approved	CAPEX Spent YTD	Forecast to Complete	Forecast Underspend / (Overspend)	Forecast Unapproved CAPEX
Project #1	10	100	50	160	80	70	10	0
Project #2		450	700	1,150	590	400	160	0
Project #3		1,700	(700)	1,000	550	600	(150)	150
Project #4								
Project #5								
Other								
Total	10	2,250	50	2,310	1,220	1,070	20	150

Unapproved items:
_____
_____

Issues:
_____
_____

Actions to be taken:
_____
_____

EXHIBIT 7.11   Example of a CAPEX approval report

The One-Page Investment Proposal

One of the important principles that make Toyota so successful is the need for transparency. This view is carried through to its investment proposals. All proposals have to fit on an A3 page (U.S. standard fanfold; see Exhibit 7.12). Condensing a major investment into an A3 page is a very difficult task. The one-page summary ensures clarity of thought and reduces the possibility that the proposal will be 50 pages because it represents a $500 million investment. Toyota has recognized that a large investment document will not be read or fully understood by all the decision makers. In fact, the larger the document, the less there is "clarity" for decision making. A must-read book to understand the guiding principles of Toyota is *The Toyota Way* by Jeffrey Liker.[4]

 MORE EMPHASIS ON DAILY AND WEEKLY REPORTING

Why is the monthly reporting so important? For leading organizations, decision-based information is based on daily/weekly information on progress within the important areas of the business. In these organizations, the month-end has become less important, and consequently, the management papers have been reduced to 15 pages or less.

In one company the senior management team (SMT) has a daily report delivery every morning called the "9 o'clock news," followed by further weekly information. At the monthly management meeting to discuss the results, even the human resources manager is able to enter the sweepstakes guessing the month-end result. Talking about the monthly numbers is a small part of the meeting, which happens in the first week of the following month.

I believe as a corporate accountant, you have become future ready when members of the management team intuitively know during the month whether it is going well or badly. This prompt information enables management to take appropriate action.

Corporate accountants should look at providing this daily and weekly reporting:

- Yesterday's sales reported by 9 a.m. the following day
- Transactions with key customers reported on a weekly basis
- Weekly reporting on late projects and late reports
- Reporting some weekly information of key direct costs
- The key performance indicators, which are reported daily/weekly (see Chapter 18)

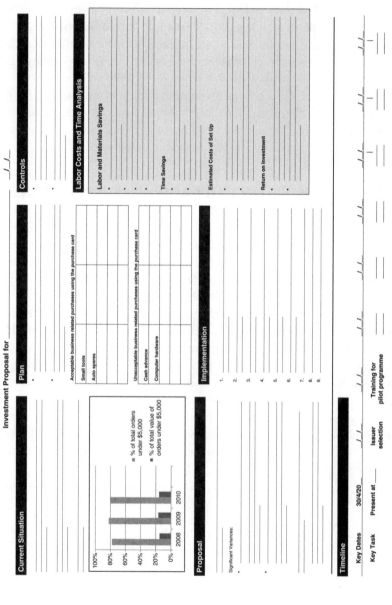

EXHIBIT 7.12 Example of a one-page investment proposal

Daily Sales Report

If the CEO and SMT receive a report on the daily sales, they will better understand how the organization is performing. Exhibit 7.13 shows the sort of detail they will be interested in.

Weekly Key Customers' Sales

In a similar vein, it is important for the SMT to monitor how products are being purchased by the key customers. This is especially important after the launch of a new product, or after your competitors launch a new competing product. In Exhibit 7.14, the organization has three main products and three key customers. Sales made on minor products have been shown in two groups.

Daily Sales Report

	$000s			
	Yesterday's Sales	Daily Average Last 90 days	Variance	>$100k & >10%
Sales by key product				
Product 1	450	400	50	
Product 2	440	560	−120	x
Product 3	375	425	−50	
Other products	185	175	10	
Total Sales	1,450	1,560	(110)	
Sale by branch				
Branch 1	580	700	−120	x
Branch 2	440	420	20	
Branch 3	220	210	10	
Branch 4	180	160	20	
Other branches	30	70	−40	
Total Sales	1,450	1,560	(110)	

--- Total Sales —— Monthly Target (average daily amount)

EXHIBIT 7.13   Example of a daily sales report

Weekly Sales of the Top Three Products to Major Customers

	$000s			
	Last Week's Sales	**Weekly Avg. Last 180 days**	**Variance**	**>$100k & 10%**
Customer #1				
Product 1	450	400	50	
Product 2	400	460	(60)	
Product 3	340	310	30	
Other products	375	425	(50)	
Other products	185	105	80	✓
Total Revenue	1,750	1,700	50	
			0	
Customer #2			0	
Product 1	340	480	(140)	×
Product 2	380	450	(70)	
Product 3	120	190	(70)	
Other products	180	190	(10)	
Other products	180	220	(40)	
Total Revenue	1,200	1,500	(300)	×
			0	
Customer #3			0	
Product 1	220	160	60	
Product 2	190	140	50	
Product 3	160	120	40	
Other products	190	150	40	
Other products	1,140	1,130	10	
Total Revenue	1,500	1,300	200	✓

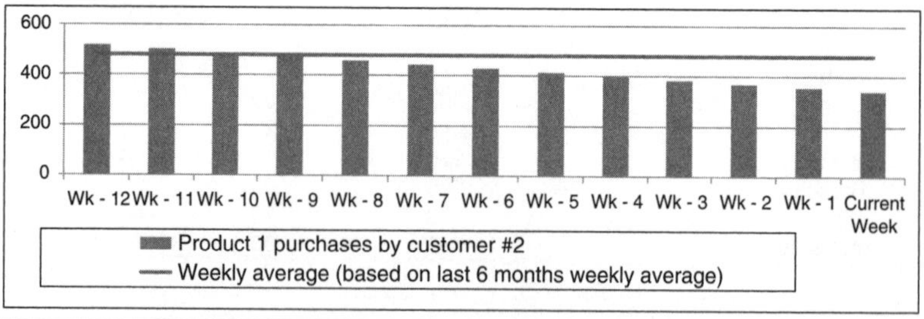
600
400
200
0
Wk - 12 Wk - 11 Wk - 10 Wk - 9 Wk - 8 Wk - 7 Wk - 6 Wk - 5 Wk - 4 Wk - 3 Wk - 2 Wk - 1 Current Week
Product 1 purchases by customer #2
Weekly average (based on last 6 months weekly average)

Areas to note:

1. ____________________

2. ____________________

3. ____________________

4. ____________________

EXHIBIT 7.14 Example of a weekly sales report

Weekly Reporting on Late Projects and Late Reports

Many managers are innovative people who love to get on with a project but often fail to tie up the loose ends or finish it. I am always encountering projects which are stuck in limbo. They will be of value to the organization only when someone refocuses on them. Exhibits 7.15 and 7.16 present two report formats that I believe should be presented weekly to senior and middle management to enable them to focus on completion. Exhibit 7.15 has a dual focus, on the project manager and the project. Exhibit 7.16 is a *shame and name* list targeting overdue reports. It focuses management on those reports that are well past their deadline. The version number helps management realize the cost of

Weekly Tracking of Projects That Are Past Their Deadline			
Manager	**Number of Projects Running Late**	**Number of Projects Running Late Last Month**	**Total Projects Currently Being Managed**
Kim Bush	7	0	8
Pat Carruthers	5	3	10
Robin Smith	3	3	12
_____	3	2	5
List of Major Projects That Are Past Their Deadline	**Original Deadline**	**Project Manager (sponsor)**	**Time to Complete**
_____	__/__	AB (YZ)	5 days
_____	__/__	DE (RS)	15 days
Strategic Plan Project	__/__	AB (RS)	90 days
Balanced Scorecard Project	__/__	DE (YZ)	15 days
Rolling Planning Project	__/__	AB (YZ)	60 days

EXHIBIT 7.15   Example of a weekly overdue projects report

Past Deadline Reports Week Beginning __/__/__				
Report Title	**Date of First Draft**	**Manager's In-Tray**	**Version #**	**Original deadline**
Annual Report	__/__	DP	>10	__/__
Annual Budget	__/__	DP	>20	__/__
_____	__/__	DP	>10	__/__
_____	__/__	DP	5	__/__
_____	__/__	DP	4	__/__
_____	__/__	PC	>10	__/__
_____	__/__	PC	1	__/__

Actions to be taken:

Annual Report	_____
Annual Budget	_____
_____	_____

EXHIBIT 7.16 Example of a weekly list of overdue reports

revisions. The manager's in-tray column focuses on the guilty manager and helps encourage action.

Daily and Weekly Reporting of Performance Measures

For a performance measure to be important, it needs to be reported *during* the month as opposed to at the end of the month. Visit Chapter 18 to understand how to develop, implement, and use winning key performance indicators.

DESIGNING REPORTS AROUND CURRENT TECHNOLOGY

It is important to design your reports based on the user's technology. Many 24/7, daily, or weekly reports will now be read via the users' phones and tablets. See Exhibit 7.17 for an example from Stephen Few.

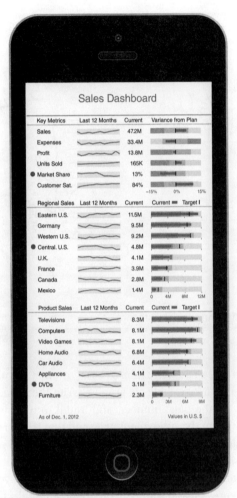

EXHIBIT 7.17 Example of a sales dashboard for a smart phone *Source:* Used with permission of Stephen Few, www.perceptualedge.com

 ERROR-FREE REPORTING

Checking Internal Consistency

We need to ensure that all reports are totally consistent internally. Many accountants are aware of a process that they first saw when they were auditors. You start off by marking all pages with a number (e.g., for a five-page

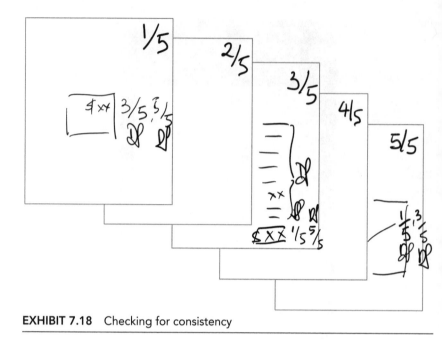

EXHIBIT 7.18   Checking for consistency

report, mark 1 of 5, 2 of 5, see Exhibit 7.18). For every number that appears elsewhere—either in a box, table, or graph—write the page reference where it appears again, by the page number, and initial to indicate that you have checked this number in the subsequent page and that it is correct.

This quality assurance document should be left around so the CEO sees it one day. When asked what are all these references and red ink, you say, "This is the quality assurance we do every time we issue a report to you." I assure you the CEO will be impressed and want you on important projects.

The Two-Person Read-Through

For all reports going to the senior management team, CEO, or board, you should use a two-person read-through. I learned this technique when I was an auditor.

The originator of a report gets another person to read aloud the report while they follow the words on another copy. By hearing the words, the writer can check the "dance of the words," their rhythm, and thus amend to correct spelling, grammatical errors, and make it an easier read. Where the reader has faced difficulties with your report, I can assure you the CEO will as well if the process of the two-person read-through has not been done.

Text-to-Voice Facility

The quick access bar on Microsoft Word, PowerPoint, and in Outlook has a "speak selected text" option. This is a valuable tool for a read back. I use this facility on all emails and smaller documents.

This facility does not replace the two-person read-through on those important reports, as you will miss out on some collective editing that occurs when two minds are working on the one document.

There are many sophisticated software applications that now will convert speech-to-text and text-to-voice. If you have one of these, I would use the text–voice capability instead of the simpler read back facility Microsoft applications provides.

The Final Check for the "Two Gremlins"

The two-gremlin rule states that in every piece of work there are always at least two gremlins that sneak through. If I find them and they are minor, I leave them and release the report. If you do not find them, look again or someone else will spot them.

Remember that you need a sense of perspective here; if minor, do not alter, as the cost both in time delays and reprinting may not merit the change. If spotted, you simply congratulate the person, saying, "Well spotted." Never, never mention these errors. Let your managers find them if they can.

I would always change typos in the first couple of pages or in the recommendations, as these can undermine the report.

 ## USING BEST-PRACTICE GRAPHICS

Everybody has a favorite graph. However, that graph might not resonate with other readers of your report. Instead of using our own viewpoint, I firmly believe we should follow the experts in data visualization.

Data visualization is an area that is growing in importance. There is a science behind what makes data displays work. The expert in this field is Stephen

Few. Stephen Few has written the top three best-selling books on Amazon in this field.[5] All corporate accountants involved in reporting should visit Stephen Few's website,[6] where he has lodged many high-quality white papers on the topic of graphical displays (www.perceptualedge.com/articles).

Stephen Few has come up with a very useful list of common pitfalls in graph and dashboard design in a must-read article available on his website (www .perceptualedge.com).[7]

Designing Dashboards

Exhibit 7.19 lists common problems with dashboards, utilizing Few's wisdom. It also includes some examples of poor dashboards, as illustrated in Few's book.

EXHIBIT 7.19   Common problems with dashboards

Problem & Symptoms	Example of Poor Graphics
Exceeding the boundaries of a single screen: Here, Few is warning us to think about the design carefully and avoid giving the reader the option to access alternatives. We need to define what should be seen instead of leaving the manager to click on an icon to get the important data.	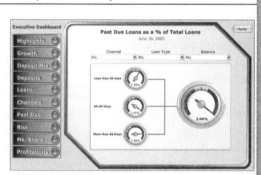
Introducing meaningless variety: Don't introduce myriad different graphs just because you can. Don't use a graph if a table would be better, and don't use a pie chart when a horizontal bar graph would be better.	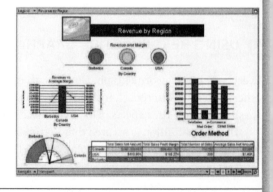

EXHIBIT 7.19 (*continued*)

Problem & Symptoms	Example of Poor Graphics

Arranging the data poorly: Make sure issues are linked together. Position graphs about the same subject together on the dashboard.

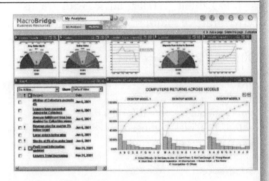

Using a lot of color to highlight everything: Few points out that many readers cannot distinguish between certain colors, and it is better to be a minimalist with color, only using red to highlight areas of concern.

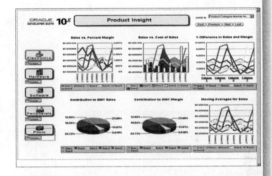

Cluttering the screen with useless decoration: Managing the white space is important. Only things that matter to the reader should be included.

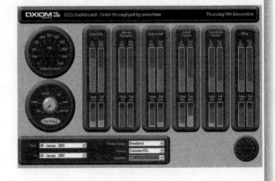

Designing Graphs

Besides the rules for dashboards there are additional rules for graphs used in reports. Exhibit 7.20 lists advice with graphs utilizing Few's wisdom and some better-practice solutions I have observed over the years.

EXHIBIT 7.20   Advice on Graphs

Advice	Graph Alternative
Supply adequate context for the data: Far too often, we show speedometer graphs that do not give enough information as to what is good or bad performance. *Source:* Stephen Few, www.perceptualedge.com	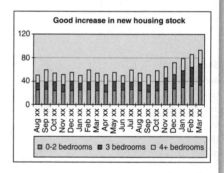
Avoid displaying excessive detail or precision: Graphs should summarize the information and be a big-picture view. The graph should have no more than a five-point scale and this should avoid unnecessary precision. For example, use $5 million instead of 5,000,000.00. Why do we need to show 23.4% when 23% would suffice?	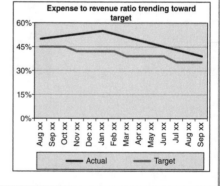
Always start the scale at zero: Often, to emphasize a point the press will show an exchange rate within a very narrow band—say US$ to euro within a five-cent range, magnifying the movement. Few is adamant that this may mislead and give rise to poor decisions. Better to express the graph starting the scale from zero.	

EXHIBIT 7.20 *(Continued)*

Advice	Graph Alternative

Avoid using these graphs: The following graphs should be banned from use:

- Pie charts
- Radar graphs
- Three-D graphs

Source: Stephen Few

Few points out that it is far better to use a horizontal bar graph instead of a pie chart.

Make one data series the baseline: Few also points out the benefit of making one data series the baseline and showing the other as a variance to it. For example, actual shown against a budget, which is on the baseline.

Source: Stephen Few, www.perceptualedge.com

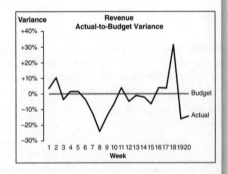

Show a minimum of 15 months' trend analysis: Trend analysis is required, going back at least 15 months to ensure any seasonality in the operations is captured. Remember, business has no respect or interest in your year-end. It is merely an arbitrary point in time.

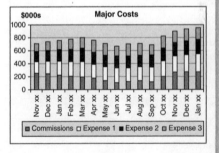

(continued)

EXHIBIT 7.20 (*Continued*)

Advice	Graph Alternative

Avoid using a YTD budget line: There is no room to show a flawed monthly or year-to-date budget line, an arbitrary apportionment of the annual planning number that was done at the last minute and was wrong from the very start.

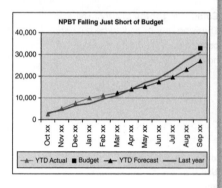

Explain turning points: Key turning points on graphs should be explained by a note on the graph, and comments need to highlight major issues.

Source: Stephen Few, www.perceptualedge.com

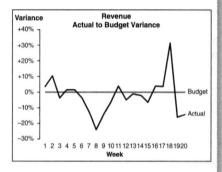

Use up to five gridlines and a yellow background: The gridlines on the graph should be limited to around five lines. I always make these a medium tone of gray. Black on yellow is the best combination for clarity, so when using color graphs, make the background a faint yellow.

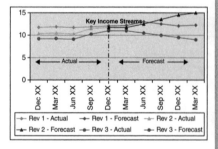

EXHIBIT 7.20 *(Continued)*

Advice	Graph Alternative

Color your combination graph axis: These are very useful, especially when comparing a financial cost against a nonfinancial.

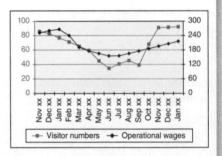

Use the graph title to say something important: Like a journalist, you need to treat the title as important "real estate." If you cannot say something important, maybe you should use a different graph.

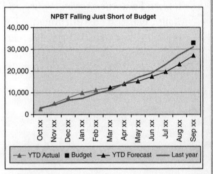

PDF DOWNLOAD

To assist the finance team on the journey, I have included some templates. The reader can access, free of charge, a PDF of the following material from www .davidparmenter.com/The_Financial_Controller_and_CFO's_Toolkit.

The PDF download for this chapter includes:

- CEO one-page fanfold report
- Board dashboard one-page fanfold report

 ## NOTES

1. Brian Maskell and Francis Kennedy, *Why Do We Need Lean Accounting and How Does It Work?* (Hoboken, NJ: Wiley Inter Science 2007).
2. Ibid.
3. Stephen Few's work is accessible from www.perceptualedge.com.
4. Jeffrey K. Liker, *The Toyota Way* (New York: McGraw-Hill, 2003).
5. Stephen Few, *Information Dashboard Design: Displaying Data for At-a-Glance Monitoring,* 2nd ed. (Burlingame, CA: Analytics Press, 2013).
6. Stephen Few's website (www.perceptualedge.com/articles) contains many useful articles.
7. Stephen Few, *The Common Pitfalls of Dashboard Design* (Proclarity, 2006).

CHAPTER EIGHT

Lean Board Reporting

OVERVIEW

Board reporting is frequently an anti-lean process. Boards often complain about getting too much information too late while management often complains about the time that is tied up in the board reporting process. This chapter explores how to get the board to agree to briefer reports that are less frequent and are received electronically. It also covers the need to cost the process, how to circumvent the amount of rewriting that occurs, the mistakes to avoid with the finance board report, and what should be in a one-page board dashboard.

It must be one of the classic Catch-22 situations: Boards complain about getting too much information too late, and management complains that nearly 20 percent of its time is tied up in the board reporting process. The process of board reporting is anti-lean in many respects. This process needs to occur more efficiently and effectively for both the board and management.

135

The corporate accountants should work with the CEO and the board to carry out these tasks:

- Commence an educational process regarding the cost versus benefit of the board reporting process; start with costing out each board paper, and the board will be the first to complain about the waste.
- Ensure all requests for information are properly scoped and costed first.
- Instigate an empowerment program so reports are not rewritten as they are reviewed by senior management unless absolutely necessary.
- Prepare an A3 (fanfold) one-page board dashboard covering both a financial and nonfinancial overview of the organization.
- Table board papers electronically, using some of the innovative applications designed for this purpose.
- Work with the chairperson to constantly reduce the number of board papers.
- Release papers to the board as they become available to give the board more time to absorb the information.
- Introduce a change to the board meeting timetable. The board should meet less frequently (four to six times a year, with board subcommittees meeting in the intervening months) and within 10 working days of the last reporting period.

 ## SELLING CHANGE TO THE BOARD

In order to sell change to the board, we need to master and promote selling change. We need to fully understand the content of Chapter 2, Leading and Selling the Change, so it would be worth rereading this chapter. In order to be able to paint the default feature, show the board the reinvented future and ask board members if they really want the default future. If they do, we need to push selling change. In preparation for this sales process, you need to work out the cost of preparing board papers over a typical year.

Costing the Preparation of Board Papers

Board papers can reach mammoth proportions, tying up vast amounts of management time in preparation. In some organizations, one week a month is written off by the senior management team (SMT) working on board papers.

	Accounting Team	CFO	Business Unit Managers	Senior Management Team	CEO
			Working days per month		
Board papers					
Preparing board financial report	5 to 8			1 to 1.5	
Review reports before they going to board	2 to 3				
Preparing business unit progress reports to the board			4 to 6		
Preparing one-off board reports each meeting	3 to 5		10 to 20	6 to 10	
Review and redrafting		1.5 to 3		0.5 to 1	3 to 5
Binding board papers and organising despatch	0.5 to 1				
Working days per month	10.5 to 17	1.5 to 3	14 to 26	7.5 to 12.5	3 to 5
Average salary cost	$120,000	$250,000	$175,000	$250,000	$400,000
Average productive weeks	42	32	32	32	32
	11 times a year			6 times a year	
	Low	High		Low	High
Annual Cost ($Millions)	$0.5	$0.8		$0.4	$0.6
Over next 10 years ($Millions)	$5.0	$8.0		$4.0	$6.0

EXHIBIT 8.1 Cost of preparing board papers for a 500 FTE organization

The result of these excesses often is late board meetings, with the papers being sent to the directors only a day or two before the meeting. The board meetings themselves can then be sidetracked by the detail, with the strategic overview inadequately addressed.

Directors themselves are often guilty parties, requesting changes to board report formats, asking for unnecessary detail, and requiring analysis without first giving staff guidelines as to how much detail is required.

What amount of SMT time is absorbed by the board reporting process? It is important to cost this out and report it to the board members. They will be horrified with the results. Based on an organization with 500 full-time employees (FTEs) meeting 11 times a year, the preparation of the board papers could cost between $5 million and $8 million (see Exhibit 8.1). This is a scary sum, one the board would want to reduce.

I base the costing on 42 productive weeks a year, having removed holidays, training, and sick leave. The CFO, CEO, and SMT's available time is only 32 weeks for the year, as I have taken off the time they spend traveling and in meetings going nowhere quickly.

SCOPING OF THE INFORMATION REQUESTS

A request for information from the board often can take on a life of its own. A simple request soon adopts "Charge of the Light Brigade" characteristics, where instructions get mixed up as the request is passed down the management tree. Often, the director who asked the question had visualized a 30-minute job, and now the staff member, assigned the task, embarks on a massive exercise. How often has your board received a lengthy report with over $20,000 of time invested, only to glance cursorily at it?

There needs to be more direct communication between the directors and the staff who are going to research the request. A discussion between the director, the researcher, and the relevant general manager will be able to scope the exercise and ensure the likely investment is worthwhile. Failing that, all directors should be asked by the chairperson to scope their requests: "I would like to know about _____. I suggest we invest no more than __days and $_____ on researching and reporting this."

 ## AVOIDING REWRITES OF BOARD REPORTS

Some organizations have made a major cultural change to board report writing, obtaining commitment from the board, CEO, and SMT that the original report can be sent, unaltered grammatically, to the board, thus avoiding expensive rewrites. The board no longer considers the quality of the board papers as a reflection of the CEO's performance. The organizations have learned to delegate and empower their staff so that SMT and board papers are being written with limited input from senior managers and are being tabled with few amendments, provided that the SMT agree with the recommendations. The CEO can choose to put a caveat on each report: "While I concur with the recommendations, the report was written by _____."

The board understands that the report is not written in SMT language. Board members are encouraged to comment directly to the writer about strengths and areas for improvement in report writing. The writers are also the presenters, where necessary. The benefits include motivated and more competent staff, and general managers being free to spend more time contributing to the bottom line.

In this regime, the CFO would not present the results. This would be delegated to the senior management accountant closest to the numbers. The CFO and other SMT members deliver more strategic papers.

PAPERLESS BOARD MEETING

Many of the procedures that support a board meeting have changed little since Charles Dickens's time. Board members receive large board papers that they have difficulty finding the time to read. In the twenty-first century, we should be using the electronic board software applications outlined in Chapter 4.

INTRODUCE A CHANGE TO THE BOARD MEETING SCHEDULING

Seek to restructure the operations of the board, setting bimonthly meetings, with the board members' investing the saved time elsewhere, such as:

■ Sitting on subcommittees that are looking at improvements in key areas of the business.
■ Assisting the organization to share specialist knowledge by making presentations on topics to management and staff.
■ Helping the company by opening doors to new markets.

Since board meetings are to be strategic, there is no need for monthly meetings, and enlightened companies now have bimonthly meetings, or, at most, eight board meetings a year.

The longer the period of elapsed time you allow for a task to be completed, the greater the chance of its being completed inefficiently. Thus, a prompt board meeting will ensure a more efficient one. The best practice is for the board to meet within 10 working days of the reporting period to avoid the process absorbing too much time.

At the other end of the spectrum, some boards are meeting six weeks after the month-end. There is another month-end in between, making for a truly ridiculous situation. Exhibit 8.2 shows an efficiency scale in the scheduling of board meetings after the month-end in question.

EXHIBIT 8.2 Efficiency Rating of Board Meeting Scheduling (Number of Working Days Since Reporting Period Ended)

Exceptional	Above Average	Average	Below Average
< 8 working days	8–10 working days	11–15 working days	> 15 working days

MISTAKES TO AVOID WITH THE FINANCE REPORT IN THE BOARD PAPERS

Here are the top mistakes, which constantly reappear, in board finance reports, as noted by Graeme Nahkies, Director of BoardWorks International.

Not using important financial ratios. Failure to calculate and present clearly to directors important financial ratios, such as the solvency ratio. All staff preparing reports for the board must remember that their job is to communicate key information to directors. Directors should not have to spend time unnecessarily analyzing and interpreting the finance or any other kind of report. Directors are just as much the CFO's customer as the chief executive and will sometimes have as much or more influence over their future career.

Lack of interpretation. Failure to interpret the ratio against target levels when it is shown. The report should comment on the ratios—for example, "The quick ratio target is two and we are now tracking down toward it because this month we have _____. Next month we will be back at a comfortable _times cover."

Meaningless graphs. While presenting financial data in pictorial (i.e., graphed) form is highly desirable as a complement to the numbers, these should focus on matters that are relevant at the board level. Cluttering board reports with graphs that are unlikely to show material change over long periods is not that helpful. Graphs should be chosen for their relevance in informing directors about the financial well being of the entity.

Assuming too much. The report is too narrative, therefore assuming that the board can remember all prior details given before. The finance story, delivered during each board meeting, should stand on its own two feet as a self-contained document that does not rely on directors' memories or ability to refer back to earlier documentation. Many board members sit on multiple boards, so do not expect them to have total and accurate recall. Also, it is worth acknowledging that not all directors are as financially literate as they would have you believe.

Thinking your financial report is the "main course." The finance report should be the first item on the agenda only in a crisis. Otherwise, if it is business as usual, place the finance report toward the back-end of the agenda. Board members should be talking about the future, for this is where they can add the most value, and it is the only thing they can influence. Finance reports being precirculated can be assumed to have been read and therefore to have informed the directors' approach to the meeting. Exception reporting means that only matters that are not as they should be are highlighted for board attention and possible discussion.

Poor quality reporting. Boards want to have confidence in the financial reporting. Poorly written and presented finance reports, which contain obvious errors even of a proofreading nature, undermine directors' confidence in their key professional adviser. Finance teams would be well advised to undertake some practical training in delivering informative and error-free board papers.

Slow month-end reporting. Slow month-end reporting leads to a narrow window for board meetings. Leading practice is now for finance teams to have the finance report to the CEO inside three working days of commencement of the new month, with the board report following the end of the first week. The board meeting can now be held in the latter part of the second week. This means that busy professional directors do not have to concentrate all their board meetings into the latter part of the month.

CONTINUALLY PURGING THE BOARD PAPERS

Does it take a 200-page board paper package to run a business? Are the key decisions a direct result of board papers or the collective experiences of the board members?

If Toyota makes investment decisions on an A3 (fanfold) one-page submission, surely we can limit many other papers to one A3 page, leaving the presentation and question and answer session to cover the detail. The benefit to the board is that management has less space to cloud a problem. Management has to set out the issues clearly and concisely.

Making the presentation slides also a board paper will backfire, as you will tend to put too much information on the slides. See Appendix B on the tips to deliver a killer presentation.

MOVING TO GOVERNANCE INFORMATION

There is a major conflict in most organizations that have boards, as to what information is appropriate for the board. Since the board's role is clearly one of governance and not of management, we should avoid giving the board a copy of the management papers. If we use an analogy of the organization being a ship, the board must focus on the horizon for icebergs or look for new ports of call. This is instead of the directors parking themselves on the bridge and getting in the way of the captain who is trying to perform the important day-to-day duties of steering the ship.

The profit and loss statement and balance sheet should be reduced to no more than 10 lines each. No number is shown unless it is material—say, over 10 percent of total expenditure (P/L) or 10 percent of capital employed for the balance sheet. You simply amalgamate and be clever with your caption headings.

A3 (FANFOLD) ONE-PAGE BOARD DASHBOARD

There is a major conflict in most organizations that have boards, as to what information is appropriate for the board. Since the board's role is clearly one of governance and not of management, it is inappropriate to be providing the board with the organization's key performance indicators (KPIs), as these should be monitored frequently, as discussed in Chapter 18.

KPIs are the very heart of management. Used properly, many of them are monitored 24/7 or at least weekly. Certainly they are not measures to be reported monthly or bimonthly to the board.

We need indicators of overall performance that should be reviewed only on a monthly or bimonthly basis. These measures need to tell the story as to whether the organization is being steered in the right direction at the right speed; whether the customers and staff are happy; and whether the organization is acting in a responsible and environmentally friendly way. In Chapter 18, I called these measures *key result indicators* (KRIs). These KRIs help the board focus on strategic rather than management issues, and should be reported in an A3 (fanfold) one-page board dashboard, as shown in Exhibit 8.3.

The key features of dashboards include:

- The financial numbers include a summary P/L and summary B/S similar to the information given to the CEO in the one-page A3 finance report.
- Commentary is restricted to bullet points covering the "areas of concern" and "areas to note."
- Use traditional graphs showing at least 15 months of trend analysis.
- Each graph has a relevant title, to explain what is happening. "Return on Capital Employed" becomes "Return on Capital Employed Is Recovering."
- You may need to maintain somewhere between 10 and 15 graphs and report the most relevant ones to the board.

Please revisit the section on best-practice graphics in Chapter 7 before you commence designing your board dashboard.

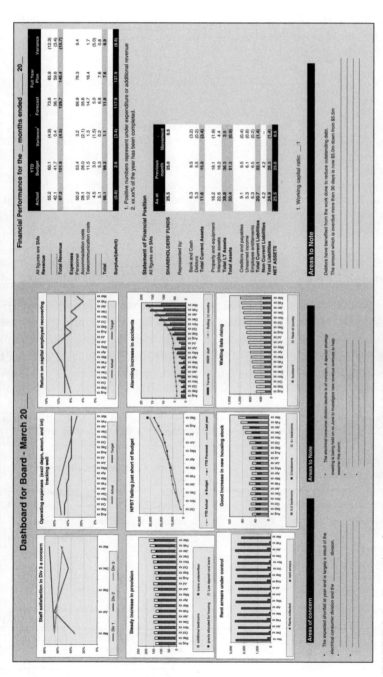

EXHIBIT 8.3 Example of an A3 page (U.S. Fanfold) board dashboard

A BOARD DASHBOARD COMPLETED OVERNIGHT

One accountant, after attending a KPI workshop, went home and prepared a board dashboard for the board meeting the following day. It was not hard, as most of the graphs required had been prepared for previous papers. He simply updated and repositioned them. He arrived early to meet the chairman and said, "I know you do not like surprises, but I have just prepared a one-page summary of the organization. I think you will find it useful." The chairman agreed and opened the board meeting by explaining the origins of this new one pager. It was such a success that the accountant was instructed to make it the first page of all future board papers.

Examples of Key Result Indicators for a Board Dashboard

Once you understand the terminology I am using, you will find that many of the measures you have been calling KPIs are in fact KRIs. Thus, the exercise of preparing a board dashboard of KRIs is very easy: It is simply a matter of recycling graphs you already have. I have included some examples of KRI board dashboard graphs that may be of interest in Exhibit 8.4.

EXHIBIT 8.4 Examples of Key Result Indicators for a Board Dashboard

Staff satisfaction:
No different or less important than customers. As one person said, "Happy staff make happy customers, which make happy shareholders." If you believe in this connection, run a survey now! A staff satisfaction survey need not cost the earth and should never be done covering all staff; instead, it should be replaced by a rolling survey.

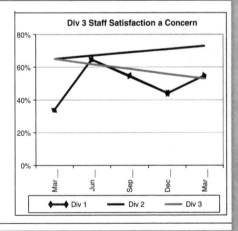

EXHIBIT 8.4 (*Continued*)

Expenses as a ratio to revenue:

The board should be interested in how effective the organization has been in utilizing technology and continuous improvement to ensure that the cost of operations is tracking down as a percentage of revenue.

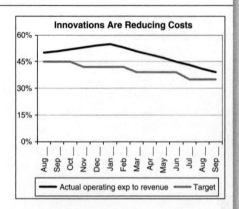

Customer satisfaction:

Customers should be set out in groups as to their importance to you. Airlines have between four and five different categories for their registered frequent flyers. Satisfaction needs to be measured at least every three months for your key customers and for the next level down. I believe the lowest customer category should be surveyed less frequently as they contain the disgruntled customer that should be abandoned in any case. Show the board only the satisfaction of the top three levels.

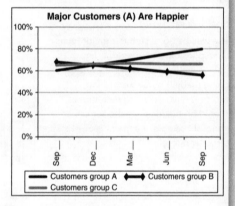

Value of new business, or amount of take-up of new services:

All businesses in the private sector need to focus on the growth of their rising stars. In the government and nonprofit sectors, take-up of new services is more important.

(continued)

EXHIBIT 8.4 (*Continued*)

Net profit before tax (NPBT):

Since the board will always have a focus on the year-end, it is worthwhile showing the cumulative NPBT. This graph will include the most recent forecast, which should be updated on a quarterly basis bottom-up. Note that the year-to-date budget line is not shown, as explained in Chapter 16.

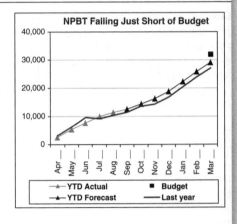

Health & safety:

The well being of staff is a major focus of responsible management, and boards are interested in the progress being made. For manufacturing, accident rate, including near misses, should be the focus. In the service and nonprofit sectors, we might look at staff turnover rate.

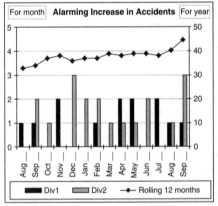

Return on capital employed:

ROCE has always been an important KRI and should never be called a KPI, as explained in Chapter 18.

EXHIBIT 8.4 *(Continued)*

Cash flow:
This would be projected out at least six months forward.

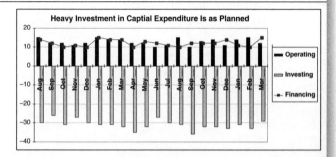

Capacity:
Monitoring the capacity of key machines and plant is always important. The graph should go forward at least 6 to 12 months. The board needs to be aware of capacity limitations, and such a graph will help it focus on the need for new capital investment.

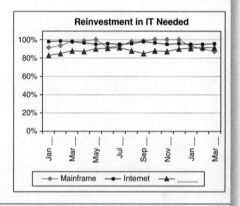

PDF DOWNLOAD

To assist the finance team on the journey, templates, checklists, and book reviews have been provided. The reader can access, free of charge, a PDF of the following material from www.davidparmenter.com/The_ Financial_Controller_and_CFO's_Toolkit.

The PDF download for this chapter includes:

- Cost of preparing board papers template
- Board dashboard template

CHAPTER NINE

A Lean Annual Planning Process—Ten Working Days or Less!

OVERVIEW

Annual budgeting and planning can be completed in two weeks provided we take a fresh look at the process. The only thing certain about annual planning is that it is wrong as soon as the ink has dried, so we need to get it wrong quicker. This chapter explores why annual planning needs to change radically. It discusses the foundation stones and better practices behind a lean annual planning cycle, and how to sell the change to management.

This sounds impossible, yet annual planning can be completed in two weeks. It takes good organization, plenty of abandonment, and awareness that the annual planning process is not adding much value to the organization as the numbers are wrong as soon as the ink has dried. Annual planning is undermining an efficient allocation of resources, encouraging dysfunctional budget holder behavior, negating the value of monthly variance reporting, and consuming huge swathes of time from all those involved.

When was the last time you were thanked for the annual planning process? You have a situation where, at best, budget holders have been antagonized; at worst, budget holders now flatly refuse to cooperate.

The future for planning in any lean organization is quarterly rolling planning, which is covered in Chapter 16 in this book and is developed from the *Beyond Budgeting* movement, which I fully endorse. However, it will take upwards of nine months to implement quarterly rolling planning, and thus your annual planning cycle may be just around the corner.

This chapter is a summary of the content in my white paper, "Timely Annual Planning Process in Two Weeks or Less."[1]

 ## LEADING AND SELLING THE CHANGE

It is important to sell to management why a quick annual plan is a good annual plan. This is not particularly difficult, because it is rare to find a manager who enjoys the process or finds it rewarding and worthwhile. The difficulty is that while managers will concur with the concept, getting them to change old and embedded bad practices requires a culture change.

As mentioned in Chapter 2, Leading and Selling the Change, it is important to start off the process by getting management to see that the default future is not what they want. We need to sell the change using emotional drivers rather than selling by logic, as already discussed.

Some Emotional Drivers

> *"It's no secret that annual budgeting processes are time consuming, add little value, and prevent managers from responding quickly to changes in today's business environment."*
> —Jeremy Hope of Beyond Budgeting fame[2]

The following points are some of the emotional drivers you would use to sell the need to streamline the annual planning process to the SMT:

Annual planning is wasteful There is a huge cost associated with the annual plan—ensuring you estimate on the high side, as costs motivate the SMT and the board.

Finance team members lose months and work many late nights and weekends, producing an annual plan that is wrong.

The board, the SMT, and all levels of management are tied up in arguments discussing a period no one can predict.

Poor allocation of resources Rational budget holders become dysfunctional requesting funds they do not need but feel they should have them just in case. Resources are thus locked away in budget holder slush funds.

Many new opportunities that become available are not taken up, as they were not funded in the budget. The funding is thus not adaptable to the changing conditions.

The finance team and budget holders are skilled staff that could be doing more meaningful activities.

Undermines reporting The monthly budgets, if set from the annual plan, create meaningless month-end targets. The June budget turning out to be closer to September's numbers and September's budget more relevant to November, and so on. The corrupted budgets lead to meaningless variance commentary (e.g., "It is a timing difference;" "It was not meant to happen this month").

I always say to attendees at my workshops, if you set your month-end budgets from the planning round, you have committed one of the greatest mistakes since Luca Pacioli invented double entry bookkeeping.

Costing the Annual Planning Process

In order to create a change in the way the SMT, board, and management address the annual planning process, you need to establish what is the full cost of the annual planning process, including CEO, CFO, SMT, the budget holders, and the accounting and planning staff masterminding the process.

Based on a costing for a 500 FTE organization, I have estimated that the annual cost is between $1.2 million and $1.7 million a year. As I like to say to senior management, "If you do nothing about this, you will be investing $12 million to $17 million over the next 10 years." Exhibit 9.1 illustrates how the sum was calculated. The times are estimates and show what a 500 FTE organization may be investing in its annual plan preparation.

As used in earlier costings, I use 42 productive weeks a year for the finance team and budget holders, having removed holidays, training, and sick leave. I take off another 10 weeks for the CFO, SMT, and CEO to account for time spent traveling and in numerous meetings.

	General Managers	CEO	CFO	Accounting & Planning	Budget Holders
Staff involved	4 to 6	1	1	3 to 5	50 to 70
	Estimated total number of weeks worked				
Budget Process (incl rework)	4 to 6	3 to 4	3 to 4	10 to 25	100 to140
Re-Budget Process (if done)	1 to 2	0.5 to 1	0.5 to 1	5 to 10	50 to 70
Reporting Against Budget	2 to 4	0.5 to 1	0.5 to 1	5 to 10	150 to 210
Re-Forecasting Y/E Result (>6 Times a Year)	1 to 2	0.5 to 1	0.5 to 1	3 to 5	100 to 140
No.of Weeks Worked	8 to 14	4.5 to 7	4.5 to 7	23 to 50	400 to 560
Average Salary Cost	$250,000	$400,000	$250,000	$120,000	$100,000
Average Productive Weeks	32	32	32	42	42
Personnel costs only	$50-90k	$60-90k	$30-40k	$60-150k	$1.0m-1.3m
Annual cost	**$1.2m to $1.7m**				
Over next ten years	**$12m to $17m**				

EXHIBIT 9.1 Cost of the annual planning process

 ## FOUNDATION STONES OF A LEAN ANNUAL PLANNING PROCESS

When discussing better practices, I separate out those practices (foundation stones) that you have to adopt to progress forward from those practices you can choose to adopt or not without adversely affecting the process.

A number of foundation stones must be laid before we can commence a project on reducing the annual plan to two weeks. When building a house, you need to ensure that all of the structure is built on a sound foundation. Lean annual planning has a number of essential foundation stones:

1. Separate targets from the annual budget.
2. Bolt down your strategy beforehand.
3. Avoid monthly phasing of the annual budget.
4. The annual plan does not give an annual entitlement to spend.
5. Commit the budget committee to a lock-up.
6. Budget at category level rather than account code level.
7. Get it wrong quicker.
8. Build in a planning tool—not in a spreadsheet.
9. Plan with months that consist of 4 or 5 weeks.

Separation of Targets from the Annual Plan

It is so important to tell management the truth rather than what they want to hear. Boards and the senior management team have often been confused between setting stretch targets and a planning process. Planning should always be related to reality. The board may want a 20 percent growth in net profit, yet management may see that only 10 percent is achievable with existing capacity constraints.

The key is to remove any deliberate manipulation related to performance bonuses. In Chapter 20, Performance Bonus Schemes, I point out that any performance bonuses should be paid on performance compared to the market rather than to an annual plan. We want management to be extracted from the annual charade of making a target easy so their bonus is secured.

DIALOGUE WITH THE BOARD

You can say to the board, "Setting a stretch target is desirable, but you must accept that we might not be able to achieve this. We understand that the bonuses might well be pegged against the goal and we are not trying to lower the threshold to get the bonus, but merely informing you of the performance gap so you can think strategically about how we are to close the gap up."

By reporting a gap, we are saying to the board that based on expected customer demand, the existing products/ services, and the relevant prices there is a shortfall. "Please help us find the missing profit." The board then might need to acquire some profit by purchasing a new subsidiary or bring forward the development of a new product, increase prices, and so on.

Exhibit 9.2 shows where management have forced the plan prepared in March to meet the target set by the board. Each subsequent reforecast continues the charade until in the final quarter reforecast, performed in March the following year, the truth is revealed. In reality, the truth was always a shortfall, as the dark line in Exhibit 9.2 illustrates.

Bolt Down Your Strategy Beforehand

Leading organizations always have a strategic workshop out of town. This session should be anticipated with a positive attitude. Normally, board members

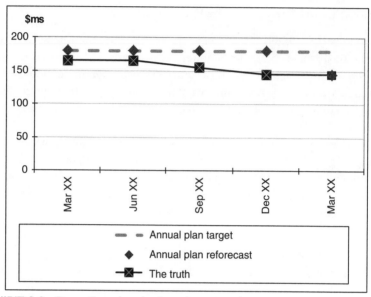

EXHIBIT 9.2 Reporting what the board wants to hear

will be involved, as their strategic vision is a valuable asset. These retreats are run by an experienced external facilitator. The key strategic assumptions thus are set before the annual planning round starts, and board members also can set out what they are expecting to see.

Great management writers, such as Jim Collins, Tom Peters, Robert Waterman, and Jack Welch, have all indicated that prominent organizations are not great because they have the largest strategic plan. In fact, it is quite the reverse; the poor-performing organizations are the ones that spend the most time in strategy and the dreaded annual planning process.

Jack Welch, in his book *Winning*,[3] talks about how he stopped business units writing large strategic documents and delivering drawn-out presentations. He forced all strategy plans to fit on to five slides. I have set out my interpretation of his slides and also include the thoughts from Jim Collins (see Exhibit 9.3).

Avoid Monthly Phasing of the Annual Budget

As accountants, we like things to balance. It is neat and tidy. Thus, it appeared logical to break the annual plan down into 12 monthly breaks before the

1. What the playing field looks like now (competitor analysis/market share)

Competitors	Global share	Market #1	Market #2
Us			
Competitor #1			
Competitor #2			
Competitor #3			

New entrants	Global share	Market #1	Market #2
New entrant #1			
New entrant #2			
New entrant #3			

1. What the playing field looks like now #2 (What are the characteristics of this business?)

Main products	Commodity / high value	Long / short cycle	Position on growth curve	Main drivers of profitability

1. What the playing field looks like now #3 (strengths and weakness of competitors)

Competitor	Their strengths	Their weaknesses
Competitor #1		
Competitor #2		

1. What the playing field looks like now #4 (main customers and how they buy)

Main customers	Preferred sales channel	Sales growth in last six months	Sales growth in last twelve months
Main Customer #1			
Main Customer #2			

2. What have the competition been up to? (main customers and new entrants)

Main competitors	Innovations in last year	Any game breakers	Revenue estimate last 12 months
Competitor #1			
Competitor #2			

New entrants	Innovations in last year	Any game breakers	Revenue estimate last 12 months
New entrant #1			
New entrant #2			

3. What have we been up to in the last year?

Key product	Innovations	Changes in sales force	Gain / Loss in competitiveness	Product sales in last 12 months
Key Product #1				

- Company purchased _____

4. What is our hedgehog?

The area where these three spheres share is your "Hedgehog" your reliable, robust, and safe place to be.

What you are deeply passionate about

What you can be the best in the world at

What drives your economic engine

5. What's around the corner?

- Competitor actions that could adversely affect us:
  - _____
  - _____
- New "game changing" technologies:
  - _____
  - _____
- Possible M&A deals that could adversely affect us:
  - _____
  - _____

6. What's our winning move?

- Actions we can do to build a bigger hedgehog:
  - _____
  - _____
- How we can change the playing field:
  - _____
  - _____
- Changes to increase key customer retention:
  - _____
  - _____

EXHIBIT 9.3 A strategy slide deck based on welch and collins

year started. Since we planned monthly, it seemed logical that July's column was July's number. In reality, July's numbers represented November's actuals and the November budget was closed to February's actuals. In other words, although the 12 columns added up to a year that maybe proved to be a reasonable guess, the monthly splits are radically wrong. If you can get your monthly splits right, you are in the wrong job, as you should be making money out of your knack of seeing into the future.

In the annual plan, we should only present quarterly indicative splits concealing the month columns. See Exhibit 9.4 for a suggested one-page summary format.

The monthly targets should be set a quarter ahead using a quarterly rolling forecasting process, which is discussed in Chapter 16. This change has a major impact on reporting. We no longer will be reporting against a monthly budget that was set, in some cases, over 12 months before the period being reviewed.

If you get the monthly budgets approved in the annual planning process, you will have created a reporting yardstick that undermines your value to the organization. Every month in the organization you will make management write variance analyses that I could do just as well from my office. "It is a timing difference," "We were not expecting this to happen," "The market conditions have changed radically since the plan," and so forth.

The Annual Plan Does Not Give an Annual Entitlement to Spend

The annual plan should not create an entitlement; it should be merely an indication, with the funding based on being allocated on a quarterly rolling forecasting and planning regime, a quarter ahead each time (see Chapter 16). Asking budget holders what they want and then, after many arguments, giving them an "annual entitlement" to funding is the worst form of management we have ever presided over.

Organizations are recognizing the folly of giving a budget holder the right to spend an annual sum, while at the same time saying that if you get it wrong, there will be no more money. By forcing budget holders to second-guess their needs in this inflexible regime, you enforce a defensive behavior, a stockpiling mentality. In other words you guarantee dysfunctional behavior from day one!

Annual plan for the year ending _____

	Quarter 1 Apr - Jun 20__	Quarter 2 Jul - Sep 20__	Quarter 3 Oct - Dec 20__	Quarter 4 Jan - Mar 20__	Y/E plan 31/03/__	Forecast for Y/E 31/03/__
			$Ms			
Income						
Income 1	13.0	12.5	12.1	12.3	50.0	46.5
Income 2	12.5	13.5	14.5	15.0	60.0	55.8
Income 3	10.5	10.0	9.5	9.0	40.0	37.2
Total Revenue	36.0	36.0	36.1	36.3	150.0	139.5
EXPENDITURE						
Personnel costs	15.1	15.7	15.3	15.5	61.6	57.3
Cost category 2	5.3	5.9	5.7	5.9	22.8	21.2
Cost category 3	3.4	4.0	3.6	3.8	14.8	13.8
Cost category 4	1.7	2.3	2.1	2.3	8.4	7.8
Cost category 5	1.6	2.2	1.8	2.0	7.6	7.1
Cost category 6	1.4	2.0	1.8	2.0	7.2	6.7
Other operational costs	2.8	3.4	3.0	3.2	12.4	11.5
Total Expenditure	31.3	35.5	33.3	34.7	134.8	125.4
Management overview					(0.2)	(0.1)
Net Result	4.7	0.5	2.8	1.6	15.0	14.1

Key Ratios	Average over last 4 qtrs						
FTEs	350	355	360	365	370	370	355
Revenue per FTE	$98,000	$101,000	$100,000	$99,000	$98,000	$405,000	$393,000
Personnel costs to total revenue	40%	42%	44%	42%	43%	41%	41%

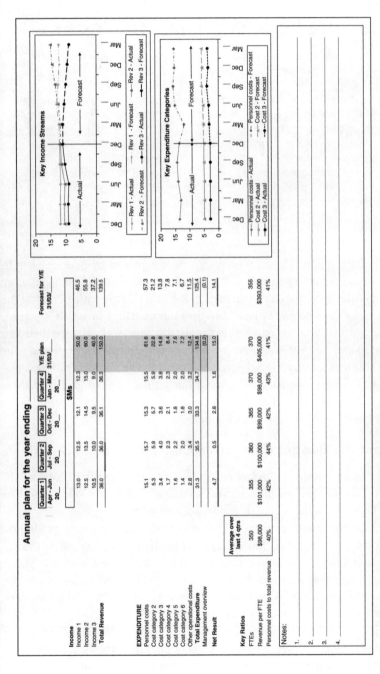

Key Income Streams

Rev 1 - Actual · Rev 1 - Forecast · Rev 2 - Actual
Rev 2 - Forecast · Rev 3 - Actual · Rev 3 - Forecast
Actual · Forecast

Key Expenditure Categories

Personnel costs - Actual · Personnel costs - Forecast
Cost 2 - Actual · Cost 2 - Forecast
Cost 3 - Actual · Cost 3 - Forecast
Actual · Forecast

Notes:

1. _____
2. _____
3. _____
4. _____

EXHIBIT 9.4 Example of an A3 (U.S. fanfold) annual plan

THE NINE-YEAR-OLD'S BIRTHDAY CAKE

The annual planning process has a lot in common with the handling of a nine-year-old's birthday cake. A clever parent says to Johnny, "Here is the first slice, if you finish that slice, and are not going "green around the gills" and want more, I will give you a second slice." Instead, what we do in the annual planning process is divide the cake up and portion all of it to the budget holders. Like nine-year-olds, budget holders lick the edges of their cake so even if they do not need all of it, nobody else can have it. Why not, like the clever parent, give the manager what they need for the first three months, and then say, "What do you need for the next three months?" and so on. Each time, we can apportion the amount that is appropriate for the conditions at that time.

The key is to fund budget holders on a rolling quarter-by-quarter basis. In this process, the management asks, "Yes, we know you need $1 million and we can fund it, but how much do you need in the next three months?" At first the budget holder will reply, "I need $250,000 this quarter," to which is replied, "Pat, how is this? Your expenditure in the last five quarters has ranged between $180,000 and $225,000." "Pat, you are two team members short and your recruiting is not yet underway; be realistic. You will only need $225,000, tops."

It will come as no surprise when a budget holder is funded only three months ahead that the funding estimates are much more precise and there is little or nowhere to hide those slush funds.

Commit the Budget Committee Commits to a "Lock-up"

It is best to have a small "budget committee," comprising the CEO, two GMs, and the CFO. Rotate the GMs each year so that all are involved over time. The GMs will, of course, be part of their relevant annual plan submission.

This committee sits in a lock-up for between three and five days. It is important to book, well forward, in the diaries of the budgeting committee the key dates when they need to be in committee to interview budget holders.

You need to ask the budget committee whether it would rather have three days or three months of pain. I cannot conceive of any CEO, who is a modern thinker, who would not take up the offer.

The role of the committee is to interview all budget holders about their annual plans for their team next year, including justifying their annual plan forecast, and the nonfinancials (e.g., staff succession, staff rotation).

During the three-day lock-up, each budget holder has a set time, up to about 45 minutes, to do the following:

- Discuss their financial and nonfinancial goals for the next year.
- Justify their annual plan forecast.
- Raise key issues (e.g., the revenue forecast is contingent on the release to market and commissioning of products __and __).

Budgeting at Category Level Rather Than Account Code Level

It is far better to budget at category level rather than account code level. A forecast is rarely right. Looking at detail does not help you see the future better. In fact, I would argue that it screens you from the obvious. Planning at a detailed level does not lead to a better prediction of the future. A forecast is a view of the future; it will never, can never, be right. As Carveth Read,[4] said "It is better to be vaguely right than exactly wrong." Planning a full final year in detail, in the dynamic world we live in, has always been, at best, naïve, and at worst, stupid.

COUNTING THE TREES IN A FOREST

Imagine that you have been asked to count the trees in a state forest that consists of 100 square miles of trees. You have two choices, the detailed way and the "helicopter" way.

For the detailed way, you could set up 10 teams of seven people. Each team is assigned 10 square miles and is given satellite navigation equipment, a different color of spray paint, safety gear, camping equipment, and provisions for three weeks or so. The teams update their count each night on a spreadsheet. At the end, the tree counts are consolidated. Some data are left out because the counters in some teams forgot to load every spreadsheet into the workbook. The final count, therefore, is wrong, although no one knows that.

For the helicopter way, satellite imaging is used to select five sample areas that are 1/1,000 of the forest. The staff are assigned to five bigger teams, and each counts their area in a day. The count of the five areas is averaged and then multiplied by 1,000. The answer is wrong. But it was wrong quickly and is still a good approximation. For forecasting, the helicopter way is usually the better option, unless you are forecasting payroll where managers can forecast by their staffs' actual salaries.

Although precision is paramount when building a bridge, an annual plan need only concentrate on the key drivers and large numbers.

Following this logic, it is now clear that as accountants, we never needed to set budgets at account code level. We simply do it because we did it in the previous year. You can control costs at an account code level by monitoring trend analysis of actual costs over 15 to 18 months.

We therefore apply Pareto's 80/20 principle and establish a category heading that includes a number of general ledger codes, as shown on Exhibit 9.5.

Helpful rules that can be used to apply this foundation stone include:

- Budget for an account code if the account is over 10 percent of total expenditure or revenue—for example, show revenue line if revenue category is over 10 percent of total revenue. If account code is under 10 percent, amalgamate it with others until you get it over 10 percent. See Exhibit 9.5 for an example.
- Only break this rule for those account codes that have a political sensitivity.
- Limit the categories that budget holder's need to forecast to no more than 12.
- Select the categories that can be automated, and provide these numbers.
- Map the G/L account codes to these categories—a planning tool can easily cope with this issue without the need to revisit the chart of accounts.

Getting It Wrong Quicker

The only thing certain about an annual target is that it is certainly wrong; it is either too soft or too hard for the actual trading conditions. If we all agree that we spend months of effort getting a number wrong, then you should agree with me that we need to get it wrong quicker, but we still need a reasonable estimate.

In the past, we have given budget holders three weeks to produce their annual plan—yet they have done it all in the last day or so. They have proved to us it can be done quickly.

If we apply the foundation stones described earlier, you will have taken the politics out of annual planning—why would budget holders spend a long time fighting for an annual plan allocation if you have told them it is not an entitlement to spend?

Forecasting at Account Code Level		Forecasting at Category Level		Notes
Stationery	40,556			
Uniforms	23,325			
Cleaning	11,245			Estimated to the nearest
Miscellaneous	17,654	Consumables	110,000	$10K.
Consumables	12,367			
Kitchen supplies	2,134			
	107,281		110,000	
Salaries and Wages	25,567,678	Salaries and Wages	27,400,000	Computed by business unit expected staff, rounded to the nearest $100k.
Taxes Levied on Gross Wages	2,488,888	Taxes Levied on Gross Wages	2,900,000	Taxes are automatically calculated by model.
Temporary Staff	2,456,532			
Contract Workers	2,342,345	Other Employment Costs	4,200,000	This number is the balancing item.
Students	234,567			
	33,090,010	Employment Costs	34,500,000	Budget holder estimates costs to the nearest $0.5m.

EXHIBIT 9.5   How a forecasting model consolidates account codes

One way to reduce the time spent in this area is to start the annual planning cycle off later. I recommend the second week of the ninth month—that is, for a December year-end, start the annual planning in week 2 in September.

The CEO needs to make a fast time frame nonnegotiable in all communication with staff. As long as the foundation stones are in place and the CEO has agreed to get behind a fast annual planning process, the program, as set out in Exhibit 9.6, will work.

From the memo that goes out to invite budget holders to the annual planning workshop, the address of the attendees at the workshop, and the daily chasing up of the laggards during the three days budget holders have to complete their annual plan, the message is clear: We want a fast, light-touch annual plan. *Fast* ensures the annual plan is completed in less than two weeks, and *light touch* avoids unnecessary detail.

As part of this foundation stone, common templates are established to replace the myriad spreadsheets. One such common template is the payroll worksheet that shows budget holders all their staff and their salaries, start date, leaving date if known, and so on (see Exhibit 9.76). This tool is discussed later on.

Process =>	Pre-work			Week 1 2 3	4	5	End	6 7 8	9	10
	Budget prework	Meeting with divisional heads (DHs)	Present budget workshop	Budget holders prepare and load their forecast	First look at numbers	Rework some budgets		Submissions by BHs to budget committee	Completion of final draft budget for board approval	Final alterations and finishing off documentation
Activities by team =>										
Strategic planning			Attend				Review to ensure linkage to plan, and advise on any discrepancies		Attend	
Senior management team (SMT)	Set assumptions	One-to-one with the finance team	Give presentation to BHs		First look at numbers			Budget committee review submissions in a "lock-up" session	Hear presentation and give instructions for final changes	
Finance team	Prepare system, the presentation, calculate known costs overheads, personnel costs etc.	One-to-one with DHs		Help BHs with budget plans (extended team)	Quality assurance	Help BHs		Further quality assurance	Complete preparation and deliver annual plan presentation	Complete documentation
Budget holders (BHs)			Attend	Prepare budget	Alter numbers after feedback	Rework numbers if necessary		Present plan to SMT when called	Attend or see presentation slides later	Document all calculations

EXHIBIT 9.6 Two-Week annual planning outline

162

Employee Name	Position Grade	Department	Current Salary	New Salary	Start Month	End Month
Jump, John	Junior Sales	Sales team 1	35,000	40,000	June *	
Host, Chris	Senior Sales	Sales team 1	70,000			
Big, Terry	Senior Sales	Sales team 1	68,000			August *
A. N. Other #1	Senior Sales	Sales team 1	70,000		August *	
A. N.Other #2	Senior Sales	Sales team 1	60,000		May *	

EXHIBIT 9.7 Payroll calculation worksheet

Built in a Planning Tool—Not in a Spreadsheet

As stated in Chapter 4, *Technologies You Must Have Before You Upgrade the G/L,* there is no place for a spreadsheet in forecasting, budgeting, and in any other core financial routine.

Acquiring a planning tool is the first main step forward, and one that needs to be pursued not only for the organization's future but also for the finance team members' future careers.

It has never been a better or easier time to do this. Planning tools are more affordable, many are cloud based, and they can work with any general ledger. I consider it unprofessional for qualified staff to be working with spreadsheets over 100 rows. If not convinced, please reread the first section of Chapter 4.

Plan with Months that Consist of 4 or 5 Weeks

The calendar in use today can be a major hindrance in forecasting. With the weekdays and number of weekend days, in any given month, being different from the next month, forecasting and reporting can be unnecessarily compromised. Closing off the month on a weekend can make a big positive impact in all sectors.

Forecasting models should be based on a "4, 4, 5 quarter"; that is, two four-week months and one five-week month are in each quarter, regardless of whether the monthly reporting has moved over to this regime. Calculating and forecasting the following items then becomes easier:

- *Revenues.* For retail, you either have four or five complete weekends (the high-revenue days).
- *Payroll.* You have either four weeks of salary or five weeks of salary.
- *Power, telecommunications, and property-related costs.* These can be automated and be much more accurate than a monthly allocation.

- *Monthly targets.* You can simply adjust back based on calendar or working days.

Simply design the model so that smoothing back to the regular calendar can be removed easily when you decided to migrate reporting to 4- or 5-week months.

To make progress in this area, I recommend to that you contact your general ledger supplier and ask, "Who is a very sophisticated user of this general ledger and who uses 4, 4, 5 reporting months?" Arrange to visit them and see how it works for them. Ask them, "Would you go back to regular calendar reporting?" Most are likely to give you a look that says, "Are you crazy?"

EFFICIENT ANNUAL PLANNING PROCESSES

I have included a checklist on "performing an efficient annual planning process" in the attached PDF files. This will help with the quality assurance process.

Hold a Focus Group Workshop

As explained in the section *The Power of the Focus Group* in Chapter 2, a focus group needs to be formed as part of the selling change process. We need the oracles in the business units to discuss what the annual planning default future looks like and agree that they do not want it. The focus group workshop is important for a number of reasons:

- Many people will doubt the organization's ability to move from three to four months to two weeks, and we need to ensure that all likely objections are aired in the focus group workshop.
- We need to reengineer the annual plan process using Post-it notes, as discussed in Chapter 10.
- The foundation stones need to be understood, agreed on, and put in place early in the project.
- A green light from the focus group will help sell this concept to the SMT.
- The focus group will give valuable input as to how the implementation should best be done to maximize its impact.

The proposed agenda for the focus group is set out in Exhibit 9.8. The suggested attendees would include: budget committee, selection of business unit heads, all management accountants, and a selection of budget holders. You will need an event secretary to document agreements, two laptops, a data show projector, and two whiteboards.

EXHIBIT 9.8 Draft Agenda for a Planning Focus Group

Location: _____

Date and Time: _____

Prework: Attendees to document forecasting procedures on Post-it stickers. One procedure per Post-it. Each team to have a different color Post-it.

8:30 a.m.	Welcome by CFO, a summary of progress to date at _____, an outline of the issues and establishing the outcome for the workshop.
8:40	**Setting the Scene**—topics covered include:

- The default future, the cost, and the major flaws
- The alternative—the proposed foundation stones, how a two-week process can work
- The proposed new annual planning foundation stones

9:40	**Workshop 1: Analyzing the foundation stones.** Separate teams look at the proposed new rules, and comment on changes required.
10:15	Morning break.
10:30	**Workshop 2: Workshop on "Post-it" reengineering of the annual planning process.** During the workshop, we analyze the bottlenecks of the forecasting process. In this workshop, we use these sticky notes to schedule the steps (e.g., yellow for budget holder activities, red for forecasting team activities, blue for budget committee activities).
12:00 p.m.	Feedback from work groups on both workshops and action plan agreed (document deadline date and who is responsible). Individuals will be encouraged to take responsibility for implementing the steps.
12:30	Lunch at venue.
1:30	Delivery of the proposed "selling presentation."
2:00	**Workshop 3: Feedback on the presentation.** Separate work groups look at different parts of the presentation.
3:00	The team presents, to an invited audience, the changes they would like to implement and when. They can also raise any issues they still have.
	Suggested audience includes all those who attended the setting the scene morning session.
4:00	Wrap-up of workshop.

The Post-it reengineering exercise is the same as the month-end process reengineering. Please see Chapter 10, Lean and Smarter Work Methods, on how to run a Post-it reengineering session.

Forecasting Demand by Major Customers by Major Products

If you have 200 products and 2,000 customers, how do you get to a reasonably accurate forecast? The answer lies in applying Pareto's 80/20 rule to the sales forecasting process. Sales need to be forecast by major customers and major products. The rest of the customers and rest of the products should be put into meaningful groups and modeled based on the historic relationship to the major customers' buying patterns. See Exhibit 9.9 for a suggested format.

Many organizations liaise with customers to get demand forecasts, only to find them as error prone as the forecasts done in-house. The reason is that you have asked the wrong people. You need to get permission to meet with the staff who are responsible for ordering your products and services.

> One financial team decided to contact its major customers to help with demand forecasting. Naturally, the team was holding discussions with the major customers' "headquarters" staff. On reflection, the financial team found it better but still error prone, so its members went back and asked, "How come these forecasts you supplied are so error prone?" "If you want accurate numbers, you need to speak to the procurement managers for our projects," was the reply. "Can we speak to them?" "Of course, here are the contact details of the people you need to meet." Several meetings were then held around the country. The team found that these managers could provide very accurate information and were even prepared to provide it in an electronic format. The sales forecast accuracy increased sevenfold due to focusing on getting the demand right for the main customers.

The lesson here is that if you want to forecast revenue more accurately, you can do this by delving into your main customers' business, by asking them on a quarterly basis, "Whom should we speak to in order to get a better understanding of your likely demand for our products in the next three months and the next five quarters?"

James Surowiecki wrote that[5] "a large group of people are often smarter than the smartest people in them." Hence the term *wisdom of the crowd* was born. In other words, a group's aggregated answers to questions that involve quantity estimation have generally been found to be as good as, and often better than, the answer given by any of the individuals in the group. Involving a

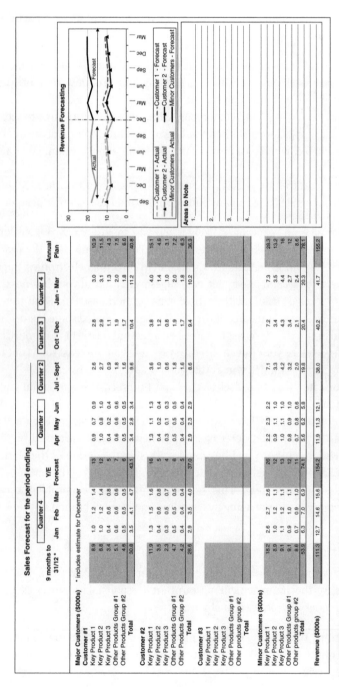

Sales Forecast for the period ending

Major Customers ($000s)	9 months to 31/12 *	Quarter 4 Jan	Feb	Mar	Y/E Forecast	Quarter 1 Apr	May	Jun	Quarter 2 Jul - Sept	Quarter 3 Oct - Dec	Quarter 4 Jan - Mar	Annual Plan
*includes estimate for December												
Customer #1												
Key Product 1	8.9	1.0	1.2	1.4	13	0.9	0.7	0.9	2.6	2.8	3.0	10.9
Key Product 2	8.8	1.0	1.2	1.4	12	1.0	0.8	1.0	2.7	2.9	3.1	11.5
Key Product 3	3.4	0.4	0.6	0.8	5	0.4	0.2	0.4	0.9	1.1	1.3	4.3
Other Products Group #1	5.1	0.6	0.6	0.6	7	0.6	0.6	0.6	1.8	1.9	2.0	7.5
Other Products Group #2	4.6	0.5	0.5	0.5	6	0.5	0.5	0.5	1.6	1.7	1.8	6.6
Total	30.8	3.5	4.1	4.7	43.1	3.4	2.8	3.4	9.6	10.4	11.2	40.8
Customer #2												
Key Product 1	11.9	1.3	1.5	1.6	16	1.3	1.1	1.3	3.6	3.8	4.0	15.1
Key Product 2	3.5	0.4	0.6	0.8	5	0.4	0.2	0.4	1.0	1.2	1.4	4.6
Key Product 3	2.3	0.3	0.3	0.7	4	0.3	0.1	0.3	0.6	0.8	1.0	3.1
Other Products Group #1	4.7	0.5	0.5	0.5	6	0.5	0.5	0.5	1.8	1.9	2.0	7.2
Other Products Group #2	4.2	0.4	0.4	0.4	5	0.4	0.4	0.4	1.6	1.7	1.8	6.3
Total	26.6	2.9	3.5	4.0	37.0	2.9	2.3	2.9	8.6	9.4	10.2	36.3
Customer #3												
Key Product 1												
Key Product 2												
Key Product 3												
Other Products Group #1												
Other products group #2												
Total												
Minor Customers ($000s)												
Key Product 1	18.2	2.6	2.7	2.6	26	2.2	2.3	2.2	7.1	7.2	7.3	26.3
Key Product 2	8.9	1.0	1.2	1.1	12	0.9	1.1	1.0	3.3	3.4	3.5	13.2
Key Product 3	9.1	1.1	1.2	1.1	13	1.0	1.1	1.0	4.2	4.3	4.4	16
Other Products Group #1	9.1	0.9	1.0	1.1	12	0.8	0.9	1.0	3.2	3.4	2.7	12
Other products group #2	8.6	0.7	0.9	1.0	11	0.7	0.8	0.6	2.0	2.1	2.4	8.6
Total	53.9	6.3	7.0	6.9	74.1	5.6	6.2	5.8	19.8	20.4	20.3	78.1
Revenue ($000s)	111.3	12.7	14.6	15.6	154.2	11.9	11.3	12.1	38.0	40.2	41.7	155.2

Revenue Forecasting

Actual — Forecast

- - Customer 1 - Actual
- - Customer 2 - Actual
— Minor Customers - Actual
- - Customer 1 - Forecast
- - Customer 2 - Forecast
— Minor Customers - Forecast

Areas to Note
1.
2.
3.
4.

EXHIBIT 9.9 Suggested level of detail in a sales forecast model

167

"crowd" in planning and forecasting can have a major positive impact on the process because:

- A great deal of trend information is being noted by those at the workplace, such as unsold products that are piling up, products that are being returned, and customer comments.
- Groups are less motivated to forecast what management wants to see.
- A small group of forecasters can only process a tiny fraction of the information available, whereas a crowd can take in an almost unlimited "harvest of data."
- Experts tend to have a bias of optimism, especially if they are looking at sales from inside the company rather than from the customer perspective.

Resistance from "experts" is likely when you suggest using the wisdom of the crowd in place of their forecast. To convince them, you copy the practice used by Best Buy, an American multinational in consumer electronics. Suggest two forecasts: theirs and one by selected sages from around your business. Ask the sages to forecast sales for the whole organization based on what they are seeing in their areas. You can tell them, "We have prepared some historic data for you and limited the forecast to some key lines and the rest is summarized in groups. Please place your forecast in the system. If your forecast turns out to be the most accurate, you will win a weekend for two at _____ resort."

Each quarter, you then disclose the experts' forecast versus actual and the wisdom of the crowd versus actual. I predict that the experts will want to duck for cover after a couple of forecasts highlight their inaccuracies. They will ask, even plead, "Please put our forecast in with the wisdom of the crowd."

The wisdom of the crowd has implications on the design of the planning tool. You can expect to accommodate possibly 20 versions of the revenue forecast and then average them. This, however, should not be a problem because you are not forecasting revenue by each line and by each branch.

Required Prework

Before the two-week lean planning cycle starts, much prework has to be performed by the management accountants responsible for overseeing the planning model. The prework includes:

- Amending the existing model to incorporate the changes in this paper
- Ensuring that the sales forecast, using the practices already discussed, appears reasonable

- Inserting the current personnel details (name, title, salary) into the payroll section of the model
- Calculating all categories that are to be based on historic trends

Accurately Forecasting Personnel Costs

Payroll often represents 30 to 60 percent of total costs, depending what sector your organization is in; thus, it is worth some extra effort to get a reasonable forecast.

Accurate forecasting of personnel costs requires analysis of all current staff (their end date if known, their salary, the likely salary review, and bonus), and all proposed new staff (their starting salary, their likely start date). This is done by each manager, who reviews a prepared schedule of current staff with the salary field populated by personnel from the most recent payroll records.

Budget holders put in a leaving date if known, their likely salary review with start date, and any possible bonus. For new staff, budget holders enter starting salary and their likely start date. No one needs to show managers the monthly and quarterly figures. The model can get it right. They simply have to get the best estimate of who will be working that year and the likely salary. Exhibit 9.7 shows an example of personnel cost forecasts.

Too many errors occur when budget holders are simply given last month's payroll total to use as a basis for annual planning. By using this number, you have multiplied the long service leave paid to employee _____ last month by 12. At the same time, you have not recognized that two staff positions were not included. Many of us have made this error.

After you have the correct salaries and wages, you can model any employment taxes paid by your organization. Then, forecast the total likely employment costs because you will have an idea about what total costs are permissible, and you can deduce the temporary, contract, and interns costs (see Exhibit 9.10). Exact numbers for these costs are not possible, no matter how much time is spent on them. In fact, the amount flexes all the time: If recruiting costs related to contract workers are late, these costs go up and the salaries and wages total is lower, and vice-versa.

Automate the Calculation for Some Expense Categories

A number of categories can be pre-populated, as the budget holder will look only at historic numbers and may even misinterpret this data. The finance team is best equipped to provide these numbers as the budgets will be

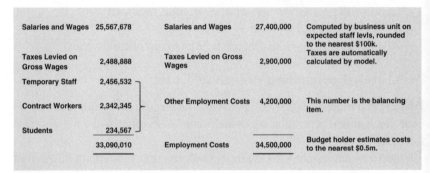

Salaries and Wages	25,567,678	Salaries and Wages	27,400,000	Computed by business unit on expected staff levls, rounded to the nearest $100k.
Taxes Levied on Gross Wages	2,488,888	Taxes Levied on Gross Wages	2,900,000	Taxes are automatically calculated by model.
Temporary Staff	2,456,532			
Contract Workers	2,342,345	Other Employment Costs	4,200,000	This number is the balancing item.
Students	234,567			
	33,090,010	Employment Costs	34,500,000	Budget holder estimates costs to the nearest $0.5m.

EXHIBIT 9.10   Forecasting employment costs (the helicopter way)

calculated based on historic trend information. The obvious categories to populate and lock down include:

- Communication costs (landlines, Internet, mobile)
- Property costs (power, lighting, property repairs, security, cleaning)
- Consumables
- Fleet costs
- Depreciation
- Miscellaneous costs

Provide Automated Calculations for Travel and Accommodation

When budget holders calculate travel and accommodation costs, they can spend hours searching the web for special deals. They then use these deals for their annual plan. I recommend that you set up a simple calculator. See Exhibit 9.11 with standard costs so all staff have to do is state the date, object of trip, select a return or one-way journey, number of staff, such as "three people going from Houston to Boston for two nights on a roundtrip."

The model then uses standard estimates to automatically calculate the airfares, accommodation, transfers, overnight allowances and other costs. For example, you might schedule the top 10 routes with standard pricing and have an eleventh flight called "Flights—other" and set a $300 return airfare. Although the forecast won't be exactly right, it is likely to be approximately right because it is based on an average calculated from the last three months of actuals.

Month of trip	Object of trip	From	To	Return trip	Nights	Number of staff traveling	Cost	
Oct xx	QRP project	Houston	Toronto	Yes	2	2	1,600	Cost is calculated based on standard flight, accommodation, and overnight allowance costs.
Nov xx	QRP project	Houston	Seattle	Yes	2	2	1,400	
Nov xx	QRP project	Houston	Boston	Yes	3	2	1,900	

EXHIBIT 9.11   Example of a travel and accommodation calculator

Prepare a Simple Reporting Template for the Annual Plan

Annual plans often end up in elaborate reports. The feeling is, "Since we spent so much time on it, we better make a great job of the write-up." In reality, nobody reads these documents. It is far better to have the documentation left mostly in presentation format along with a key summary page for each business and one for the consolidation. We do not need to report the annual plan to the board in monthly splits. A quarterly analysis of the annual plan will suffice, as shown in Exhibit 9.4.

Have Trend Graphs for Every Category Forecasted

Better quality can be achieved through analysis of the trends. There is no place to hide surplus funding when a budget holder has to explain why the forecast trend is so different from the past trend. The graph shown in Exhibit 9.12, if made available for all the categories budget holders are required to forecast, will increase forecast accuracy. Budget holders will want to ensure their forecasts make sense against the historic trend.

If Using a Spreadsheet, Simplify the Model to Make It More Robust

As explained, forecasting requires a good robust tool, not a spreadsheet built by some innovative accountant that no one can understand now. However, you may not have the time to replace the existing Excel model. A new planning tool will take at least six months for researching, acquiring, and implementing for organizations with over, say, 500 full-time staff. In this case, you can:

■ Improve the revenue predictions by focusing in on major customers' demand for the major products. You can automate the rest of the sales based on historic relationships between sales of minor products and major products and sales to minor customers to those made to major customers.

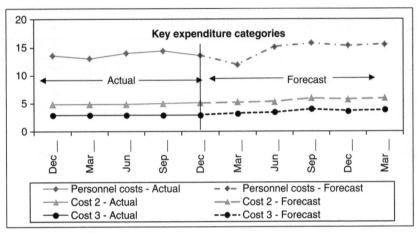

EXHIBIT 9.12 Expenditure trend graph

- Budget at category rather than account code level, hiding the rows not required.
- Forecast the annual plan using quarterly figures rather than monthly (hiding two of the monthly columns for each quarter).
- Consolidate via the G/L instead of the spreadsheet (if you can add the category headings easily into the G/L).

Expand Your Team, as Budget Holders Will Need One-to-One Support

Many budget holders will need one-to-one support. Yet, as seen in Exhibit 9.6, we are to do this all in three working days. We thus need to expand the support team. Some suggestions to expand your team are:

- Get all the qualified accountants involved, even those not working in the finance team (e.g., get the CFO involved as well).
- Ask the auditors to loan some audit seniors from their local offices to cover those remote locations—the audit seniors will be happy to be involved in an interesting task (those who have been auditors will know what I mean).
- Bring in some temporary staff with budget experience.
- For smaller budget holders, the senior accounts payable staff would be ideal.
- Offer remote budget holders one-on-one training with Skype-based virtual meeting technologies.

Thus, all budget holders who need help, wherever they are located, can be supported during the three-day window for data entry.

Hold a Briefing Workshop for all Budget Holders

Never issue budget instructions, for you already know they are never read. Follow the lesson of a leading accounting team that always holds a briefing workshop at which attendance is compulsory. With today's technology, you also can hold the workshop simultaneously as a webcast so budget holders in remote locations can attend, albeit electronically. (Attend a webcast to see what I mean.)

Hold a "budget preparation" workshop (see Exhibit 9.13 for an agenda example) covering how to complete the input form and explaining why budget holders do not need to forecast monthly numbers, only quarterly; the three-day window; the daily update to the CEO; and the fact that late returns will be career limiting. Stress that the bigger items should have much more detail. Explain why you have automated some of the categories and the help they will receive, and so forth.

Make sure that at the workshop, the CEO makes the following clear.

- **Fast light touch**
  - Everybody has to cooperate to achieve the three-day window to enter data.
  - Late forecasting will be a career-limiting activity.
- **Help at hand**
  - Help will be provided on a one-to-one basis.
  - How to use the planning tool (attendees will already have some training on this).
  - Forecasting by the categories, and why some categories are now automated.
- **Level of detail required**
  - What they should prepare for their presentation to the budget committee.
  - No monthly breakdown in annual plan, as the monthly numbers are to be set just before each quarter starts.
  - Stress the fact that only the more material categories will have more detail (e.g., payroll).
  - Sales forecast has been already made and is _____.

EXHIBIT 9.13 Draft Agenda for the Annual Plan Briefing Workshop

---

Location: _____

Date and Time: _____

Suggested attendees: all budget committee, all business unit heads, all management accountants, and all budget holders

Requirements: event secretary, desk top for every seven attendees, data show, two whiteboards

8:30 a.m.	Welcome by CEO and why this is a nonnegotiable event.
8:40	**Setting the scene—**topics covered include:

- Why we cannot afford the current annual planning process
- Better-practice stories and research we have done
- Some of the major flaws with the annual planning process
- The new rules that have been vetted by the focus group
- Proposed two-week annual planning process
- The setting on monthly targets a quarter ahead, instead of annually

The senior management team may wish to leave after this session.

9:30	**Present the new planning tool.**
10:00	**Workshop 1: Looking at the planning tool:** In small groups, no more than seven, each attendee gets a chance to play with the tool. Each group has a member from finance facilitating this process.
10:30	Morning break.
10:50	**Feedback on the package from the workgroups.**
11:20	Wrap-up of workshop by CFO, reminder about deadlines, help available, and to keep to the bigger picture.

 PDF DOWNLOAD

To assist the finance team on the journey, templates and checklists have been provided. The reader can access, free of charge, a PDF of the suggested worksheets, checklists, and templates from www.davidparmenter.com/The_Financial_Controller_and_CFO's_Toolkit.

The PDF download for this chapter includes:

- Costing of the annual planning process
- Performing an efficient annual planning process checklist
- Planning focus group agenda
- Annual plan briefing workshop agenda

NOTES

1. David Parmenter, "Timely Annual Planning Process in Two Weeks or Less," www.davidparmenter.com, 2015.
2. Jeremy Hope, *Reinventing the CFO* (New York: Harvard Business Press, 2006).
3. Jack Welch with Suzy Welch, *Winning* (Cambridge, MA: HarperBusiness, 2005).
4. Harry Read, Carveth, Logic, Deductive and Inductive (1898), *Artful Persuasion: How to Command Attention, Change Minds, and Influence People* (New York: AMACOM, 2000).
5. James Surowiecki, *The Wisdom of the Crowds* (New York: Anchor, 2005).

CHAPTER TEN

Lean and Smarter Work Methods

OVERVIEW

Around the world, teams are challenging old out of date work methods, "other people's thinking" as Steve Jobs called it, and replacing this thinking with twenty-first-century smarter work methods. This chapter covers; how to Post-it reengineer, scrum meetings, Kanban boards, lean management techniques, and Toyota's 14 management principles. This chapter also explores some of the management lessons I have gathered on my journey to writing *The Leading-Edge Manager's Guide to Success*.[1]

In this chapter I have extracted some lean and smart work methods gathered from witnessing a number of amazing teams and my research on the writings of the great paradigm shifters (Drucker, Hope, Collins, Hamel, and Peters and Waterman).

TECHNIQUES TO ADOPT FROM THE LEAN MOVEMENT

As mentioned in Chapter 1, the *lean movement*, which started in Japan during the rebuild after the Second World War, had an American influence, Edwards Deming.[2] The lean methods developed by the Japanese multinationals have now spread far and wide and should find a home in the finance team. These include:

- Post-it reengineering of inefficient routines such as: month-end, annual planning, and the annual accounts
- Adopting stand-up scrum meetings everyday during the delivery of a project, report, annual plan
- Having a Kanban board for each key process while it is in play

 ## POST-IT REENGINEERING WORKSHOPS

Re-engineering can be a complex or a relatively easy one—the choice is yours. Many organizations start off by bringing in consultants to process map the existing procedures. This is a futile exercise; why spend a lot of money documenting a process you are about to radically alter and when it is done only the consultants will understand the resulting data-flow diagrams?

You should Post-it reengineer the following:

- Month-end routines
- Annual planning routines
- Rolling forecasting and planning routines
- Annual accounts routines
- Inefficient processes

Reengineering Month-End Routines

The first place to start is to Post-it reengineer your month-end procedures in a workshop. This takes a full day and involves seven stages.

Stage 1 Invitation

Having set the date, ask the CEO to send out the invites for the workshop; see Appendix A for a draft. The finance team needs to send out instructions, a week or so prior to the workshop, outlining how each team is to prepare their sticky notes; see Exhibit 10.1.

Suggested attendees include all those involved in month-end, including accounts payable, financial and management accountants, and representatives from teams who interface with month-end routines (e.g., someone from IT, payroll).

EXHIBIT 10.1   Post-it Reengineering Instructions

Although our month-end has been streamlined in our pursuit of continuous improvement, we need to eliminate more waste from the process. I have organized for _____ to run a breakthrough lean technique to streamline the processes. During the session, _____will talk about the leading practices from around the world. This session will enhance your job satisfaction as you spend more time in the future scoring goals.

Date & Time: _____ 8:45 a.m. for refreshments, start 9 a.m., finish at 4:45 p.m.

Location: Room_____, _____

Your presence at the workshop is important. In order to run this workshop, we need you to prepare a list of all the processes you undertake as a team at month-end.

This process is quite simple. All it requires is:

■ Teams list all their processes onto the "Post-it" stickers allocated to them prior to the workshop and document each process with the whiteboard pen, enclosed. It is important that these stickers can be read from four to five yards. Please do not use pencil or ballpoint pen.

+2

Close-off Accounts Payable

■ List one procedure/process per Post-it note (please note, every Excel spreadsheet is a process and thus should have a Post-it note).
■ State when it is done, using the following time scale: –2, –1 (last working day), +1 (first working day), +2, etc.

EXHIBIT 10.2   Allocation of Colored Post-it Stickers

AP	Yellow
AR	Green
Financial Accounting team	Blue
Management Accounting Team	Purple
Capex	Pink
Payroll	Turquoise

Set up a schedule to ensure all the main teams have a unique color of notes (see Exhibit 10.2).

Stage 2 Stand-up Workshop around the Whiteboard

With everyone assembled, go through the agenda items, starting off with an introduction to best practice. See Exhibit 10.3 for an outline of the workshop agenda.

Assemble everyone to go through the agenda items, starting off with an introduction to best practice. You can access one of the many webinars I have recorded with accounting bodies and play this to the attendees. I recommend you only play ten minutes and then pause the webinar and ask attendees to pair off and discuss what they agree with and what they disagree with. These webinars can be accessed from www.davidparmenter.com.

When you get to the stage in the agenda for the Post-it reengineering, you ask a representative of each team to place the Post-it stickers in time order under column headings day –2, day –1, day +1, day +2, and so forth using a whiteboard. When all the stickers are on the board, it will look like Exhibit 10.4.

Then remove all desks near the whiteboard, and ask all the staff present to come and stand in a semicircle in front of the whiteboard. All staff members need to have a clear view of the board. Having the attendees stand up is important, as it brings everybody in sight of the stickers and, more importantly, as the meeting progresses ensures swifter agreement, as nobody will enjoy standing for over two hours.

Stage 3 Missing Processes

Then you ask, "What is still missing from the list?" There will always be a forgotten process. I probe until at least two additional processes are put on the board, and I ask each person in turn to acknowledge that they are in agreement that the whiteboard represents all the processes.

EXHIBIT 10.3   Workshop Agenda

Reengineering Month-End

Agenda for Workshop

Learning Outcomes: After this workshop, attendees will be able to:

- Discuss and explain why _____ should have quicker month-end reporting.
- Implement the steps required to move month-end reporting back to day 3 or less.
- Describe better-practice month-end routines.

9:00 a.m.	Welcome by Financial Controller
9:10	**Setting the scene**—a review of better practices among accounting teams that are delivering swift reporting; topics covered include:

- Cost of reporting in _____
- Benefits of quick reporting to management and the finance team
- Advice from Steve Jobs and Peter Drucker
- Lean month-end better practices

Senior management and a selection of budget holders (who are based locally) will be invited to attend this session, "setting the scene."

10:30	**Workshop One, When activities should start and finish,** where separate teams look at the different issues (we will cover month-end close-off of the various teams, listing bottlenecks within and between teams, reporting and forecasting issues, reconciliation issues, etc.)
10:45	Morning break
11:00	**Workshop Two, To analyze the month-end procedures,** using each team's colored sticky notes
12:40 P.M.	Lunch
1:00	**Workshop Two, To analyze the month-end procedures,** continues
2:00	**Agile processes (scrum and Kanban) and quality assurance steps to make the reports bulletproof**
2:30	Afternoon break
2:45	The changes one can make in the next six months to month-ending reporting
3:15	**Workshop Three, To set out the appropriate implementation steps to implement quick reporting.** Each team prepares a short presentation of the key steps it is committed to making (teams will use PowerPoint on laptops).
4:00	Each team presents reports to the group regarding what changes it will implement and when. The team can also raise any remaining issues.
	Those SMT and budget holders who attended the first session will be invited to attend this session.
4:45	Wrapup of workshop by the financial controller
5:00	Finish

EXHIBIT 10.4 Post-It reengineering month-end reporting on a whiteboard

Stage 4 Removal of Duplication

I then ask, "What processes have two stickers when there should only be one?" (We want to remove any duplication.) These stickers are removed; see Exhibit 10.5.

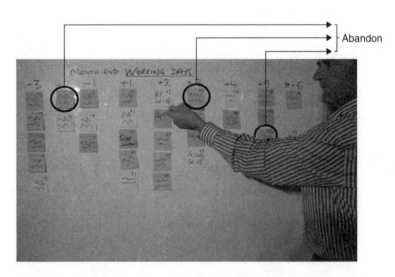

EXHIBIT 10.5 Abandoning processes by removing the "post-it" stickers

Stage 5 Abandonment

The next question I pose is, "What processes do you not need to do anymore and therefore should you abandon?" There is often a pause here, as staff look bewildered. "Why would we do something that is not required?" they are thinking. At this stage, I talk about Peter Drucker, the great management thinker's abandonment philosophy, discussed in Chapter 1.

I recommend that you buy a dozen movie vouchers before the workshop so you can give one to every attendee who points out a process that can be removed because it is not necessary (the process was done because it was done last month)—each procedure that is removed is like finding gold because it means less work, fewer steps. After the first movie ticket handout you will notice a greater focus from the attendees!

I normally will, when running the workshop, spend up to two hours to ensure all the superfluous processes are removed.

Stage 6 Rescheduling

The next stage is to reorganize the key processes and bottlenecks based on better practice. I start off by pulling off the AP close-off sticker and ask, "When could we finish this exercise if we were to adopt best practice?" The answer I am looking for is "Noon on the last working day," which has been discussed in an earlier section.

With each rescheduling of a process it is important to seek consensus. Invariably, some members of the team will believe the world will end if the cut-off is moved earlier. I simply question the logic and allow a dissenting group to note objections. "If you are proved correct, next month, we owe you a coffee and donut. If, however, you are proved wrong you owe all of us a coffee and donut." With that statement, I move the sticker to where the majority have agreed (see Exhibit 10.6).

After 45 minutes of standing, these disagreements will recede due to peer pressure.

Stage 7 Spreading the Workload

Look at day −1 steps, as you may have too many. Move the non-time-critical ones between day −2 and day +1 to better spread the workload.

Document the stickers on a spreadsheet. This is the only record you need. Any person who for health reasons cannot stand for the couple of hours, can be assigned this documentation process.

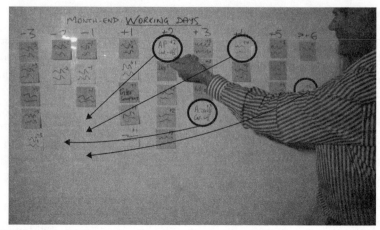

EXHIBIT 10.6 Moving the bottlenecks to the earliest time they can be completed

You will find it hard to justify any task needing to be done after day 3! You can view a YouTube video of me demonstrating a reengineering exercise on www.quickmonthendreporting.com. Please note that this was held in a training workshop so the attendees were allowed to sit at their desks.

Some Case Studies Who Used Post-It Reengineering

Organizations in both public and private sectors have improved their month-end reporting using the Post-it reengineering workshop.

The CFO of a famous entertainment center in Australia brought 20 of his team to a training session one September. They all went back and reengineered their month-end. Six weeks later, the CFO announced that his team had the final accounts in his hand—day 3 reporting within six weeks! The CFO had for years been used to very quick reporting with an American company, so you can imagine his frustration when he first arrived at his new position. The Post-it reengineering process unlocked the potential he knew was there.

After holding a one day in-house workshop to reengineer the month-end, a regional council accounting finance team moved the next month-end from seven to two working days. The team embraced both the reengineering exercise and abandonment of the processes that were no longer purposeful. They adopted the day 1 flash report and the daily scrums and noticed much more cohesive teamwork. There is now a much better awareness of what is important and a common view on materiality.

A CFO of a radio station conglomerate flew all her management accountants from around the country for a one-day Post-it reengineering workshop. For some, it was the first time they had met. The workshop was a fun day, and members could laugh at the bottlenecks that they, in some cases, had created. Excel spreadsheets were tossed out, along with other low-value month-end activities. Two weeks after the end of their training, the CFO was asked how the month-end was going. She replied, "What do you mean going? It is finished." She achieved day 2 month-end reporting, down from day 8, in two weeks.

Post-it Reengineering of Annual Planning and Annual Reporting

The Post-it reengineering of annual planning differs from the reengineering month-end process only in that:

- The time scale is Week −2 Week −1 (last week before annual planning kicksoff workshop), Week +1 (first week of annual plan), Week +2, etc. instead of Day−2, Day −1, etc.
- There will be different attendees at the workshop.

The Post-it reengineering of the annual reporting differs from the reengineering month-end process only in that:

- The time scale is Week −Two, Week −One (last week before year-end), Week +One (first week of the new financial year), Week +Two, etc. instead of Day −Two, Day −One etc.
- The audit manager will be invited to attend along with those involved in drafting content for annual accounts.

The invites to attend both of these workshops come from the CEO, and I have included suggested drafts in the web-based toolkit.

ADOPTING SCRUM STAND-UP MEETINGS

Scrum meetings are stand-up 15-minute meetings held first thing each morning, where team members are asked to talk about:

- What they did yesterday
- What are they doing today
- What are the barriers to progress

The debrief, for each team member, is to take no more than a minute or so. Some teams even have a dumbbell weighing 10 pounds to be held out horizontally, with the weaker arm, with the rule you can only talk as long as you can hold the weight horizontally. At the end of the session, the group ends the session by touching fists, an homage to the source of this technique.

The financial controller/CFO, renamed the *scrum master*, notes all the roadblocks and immediately sets about removing them with an appropriate phone call or walkabout: "Pat, will you please make time this morning to see my corporate accountant? I understand Sam has being trying, for the last few days, to meet you. This is now holding up the _____ and the CEO and _____will soon be on my and your back if we cannot resolve the issue today."

This scrum stand-up meeting does many things; it replaces loads of emails, as the team members get to know what has been done and is going to be done and by whom. It makes everyone accountable. There is no place for a cruiser. Scrums should be used by the finance team:

- Every month-end, starting at day –2, the scrum reducing in numbers as people complete their month-end routines
- During the planning process, starting with those involved in the prework and expanding the attendance when the three-day period starts for the annual plan completion by the budget holders
- During the annual accounts preparation
- For team debriefs

History of Scrum

The scrum technique was developed to radically reduce the time it takes to write new software applications. It recognized that teams in very intense work periods do not always function properly. Scrum (a technique developed in accordance with the *Manifesto for Agile Software Development*[3])—started off as a rethinking of the project management process by Jeff Sutherland, a software developer and onetime fighter pilot. He saw that combat fighter planes and big software development projects had a lot in common. They both had to avoid being shot down. He noticed that large projects were:

- Typically late, with lots of pressure and no fun.
- Run even later as more resources were applied to help speed things up. Typically, the new staff were "tripping over each other" and spending time in long, dysfunctional meetings.
- Frequented with duplication of effort.

- Often over-planned, only to find the "game had changed."
- Constantly hitting roadblocks. Team members were unable to surmount the roadblocks because they did not have the skills or sufficient clout within the organization.

Sutherland was challenged to produce a new product in six months. He discovered two things: a 1986 *Harvard Business Review* study, "The New Product Development Game," by Hirotaka Takeuchi and Ikujiro Nonaka, which noted that the best product development teams looked like sports teams, united in overcoming obstacles with intensity, and a company called Borland, which thrived on daily stand-up meetings.

Sutherland soon developed the "scrum" system (named after a formation in the sport of rugby), which was successful due to the following points.

Instead of spending months planning, you need to have a clear vision of what you are after. With this shared vision, you take a small chunk of work, saying, "If we deliver this feature, we will progress the project." This chunk is called a *sprint* (see number 2 in Exhibit 10.7). The key is that this chunk is about two weeks of effort (see number 3 in Exhibit 10.7) and is an isolated

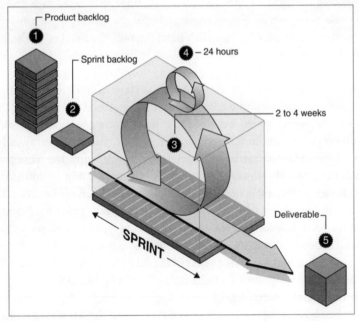

EXHIBIT 10.7   The daily scrum is part of a two-week sprint   *Source:* Boost Agile.[4]
Visit www.boost.co.nz/blog

standalone part of the project that can be signed off by the customer as, "Yes, that is what I want" (see number 5 in Exhibit 10.7).

Each day, during a two-week sprint, the team meet for a scrum (see number 4 in Exhibit 10.7). The scrum master's task is to manage team members who appear to be slowing down, and to clear the bottlenecks that are holding up progress.

Although scrums typically happen first thing in the morning, you could put them at the end of the day. The key is to restrict the topic matter and make sure it is a stand-up meeting.

Visit Jeff Sutherland's YouTube presentation to help you understand more about this great technique. Search "scrum+Jeff Sutherland+YouTube" in any search engine.

ADOPT KANBAN BOARDS

Here we need to adopt visual control techniques that are part of the lean or agile movement.

Creating a Kanban board to visually manage your work is a great way to increase your overall effectiveness and efficiency. Kanban is also a great way to instill a sense of accomplishment among a team. Let's take a look at why this is the case.

A Kanban board is a visual process and project management tool that helps teams organize and manage their work. Kanban boards allow teams to visualize their work and understand what is going on at a glance. Using note cards or sticky notes to represent work items, you can show any sized body of work such as a project (involving numerous tasks) or a task (usually involving only one person). Different colors are for different staff or work groups. The whiteboard is divided into three columns to represent backlog (to do), doing, or done. A small box is also set up for any processes that are stuck, as shown in Exhibit 10.8.

Kanban boards visually show the work in progress. This way, everyone is kept in the loop. Kanban boards work well for any type of work. It's so flexible that you can start with whatever process you already have.

The Kanban method uses a pull system. Instead of trying to do 10 things at once, manage your personal tasks by "pulling" in new work only when you have completed the current work.

Kanban boards show a team's accomplishments. Have you ever had a hard time explaining to your boss what you're working on because you have so many things on your to-do list that you don't know where to begin? By showing him

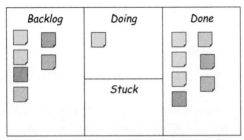

EXHIBIT 10.8 Kanban board used to help staff manage daily workflow

your Kanban, your boss will instantly see all of your work and understand your workflow.

TOYOTA'S 14 MANAGEMENT PRINCIPLES

I believe Toyota to be possibly the greatest company in the world. It has 14 management principles that are the backbone to its culture and Toyota can embed these principles in all countries it operates within. To understand the Toyota principles, read Jeffrey Liker's book *The Toyota Way*.[5] He has broken them down into four categories as set out in Exhibit 10.9.

I believe that Toyota's 14 management principles should be embedded in all organizations as best they can. The finance team can start this process by focusing on Exhibit 10.10.

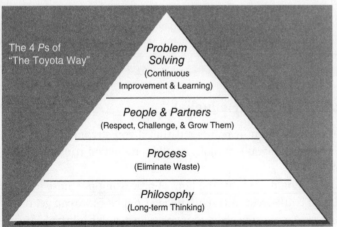

EXHIBIT 10.9 Jeffrey Liker's analysis of Toyota's 14 management principles

EXHIBIT 10.10 Toyota's 14 Principles

Philosophy	Principle 1: Base your management decisions on a long-term philosophy, even at the expense of short-term financial goals.
Process (Eliminate Waste)	Principle 2: Create continuous process flow to bring problems to the surface.
	Principle 3: Use "pull" systems to avoid overproduction.
	Principle 4: Level out the workload (Heijunka).
	Principle 5: Build a culture of stopping to fix problems, to get quality right the first time.
	Principle 6: Standardized tasks are the foundation for continuous improvement and employee empowerment.
	Principle 7: Use visual control so no problems are hidden.
	Principle 8: Use only reliable, thoroughly tested technology that serves your people and processes.
People and Partners (Respect, Challenge, and Grow Them)	Principle 9: Grow leaders who thoroughly understand the work, live the philosophy, and teach it to others.
	Principle 10: Develop exceptional people and teams who follow your company's philosophy.
	Principle 11: Help your extended network of partners and suppliers to improve.
Problem Solving (Continuous Improvement and Learning)	Principle 12: Go and see for yourself to thoroughly understand the situation (Genchi Genbutsu).
	Principle 13: Make decisions slowly by consensus, thoroughly considering all options and then implement the decisions rapidly.
	Principle 14: Become a learning organization through relentless reflection (Hansei) and continuous improvement (Kaizen).

Level Out the Workload (Heijunka)

This is a major breakthrough. It points out that if you streamline processes and eliminate bottlenecks, you can make smaller production runs viable and indeed desirable.

Finance teams should even out the flow of processing purchase invoices to avoid month-end bottlenecks. As mentioned in Chapter 5, we can get major suppliers to send electronic consolidated invoices in regular intervals during the month; minor invoices can be paid by the alternative payment system (the purchase card) and invoices are trapped by the accounts payable.

Build a Culture of Stopping to Fix Problems, to Get Quality Right the First Time

This is an important principle for the finance team to master. Finance teams invariably go from:

- One month-end to another without improvement
- One annual plan to another without improvement
- One year-end to another without improvement

If we adopted this Toyota principle, we would evaluate, after the process has finished, and ask, "What can we do better next month, next year?"

We should reduce the number of internal transactions, the number of spreadsheets, and constantly review each process's timeline to further eliminate waste and shortened timelines.

Use Visual Control So No Problems Are Hidden

Toyota is famous for its "Andon Cord" if problems occur. *Andon* refers to the pull cord where any worker on the production line can stop production, and ask for help, if they see a fault that cannot be fixed by them or the next group of workers before it will be covered up by a panel. Immediately, lights flash and that part of the production line is halted. The workers further down the line are unaffected, as there is a feed in line with about eight minutes of product to work on. Trained engineers rush in and fix the problem. They have up to eight minutes before the whole production line will be halted. The ability of anyone to stop production and activate the flashing lights to get the roaming engineers to the spot quickly is a major advantage Toyota and other manufacturers have when using this visual control.

Visual control is an important principle for the finance team to master as many reports need a rocket scientist to read them. If we adopted this Toyota principle, we would follow these guidelines:

- All major reports reduced to fit on an A3 (U.S. fanfold) page.
- Use a Kanban board to highlight when staff are having a problem that might delay an accounting process, at month-end/annual planning/ annual accounts.
- Use staff notice boards, screens in canteens to report daily progress with the KPIs and KRIs.
- Use only reliable, thoroughly tested technology that serves your people and processes.

- Toyota is never the first to use a new technology developed by third parties. It lets others break new ground. Toyota is, without doubt, the best user of a new technology once it has ascertained that it will serve Toyota's staff and processes.
- This has important ramifications for the finance team in the selection of a new G/L, a planning tool, and a new accounts payable system.

Help Your Extended Network of Partners and Suppliers to Improve

This is an important principle for the finance team to master, as it will involve:

- Ensuring all transactions from major long-term suppliers are paperless.
- Streamlining certain processes to one national supplier (e.g., the purchasing stationery and travel).

Go and See for Yourself to Thoroughly Understand the Situation

Toyota supervisors and managers are always expected to "walkabout" to see for themselves what is happening (Genchi Genbutsu). They do not rely on written reports or meetings; instead, they participate in walkabout.

Staying behind one's desk or around a meeting table will lead to a common perception that the finance team is not adding much value. Staff will be frequently wondering, "What on earth do our accountants do all day?"

Make Decisions Slowly by Consensus, and Then Implement the Decisions Rapidly

Toyota is very slow in the planning stage, thoroughly considering all options, but very fast in the implementation and commissioning, as everything, I mean everything, has been discussed and contingency plans agreed, ready for action if required. The finance team should take heed of this principle, especially with the:

- Changing of the general ledger
- Purchasing of a planning tool
- Migration from annual planning to quarterly rolling forecasting

Become a Learning Organization through Relentless Reflection and Continuous Improvement

One thing that sets Toyota apart from nearly all organizations is its continuous improvement (Kaizen). Every employee is expected to reflect (Hansei) each day,

"What could I do better tomorrow?" and come up with at least one innovation per month, no matter how small. The Toyota average, internationally, is ten innovations per employee per year.

All the great paradigm shifters such as Peter Drucker, Jim Collins, and Peters and Waterman have preached the need to innovate and not spend too much time trying to second guess whether it will work.

All the "Built to Last" companies featured in Jim Collins's book came up with their big ideas through a bit of serendipity. Jim Collins refers to it as very much like Darwin's survival of the fittest. Try a lot of things, and only let the strong ideas survive. In the Motorola example, he points out that Motorola sees innovation very much like a growing tree—you let it branch out but you are also constantly pruning.

Finance teams should:

- Hold an abandonment and Kaizen session once a month after the month-end is complete. Ask each finance team member to come to the meeting with one innovation and one abandonment. Using a scrum meeting, ask those assembled:
    - Will this abandonment/innovation be of concern if it fails?
    - Is there any reason why we *should not* undertake this abandonment/ innovation?
- The goal is ten innovations/abandonments per year per finance team member.
- Maximize use of the G/L, planning tool, reporting tool by constantly adopting more of their features.

 ## GOLDEN RULES WITH EMAILS

In any working week, many of us are spending up to 20 percent of our time reviewing and processing emails. In many cases, workflow is simply being pushed around the organization for no tangible gain. Here are some rules to save you time.

Rule 1: Never Open Emails before 10:30 a.m.

In the good old days, we would handle mail at 10:30 a.m. when the mail finally arrived from the mailroom. We thus started the day with scoring a goal—undertaking a service delivery activity. Now the first thing we do is open up the email, and suddenly one hour has evaporated. Some of us have not disabled the email alert, so we get interrupted every time a new email arrives. As a therapy, I suggest not opening your email until after your morning coffee and then looking at emails only once or twice more during the day. If something is very important, you will get a phone call. This technique will help you get more 1.5-hour blocks of concentrated time in your day. If you do receive the odd urgent email, you could, as a friend of mine does, scan for these at 8:30 a.m. My friend, however, has the control only to handle these urgent emails and then moves on with the day, leaving the replies to the bulk of the emails to late in the day. For me, even looking at the in-box before 10:30 a.m. is too risky as curiosity wins every time.

Rule 2: You Are Not the President, So Do Not Live and Sleep with Your iPhone!

Most of us (fortunately or unfortunately) are not heart or brain surgeons. Our work is not critical to life. Many emails we handle have little or no relevance to where we or our organizations want to go. The silliest thing is surely to handle an email twice, once on the iPhone, "Will get back to you when in the office," and once in our office.

It is particularly sad when it becomes a part of the company culture for the senior management team to text each other about Monday's schedule during the add breaks on the Sunday night.

I may send the odd email on a wet Sunday afternoon when a round of golf is not so enticing, but I never expect it to be read until business hours.

Rule 3: The Five-Sentence Rule

Treat all email responses like text messages and limit them to something you can count easily: five sentences. With only five sentences, the writer is forced to ensure that all terms, conditions, and papers are attached to the email. This has the added benefit of ensuring the saving of possibly important documents in the document management system.

Rule 4: Have an Attention-Grabbing Header

Make the header the main message of the email. For example: Freeing up more time—reengineering of_____. Never recycle the header you received in previous correspondence. Make the header more meaningful. If you cannot think of a good email header, maybe you should not send the email.

Rule 5: Actively Terminate Email Exchanges

Manage your email exchanges. If you needed feedback in order to get to closure, often a phone call is better. Ping-Pong emails on the same topic are screaming out for, "Let's speak tomorrow!" Think about your desired outcome and promote a course of action to avoid the table tennis. If necessary, use the sentence, "No more emails on this one, thank you."

Rule 6: Only Send Your Email to Those People Whom You Are Prepared to Phone

Promote yourself by your endeavors, not by your use of broadcast emails, reply all, or copy correspondence. Avoid sending broadcast emails unless you are prepared to call up each person to advise them that there is a key document that they need to read.

Ensure that you do not add to the spam in your organization as it is creating havoc in many organizations, with some managers receiving up to 200 emails a day.

Rule 7: If You Would Not Put Your Words in a Letter, Do Not Put Them in an Email

Far too often, the content of emails, while amusing, is not appropriate. Be careful about being the bearer of silly jokes. Today many people seem to want to be remembered by their joke telling. Now, don't get me wrong, I love a joke, but when the same people send a couple a week, you do wonder what they do all day. Remember, perception rules everything. You do not want to be perceived as a person whose prime focus is to entertain, such as Ricky Gervais in the UK version of *The Office*. You want to be thought of in more positive terms.

Rule 8: Master Email Applications' Tools Section

The experts have been busy improving the ways we can handle emails. The applications you use for emails will have many features you have never opened. Many readers have mastered word and spreadsheet applications, yet they know least about the one application they use the most. Master the new features; it will take a 30-minute session with an expert. You need to know and master:

- How to turn off the Outlook automatic notifiers
- How to use filters to sort and prioritize
- How to get newsletters automatically sent straight to a folder that you access twice weekly
- How to set up auto-responders to acknowledge and advise response time
- How to use filters, flags, colors, and sorting tools

Rule 9: Your Inbox Is Not a Storage Area

The inbox should be for collection only, just like your desk inbox. Messages should be deleted, actioned, or filed. Do you keep all your texts and phone messages? *No!* Be ruthless with deletions. You have only deleted enough when you, on occasion, have to ask people to resend their email.

Rule 10: Have a Night's Sleep before You Send a Complaint/Rebuff Email

For complex responses, complaints, rebuffs, and the like, draft the email and file in the drafts section of your email application overnight, as you may well have second thoughts. It is a good idea to send these draft emails to your mentor. Many a career has been dented by a poorly thought-out email written in anger.

Rule 11: Monkey-on-the-Back Emails

Many people are using the email system to pass their workload on to others. In many cases, people contact known experts and ask for their help without having done any research themselves. In other words, they are passing the monkey on their back to the expert.

My friend, an internationally recognized expert, advised me that the best way is to politely thank the sender for the email and then say, "Please call when convenient to discuss." Based on his experience, this gets rid of 95 percent of the requests.

 THREE BOOKS TO READ

As I know that many people reading this book will be very busy people, I have only listed three out of my top ten books of all time for you to read. These are:

- Elizabeth Haas Edersheim, *The Definitive Drucker*[6]: Drucker, the father of management, or as I like to call him, the Leonardo De Vinci of management, will be better understood 400 years from now. There is not a problem that you will have faced or are about to face that he has not already provided the answer for. Read this brilliant book, as it summarizes 32 Drucker volumes, which one could argue are a much more challenging read.

- Jack and Suzy Welch, *Winning*.[7] Jack Welch was named the best CEO of the twentieth century for his performance at General Electric. He was greatly influenced by Peter Drucker.
- Jeffrey Liker, *The Toyota Way: 14 Management Principles from the World's Greatest Manufacturer*. It will help you understand the traits that your finance team and organization should seek to gain.

PDF DOWNLOAD

To assist the finance team on the journey, templates and checklists have been provided. The reader can access, free of charge, a PDF of the suggested worksheets, checklists, and templates from www.davidparmenter.com/The_Financial_Controller_and_CFO's_Toolkit.

The PDF download for this chapter includes:

- The complete set of reengineering instructions for year-end accounts and annual planning
- A memo a CEO might send out to staff to attend a reengineering exercise
- Book reviews of Elizabeth Haas Edersheim's *The Definitive Drucker*; Jack Welch with Suzy Welch, *Winning*; Jeffrey Liker's *The Toyota Way*

NOTES

1. David Parmenter, *The Leading-Edge Manager's Guide to Success* (Hoboken, NJ: John Wiley & Sons, 2011).
2. W. Edwards Deming, *Out of the Crisis* (Cambridge, MA: The MIT Press, 2000).
3. Kent Beck et al., *Manifesto for Agile Software Development*, 2001, http://agilemanifesto.org/.

4. Visit www.boost.co.nz/blog/2011/11/scrum-a-beginners-experience/.
5. Jeffrey Liker, *The Toyota Way: 14 Management Principles from the World's Greatest Manufacturer* (New York: McGraw-Hill, 2003).
6. Elizabeth Haas Edersheim, *The Definitive Drucker: Challenges for Tomorrow's Executives — Final Advice from the Father of Modern Management* (New York: McGraw-Hill, 2006).
7. Jack Welch with Suzy Welch, *Winning* (New York: HarperBusiness, 2005).

11

Effective Leadership, Growing and Retaining Talent

OVERVIEW

Being good with numbers and systems is one thing, but far more important is growing, and retaining talent. It is a far greater challenge and the impact is much more profound. This chapter explores why you have to start with fine tuning your leadership skills, and then focus on creating a more attractive work environment. This chapter also explores how the finance team can network better within the organization, and how the senior members of the finance team can market themselves with greater success. It also looks at presenting a more service-centered culture to the budget holders.

These lessons have been gathered on my research during the writing of *The Leading-Edge Manager's Guide to Success.*[1]

"Why is it that when I actually find some talent, they never stick around?" a troubled CFO asks.

"Where is the talent, for I cannot find them!" another adds.

The first place to examine if your finance team finds it difficult to attract and retain staff is your leadership. Poor performance in this vital area will lead to a high staff turnover. We then need to make the finance team a more attractive place to work. Once we have been able to create a more pleasant environment for potential and current staff, we need to "get the right people on the bus" and give them a substantial start and an appealing future.

FOUNDATION STONES FOR LEADERSHIP THAT ATTRACTS

Getting competent staff to stick requires you to be a good, if not great, leader. The favorable news is that this can be learned. One of the most interesting findings in the work of Collins and Porras[2] was that most of the "Built to Last" organizations researched had CEOs who got on with their job without too much fanfare. In other words, being charismatic may be useful but it is not a requirement for a good leader.

In order to succeed as a leader, you need six foundation stones to provide you with a sound platform from which you can lead. In Jack Welch's[3] terminology, these foundation stones are "tickets to the game" a given, a must have.

Foundation Stone #1: Minimize Personal Baggage

From the time we enter this world, we develop traits and habits that will be limiting factors in our management and leadership of people. We will always be running with a few cylinders misfiring unless we fully understand our behavior patterns and those around us.

It is important to understand that to be a leader today you do not have to have handled all of your personal baggage; the key is the awareness of your weaknesses. There are plenty of "crippled" CFOs and financial controllers causing havoc in every organization that they work for. Yet there are also some who are a pleasure to work with and who also will have a more rewarding life at home as well. My point is that you owe it to your colleagues, your staff, your suppliers, contractors, family, partner, and offspring to do something about your own personal baggage.

Here are four courses that will aid you immensely.

The Enneagram. The Enneagram is a profound approach to people and their relationships. It describes nine personality types and you will find that one fits you. It will predict your behavior and the likely pitfalls which you can avoid with some minor modifications. It is best learned by attending a course, with your partner or a friend, and sharing your life experiences with others with the same traits. (See www.enneagraminstitute.com/ ennagram.asp.)

Hermann's Thinking Preferences. This looks at the way people think. It is broken into four types. It is important to understand the thinking preference of yourself, your boss, colleagues, and staff reporting to you so you can communicate effectively with them. A great in-house team building and awareness workshop (www.hbdi.com/).

Neuro-Linguistic Programming. NLP will have a profound impact on your leadership, your hobbies, and your relationship at home. By using your five senses you create visions of achievement you have yet to attain. You smell, you see, you feel, you hear, you touch, all in your mind, the event you want to achieve. Your subconscious will now set about closing the gap between now and this future reality. Go online and search "NLP+course + _____" (your location) to find a local course.

Intensive Life Skills Course. Life skills courses have various titles (e.g., The Landmark Forum). Ask around and find a course that has made a difference to others. The personal development courses of longer duration have the most chance of changing your behaviors. The experts in behavioral change say that it takes up to 12 weeks of weekly exercises to change behavior.

I went to one life skills course, as a skeptical accountant would, expecting to be mildly challenged. It turned out to be a vastly more challenging and rewarding experience. I soon realized the extent of my baggage. I realized that I had never grieved properly for the loss of a close relative. I had in fact successfully shut down my emotional side and not shed a tear for over twenty years. I now am able to express sadness and loss as any normal person would do.

Foundation Stone #2: "Love Thy Neighbor as Thyself"

Many in the corporate world do not abide by "Love thy neighbor as thyself," and that is why we quite happily create conflict in our working environment. Corporate life is littered with examples of unnecessary litigation, which has led to poor health in those individuals who are caught up in this self-inflicted process.

As a good friend said to me the other day, "People don't care how much you know until they know how much you care." Respect, hostmanship, humility, integrity, and candor all form the building materials for this foundation stone.

Respect

We all have experienced the impact of respectful and disrespectful behavior. Respect should be evident with:

- The way you treat your colleagues' and your team members' time (i.e., allowing them quality time to process initiatives rather than interrupting them with another meaningless task).
- Your working relationships with all colleagues, even those whom you would never invite to your weekend barbecue.
- The setting of deadlines (e.g., avoid asking for a report by 9 a.m. tomorrow when you will only get around to reading it three days later).
- The way you handle stress—your own, your staff's, and your colleagues'.
- The way you treat suppliers.

Hostmanship

Jan Gunnarsson[4] says that hostmanship is the way we make people feel welcome. His hostmanship approach has the approval of Tom Peters, and has had a profound impact on organizations applying it, on both the organization's culture and its interfaces with the outside world.

It is interesting to note that one's ability to be a host is influenced by one's past, both in experiences at home and with one's role models. It is no wonder so many of us have issues here.

If you have a visitor, good hosts greet them in the foyer and take them back down to the foyer when they are departing. This happened to me when I interviewed a CEO and it made a lasting impression on me.

Humility—Treat Everyone as Equals

Jim Collins in his book, "How the Mighty Fall and Why Some Companies Never Give In," noted that the first stage of corporate collapse is "Hubris born of success." He was talking about "excessive pride or self-confidence." If it is the downfall of a company, so it is the downfall of us, whether we be the CFO, a CEO or even the Prime Minister.

The day we cease dealing with individuals as equals is the day of our decline.

Integrity—Set Values, Live by Them, Recruit by Them

In organizations where "Money is God," you will constantly see lack of integrity and types of behavior, among executives and staff, fit only for the wilds of the

Serengeti. When you look at the collapses of major companies, you will always find a lack of values. Great organizations with high-meaning values can become compromised if these values are not maintained. The CFO must always be looking for breaches and ensuring that these are pointed out to all staff immediately.

You can train many things but Values are not amongst them. You need to recruit around them. It is among the most important parts of a recruiting process.

Candor

Jack Welch, CEO of General Electric, was one of the first CEOs to talk about *candor,* the quality of being open, honest, and frank. He calls it the biggest dirty secret in business.[5] He said it is a leader's obligation to tell staff how they are doing and what they can improve in a candid way.

One has to realize that underperforming staff members may well be in the wrong place at the wrong time, and thus, encouraging them to follow their passion to find the job in which they will excel is the kindest thing you can do for them. As a good friend of mine and writer, Bruce Holland, says, "There is a golden Buddha in all of us."

Jack Welch pointed out that candor is important:

- When giving feedback to underperforming staff
- When evaluating a business proposal
- In daily discussions with staff and colleagues
- In contact with customers and suppliers

Foundation Stone #3: Mastery of Communication and Public Relations

You cannot lead unless others understand your vision and are sold the "flight tickets" for the journey. Mastering communication means understanding the importance of one-to-one communications, being seen by your staff, working the public relations machine, and mastering the written and spoken word.

This has been further emphasized to me by Zaffron and Logan's *Three Laws of Performance*[6] outlined in Chapter 2.

Master the Oral and Written Word

CFOs must realize that being a good orator is a vital part of leadership. Time and effort need to be devoted to delivering a meaningful message. Special coaching and endless practice should be seen as an important investment rather than a chore before delivering an important presentation. See the 25+ tips to improve your presentations in Appendix B.

Seek help from the SMT member who writes in a style you want to emulate. Attend some business writing courses where you will learn techniques, such as writing in the reverse pyramid style, as discussed by Mary Munter.[7]

More Scrums and One-to-One Sessions

The key to effective management is to hold fewer meetings, and replace with more scrums and one-to-one sessions. They do not have to be long if you are doing plenty of walking around among the staff. Scrums were discussed in Chapter 10.

Work with Your Adversaries

All great leaders realize that the world is a small place, and "what goes around comes around." They take care to avoid alienating themselves from individuals who frequently see things from a different perspective. Always approach those who are your adversaries, your roadblocks, and take them out for coffee or lunch. It is the hardest thing to do and yet the most effective.

Walkabout among Your Staff

Great leaders take a walkabout at least twice a day when they are in the office. Not only does it give them some much-needed exercise but it allows them to be "ambushed" by staff who have may have an issue but would like to talk about it more informally. It is also a good way, by subtle questions, to show you are up with the play and to keep the staff on their toes.

Unfortunately, today, more often than not it is only the older, more experienced managers who walk around the office—the younger managers believe that an email will do! Drucker was very scathing about leaders who communicate by email. His advice was, "Go and ask."

Finance team staff need to be encouraged to do more walkabouts so that instead of sorting out the bodies at the bottom of the cliff, they put fences at the top. Finance team visits could be used for:

- Increasing the usage of the purchasing card or the _____ system.
- Increasing compliance within accounts payable, especially by raising electronic orders and the subsequent electronic receipting.
- Seeing how things are being done rather than relying on progress reports that might be scripted to reflect what you want to hear.

- Setting up new "paperless processes" with key suppliers.
- Undertaking exercises to reduce waste within operations.
- Visiting better-practice sites using the intended technology you wish to implement.

Foundation Stone #4: Have a Cluster of Mentors and a Safe Haven

Over the last ten years, I estimate that less than 10 percent of all accountants at my seminars and workshops have mentors—it is no wonder corporate accountants are so isolated.

Having a Cluster of Mentors

In his book, *Winning*, Jack Welch says that one mentor is never enough. Anyone who thinks they have arrived and do not need a mentor is like a matador who turns away from the bull to the adoring crowd to show how brave he is—a gesture of stupidity that will ultimately bring about a painful end.

Mentors have many functions, from advising you on tricky stages in your career and managing work relationships to getting great career opportunities. Asking someone to become your mentor is one of the finest compliments you can give.

Mick Ukleja and Robert Lorber[8] have talked about four different types of mentors:

Upward Mentors. These are the people to whom you look up and admire. They are older than you, wiser, with more gray hair—a Obi-Wan Kenobi. It could be a retired CEO or a retired board member whom you once worked for, or a professional mentor.

Friendship Mentors. These are the people with whom you have experienced life so far. You have gone through various stages with them—college, career, or family and work life. They are your peers and are able to share knowledge they have gained. They are fully aware of your strengths and weaknesses.

Sandpaper Mentors. We all have work colleagues, who, after a five-minute discussion, make you feel like pulling out your hair. They see the world in a totally different way. Some of us have a life partner, whom we chose, who constantly challenges us. These are sandpaper mentors whose views should be embraced, for they are another pair of eyes for us. They will see the crevasse when we are oblivious to it.

Downward Mentors. We all have noticed how we ourselves learn through the process of training others. When you mentor someone else, you actually learn a lot about yourself. You experience what's important to you and what should be emphasized and reinforced in your own professional and personal life.

Having a Safe Haven—A Second Passion

All leaders will have many soul-searching moments during their journey. The magnitude of these can be quite severe if the leader is taking their team/organization on a significant conquest. In order to cope with these "downs," you need to have built a safe haven for yourself, a place where you can retreat and recover. Leaders need to nurture close relationships and hobbies that offer relaxation and enjoyment. Without a safe haven, leaders will succumb to the sense of failure that can permeate them when all they have in their life is their chosen conquest that has now gone off the rails.

When you analyze great leaders, you tend to find their safe haven (e.g., for Jack Welch it was golf). Peter Drucker[9] talked at great length about the importance of having another passion other than your job. Drucker noted that a safe haven acts as a failsafe and at the same time stimulates the brain in different ways, leading to clearer thought patterns and better decision making.

Foundation Stone #5: Fearless in Pursuit of Legacy

Being fearless, leading from the front, is another of the givens for a leader. One of the messages from Peter Drucker was that outstanding performance is inconsistent with fear of failure.

I firmly believe that the meaning of life for the human race can be summed up in one word—*legacy*. We all have a driving force to leave something behind to say we were here. It can be through our family, through our work, or through our devotion to others. This legacy says, "I was here; I added up to something; I had something to say; I changed peoples' lives for the better." Understanding one's legacy is important: it is a directional beacon that will guide you through life in a more purposeful way.

Peter Drucker made reference to it. He would ask, "What do you want to be remembered for?"

If you were to make a one-paragraph statement as to what your legacy is to be, what would it say? Forming this legacy in your mind gives meaning to life and puts up a guiding star in the sky that will shine brightly, guiding you forward, no matter what dark clouds are around you.

Foundation Stone #6: Be a Follower of the Paradigm Shifters

The father of management, Peter Drucker, sadly passed away in 2005. His work contains many gems that have been overlooked. Alongside Drucker, there are some brilliant writers like Jack Welch, Tom Peters, Robert Waterman, Gary Hamel, Jeremy Hope, and Jim Collins who have now taken the batten. The only problem is that many of us are too busy to read and absorb their work.

It should never be underestimated the impact these great writers can have if one spends enough time understanding their wisdom. To assist you on your journey of discovery, I have set out in the PDF download some of the paradigm shifters' leadership lessons.

 # MAKING THE FINANCE TEAM A GREAT PLACE TO WORK

Team Building-Lessons from a World-Class Coach

A coach of a national team who had won three consecutive World Cup finals gave me some tips about building a team:

- Find out what makes each of your team members tick—this requires a number of meetings outside the work environment.
- Always remember that an emotional outburst may create emotional damage, which takes a long time to heal.
- Remember that selling the message to your team is important.
- Focus on shared leadership—be a facilitator rather than a leader.
- Team building is vital—take your team away to outdoor pursuit centers.
- Ask your team members individually, "What do you want from me?"
- Be accepting of mistakes and analyze the decision making that led to the mistake; both you and the staff member will learn something.

Outdoor Adventure Learning

The same coach of the world-champion team always had team-building exercises in an outdoor adventure center where there were basic accommodation amenities (e.g., no television in the rooms). He wanted the team to always be together, learning more about one another.

I also have met a senior partner in an accounting firm who recalled that one weekend a group of staff got together and went on an overnight hike. It turned out to be more of an adventure than most had anticipated. The team dynamics after the hike were truly amazing. Those who went became known as the *A-framers*, named after the shape of the huts that offered them shelter overnight. Even 20 years later, the group had reunions, with members flying in from abroad.

Reduce Time in the Three Potholes

Reduce time in three potholes, the three areas where we invest much for little reward—month-end reporting, annual planning, and the annual accounts process. Your hairy, audacious goal is for the qualified accountants in the team to spend less than 30 percent of their time in these three areas. Please refer back to Chapters 3, 9, and 12.

Adopt Lean Management Techniques

Being lean also means adopting the better management practices that are used by successful managers such as:

21st century office environment	Stand-up desks and work stations. Research points out that it will increase life expectancy and your productivity. I have one, and now use my chair three to four hours a month. The article *"Five Health Benefits of Standing Desks"*[10] if read, will get you over the line.
Revolving work areas	Modern offices prevent personal filing systems as they are a disaster when the individual is suddenly indisposed. In one office I have been in, staff arrive in the morning to collect their three-drawer desk cabinet and wheel it to the work area. They sit in a different place each day, alongside colleagues from different teams. This approach forces staff to mix better, have less paper, have a clean desk at the end of the day, and to use a centralized electronic filing system.
Blue sky Fridays	Have one half day a week or every two weeks where you work in a quiet space, away from; the office, to work on the finance team's future. You are not allowed to handle daily tasks (email, receive calls, have meetings), instead you do all the things that will make the future happen.

Manage Your Meetings

Meetings today are taking too long, achieving very little, and are scheduled for maximum disruption of your efficiency. Here are three ways to get control over your working day.

Banning Morning Meetings for the Finance Team

A good start is to avoid having meetings during your productive time (e.g., mornings). I fail to see why CEOs feel the need to have meetings with their direct reports at 9 a.m. on Monday mornings. Such meetings often are followed with more meetings as the debriefing is passed down the chain in the finance team. Why not have this meeting at 4:30 p.m. on a Friday? It certainly would be a quick meeting.

Ask anybody about their productivity, and you will find frustration about how time has been taken away with nonproductive activities. Would it not be better to schedule meetings toward the tail end of the day and leave the morning for service delivery? Exhibit 11.1 shows how a manager's calendar often looks

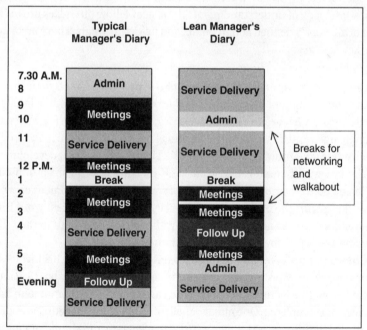

EXHIBIT 11.1   Impact of rescheduling meetings in a working day

and how it could look. The main change is bigger chunks of service delivery time, delaying email duties, and meeting time rescheduled to the afternoons, allowing us to be more relaxed because we have scored some early goals.

We have to make these rescheduled meetings more productive.

Have Action Meetings

A majority of meetings are totally flawed. They are held because they were held last week, two weeks ago, last month. The fundamental purpose of the meeting has long ago been forgotten.

Most managers at some time have received training in managing meetings, yet the level of frustration with meetings remains the same. The problem has been that the training has not looked at all the core reasons for failure. Even the legendary John Cleese's training video, *Meetings, Bloody Meetings*, serves to entertain rather than tackle these issues.

Two management consultants, Mike Osborne and David McIntosh, have developed a methodology that is breathtaking in its simplicity yet profound in its impact. Action Meetings has attacked the core of dysfunctional meetings and their common features: unclear agendas, lack of engagement, rambling discussions, a total lack of understanding of "the space" fellow attendees are in, and, worst of all, poorly defined action points and follow-through. There are a number of key features:

- **Get people properly into and out of the meeting.** This is done through the introduction of a first word and last word, where attendees briefly say what state they are in. The first words could range from "I am very time challenged and this meeting is last thing I need," to "Eager to make progress with this assignment and to hear Bill' s view on the _____ development." The last words could range from "This meeting once again promised little and delivered nothing," to "I look forward to receiving Pat's report and working with the project team." The key to the first and last word is that attendees can say anything about how they feel at that point in time. Their comment is just that and is to remain unchallenged.
- **Construct an effective agenda based on outcomes.** This involves the use of precise wording about meeting outcomes (see Exhibit 11.2). Outcomes provide focus and the ability to easily check whether an item has in fact been completed. One major benefit of establishing "meeting outcomes" worded in this way is that requested attendees can and should not attend if they do not think they can add value or assist in achieving the outcomes.

EXHIBIT 11.2 What Meeting Outcomes Could Include

1.	Project ____ progress **examined and understood**
2.	The monthly results **understood**
3.	The next steps for project ____ **agreed and assigned**
4.	This month's key initiatives **agreed**
5.	The responsibilities on the acquisition of ABC Limited **assigned**

- **Meetings are participant-owned, not chairperson-owned.** All attendees are trained in the new methodology. Thus, meetings are owned and policed by all participants and are less reliant on the capability of the chairperson.
- **Once an outcome is closed, it remains closed.** During the meeting, remind anyone who is opening a closed item that the item has been closed.
- **Park nonrelated issues.** Any issues raised that are not related to the outcome under discussion are tabled for another, future discussion.
- **Write action steps.** Action steps are written carefully on a special pad and then entered into a web-based application so all can see the progress.

Hold Finance Team Scrums

Replacing sit down finance team meetings with 10 minute scrums will be more productive with higher attendance. Take care not to mix your scrums together. If you are in month-end, have a separate scrum from the abandonment scrum that might be scheduled for that day as well.

Adopt Agile Techniques

There are a number of tools in the lean toolkit that should be used by the finance team:

- Post-it reengineering to replace month-end routines, annual planning routines, annual accounts routines, and any other inefficient processes
- Adopting stand-up scrum meetings every day during the delivery of a project, report, annual plan
- Having a Kanban board for each key process while it is in play

These were discussed in Chapter 10.

Embrace Technology

Not only will technology reduce the time spent processing data, it will help the careers of all accountants that work with it. Using twenty-first-century technology will make your finance team more attractive to prospective staff and help retain them once you have secured their services. The minimum technology, as discussed in Chapter 4, that a finance team needs to master these days includes:

- A planning and reporting tool
- A consolidation tool
- A paperless flow tool for accounts payable
- A friendly drill-down tool to sit on top of the GL

Having Fun in the Workplace

Finance teams need to be seen as teams that work hard and have fun doing this. Why would you wish to stay in a miserable team? Some initiatives you can undertake to improve the work environment are:

Hold off-site meetings. Some teams hold a half-day, off-site meeting every month after they have completed their month-end. Others have an off-site team training session every three months. At the very least, hold one session a year. Exhibit 11.3 shows the agenda items of a typical off-site meeting.

Café meetings. Hold a staff meeting in a coffee shop once a month, and treat the team. This should be considered a business expense. You can link it with an abandonment and Kaizen session.

Birthdays. Set up a routine where birthdays are acknowledged and celebrated where the staff person is actively encouraged to take that day off (out of their vacation allowance) and then celebrate the birthday the next day in the office.

Recognition. Giving recognition freely makes us a person whom people like to work for and one we naturally gravitate toward. Many of us will need to count the recognitions we give, until doing so becomes a natural part of our makeup.

During team meetings, ensure that you find at least three team members to thank and recognize their achievements, some of which may have occurred outside work.

EXHIBIT 11.3   An Agenda for an Offsite Team Meeting

Meeting Agenda

Location: _____

Date: _____

Attendees: All the accounting team with special guests _____

Requirements: **session secretary (Pat Carruthers), lap tops x2, data show, whiteboards x2**

8:30 a.m.	Welcome by CFO, a summary of progress to date, an outline of the issues, feedback from the in-house customer survey (if one has been done recently), and establishing the outcome for the workshop
8:40	**Setting the scene**—A talk by a member of the senior management team (SMT). Topics covered include:

- Importance of the finance team in the organization
- Future direction of _____
- Areas where the SMT are keen to see improvements
- Where the accounting team can score more goals for the SMT

9:00	**Presentation by external party on a new methodology or tool**
	Topics covered could include:

- Improving the use of the G/L (revisiting the time saving features)
- Demonstration of a planning tool
- Accounts payable better practices
- Team-building exercises (Hermann's thinking preferences or the Myers Briggs, team wheel, etc.)
- Other better practices taken from this book

10:15	Morning break
10:30	**Workshop 1** How to implement changes to increase values to the SMT and in-house customers (utilizing findings from survey and talk from SMT member)
11:00	**Workshop 2** How to implement _____ better practice
12:15	Lunch at venue
1:00 p.m.	Wrap up of workshop

Simple cost-effective recognitions are handing out film tickets, or vouchers for two at a restaurant, to reward accounting staff who have gone the extra mile.

Celebrate every success. In going from one deadline to the next, often deferring a celebration to the never-ending future, corporate accountants are missing a vital PR trick. A celebration is a great communicator of success. It tells others you have performed well. Let's face it, the marketing team celebrates all the time by sharing success stories both externally and internally within the organization.

"Work is too much a part of life not to recognize moments of achievement," Jack Welch.[11]

If you have not celebrated something in the last two months, find something worthwhile, organize a function and hold the celebration.

20 percent discretionary time to pursue their ideas. Finance teams should, like Google, give the talented staff 20 percent of discretionary time, to pursue their ideas on initiatives that would benefit the organization. This is how the idea for Google Earth happened.

In-House Training

Far too much of accountants' training is done on their own. Aim to have at least one in-house training day for the whole accounting team. You will gain much from the team building that occurs during the day. Suggestions include: reengineering exercise, Hermann's thinking preferences, neuro-linguistic programming, interpersonal skills, client management, and consultancy skills (for the management accountants and advisers).

In addition, you can offer, after ___years of service, support for further tertiary education (e.g., MBA programs) for the CFO protégés.

One-on-One Progress Meetings

Set up monthly progress meetings with your direct reports in the first week of the month and on the same day (e.g., Ted, 2 p.m. first Tuesday of month; Sarah, 3 p.m. first Tuesday of month; etc.) and give them performance feedback, which in most cases will be just verbal. In this meeting, ask them to prepare a few PowerPoint slides rather than a written report and suggest a maximum of 30 minutes' preparation time. These meetings also will replace the need for project progress meetings. The content for the PowerPoint would include these questions:

- What have I done well last month?
- What did not go so well last month?
- What lessons have I learned?
- What am I planning to do this month?
- What training am I going to organize?

Finance Team Balanced Scorecard

Organizations that have adopted balanced scorecard reporting have introduced team scorecards. These help the team score goals in a balanced way and increase the alignment of the individual members' work with their team's and organization's goals. Even if the organization has not adopted the balanced scorecard, the accounting team can add value by leading change in reporting team performance in a balanced way by introducing the concept for their team. Exhibit 11.4 shows a team scorecard designed in Excel. Excel is an excellent tool for designing a template and testing it over a couple of months, after which it should be installed in a proper balanced scorecard system.

 ## PUTTING THE FINANCE TEAM ON THE MAP

If accountants were natural marketers, many may well have chosen a different career path. It is thus important for accountants to recognize these shortcomings and to fill the gap with training, advice from their mentor, and the implementation of the practices set out below.

Networking within the Organization

Only fools believe one's achievements speak for themselves. The modern finance team needs to master networking. Some ways you can improve your networking include:

Acquire a marketing mentor. Find yourself a marketing mentor, touch base with your in-house public relations (PR) expert, or acquire some PR external advice—you will not regret it.

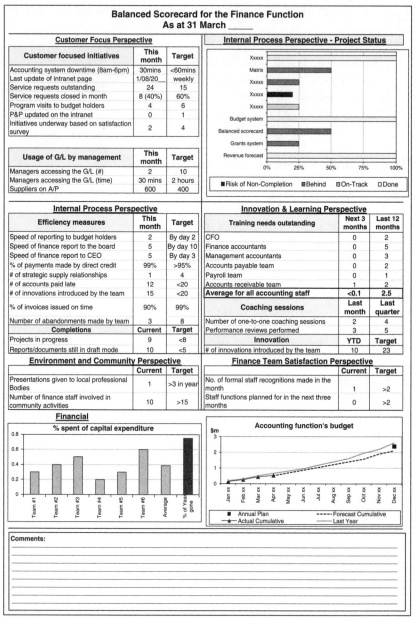

Balanced Scorecard for the Finance Function
As at 31 March ____

Customer Focus Perspective

Customer focused initiatives	This month	Target
Accounting system downtime (8am-6pm)	30mins	<60mins
Last update of intranet page	1/08/20__	weekly
Service requests outstanding	24	15
Service requests closed in month	8 (40%)	60%
Program visits to budget holders	4	6
P&P updated on the intranet	0	1
Initiatives underway based on satisfaction survey	2	4

Usage of G/L by management	This month	Target
Managers accessing the G/L (#)	2	10
Managers accessing the G/L (time)	30 mins	2 hours
Suppliers on A/P	600	400

Internal Process Perspective - Project Status

Chart showing project status bars (0% to 100%) for: Xxxxx, Matrix, Xxxxx, Xxxxx, Xxxxx, Budget system, Balanced scorecard, Grants system, Revenue forecast.

Legend: ■ Risk of Non-Completion ▨ Behind ▨ On-Track ☐ Done

Internal Process Perspective

Efficiency measures	This month	Target
Speed of reporting to budget holders	2	By day 2
Speed of finance report to the board	5	By day 10
Speed of finance report to CEO	5	By day 3
% of payments made by direct credit	99%	>95%
# of strategic supply relationships	1	4
# of accounts paid late	12	<20
# of innovations introduced by the team	15	<20
% of invoices issued on time	90%	99%
Number of abandonments made by team	3	8

Completions	Current	Target
Projects in progress	9	<8
Reports/documents still in draft mode	10	<5

Innovation & Learning Perspective

Training needs outstanding	Next 3 months	Last 12 months
CFO	0	2
Finance accountants	0	5
Management accountants	0	3
Accounts payable team	0	2
Payroll team	0	1
Accounts receivable team	1	2
Average for all accounting staff	<0.1	2.5

Coaching sessions	Last month	Last quarter
Number of one-to-one coaching sessions	2	4
Performance reviews performed	3	5

Innovation	YTD	Target
# of innovations introduced by the team	10	23

Environment and Community Perspective

	Current	Target
Presentations given to local professional Bodies	1	>3 in year
Number of finance staff involved in community activities	10	>15

Finance Team Satisfaction Perspective

	Current	Target
No. of formal staff recognitions made in the month	1	>2
Staff functions planned for in the next three months	0	>2

Financial

% spent of capital expenditure — bar chart (0 to 0.8) for Team #1, Team #2, Team #3, Team #4, Team #5, Team #6, Average, % of Year gone.

Accounting function's budget — line chart ($m, 0 to 3) over Jan xx–Dec xx.
Legend: ■ Annual Plan ----- Forecast Cumulative ▲ Actual Cumulative — Last Year

Comments:

EXHIBIT 11.4 Example of a finance team balanced scorecard

Connect better with the subsidiaries. Invite new staff from major subsidiaries or departments to call in when they are next in the head office.

Use your coffee breaks wisely. Ensure that you take a morning and afternoon break and use these times for catching up with your team and networking with budget holders and other stakeholders. From now on, see working through these breaks as a lost opportunity rather than a badge of honor.

Coffee for a cause. Consider organizing a "coffee for a cause" event where the finance team raises funds for a local charity. Invite all your budget holders and stakeholders, asking them to donate a dollar or so and enjoy some hospitality at the finance team's office. You will have scored a goal by just organizing such an event.

Attend all corporate functions. Ensure that at least one member from the finance team is attending the organization's corporate functions.

Walkabout more. Encourage the finance staff to spend more time on proactive visits. This has been covered in the leadership foundation stone "mastery of communication and public relations."

Finance team intranet site. Have an informative intranet finance team home page, as discussed in the following section.

Newsletter contributor. Contribute to your organization's newsletter. Quantify savings in meaningful numbers, promote new processes, and emphasize success stories of other departments.

One-page insights. Spend time adding value to the senior management team by increasing their understanding of the business. Prepare one-page useful insights.

Have a Useful Finance Team Intranet Page

The finance team should aim to have the most interesting and best-maintained team page on the organization's intranet. Have informative intranet pages, including:

- Success stories of finance team projects.
- Photos and short-form CVs of all of the accounting team members. If some staff are reluctant to have their picture taken at the next celebration, take a team photo and load it.
- Quick tips to make better use of the key finance systems.
- Have a link to your accounting procedures manual.

See Exhibit 11.5 for an example of a team's intranet page.

Accounting function home page

Our mission is to be a leading accounting function which provides better practice services and is an awesome place to work

CFO's Introduction
New budget holder's section
Delegations authorities
Policy & procedures
Summary of last month's financial results
Contact the team
User feedback form
Profile of the team
Useful links

The Accounting team's balanced scorecard KPIs:

- Customer satisfaction initiatives
- Continuous improvement & innovation
- Learning & growth
- Progress against budget

Projects in progress:

- Developing winning KPIs
- Streamlining board papers
- Reducing month-end reporting to day 3
- Eliminating the company check book
- Reducing suppliers to <400
- Streamlining budget and forecasting process

Recent success story: the accounting function in conjunction with budget holders and suppliers have been able to increase the number of direct credits from 66% to 95% creating a saving of over $20,000 PA.

Recent success story #2: the savings to date with the national contract for travel have been $8,000 which represents £48,000 PA

EXHIBIT 11.5 Team's intranet site example

Marketing Yourself

Although marketing the team is important, one must not forget to market oneself. Here are some suggestions for you to consider.

Key contacts. Make a list of the top ten contacts you have outside the finance team. Ensure you have coffee or lunch with at least one of these contacts every week. Over 10 to 12 weeks, you will have covered everyone.

Wardrobe makeover. If you look like a million dollars, then you will feel like a million dollars. Note that most of your organization's successful managers actually *look successful*. Observe them and create a look of success that you are comfortable with. Acquiring a good wardrobe of quality business attire, maintaining a well-groomed appearance and having a smile you can be proud of should be seen as a ticket to the game and a sound investment.

Radiate a positive attitude. Ensure that you talk positively to others. Popular people are seldom the fountains of negativity—so learn to keep your negative thoughts private.

Report on a page. Avoid writing long reports, as nothing was ever changed by a report; it was the follow-up action that made the change. Be a master of the one-page A3 (U.S. fanfold) report discussed in Chapter 7.

Learn about enchantment. Guy Kawasaki has written about *Enchantment: The Art of Changing Hearts, Minds, and Actions*.[12] He talks about how to become likable through some simple steps, such as how people connect better to other people when they are welcoming and positive.

See the big picture always. Remember to always try to see the bigger picture—nobody, to my knowledge, ever died because a corporate accountant's work was late; fortunately or unfortunately, our work is not that critical in regard to life or death.

We all need to work long hours when it is important to the organization. The key is to understand what is important and what is not. Working long hours on unimportant activities sends the wrong message. That is basically shooting yourself in the foot.

Fountain of recognition. Learn to give recognitions more freely. It will add to your workplace enjoyment and attract others to include you in their network.

Learn How to Sell Change

This has been covered in Chapter 2. Please use this resource on every new initiative you undertake.

Deliver Killer Presentations

Far too often, the accountant will short-change themselves by undercooking their preparation and practice time before giving a presentation. Being great on your feet is a skill you need to master in order to be a prominent corporate accountant.

Many readers will have already attended a presentation skills course—a prerequisite to delivering bulletproof presentations. The speed of delivery, voice levels, use of silence, and getting the audience to participate are all techniques that you need to be familiar with and comfortable using.

I have prepared 25 rules for a good presentation, and these are available in the PDF download and in Appendix B. I set out a few of these for you to consider:

1. At least 10 to 20 percent of your slides should be high-quality photographs, some of which will not even require a caption.
2. Read *Presentation Zen*[13] by Garr Reynolds, *Slide:ology*[14] by Nancy Duarte, and "The Presentation Secrets of Steve Jobs"[15] by Carmine Gallo.
3. Use Kawasaki's 10/20/30 rule for a sales pitch presentation. Have ten slides that last no more than 20 minutes and ensure all text is no smaller than 30 points in size.

4. Bring theatrics into your presentation, use memorable props, be active, and have a bit of fun. This will fully engage your audience.
5. Practice your delivery. The shorter the presentation, the more you need to practice. An important 15–20 minute pitch to the board should be practiced more than ten times in front of a sample audience.

Improving Relationships with Budget Holders

The accounting teams need to focus much more on client management. Too much time is spent sitting behind a desk instead of scoring goals in front of managers and the senior management team (SMT). Accountants need to be business advisers first. Here are some ways you can improve your relationships with budget holders:

- Give them new insights into their operations.
- Include trend information (rolling 15- or 24-month graphs) and key performance indicators in the reporting.
- Talk through the monthly results with them—they might not understand the reports.
- Provide training sessions for budget holders' staff.
- Help budget holders with their new reforecast—you can expand your team temporarily for this purpose.
- Help budget holders with the task of bringing forward projects.
- Run a satisfaction survey on your in-house customers and implement the recommendations.
- Give a small gift to the first budget holder to submit a correct monthly return.

 PERFORM AN IN-HOUSE CUSTOMER SATISFACTION SURVEY

One way to show that you are customer orientated is to run a short in-house customer survey. There are many survey tools that will allow you to get this up and running in less than two hours. Initially, once a year and then twice a year, run a statistically based sample survey on your in-house customers. Send the survey set out in Appendix C. The key features are:

- When asking about the variety of services you offer, put the survey statement in the positive: "I am happy with the monthly report I receive."

- Use a five-point rating scale (5 = strongly agree, 4 = agree, 3 = sometimes agree, 2 = disagree, 1 = strongly disagree, X = not applicable/cannot rate).
- Ask two open-ended questions that will generate most of the benefit of the survey: "What are the three things we do well?" and "What are the three things we can improve on?" Never ask about the problems, as half of them will not be fixable.
- Categorize all responses to these open-ended questions in a database and sort by positive comments (bold) and suggestions for improvement (see Exhibit 11.6).

EXHIBIT 11.6 Extract from a Commentary Section Showing Identification of Positive Comments (Bold) and Negative Comments

Customer focus	**Staff prepared to go the extra mile**
	The team has an excellent personal assistant who is very helpful.
	Adept ability to respond to circumstances and needs that change rapidly
	Fairness and courtesy to all
	Staff willingness and very positive attitude
	Supportive well-trained support staff
	Client focused
	I attended a meeting and it was quite clear that the finance staff were uninterested and showed their boredom.
	A couple of the finance team presentations I have attended have, quite frankly, been appalling. Poor content, poor delivery showing little regard to all the attendee time wasted.
Communication	**Initiatives to improve communication within the _____ have been positively received and changes (for the better) have been made.**
	Good communications
	Good liaison with the _____ and _____
	_____ and _____ weren't told that they were not needed for the meeting in _____ when it was canceled. Much time was wasted!
Database	Improvement of the database
	Computer database inadequacies are causing major problems for us.

- Separate accounting system dramas from the services your team provides by asking a series of system-related questions.
- Use a web-based survey package to avoid rekeying responses.
- Never ask for feedback in areas where you do not have the funding or the resources to solve the issue.
- Make the questionnaire simple and able to be completed in ten minutes.
- Implement the top five services improvements, identified in the survey, within six weeks of the published survey results.

One CFO who has experience with running satisfaction surveys wanted to improve results. So he went around to every budget holder and member of the senior management team and asked, "What would the finance team need to do to get at least a very good rating from you on services our team provides?" Surprise, surprise, the team listened and acted on the suggestions, and in the next survey, it got the best results out of all teams.

—CFO from the electricity sector

 ## PDF DOWNLOAD

To assist the finance team on the journey, templates and checklists have been provided. The reader can access, free of charge, a PDF of the suggested templates, checklists, and templates from www.davidparmenter.com/The_Financial_Controller_and_CFO's_Toolkit.

The PDF download for this chapter includes:

- Other Leadership traits from *The Leading-Edge Manager's Guide to Success*
- Some leadership articles
- An agenda of a team offsite meeting

- Summary of the lessons from the paradigm shifters
- Locking in Good Leadership Habits—a Thirteen-Week Program

NOTES

1. David Parmenter, *The Leading—Edge Manager's Guide to Success* (Hoboken, NJ: John Wiley & Sons, 2011).
2. Jim Collins and Jerry Porras, "*Built to Last: Successful Habits of Visionary Companies* (New York: Harper Business Essentials, 2004).
3. Jack Welch and Suzy Welch, *Winning* (New York: HarperBusiness, April 2005).
4. Jan Gunnarsson and Olle Blohm, "The Art of Making People Feel Welcome," *Dialogos* (2008).
5. Welch and Welch.
6. Steve Zaffron and Dave Logan, *The Three Laws of Performance* (San Francisco: Jossey-Bass, 2011).
7. Mary Munter, *Guide to Managerial Communication*, 10th ed. (Prentice Hall, 2013).
8. Mick Ukleja and Robert Lorber, *Who Are You and What Do You Want?* (New York: Perigee, 2009).
9. Elizabeth Haas Edersheim, *The Definitive Drucker: Challenges for Tomorrow's Executives—Final Advice from the Father of Modern Management* (New York: McGraw-Hill, 2006).
10. Joseph Stromberg, *Five Health Benefits of Standing Desks*, smithsonian.com (March 26, 2014).
11. Welch and Welch.
12. Ibid.
13. Jim Collins and Jerry Porras, *Built to Last: Successful Habits of Visionary Companies* (New York: Harper Business Essentials 2004).
14. Jack Welch and Suzy Welch, *Winning* (New York: HarperBusiness April 2005).
15. Jan Gunnarsson and Olle Blohm, "The Art of Making People Feel Welcome," *Dialogos* (2008).

12

Quick Annual Reporting: Within 15 Working Days Post Year-End

OVERVIEW

If you are not careful, your year-end accounts can take on a life of their own. Led by the auditors, who delay the audit to fit it into their work schedule, giving them the luxury of hindsight. The delay encourages the accounting team to process adjustment after adjustment only to find the accounts have gone full circle with the year-end audited accounts within 5 percent of the starting numbers. This chapter covers the need for change, how to get the year-end organized, the technology to adopt, the steps to minimize the stress, and how to control all the data coming in from different sources.

The annual reporting activity is part of the three major lost opportunities for the finance team. Slow month-end reporting, long annual planning, and a never ending year-end suck the life out of far too many accounting teams.

While annual reporting is an important legal requirement, it does not create any value within your organization, and thus seldom is it a task where your team has received any form of gratitude. Accounting functions therefore need to find ways to extract value from the process, while, at the same time, bringing it into a tight time frame.

Before you can have a quick year-end, you need to speed up month-end reporting monthly so staff are disciplined to a tight month-end. Your goal should be reporting monthly numbers and comments by day 3 (see Chapter 3 on quick month-end reporting).

This chapter is a summary of the content in my white paper, "Quick Annual Reporting: Within 15 Working Days Post Year-End."[1]

THE FIVE STAGES FOR A QUICK YEAR-END

There are many ways in which we can improve how we process the year-end reporting, and they can all be grouped in five ways:

1. *Sell the need for change.* To the finance team, the CEO, and the board.
2. *Get organized.* Embrace best practice year-end rules, preparing a comprehensive auditors' file, agree the audit deadlines, with effective communication between the auditors and finance team.
3. *Use technology to save time.* Use consolidation, intercompany, and disclosure management software.
4. *Minimize year-end stress.* Establish an audit coordinator role, efficient stock, debtors, and fixed-asset procedures; hard close at month 10 or 11.
5. *Control the last mile and maintain quality.* Handle the myriad data, quality assurance of the annual report, and avoid the number noise of a constantly shifting bottom line.

SELL THE NEED FOR CHANGE

As stated in Chapter 2, before we can make progress, we need our organization to see the need for change. We need to change its default view so leaders can persuade themselves that changes are not only necessary but desirable. Please reread Chapter 2 for greater detail.

The costs of a slow year-end include:

- Months where the accounting team is simply doing annual and monthly reporting—thus, little added value is created by the finance team in that time.
- Too much time goes into the annual report as we lose sight of Pareto's 80/20 principle.
- Little or no client management during this time; thus, budget holders pick up bad habits.

"Accounting teams are often hijacked by the annual reporting process."

—CFO with international blue chip experience

"Given the amount of time this activity takes, the 80/20 rule still applies. Most organizations look at the annual report financials as being special numbers that they have reworked many times. There is absolutely no reason in 99 percent of the cases why the first cut of year-end for internal reporting should not be the same as the last cut for external reporting. Most adjustments are trivial and result in printing delays. The annual report comes out so late virtually nobody reads it anyway!"

—CFO with international blue chip experience

Cost the Annual Accounts Process

In order to create a change in the way the senior management team (SMT), board, and management address the annual accounts, you need to establish what is the full cost of the annual accounts process, including all board, management, and staff time, and all external costs (audit fees, printing costs, public relations, and legal fees, etc.). Exhibit 12.1 shows how to calculate the costs of an annual accounts process. The times are estimates and show what a typical 500 full-time-equivalent organization might be investing in the annual report preparation. It does not include investor relations, and so forth.

The SMT has lower productive weeks in a year because you have to take out, in addition to holidays, training, and sick leave, the time they spend traveling and in general meetings.

	Accounting Team	Budget Holders	Senior Management Team	CEO
Staff involved	3 to 4	10 to 15	3 to 4	1
	Estimated total number of weeks worked			
Liaison with auditors throughout audit	3 to 5		1 to 2	
Planning audit	1 to 3			
Interim audit assistance	4 to 6	20 to 40		
Preparing annual accounts	2 to 5			
Preparing audit schedules	2 to 5			
Extra work finalizing year-end numbers	20 to 30			
Final audit visit assistance	10 to 20	20 to 40		
Finalizing annual report	10 to 20		5 to 8	1 to 2
Total weeks of effort	52 to 94	40 to 80	6 to 10	1 to 2
Annual salary cost	$130,000	$80,000	$200,000	$350,000
Average productive weeks in a year	42	42	32	32
	Low	High		
Personnel cost	$290,000	$530,000		
Printing costs	40,000	70,000		
Audit fees	270,000	300,000		
Estimated cost	$600,000	$900,000		

EXHIBIT 12.1   Costing the annual accounts process

A Quick Year-End Is a Good Year-End

Many top U.S. companies report very quickly to the U.S. stock exchange. In my days as an auditor, IBM was well known for its speed of reporting. If your organization reports very quickly at year-end, ignore this chapter; otherwise, read and implement, as you and your organization are wasting too much time in this area. There are a number of benefits, including:

- Better value from the interim and final audit visits
- Improved data quality through improved processing
- Reduced costs, both audit and staff time
- More time for finance staff for critical activities, such as analysis, decision making, and forecasting
- Improved investor relations

Exhibit 12.2 shows a rating scale, based on my observations and benchmarking, for the time frames to have an audited and signed annual report (time from year-end date).

EXHIBIT 12.2 Year-End Reporting Time Frames (from the Year-End to Signed Annual Report)

Exceptional	Outstanding	Above Average	Average
Less than 15 working days	15–25 working days	26–35 working days	35–45 working days

GET ORGANIZED

We need to treat every year-end like a military operation. Getting organized, and getting organized early, is the key.

Establish Year-End Reporting Rules within the Finance Team

I always point out to accountants that we are all artists. Each year-end, we sculpt the result, and it can never be the right number, as there is no such thing as a "right" number—it can only be a "true and fair" number. If ten accounting teams prepared the year-end numbers for one company, there would be ten different results. Each accounting team will have made different judgment calls, different calls on materiality, accruals, and accounting treatments.

As mentioned previously, the finance team has to realize that they only need to do enough work to arrive at a true and fair view. All work done after this point has been reached will thus not be adding value. We therefore need some rules that the year-end reporting (YER) should adhere to:

- Month 12 numbers are the year-end numbers.
- YER should not be delayed for detail.
- Materiality for a misstatement to the year-end result is _____.
- Ban spring cleaning at year-end and allow adjustments to offset each other on the "overs and unders" spreadsheet.
- YER can only be a true and fair view. (e.g., Hunting for the perfect number is now unacceptable.)
- The final year-end report will have extensive quality assurance checks to ensure it is free from any report-writing errors.
- Spreadsheets will not be used for key routines, such as the consolidation.

Year-end reporting is not the time for spring cleaning no matter how tempting it can be. This requires a reeducation within the finance team and with budget holders.

We want to have a regime where we catch all material adjustments and see the net result of them before any decision is made to adjust—for example, only a material year-end misstatement will result in processing an adjustment.

A draft finance team year-end rules is in the accompanying pdf download.

Help Get the Auditors Organized

An audit can very easily get disorganized. The audit firm will more than likely have a change in either the audit senior or audit staff, and first-year staff members will know little about what they are trying to audit, no matter what training they have had. So, help the audit team (it is in your interests) by:

- Allocating appropriate facilities for the audit room (desks, phones, security).
- Providing an induction session for new audit staff, as up to 40 percent of junior audit time is wasted in an unknown environment.
- Preparing all the financial schedules, in the agreed format, in an electronic file ready for handing over on day 1 of the final visit.
- Advising staff to assist the auditors and having a specific person designated as the audit coordinator, who should be contacted first, should the auditors need assistance.
- Holding meetings at key times with the auditors (e.g., the planning meeting, the interim meeting, and the meetings to discuss the final results).

The steps in each of these stages are set out and analyzed in detail in the annual accounts checklist, which is provided in the accompanying PDF download.

Renegotiate the Auditor's Sign-off Deadline

Your auditors have probably delayed the audit to fit it into their work schedule. We therefore need to renegotiate the auditor's sign-off deadline. The message is, "We are going to be quick, and so are you. If you cannot make this tight deadline, we will need to go elsewhere."

Most auditors have already signed a set of audited accounts quickly. Sometimes it is because the companies wish to seek additional finance or want to be seen as a leading organization. The auditors have standard processes in these events. The benefits include:

- A level playing field—you have closed the numbers quickly and they also have to report back quickly.

- Any dirty laundry is not hanging on the line for very long—the auditors do not have the benefit of three to six months of hindsight to say, "Look what we have found."
- It encourages good practices, such as using the Pareto 80/20 rule, Post-it reengineering of year-end processes, a hard close at month 11, and so on.

Have a Month 10 or 11 Hard Close

To enable the auditors to come in and commence their audit earlier, leading finance teams have negotiated a hard close on a shorter period. In most cases, month 11 suffices. Effectively, month 11 becomes the year-end, with all major assets, such as debtors, stock, and fixed assets, being verified. If a debtors' circularization is to be performed, this will need to be performed on month 9 or 10 balances, thus allowing enough time for responses.

Once the auditors have formed an opinion as to the P/L and balance sheet for this period, they need only to audit the movement of the numbers for month 12 transactions.

The larger and more complex the organization is, the greater the need for a hard close at month 10 results.

Assembling a Well-Structured Financial Statement File

This electronic file, if scoped with the auditors and diligently completed by the finance team, will save hours of audit and finance team time. The electronic file:

- Supports all numbers in the financial statements
- Supports all numbers presented in the notes to the annual report
- Includes all schedules and reports used to compile the financial statement numbers
- Shows the links to the G/L
- Is organized in four sections: revenues, expenses, assets, and liabilities
- Contains explanations for significant variances between the current and the previous year numbers
- Contains copies of all monthly management reports

Embrace Abandonment

The lessons of abandonment (Peter Drucker) and how not to be trapped into living with the results of other people's thinking (Steve Jobs), outlined in Chapter 1, need to be embraced. Your year-end processes, spreadsheets, and documentation are the "result of other people's thinking." We need to abandon the processes that have no purpose other than doing it because we did it last year. Some easy and common abandonments to embrace:

- Using a spreadsheet for the consolidation
- Using year-end as a time to tidy up the accounts by processing many minor adjustments
- Showing additional analysis in the annual report that is not required by company law (It is sad but true—the annual report will be largely unread).

Post-it Reengineering

The Post-it reengineering process was outlined in Chapter 10, and you will need to reread this section to understand the process. The suggested attendees for the reengineering of the year-end will include all those involved in year-end including accounts payable, financial and management accountants, a representative from the auditors (the audit manager), and representatives from teams who interface with year-end routines (e.g., someone from IT, payroll, and the chairman's office). The agenda for the session is set out in Exhibit 12.3.

Scrum First Thing Every Morning

The scrum techniques outlined in Chapter 10, are ideal for the annual accounts process. On the year-end accounts, those involved in the preparation would meet, every morning, for anywhere from 10 to 20 minutes in a stand-up meeting. The importance of a stand-up meeting is that it is quicker, as we are more alert. At each session, attended only by those who are currently involved in a year-end accounts activity, they are asked to talk about:

- What they did yesterday on the annual accounts
- What they are doing today on the annual accounts
- Roadblocks that are barriers to progressing the annual accounts

At the end of the session, the group ends the session touching fists, an homage to the source of this technique. When the auditors arrive it may be appropriate for them to join the scrum. Would it not be nice to know what they have achieved yesterday?

Please reread the section in Chapter 10 to understand all the procedures of this important process.

EXHIBIT 12.3 Draft Agenda for the Quick Annual Reporting Workshop

Date & Time: _____

Location: _____

Learning Outcomes:

Attendees after this workshop will be able to:

- Discuss and explain to management why their organization should have quicker year-end reporting.
- Use better practices to streamline their current bottlenecks.
- Use a step-by-step implementation framework.
- Describe better practice year-end routines.
- Recall all agreements made at the workshop (these will be documented).

9:00 a.m. Welcome by Financial Controller

9:10 **Setting the scene**—a review of better practices among accounting teams that are delivering swift annual reporting. Topics covered include:

- What is quick year-end reporting?
- Benefits of quick annual reporting to management and the finance team
- Better practice year-end procedures/stories
- Current performance gap between _____ and better practice
- Precision versus timeliness

Senior management, PR expert involved in annual report, representative from the legal team, and a selection of budget holders (who are based in locally), will be invited to attend this session "setting the scene."

9:50 **Agreement on the current key bottlenecks of year-end reporting, presented by CFO or the financial controller**

- Current cost estimate of year-end reporting
- Human cost of the annual accounts process (weekends and late nights away from home)
- What processes we are doing well
- The need to work within existing systems
- Goal is "signed annual accounts by ____ working days"

10:05 **Workshop One to analyze the year-end procedures using Post-its** (different color allocated for each team involved, see Exhibit 12.4)

10:30 Morning break

10:45 **Workshop One continues**

(continued)

EXHIBIT 12.3   *(Continued)*

11:20	Feedback and pulling it together. Participants will document agreed changes and individuals will be encouraged to take responsibility for implementing the steps.
12:00 p.m.	**Workshop Two to set out the appropriate implementation steps to implement quick annual reporting.** Each team prepares a short presentation of the key steps they are committed to making (teams will use PowerPoint on laptops).
12:30	Lunch
1:15	**Workshop Two continues**
2:00	Each team presents reports to the group about what changes they are going to implement and when. Each team can also raise any issues it still has.
	The members of the senior management team and budget holders, who attended the first session, will be invited to attend this session.
2:30	Wrap up of workshop by CFO or financial controller
2:45	Finish

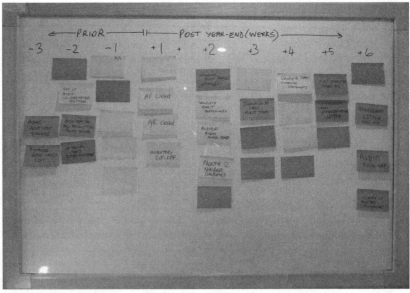

EXHIBIT 12.4   Post-it reengineering the year-end on a whiteboard

USE TECHNOLOGY TO SAVE TIME

The use of modern technology is important, no matter what size your organization is.

Consolidation and Intercompany Software

Your year-end will only be efficient when you have utilized consolidation software so that you can consolidate without fear of a screen full of REF! REF! REF! As mentioned in Chapter 4, performing a consolidation in a spreadsheet is inappropriate, and adds unnecessary error factors to the process.

There are now excellent systems that organize this for you and enable the subsidiaries to have their own general ledger and account code structure. Their trial balance is simply mapped into the consolidated entity's account codes. A search with any search engine will also find some freeware, robust older versions available at no cost. Try this search in your search engine, "consolidation+software+freeware." It worked for me.

Larger conglomerates need to have a sophisticated communication system between all related companies. Far too many finance teams are conned into thinking that they need to standardize the G/Ls for this. Yes, it will do the job, but at what cost? The primary beneficiaries are the G/L providers and the associated consultants who, no doubt, can now buy that second summerhouse that they so badly need, by their favorite lake.

The answer lies with accessing sophisticated intercompany software that enables an automatic interface for intergroup transactions where one party to the transaction does the entry for both G/Ls. This software, like the consolidation software, allows subsidiaries to keep their own G/L and account codes.

Reread Chapter 4 for a list of the intercompany and consolidation software applications.

Maximize the Use of the Existing G/L

Your G/L will have many unutilized features. So ask your G/L consultant to come for a day to see where the finance team can better use the G/L's built-in features for monthly and year-end reporting.

Collaborative Disclosure Management

As mentioned in Chapter 4, this software ensures that you have one database that is the sole source of the truth. For the year-end accounts, the input into the notes to the annual accounts would be controlled this way.

I would consider this software a must have for any organization over 500 full-time equivalents. It will be invaluable for year-end, month-end, and annual planning documentation.

 ## MINIMIZE YEAR-END STRESS

The year-end is a busy time, and there is a premium on being organized, as already covered, and ensuring that we undertake tasks efficiently, always using Pareto's 80/20 rule.

Appoint an Audit Coordinator

The first step to reducing stress and improving communication between staff and the audit team is to have a full-time audit coordinator. This person should be a staff member, not necessarily in finance, who knows most people in the company and knows where everything is, in other words, an *oracle*.

You may find the ideal person is someone in accounts payable or someone who has recently retired. The important point is that the individual should have no other duties during the audit visits (both interim and final) than helping the audit team. Give the individual a pleasant room and say, "When not helping the audit team, you can simply put your feet up." Do not get tempted to give the person additional duties. The audit coordinator's tasks include:

- Providing an induction session for new audit staff
- Gathering any, and so forth, that the auditors need
- Responding to information requests the auditors have made that are still outstanding
- Setting up designated contact points in every function (e.g., whom to speak to in the marketing department)
- Organizing meetings with the designated person in the section they need to visit

Complete the Drafting of the Annual Report before Year-End

It is desirable to complete the annual report, other than the final year's result, by the middle of month 12. This will require coordination with the public relations consultant who drafts the written commentary in the annual accounts and discussions with the chairman of the board and the CEO. Your last month's numbers will not greatly impact the commentary.

As mentioned, the annual report is not an eagerly awaited document. If you are a publicly listed company, the stock market analysts rely more on the in-depth briefing your organization provides them. Your shareholders access a summary of the results from their broker.

Limit When Changes Can Be Made

Year-end is not a time for spring cleaning. We will apply the rules already mentioned in this chapter. We will make the month 12 numbers the final-year numbers. The "overs and unders" schedule, as shown in Chapter 3, will be maintained, and we will record any major adjustments on this schedule. When the auditors arrive, we hand over the "overs and unders" schedule informing them that these are the adjustments to date. The auditors take ownership and update with any other subsequent adjustments.

You will often find that adjustments have a tendency to offset each other. If the auditors find a major adjustment, look in the opposite direction and you no doubt will find another to offset it.

The year-end adjustments will be reviewed as follows:

- Stage 1: Close of first working day (part of preparing the flash report for month 12)
- Stage 2: Day 3 when we finally issue month-12 results
- Stage 3: The morning when final audit starts so auditors have the bottom-line number
- Stage 4: When the final tax entries are known
- Stage 5: Final audit agreement meeting

Effective Stock Takes

Stock takes should never be conducted at any month-end, let alone at year-end. There is no need to do this, as your stock records should be able to be verified at any point in time. It is a better practice to conduct rolling stock counts rather than one major count that closes all production. A well-organized stock take includes:

- Trained stock takers working in pairs, each from a different department, to enhance independence and thoroughness.

- Highlighting obsolescent stocks, which can be targeted in the preceding months to reduce the write-down at year-end.
- Rolling stock inventory (counts) throughout the year (e.g., a jewelry company with a chain of stores counts watches one month, engagement and wedding rings the next month, in the quiet times during the month).
- Ensuring the stock area is clean and organized before the counting, to ensure a more accurate count (e.g., same stock items are together).
- Adding visible tags to counted items.
- Having a good celebration once the count has been done (this will ensure willing helpers next time).

Estimating Added Value in Work in Progress and Finished Goods

Auditors can get lost very easily in auditing the added value in work in progress (WIP) and finished goods. On one audit it took me a couple of weeks of elapsed time to trace the WIP through its stages, using random samples. In the second year, it was suggested that I look at how many weeks of production there were in WIP, which was easy to confirm, then at how many weeks of direct and indirect overhead could and should be absorbed. The audit of WIP took less than four hours. Thus, help your auditors by providing working papers to verify the reasonableness of complex valuations such as WIP.

Effective Fixed Asset Verification

The key to a better use of the fixed asset register (FAR) is a good attitude. Many finance teams see the FAR as a necessary evil, and thus little focus is given to really driving it properly. Few finance teams grab the opportunity and turn the FAR into a valuable system:

- Use bar codes on all assets so asset verification is a paperless exercise with a scanner.
- Set higher capitalization levels than those stated by the tax authorities, radically reducing the volume in the FAR—it being recognized that a tax adjustment can be performed easily, if necessary.
- Log maintenance for key plant as well as the up-to-date expected life, so useful graphics of expected lives of key assets can be shown to the board.
- Reduce the number of fixed asset categories, as every extra coding serves only to create more chances for miscoding (remember that we are to apply Pareto's 80/20 rule).

- Perform rolling fixed asset counts rather than doing it all at one time (e.g., verify equipment in the factory this month, computer equipment next month, etc.).

Importance of the Internal Auditors

The internal auditors can significantly reduce the external auditors' work. Many organizations contract out this function to an independent firm. I believe an in-house internal audit team will pay for itself many times over by:

- Increasing the use of efficient and effective procedures.
- Providing a great training ground for new graduate accounting staff.
- Focusing on reengineering exercises and other revenue-generating or cost-saving activities (e.g., in a one-week exercise, most internal auditors would be able to save 5 percent off the future telecommunication costs).
- Providing the external auditors with all their main working papers filled out—the internal auditors will know how to do this if they have attended the external auditor's staff training courses.

Manage the Management Letter

It is important that you insist that the auditors put a bit more care and attention into the management letters and that they are delivered within two weeks of the interim and final visits. Prompt management letters mean that management can rectify a problem immediately.

Management letters are often an afterthought, completed many months after the final audit, when much has been forgotten. The audit staff assigned to write the management letter are often relying on inadequate notes. The resulting letter is poorly constructed, with comments about a minor procedural failure easily being taken out of context by the board.

We need to ensure that all errors noted should be stated in context (e.g., We found 20 invoices with the wrong prices. We understand this was because _____. Management has rectified this situation and we tested a further sample of _____ and found no further errors. We note that of all the other price tests we performed, there were no other errors. We do not believe this has led to a loss of profits greater than $_____).

Also, we want the auditors to comment on our strengths (e.g., "We would like to comment that the new monthly report formats are the best we have seen; they are clear, concise, and efficiently produced").

I recommend that you insist that the draft letter is prepared before the audit team leave. Say to the visiting audit team, "We will go to the end-of-audit function when we have seen the letter." They will thank you for making them more efficient.

> "During the audit, we commented to the auditors that we had found a better way of carrying out a process. They turned around this knowledge and noted the current process as a weakness in the management letter, when in fact it had not created a problem. I blew up at the audit partner and they apologized and removed the comment."
> —*CFO with international blue-chip experience*

Derive More Value from the Interim Audit

In conjunction with the external auditors, look at making more use out of the interim audit. You may have implemented a new expense system, so ask the auditors to spend some time testing compliance. Ask them to cover more branches, ensuring nearly all branches are covered every two years. This will cost more but will be worthwhile.

Always remember that it is perception that rules the roost; staff members in remote branches will begin to conform to company policies if they know that auditors are to arrive and that they always test the compliance of the key systems along with all the new systems.

It is a good practice to have the first interim visit in the first half of the year to assure that the organization's staff maintains vigilance on compliance.

Restrict Access to Confidential Information to the Audit Partner

It is important to inform the staff and audit team about what is subject to restricted access (e.g., it might be that only the audit partner is able to see the senior management team's payroll). I remember the days when the audit team would fight over who was to look at the payroll; just remember, it is human nature to be nosy.

CONTROL THE LAST MILE AND MAINTAINING QUALITY

In order to achieve a fast year-end, Excel has to be replaced by twenty-first-century systems. There are several potential areas to consider if an organization is to achieve substantial time savings in the reporting supply chain. The main areas to tackle here include:

- Data capture from reporting entities (including minimizing their returns)
- Mapping to group systems and control
- "Last-mile" information handling
- Having a robust quality assurance process

Data Capture from Reporting Entities

Those of us who have reported to a finance department in an international conglomerate will know that the reporting pack was designed by a rocket scientist without any regard to materiality. Endless pages of data are gathered and sent, most of it meaningless. "It could be useful to have this," "Better ask for that in case I might get a question." The result is hours upon hours spent around the world gathering the data, which, by the way, are never used by the subsidiaries to manage their business.

How did this happen? First, the CFO delegated the task and then took little or no interest in how big the reporting pack had grown. The CFO may have observed, "The reporting pack looks a bit large. Are you sure you need all of this information?" Second, nobody ever calculated the full cost of the data-gathering process and compared it against the benefit. If this task was done, common sense would have won out. Third, there are seldom effective forums for management accountants in the subsidiaries to challenge those in the head office by saying, "Why do you need this?" or, "Tell me what you do with all of this."

Mapping to Group Systems and Control

Often, the mapping of data from reporting entities involves extensive manual procedures, spreadsheets, and the batch transfer of files, all of which introduce the potential for serious error every step of the way. It is often very difficult to spot these errors, which have a nasty habit of rearing their ugly heads during the final audit. In addition, the scope for mistakes increases by the number of entities involved and the frequency of changes in the group's reporting pack, brought about by management accountants having brain waves and the need to meet regulatory changes.

"Last-Mile" Information Handling

The efficient marshaling of information post consolidation is vital and is known as the last mile in annual reporting. In the last mile, there are PDF files, spreadsheets, PowerPoint slides, Word documents, and email communications, all of which provide input for the notes to the annual accounts. It is important that they are accessible to all those on the annual accounts team rather than residing in individuals' email inboxes and C drives.

Robust Quality Assurance Process

The quality assurance steps from Chapter 7 apply here. They include:

- Ban all late changes to the annual accounts (use the "overs and unders" schedule as discussed).
- Cross check all numbers for internal consistency.
- Use the two-person read-through.
- Look for those last two errors.

 ## SOME CASE STUDIES

Here are some case studies; many more can be found on the Internet.

IBM'S APPROACH TO FASTER CLOSING HAS FOUR STAGES

Evaluation involves understanding the current process and building a vision for the future. Benchmarking, supported with illustrations of how other organizations have achieved a faster close, can stimulate a project.

The second stage is called ETA—eliminate, transfer, and automate. Eliminate non-value-added tasks. Getting quality right at the source avoids the cycle of reviews, corrections, and resubmissions that occur too often. Transfer tasks such as intercompany reconciliation off the critical path. Then, finally, automate. They found that standardizing master data—for example, through a standard chart of accounts—is a crucial step toward flowing data without manual intervention from source systems to final reports.

The "empower" is the third stage, which is about allowing the project team to be able to make the key decisions during implementation. They are the experts, so the delegation of decision making makes sense.

The final stage, "excel," is about continuous improvement—recognizing that the pressures for continued speed and efficiency are likely to continue.

Source: Insight CIMA

ROCK-TENN USES A COLLABORATIVE DISCLOSURE MANAGEMENT SYSTEM

Rock-Tenn, a $US2.1 billion manufacturer of paperboard products, found that the year-end close had been a perfunctory process-no one really looked at it. Then Sarbanes-Oxley came along, exposing all the touch-points in the process where errors could creep in.

They have 90-plus locations, with people doing accounting functions in the field. Getting everybody to do what they need to do is like herding cats. In addition, a string of acquisitions led to a patchwork financial processes.

The first step was to create standard checklists for all Rock-Tenn financial and accounting staff. Then they launched a project to replace its aging ERP system with one that supports Sarbanes-Oxley processes out of the box. The new system replaces the spreadsheets, email, and PowerPoints that littered the previous processes.

Source: CIO

AT&T HAS ITS RESULTS AVAILABLE BY 4TH WORKING DAY

AT&T has a month 10 close, with full stock take at end of month 10. The auditors audit the ten months and then the remaining two months. They ensure comprehensive coordination and communication exists between the company and the auditors.

PDF DOWNLOAD

To assist the finance team on the journey, templates and checklists have been provided. The reader can access, free of charge, a PDF of the suggested worksheets, checklists, and templates from www.davidparmenter.com/The_Financial_Controller_and_CFO's_Toolkit.

The PDF download for this chapter includes:

- Costing the annual accounts process
- A draft finance team year-end rules
- The annual accounts checklist
- The Post-it reengineering instructions
- Agenda and outline of the Quick Year-End Workshop
- Useful draft letters

 NOTE

1. David Parmenter, "Quick Annual Reporting: Within 15 Working Days Post Year-End," www.davidparmenter.com, 2015.

CHAPTER THIRTEEN

Managing Your Accounts Receivable

OVERVIEW

P oor management of the accounts receivable can put your organization in a crisis. This chapter explores some of the smart practices I have come across while benchmarking organizations.

M any courses are offered on the subject of debt management and collection practices. This chapter assumes that your accounts receivable staff are well trained, and thus, I will only cover a selection of the intelligent practices I have come across while benchmarking organizations' practices.

OPERATIONAL IMPROVEMENTS TO ACCOUNTS RECEIVABLE

Some better practices you may wish to adopt are:

- Have the right mental attitude about credit control (e.g., when asking for your money, be hard on the issue but soft on the person).
- Provide immediate notice of overdue debt to the sales team.
- Establish clear credit practices and communicate these credit practices to staff and customers.
- Be thorough when accepting new accounts, especially larger ones (e.g., perform the credit checks that a bank would when lending the same amount).
- Continuously review credit limits, especially for major customers, if tough times are coming or if operating in a volatile sector.
- Monitor sales invoicing with promptness and accuracy.
- Charge penalties on overdue accounts.
- Accept credit cards for smaller high-risk customers.

> "People will take as much credit as you give—and that doesn't mean what your credit policy allows, it means what you let them take. A lot of bad practice has grown around the giving and taking of credit. Conventional wisdom says that the less credit you give and the more you take, the better off you are. However, this ignores the real overhead cost created by tracking and reconciling *overdues* and *outstandings*. It also makes your suppliers dislike you. They won't support you when you need them if you constantly pay late. Credit is best minimized on both sides. Demand quick payment and provide incentives. Pay your bills right away. Your administration costs will fall."
> —*CFO with international blue-chip experience*

REPORTING ON YOUR ACCOUNTS RECEIVABLE

The graph shown in Exhibit 13.1 will reduce much of the need for a larger debtor report. This exhibit focuses on debtors' aging trend. You need to go back at least 12 months, preferably 15 to 18 months, to catch the impact of last year's seasonal fluctuations.

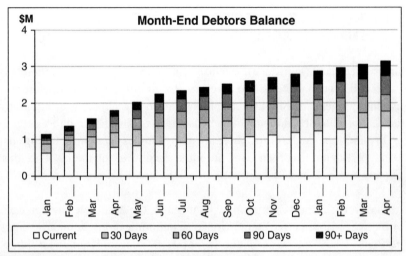

EXHIBIT 13.1 Example of an aged debtors graph

 AVOIDING ACCOUNTS RECEIVABLE MONTH-END BOTTLENECKS

Once again, electronic interfaces with key customers and electronic cash receipting are the keys to moving out of the processing battle at month-end within accounts receivable. Some better practices are:

- Cut off accounts receivable at noon on the last working day, with the afternoon sales being dated as the first day of the new month—you will need to ensure that customers still pay invoices according to your terms.
- Change the sales invoice cycle for all "monthly sales invoices" to customers (e.g., May 26 to June 25) or invoice all transactions to the 25th of the month, with a second invoice for the remaining period of the month.
- Send electronic invoices to your major customers, including their general ledger codes—the easier you make it for them, the better for both parties.
- If you need details from subcontractors in order to invoice, look to streamline processes in a meeting between your customers and your main subcontractors to ensure a prompt and accurate billing process.
- If you have a lot of subcontractors, consider offering them a free accounting system that has an automatic link to yours for all invoices relevant to you.

INCREASING THE USE OF DIRECT DEBITING CUSTOMERS' ACCOUNTS

Many retired people will make a special trip into town to pay many of their bills by check. It is good exercise and an excuse to get out of the house. However, this activity is very costly to the receipting supplier, typically some utility. Many organizations have tried in vain to get customers to allow them direct debit to the customers' bank accounts. There are many hurdles to cross, including customers' perception that their bank accounts are now at the mercy of another company. Some of the better practices to sell this change are:

- Offer a cash draw each month, financed by the cash flow savings from receiving prompt payment. One telecommunications company offers three $10,000 prizes each month. Many retirees would sign up for this.
- Offer to waive your next price increase for all those who sign up for direct debiting.
- Offer a direct debiting discount each month on the total invoice, splitting the benefit you gain between you and the customer. You can make this appear more attractive by offering a large discount on a small, fixed-price component of the transaction (e.g., energy retailers have a fixed and a usage charge, so one gave a 20 percent discount on the fixed charges, which was only $4 per customer, for every month where a direct debiting authorization was active).

 ## DEBTORS' COLLECTION BEFORE YEAR-END

Although debtors should be a focus all year round, and in some cases involve the CFO and CEO in direct contact with their counterparts, there needs to be an added drive from month nine onward to clean up everything over 60 days old. A phone call from your CEO to the other CEO could save thousands in legal fees and possibly the whole debt, if you collect it before the company has gone into receivership. Remember, if it takes 10 hours of CFO time to collect $50,000 from a high-risk account, that is a very good return on time—$5,000 per hour.

CHAPTER FOURTEEN

Attracting and Recruiting Talent

OVERVIEW

CFOs and financial controllers need to improve their ability to recruit in order to select talented staff. This chapter explores how to become a finance team of choice, the importance of a succinct advert, the value of staying the distance in the recruiting marathon, and the importance of a successful induction.

I n every workshop, I ask one question, "Who has made a recruiting decision they have lived to regret?" Every finance manager puts his or her hand up. The carnage caused is relived in their facial expressions. Why does this happen so often?

I suspect that many readers will recall instances when the interviewee has arrived and you realize, with a degree of horror, that you have not yet reviewed the CV, nor prepared enough for the interview. You where on the back foot, and the smart interviewee was now in control, painting a picture that impressed you and hiding any issues that might have caused you concern.

Far too often, managers, when looking at their calendar, throw up their hands when they realize that they have another recruitment interview to do. It is the last thing they need at this point in time. Recruitment should be seen as the most important activity a CFO and financial controller ever does. It should be the most prepared exercise we ever do, for the following reasons:

- Recruiting properly is like putting a fence on the top of a cliff—it is better to spend 40 hours recruiting a candidate properly than to spend 400 hours cleaning up after a recruiting mistake.
- You can recruit for technical skills and through training improve skill levels, but you cannot change a person's values. If an individual's values are different from those of the organization, you will always have conflict.
- Better recruits will lead to more internal promotions, both saving costs and retaining institutional knowledge.

To have a first-rate team it is desirable to start with the best resources available. There are still too many staff selections made via an antiquated interview process accompanied by some cursory reference checking; the result is a high failure rate among new staff. Greater effort needs to be injected into the selection process along with the adoption of reliable recruiting techniques.

Management guru Peter Drucker once observed General Motors, "top committee" spending hours discussing the promotion of one employee. On questioning management about the effectiveness of this, the reply from the CEO was, "If we didn't spend four hours on placing a man and placing him right, we'd spend 400 hours on cleaning up after our mistake."

I will now talk about comprehensive recruiting practices that will help you "get the right people on the bus" as advised by Jim Collins, of *Good to Great* fame.[1]

EVER-PRESENT DANGER

Let's recall the last recruitment you did that went radically wrong. Can you recall how impressed you had become with the interviewee who could not put a foot wrong? They, of course, were much more prepared than you by a factor of 5 to 1. You really did not have a chance for you were dealing with a chameleon. They appeared to be the ideal candidate for the position. They would mirror your sentiments, so, before long, you were falling for your own image. Thus, before we start, let's remind ourselves of what you need to avoid:

- Going into an interview process unprepared. If you have not had training in behavioral event interviewing and competency-based questions, make sure you are accompanied by someone who is trained.
- Always filling up the silences (let the interviewee complete their answers or ask their own questions).
- Missing the clues to possible issues in their employment history—the inability to explain job moves or employment gaps.
- Missing red flags about their personality and working style, for example, if they speak negatively of others, make obvious exaggerated claims about their ability, and appear too self-centered and egotistical rather than being a supportive team player.

 ## THE NEED TO UP-SKILL

There is no other area in your field of expertise where training will have a bigger payoff than learning to recruit successfully. You might be recruiting until you retire from full-time work, and even then it might still come in handy when you become a board member sitting on the executive recruiting panel.

So, what skills do you need?

1. A sound understanding of the differing personality types and your own personal baggage. See "The Six Leadership Foundation Stones" in Chapter 11.
2. Be acutely familiar with twenty-first-century recruitment processes outlined in this chapter.
3. Be able to frame behavioral event and competency-based questions—and understand the significance of the answers. No longer will you ask leading questions that make it clear to the candidate how they should respond.
4. Be able to spot behavioral traits that might indicate a divergence between your organization's values and their values.

 ## LAW OF ATTRACTION

Successful organizations have known for years that to attract the cream to their organization they need to overtly promote how wonderful they are. This has to be embraced by the public relations team and the CEO. I always think of Richard Branson and the way he has branded his empire. He has been so successful that I suspect many of us would jump at the chance if a headhunter tapped us on the shoulder for a good position in the Virgin Group. A picture has been painted for us and we have bought it. This branding is a long-term investment and unfortunately there are no quick fixes.

Organizations that embrace modern management techniques, such as Google and Netflix, will naturally have an easier job in selecting talent as these organizations are seen as attractive places to work by many applicants. Netflix has even adopted a policy of unlimited holiday entitlement. They tell staff take what you need so you can deliver at the high end of the spectrum we demand. The executives regularly take six to seven weeks a year.

During the whole process from the advert to the final offer, we need to maximize the promotion of the organization's and finance team's brand.

Promote Your Finance Team to the Outside World

With your journey to becoming "future ready," you will have achieved some success stories. These will start making the accounting team a preferred team to join, providing you broadcast this message. You can do this by:

▪ Establishing a relationship with your local universities by offering prizes to the best accounting graduates, delivering guest lectures (such as "A day in the life of a corporate accountant"), and offering holiday jobs. These activities will increase the profile of the team and enable you and your organization to try before you buy.

▪ Writing articles/case studies in your accounting institute's journal and delivering presentations for your local institute branch.

▪ Being active in the local institute branch.

These activities are termed *magnetic marketing initiatives*; they will attract the high-caliber candidates who tend to do more research.

 ## THE RECRUITING MARATHON

To have a leading-edge finance team requires being able to sift the wheat from the chaff in the recruitment process. It is time to revamp the process from the antiquated interview process and accompanying cursory reference checking.

Look for Values and Fit before Focusing on Expertise

A common recruiting failure is to focus on expertise and experience. If you come across the perfect fit with a candidate, it is all too easy to brush aside all the warning signals and rush into signing them up.

Jim Collins points out the importance of organizations having a core ideology, which he defines very succinctly in the formula:

Core ideology = Core values + Purpose

There are some very good examples of organizational core values and purpose statements (mission statements) in Chapter 3 of his book, *Built to Last*, that are well worth reading.

Recruiting will never be successful if the recruiters do not have a shared understanding of the organization's core values and purpose. The primary objective should always be to weed out candidates who do not share the same values and who will not buy into the organization's purpose.

It is wiser to recruit someone slightly less experienced who is clearly able and has a close fit with the organization's core ideology than to recruit an expert who will not fit from day one.

Paint the Picture First

Peter Drucker advised that you understand the job so you have a better chance of getting a good fit. Here we need to understand not only what the duties are, but what skills and expertise are required. If you have a previous high performer in that role, model the job on that person's traits.

Far too often, the only time spent painting the picture is drafting a job description based on a format from the HR department. These job descriptions may not paint the right picture. We thus need to further touch up the picture in the job advert and during the first interview.

A retired, very well-respected CEO recommended setting the bar higher than the person leaving that position. That way, your organization's talent pool has been enhanced.

Never Give a New Job to a New Person

Drucker stated that you should never give a "new job to a new person." Drucker believed that outsiders do not stand a chance implementing new systems in an organization due to concerns over change, a lack of credibility, and the overpowering nature of the default future. Instead, you need to appoint and train an in-house manager who is well respected in the organization and who has a pile of "I owe you" favors that they can call on.

If the position is new to the organization and there is to be likely resistance (e.g., implementation of a new system, new general ledger etc.), you will be far more likely to succeed by utilizing the best person within the organization than any very skilled external person.

Seek Internal Referrals First

Great organizations recruit heavily from internal referrals. They target their high-performing staff and ask them if they know a person who would fit in the team before they advertise a position. Often, this has proved successful in saving hours of sifting through the great unknown.

Google is famous for its referral recruiting. Staff members who recommend candidates are rewarded for their efforts if and when their contact becomes an employee.

Recruiting Agency or Not

You will already have a preference as to whether you use agencies with regard to recruiting finance team members. The reasons for using agencies include:

- An agency specializing in recruiting finance team staff will be in constant touch with the market. They will know the available talent pool.
- In smaller cities they are likely to know most of the senior accountants, how they perform, and what environments suit them best.
- If you are going to be busy and not able to contribute to the process fully, then they will act as a great safety net.
- The more senior the role, the more benefits there are in using a specialized agency.

When selecting an agency for the first time, ensure they specialize in recruiting accountants. In addition, as a friend in the recruiting business warned, make sure they are not currently overloaded with active positions; otherwise, your recruitment exercise may become compromised.

Begin with a Good Advert

You need to sell the position using the emotional drivers of the potential recruits. Do not let the recruiting agency draft the advert without your active involvement. The job advert should include:

- Career prospects
- Technology they will be working with
- Working conditions of the finance team
- The scope for them to make a difference
- 10 to 20 percent of time to pursue ideas that might make a substantial impact on the organization

Harry Mills,[2] a prolific business writer, has just written a great book on drafting compelling messages. In the book, he has designed some tests that you should use on all your correspondence, including your job advert. It needs to be simple, appealing, have an emotional connection, exude credibility, and have some "unexpected" content.

The use of job boards and LinkedIn can also increase the pool of potential candidates.

Commit to Communication

Throughout the process, your communication must be seamless to the potential recruits. If some candidates are no longer on the list, inform them, offer some guidelines, and remember—they may well come across your path again.

If candidates are having to chase you about where their application stands, you can rest assured that they have been thinking about it for some time already. Great communication with candidates augers well for the future and could be the deciding factor in a competing-offer scenario.

The First Round

Here we are trying to sift out those candidates who are definitely not suitable. As Dr. Richard Ford, a specialist in senior executive assessment, has suggested, it is useful to send information about the job to the candidates and ask them to assess themselves against the key knowledge-specific, role-specific, team-specific, and culture-specific competencies required for the role. This can be handled by having candidates complete a web-based application form. As Ford points out, candidates with limited insight, self-awareness, and understanding of the role can be easily eliminated.

You may also wish to review the LinkedIn and Facebook profiles for those you are unsure about.

CATHAY PACIFIC RECRUITMENT

Cathay Pacific constantly seeks frontline staff who were born with the desire to serve. They firmly believe you cannot *train* staff to be as good at serving as Cathay Pacific requires; "They have to be born that way."

(continued)

(*continued*)

In order to sort the wheat from the chaff, all frontline applicants have to go through an arduous five-interview recruitment process that often takes about three months. Only applicants who are committed to joining Cathay Pacific get over this hurdle. During these interviews management is looking for the traits they need. The investment in the front end pays off with a quicker and more successful training process and one of the lowest staff turnover ratios in the industry.

The Second Round

The next session could be a 30-minute screening phone conversation for those who have provided adequate self-assessments. You could ask them the following questions:

1. Describe your proudest achievements.
2. What has been the hardest decision you have had to make that may have made you unpopular?
3. What are your strengths?
4. What will reference checks disclose about the way you operate?
5. How will your style impact on other team members?
6. How do you plan to grow and stretch yourself in the next five years?

Study candidates' performance records to find their strengths so that you can ascertain whether these strengths are right for the job. Drucker was adamant that you should focus on the interviewee's strengths and if these fitted the job specifications, the candidate could progress in the selection process. He saw no purpose in delving into weaknesses that often are not going to be exposed in the job.

The Third Round

Consider three to five people in the shortlist to maximize your chances of getting the best fit. Often, we only have one or two suitable candidates. Drucker warns us that this is not enough. Cast your net wider to attract more interest.

Ford has written a useful article on "how to hire the 'A' players."[3] I have incorporated his questions in line with the thinking of business book writers Peter Drucker and Jack Welch.

1. Why did you leave your last job?
2. Why do you want to leave your current job? You then ask, "Why was that?" Welch says you should drill down to the truth.
3. What sorts of things irritate and frustrate you most?
4. What would your colleagues say is the best thing about you?
5. Give examples of your commitment to innovation?
6. Tell me about a time when you had to persuade people to do something they did not want to do. What happened?
7. When I call your last boss, how will he/she rate your performance on a 0 to 10 scale, and why?
8. What preparation have you done for this interview?
9. Why do you want this job?

Involve the Human Resources Team

One of the most disconcerting departures from better practice has been the demise of the human resources (HR) team's influence in organizations. Where recruitment is left to managers, chaos ensues. Welch states very strongly that the HR team should have the same standing as the finance team—for example, the head of HR should have the same pay and conditions as the CFO.

Most readers can reflect back to a recruit that they approved that did not work out. In most cases, this would have been based on interviews and references. HR practitioners have found there are far more effective ways to recruit, starting by making an in-depth focus on the job requirements and followed by behavioral event interviews, simulated exercises, and assessment centers. All of this takes experienced in-house resources to manage and deliver. As we all know, the cost of appointing the wrong person can be much greater than just the salary costs.

Use Simulation Exercises and Psychometric Testing

The basic interview is a totally flawed tool; we tend to warm to those candidates who are similar to us. Clever interviewees realize this and will mimic back to us what we want to hear. Situation, role-playing, or scenario exercises are thus becoming more common in the recruitment process in an effort to find out more about the candidates.

It is now quite common for report writing and presentation exercises to be set during the final interview round for the more senior roles.

Many organizations that I have surveyed report that they have been burned by new staff who describe themselves as competent on an important skill, only to find out in practice that they were not nearly so competent.

Psychometric tests, especially arithmetical and verbal reasoning, are found to be valuable predictors and should be used when sorting out which of the short-listed candidates. High scores in these two tests is seen as a sign of a high performer.

One organization comments on the usefulness of a simple scenario exercise as part of the recruitment process, with the candidate and the panel playing their respective roles. The organization says that it is not hard to set up, and yet it helps significantly in the selection process. Candidates are given only 15 minutes' notice of what the scenario is going to be.

Assessment Centers

First used in the British army, assessment centers have long been recognized as a thorough way to recruit staff. They work particularly well when you are recruiting a group of staff or when you are looking to select senior and middle-management internally.

A manufacturing organization has a substantial investment in assessment centers for graduate recruitment. At their initial expression of interest, the graduates complete a comprehensive self-assessment questionnaire. From these returns, preselection of possible candidates is made and interviews carried out at the universities. Up to 24 graduates are selected to take part in the assessment centers. Two assessment centers are then run, each one day in duration, with 12 graduates plus up to 24 managers from the organization. Activities include an impromptu oral presentation, group work exercises, plus rigorous interviews. Usually about 50 percent of the graduates being assessed are chosen.

A finance organization has been using assessment centers successfully to identify their best staff candidates for branch manager positions. Two years on from the first assessments and placements, they have experienced 60 percent success in the selections made. The core competencies in these generic positions have been clearly identified and are reflected in the assessment center tasks and activities. They have continuously modified and refined their assessment centers with input from outside consultants.

The Forth Round

A reference check has little or no validity unless it is from a person known to your organization or a past employer whom you can rely on.

Random references, especially if they are received attached to the resume, should be treated with caution.

Reputable recruiting agencies use a landline number to verify the person and organization. At the very least, you should phone and ask questions about the candidate's (Pat's) skill base, such as:

- "Can you give me some instances where Pat has shown her ability to complete what she has started?"
- "Can you give me some examples where Pat has shown initiative?"
- "Are you able to illustrate a situation where Pat has shown his ability to handle pressure?"
- "Does Pat have any special needs we should be aware of?"

One important government organization asks all shortlisted candidates to find a referee who is known by the organization. If none can be found, they ignore this step. Naturally, this would count against an applicant. They believe a reference is worth getting only if it can be relied on. They know that a referee who is aware of the organization, how it operates, and its values and staff would be unlikely to give an unreliable reference if he wants to retain his relationship with the organization.

A common mistake is not to verify the academic record. Newspapers are littered with cases where high-profile appointments have been made where the individual has claimed a master's or PhD degree, only to be found out when poor performance brings their claims into question. Always check against the university records where the appointments are very important to the organization.

If money is involved, for example, in accounts payable or accounts receivable, it is also a good practice to perform criminal and credit checks.

The Previous Boss Check

Drucker was adamant that you should talk to candidates' previous bosses. Obviously not their current employment, but those organizations where they used to work. Jack Welch would call a previous employer and ask, "We have Pat Carruthers short-listed for a general manager position. I was wondering, if Pat was reapplying for a similar position in your organization, would you want him back?" As Jack says, he was surprised at the honesty. If he got a no, that was enough for him to cease the recruiting of that candidate. He wanted to hear, "We would very happy to have _____ back; _____ made a significant contribution while he (she) was with us."

A retired, very well respected CEO recommended performing two of these checks.

Involve the Finance Team in the Final Selection Process

Far too often, a new staff member is soon found to be deficient in a key process he or she claimed expertise in. This is a shame, as a brief exposure to the team during a casual walk could have exposed a potentially serious weakness in the candidate's skill base.

It is a good idea to have staff on the team involved to some extent in the final selection from the short list of candidates. This need not be too complex. A meeting over an afternoon cup of coffee can give the staff a chance to subtly quiz candidates on the claimed "expert knowledge." It is useful to see how they interact with the staff.

One technology team had interviewed an impressive candidate and duly shortlisted him. In the second round of interviews, they found that the candidate, albeit a certified Microsoft engineer, had little or no practical experience. This was discovered by the team members when they gave him a tour of the team's IT equipment.

The Final Check Against Requirements

It is a good idea to summarize your findings of the shortlisted candidates on a one-page matrix; see Exhibit 14.1. Although it might be tempting to perform some form of weightings, I would advise against this. You are trying to put objectiveness in a subjective exercise. Simply review the table. If two candidates are about even, then other considerations need to be evaluated.

Closing the Deal

You have done all the hard work, found a star, and offered the job. Time to relax? Hell, no! Get the CEO involved to make a call; just a 5- to 10-minute call can make all the difference in closing the deal. Remember, talent is sought after; it is a competitive market. Tell the CEO those 10 minutes could be worth $20,000, which is $120,000 per hour.

 ## DELIVER A GOOD INDUCTION

Drucker advised that once the employment decision is made, make sure the appointee understands the assignment. He is talking about a thorough

EXHIBIT 14.1   Candidate Comparison Matrix

Factors	Candidate names			
	_____	_____	_____	_____
Level of experience				
Technical skills				
Drive				
Planning and organization				
Team leadership				
Influence and impact				
Team fit				
Culture fit				
Potential for growth				
_____				
_____				

Scoring 1 = below average, 2 = average, 3 = good match, 4 = very good match

induction process. So often, good candidates are set up to fail by a poor induction process.

All high-achieving finance teams put a lot of time and effort into a proficient induction process. This process is a commitment not only by the CFO and financial controller but by all other finance staff as well. Far too often, the induction process gets relegated to an item on the agenda. The new staffperson arrives and is given the feeling that he or she is a burden. An induction should include:

- Detailed handover with the person leaving, or the phone number and email address of the previous person who did the job, if permission has been sought and granted.
- Morning or afternoon coffee with some of the general or middle managers, depending on seniority of new recruit.
- Specified meeting times with their manager (e.g., 3:00 p.m. Wednesday, 3:00 p.m. Friday) to pick up any loose ends, give feedback, revise the training program, and plan the week ahead.
- Meeting with a representative from the human resources team, scheduled for three months after joining date.

- Meeting with help desk and information technology support to cover intranet, systems, email, hours of operation, remote access, security, and so on.
- The setting up of some easy goals for the appointee to score.
- Visits to the operational business units and relevant key stockholders.

For the graduate accountant intake, think about placing the graduate into accounts payable with the brief to introduce twenty-first-century systems and processes. It will be a good exposure to the power of technology in business. You can then rotate them to an internal audit—a good reason to bring this function back inside the organization.

A very successful CEO mentioned to me about a situation where 13 mid-management positions were being recruited as part of a major restructuring. He told the manager in charge of the recruitments that this exercise will be the most important task he would ever be involved in and the legacy would live for a long time. There were 113 interviews and the CEO attended nearly all of them. Of the 13 places only 2 were filled by internal candidates.

The CEO ensured, on commencement, that the 13 managers met every month so they became a powerful cohort. The CEO also had one-to-one meetings with them. The recruitment and induction process was very successful with the newly appointed managers actively transforming the organization. He went on to say;

"Remember a good vacancy will always be better than a bad recruitment."

PDF DOWNLOAD

To assist the finance team on the journey, templates and checklists have been provided. The reader can access, free of charge, a PDF of the

suggested worksheets, checklists, and templates from www.davidparmenter
.com/The_Financial_Controller_and_CFO's_Toolkit.

The PDF download for this chapter includes:

- 14 questions you should consider asking in an interview

NOTES

1. Jim Collins, *Good to Great: Why Some Companies Make the Leap … and Others Don't* (William Collins, 2001).
2. Harry Mills, *Secret Sauce—How to Pack Your Messages with Persuasive Punch* (Amacom, February 2017).
3. Dr. Richard G. Ford, "How to Hire the 'A' Players," *Finance & Management ICAEW* (March 2010).

CHAPTER FIFTEEN

Lean Accounting

OVERVIEW

The lean movement gave the impetus for a new look at accounting called lean accounting, which had its beginnings around 2004. Lean accounting offers the accountant many profound insights. This chapter explores streamlining the chart of accounts, questions the validity of cost apportionment and activity-based costing, outlines value-stream accounting, demonstrates the danger of absorbing overhead and labor into closing WIP and finished goods, and revisits product costing.

The lean movement gave the impetus for a new look at accounting called lean accounting, which started around 2004. Lean accounting offers the accountant many profound insights and will improve the way we report costs. Lean accounting has progressed to such an extent that there is now an annual lean accounting summit. The key writers in this space include:

- Jeremy Hope[1]
- Brian Maskell and Bruce Baggaley[2]
- Orest Fiume and Jean Cunningham[3]
- Frances Kennedy[4]

STREAMLINING THE CHART OF ACCOUNTS

The chart of accounts is where many problems start. The complex GL packages have made a serious misjudgment with regard to the need for myriad accounts. The financial controller and CFO need to be alert to the problems of a large chart of accounts.

Limit the P & L to Fewer than 60 Account Codes

Show me a company with fewer than 60 account codes for its profit and loss statement (P & L) and I will show you a CFO or financial controller who has seen the light. However, I have seen many charts of accounts with more than 300 expense account codes in the general ledger (G/L), with up to 30 accounts for repairs and maintenance.

Why is it that the least experienced accountant volunteers for resetting the chart of accounts? I think I know the answer! All the wise owls duck for cover. Common sense goes out the window. The CFO's eyes glaze over at the chart of accounts progress meetings, the objective to reduce the account codes by over 40 percent gets lost, and slowly but surely, the chart of accounts takes on a life of its own.

A poorly constructed chart of accounts leads to many problems:

- It encourages detailed reporting, with budget holders getting a 60- to 70-line P & L.
- Budgeting is at the account code level instead of at category level.
- Excessive codes increase the number of coding errors and time wasted.
- A finance team is wedded to detail.
- It is a project accounting nightmare.
- Subsidiaries slowly suffocate under the weight of their holding company's process and procedures.

Here are some rules to stop this from happening:

- Allocate an expense account code when the relevant annual expenditure represents 1 percent or more of total annual expenses. This will limit your expense items to less than 50 account codes.
- Allocate a revenue account code when the annual revenue stream represents 3 percent or more of total annual revenue. This will limit your revenue account codes to less than 20.
- When you are questioned about an obscure cost, ask what decision is going to be made based on the information requested, or tell the questioner the answer is "42."
- Where the information requested has a purpose, ask a skilled management accountant to investigate how much has been spent in the last 5 or 10 weeks and then annualize the number.

Project Accounting

One of the common reasons for a chart of accounts nightmare is setting up myriad projects and then duplicating the account codes within them. Such nightmares end up with 30 to 50 pages of codes. Pareto's 80/20 rule needs to be applied to project accounting. Work out at what level you need to manage projects (e.g., all projects where expenditures are over $50,000 or $500,000). Small projects should be reported together under the project manager's name: "_____'s other projects." This will allow the project manager to use the bulk funds as they see fit.

Subsidiaries' Chart of Accounts

With a twenty-first-century consolidating tool, all subsidiaries can have a chart of accounts that is relevant to them. All the holding company accountants have to do is map the chart of accounts in the consolidation tool, which is a simple one-off exercise.

All new codes established by the subsidiary must be communicated to the parent company in advance to avoid consolidation issues at the eleventh hour.

AVOID MONTHLY COST APPORTIONMENT

Traditionally, we have spent much time apportioning head office costs to business units to ensure they have a net profit bottom line. However, few ask the budget holders and business unit managers whether they look at these apportioned head office costs. I have never found any business unit managers who showed much interest other than to complain about the cost of information technology (IT), accounting, and other apportioned costs.

In fact, these cost apportionments, besides slowing down reporting, often lead unit managers to complain about strategic costs, which cannot be reviewed for a few years due to locked-in agreements (e.g., the accounting system).

The hours spent processing levels upon levels of apportionments to arrive at some arbitrary full costing are not creating management information that leads to decision making. Corporate accountants can arrive at full costing approximations through a more simplistic route. Some better practices are:

- Keep head office costs where they are, as budget holders see them as uncontrollables in any case.
- Use product costing as periodic one-off exercises to understand a full costing situation, after you have understood value stream accounting.
- Analyze head office costs by activities rather than account codes, for example, where the head office IT costs are spent—delivering new projects, correcting errors, providing one-to-one training, provision of equipment, and so forth. Compare these over time and against third-party benchmarks.
- Set targets in the future where you expect to see head office costs, and show this as a baseline in your graphs of the historic trend. These can be expressed as acceptable ratios to sales. Naturally, you will have researched the lowest-cost operators as benchmarks (e.g., By 20__, we want finance cost to be between __ percent and ___ percent of revenue). This sets a general direction for the head office teams and helps curb empire building.

If you have on-charged head office costs to the operations and it is creating the right environment, then continue with the process. There are a number of case studies where on-charging head office costs appears to work well. They, however, are the exception rather than the rule.

 ## VALUE-STREAM ACCOUNTING

A good definition of a value stream is that it is a sequence of steps, both value adding and non–value adding, required to complete a product, document, or service from beginning to end.

As Brian Maskell and Frances Kennedy[5] point out, "For companies that have chosen the lean journey, it is important that their accounting, control and measurement methods change substantially."

The Finance and Management Faculty of the Institute of Chartered Accountants in England and Wales is an excellent source of cutting-edge articles, and it was the first place where I read about value-stream accounting. The faculty welcomes membership from other accounting bodies, and I am sure that you will find it the best-spent US$130 annual subscription you have ever invested.

Value stream accounting takes a different look at what is a variable cost and divisional accounting. The differences include:

- The existing labor force is not treated as variable unless you need to employ extra staff.
- Value streams are cross-functional, including all people and resources involved in the value stream.
- Value streams are a collection of products that share the same processes.
- Standard costs and price and volume variances, a backbone of Charles Horngren's work, are abandoned.
- Very few allocations are used other than allocation of occupancy costs.
- No manufacturing variances are calculated as we are producing to customer orders, not to budget.
- Costing of a product is not related to the amount of labor or machine time expended; it is based upon the rate of flow through the value stream. This impact is shown in a later section.

There is a marked change in the way we report performance to management when using lean accounting. Instead of showing performance in a conventional way, as shown in Exhibit 15.1, we now look at the value

Traditional Income Statement	
	$'000
Sales	100,000
Cost of goods sold	−70,000
Gross profit	30,000
Operating expenses	−28,000
Net operating income	2,000

EXHIBIT 15.1 Traditional reporting for a manufacturer

	Value Stream Income Statement			
		$'M		
	Car	Truck	Sustaining	Total Plant
Sales	60.0	40.0		100.0
Material costs of goods sold	(20.0)	(15.0)		(35.0)
Employee costs	(9.0)	(8.0)	(5.0)	(22.0)
Machine costs	(10.0)	(5.0)		(15.0)
Occupancy costs	(6.0)	(4.0)	(5.0)	(15.0)
Other costs	(1.0)	(1.0)		(2.0)
Value stream costs	(46.0)	(33.0)	(10.0)	(89.0)
Value stream profit	14.0	7.0	(10.0)	11.0
Inventory reduction (labor and overhead from prior periods)				0.0
Inventory increase (labor and overhead carried forward)				3.0
Plant profit				14.0
Corporate allocation				(12.0)
Net operating income				2.0

EXHIBIT 15.2   Reporting using value streams

streams (see Exhibit 15.2). These value streams can be one product, or a cluster of products that go through a similar process. In Exhibit 15.2 we are looking at a company that makes only two products, which in this case are quite different.

The main differences between the conventional way and value stream accounting include:

Removal of the budget and variance column, as manufacturers are producing to customer orders, not to budget. Reporting against standard costs and prices and volume variances are also abandoned.

Value streams are cross functional, including all people and resources involved in value stream. For example, the accounts payable and receivable staff would be allocated to value streams, as their work is critical for the purchasing of supplies and the eventual sales of finished products. Value streams are a collection of products that share the same processes.

Labor and machine costs are assigned directly to value streams using some simple cost drivers, but such allocations are held to a minimum, certainly not using activity-based costing models. The existing labor force is not treated as variable unless you need to employ extra staff.

Sustaining costs are necessary costs that support the entire facility, but cannot be directly associated with particular value streams, and are shown in a separate column. Sustaining costs include management and support, facility costs, information technology, and human resource management costs that are not associated directly with a value stream.

The corporate overhead is shown here as the corporate allocation. This would comprise costs that do not have a direct link to the value streams. The salary and related costs of the accounts payable and accounts receivable staff are now treated as a direct cost as you cannot produce anything without buying supplies and selling the finished product.

The inventory movement is reported separately as below-the-line adjustments and reported for the entire entity, not the separate value streams. This allows the value stream managers to assess their individual value streams without the complexities of the inventory changes affecting the value stream profit. If the company succeeds in adopting just-in-time inventory methods, the issue would largely disappear. Consequently, the motivation for manipulating inventory values also disappears.

Occupancy costs are actually assigned to value streams according to the amount of space used. Such items as utilities and property taxes are included here. Assignment of these costs provides motivation for the value stream teams to reduce occupancy costs. However, no attempt to absorb all of the occupancy costs is required. Space not used by a value stream is charged to sustaining costs. As a result, occupancy costs are handled in a similar manner to traditional accounting, but they are assigned to value streams instead of other cost objects such as products or divisions.

Why Profitability Dips as You Embrace Lean Manufacturing

When a manufacturer moves to producing to order and not to stock, the accounts are hit by a double charge of overheads and direct labor. Since we are now producing goods for confirmed orders or projected sales in the month, production levels drop swiftly so existing stock levels are used up first. In these months of transition, all overheads and labor of the current period are charged to the P/L, along with a portion of the prior period's labor and overhead, absorbed in the existing stock, which we have now sold.

Imagine two identical plants. One is not lean and has in fact increased inventory levels at month end and the other, an adopter of lean, has reduced production, sold off excess inventory, and reduced overtime. The comparison requires a careful eye.

Looking from the traditional accounting standpoint, the lean operation has been disappointing. Profit is down from $390,000 to $280,000 and return on sales is 8 percent, down from 11 percent, as shown in Exhibit 15.3.

But in reality, the lean plant had:

■ Trained all the plant's employees in lean concepts and had deployed them in small teams to make improvements to the equipment setup, placement, and maintenance

	Plant 1	Plant 2 (Lean)
	$'000	
Sales	3,940	3,940
Opening Stock	2,000	2,000
Material Costs	1,850	1,450
Employee Costs	550	500
Equipment-Related Costs	160	160
Less Closing Stock	(2,140)	(1,580)
Cost of Sales	2,420	2,530
Gross Profit	1,520	1,410
Occupancy Costs	240	240
Sustaining Costs	210	210
Corporate Allocation	480	480
Other Costs	180	180
Operating Costs	1,110	1,110
Net Operating Income	410	300
Return on Sales	10%	8%

EXHIBIT 15.3 Reporting the comparison in the traditional way

- Reduced overtime, saving $50,000 this month
- Reduced batch size, resulting in lower finished goods levels and faster lead times
- Generated extra cash flow through eliminating large amounts of WIP and finished goods and reducing overtime payments

So we need to show the lean operation in a different way, as set out in Exhibit 15.4. We now focus on the value stream profitability. We split the inventory movement between materials that are a direct cost and the overhead component.

	Plant 1		Plant 2 (Lean)	
		$'000		
Sales	3,940	100%	3,940	100%
Material Costs in Month	1,850		1,450	
Net Movement in Materials	(100)		300	
Employee Costs	550		500	
Equipment Related Costs	160		160	
Occupancy Costs	240		240	
Other Costs	180		180	
Value Stream Costs	2,880		2,830	
Value Stream Profit	1,060	27%	1,110	28%
Sustaining Costs	(210)		(210)	
Inventory Reduction (labor and overhead from prior periods)	0		(120)	
Inventory Increase (labor and overhead carried forward)	40		0	
Plant Profit	890		780	
Corporate Overhead Allocation	(480)		(480)	
Net Operating Income	410		300	
Return on Sales	10%		8%	

EXHIBIT 15.4 Reporting the comparison using value stream accounting

Now the lean plant shows a $50,000 advantage and operating drop is seen as a one-off cost of direct labor and overhead from prior periods being charged to the P/L.

For a quoted company, you could calculate the adjustment to generally accepted accounting principles, but I would not book it. Leave it as an adjustment in the "overs and unders" schedule maintained at year-end. As night follows day, it will be offset by some other adjustment.

Costing of a Product by Rate of Flow

Costing of a product is not related to the amount of labor or machine time expended; it is based on the rate of flow through the value stream.

In Exhibit 15.5, the three products are all part of a value stream. Total production costs are $3,000 per hour for the processes. In a traditional view management would cost product A as the cheapest as less process time is absorbed. Management in its pursuit to maximize plant use would produce more of product A in process 1 than could possibly be processed in process 2 thus leading to WIP stockpiling after process 1.

Lean looks at things differently. As mentioned, we only want to produce at a rate that can be continuous. One can only produce 8 units of products A per hour to avoid stock piling, whereas Product B can be produced at a rate of 10 units per hour.

Based on the $3,000 production costs we now cost product B as $300 per unit and product A as $375. This is a radical departure from traditional accounting where product A would have had a lower cost as less processing time was involved.

	Process 1		Process 2		
Product	Minutes to produce	Maximum production	Minutes to produce	Maximum production	Rate of flow
A	4	15	7	8.6	8
B	6	10	6	10	10

EXHIBIT 15.5   Example of a rate of flow calculation

This new thinking has a major impact on the design of costing systems. Why would we need a complex apportionment system such as activity-based costing when we can, as Jeremy Hope[6] points out, simply divide the number produced in an hour, day, or week into the value stream production costs?

Lean recognizes that product costing is at best a guess and at worst an error-prone figure that is time consuming to arrive at. Instead, we focus on the value stream (a cluster of products) profitability as a whole from procurement, production, delivery, and accounts receivable. We only attribute costs to a product that add value to the customer. Thus we would include new product development, but exclude all costs that are deemed sustaining costs such as head office support costs.

Our old friend gross margin or gross profit is no longer used, as it has always been corrupted with costs that are not truly variable and benefited from production of goods to stock as overhead has been capitalized and thus transferred to a subsequent period when that stock is sold.

Costing One-off Deals

Lean accounting also helps us look at one-off deals, as shown in Exhibit 15.6. It makes you show a clear message that the fixed costs are fixed and thus do not change. We now just think about any possible impact on future sales from doing a one-off discounted deal. Only truly variable costs are variable, such as additional labor required. In this case, the extra assignment will not involve extra staff but utilize spare capacity. The decision we make is based solely on the fact that as long as the one-off sales will not reduce the profitability of traditional sales from existing customers, in future periods, we should make the one-off sale.

 ## ACTIVITY-BASED COSTING IS BROKEN

Many of us have gazed wistfully into the distance, thinking how marvelous it would be to have the cost of producing a product at any time of day. Activity-based costing seduced the accounting profession, very much like the sirens in Greek mythology.

Right from the start, the writing was on the wall. The consultants were more expensive, they talked in a language we hardly understood, and they

	Repeat Sales	One-off Sales	Total Firm
		$'000	
Sales	550	92	642
Variable Costs			
Commission	(40)	(13)	(53)
Bonus	(45)	(15)	(60)
Travel	(80)	(27)	(107)
Advertising	(35)	(12)	(47)
	(200)	(67)	(267)
Value Stream Profit	350	25	375
Fixed Costs			
Employee Salaries	(150)	No charge	(150)
Office Cost	(60)	No charge	(60)
Marketing Cost	(30)	No charge	(30)
Owner Cost	(25)	No charge	(25)
	(265)	0	(265)
Operating Profit	85	25	110

EXHIBIT 15.6 One-off deals approached from a lean way

disappeared into the bowels of the organization for months on end. We knew they were somewhere, as their Porsche was parked in the visitors' parking lot.

In a lean company, the cost of a product can be derived by dividing the value stream costs by the units of production. Yes, it is a primitive number, but certainly good enough. A lean company's closing inventory could be as little as a few days of production with some longer-term holding in strategic stocks for overseas sourced materials. So why have an ABC system?

Given that we are not expecting much movement in closing inventory, we can now just charge the current period with all overheads incurred. We can take the view that the overhead is a sustaining cost and fully absorbed in the current period.

PDF DOWNLOAD

To assist the finance team on the journey, templates and checklists have been provided. The reader can access, free of charge, a PDF of the suggested worksheets, checklists, and templates from www.davidparmenter.com/The_Financial_Controller_and_CFO's_Toolkit.

The PDF download for this chapter includes:

■ Some examples of lean accounting articles first published in ICAEW's *Finance & Management* journal

NOTES

1. Jeremy Hope, *Reinventing the CFO: How Financial Managers Can Transform Their Roles and Add Greater Value* (Boston: Harvard Business Press, 2006).
2. Brian H. Maskell, Bruce Baggaley, and Larry Grasso, *Practical Lean Accounting: A Proven System for Measuring and Managing the Lean Enterprise*, 2nd ed. (New York: Productivity Press, 2011).
3. Orest J. Fiume and Jean E. Cunningham, "Real Numbers: Management Accounting in a Lean Organization," *Managing Times Press* (2003).
4. Frances Kennedy, "Why and How Lean Accounting Works," *Finance & Management Special Report* (2012).
5. Brian Maskell and Francis Kennedy, *Why Do We Need Lean Accounting, and How Does It Work?* (Hoboken, NJ: Wiley Interscience, 2007).
6. Hope.

V

How Finance Teams can Help their Organizations get Future Ready

CHAPTER SIXTEEN

Implementing Quarterly Rolling Forecasting and Planning

OVERVIEW

With many organizations questioning the validity and usefulness of annual planning the search is on for an alternative. Quarterly rolling forecasting and planning appears to solve all the major issues. This chapter explores the foundations stones and the key implementation steps required for a rolling forecasting and planning process to work.

As mentioned in Chapter 9, the annual planning process takes too long, leads to dysfunctional behavior, builds silos, and is a major barrier to success. Organizations around the world are questioning the value of the traditional annual budgeting process.

This chapter is a summary of the content in my white paper "How to Implement Quarterly Rolling Forecasting and Quarterly Rolling Planning—And Get It Right First Time"[1]

SELLING AND LEADING THE CHANGE

It is important to sell to management why they need to move to a quarterly rolling forecasting and planning regime. As mentioned in Chapter 2, Leading and Selling Change, it is important to start the process off by getting management to see that the default future is not what they want. We need to sell the change using emotional drivers rather than selling by logic, as already discussed.

In Chapter 9, I have set out the emotional drivers regarding why annual planning needs to change. The following points are some of the additional emotional drivers you could use to sell the need to move to quarterly rolling forecasting and planning process to the SMT:

Rolling forecasting and planning is now considered a best practice. It is better practice to implement quarterly rolling forecasting and planning (e.g., 70 percent of top performing organizations undertake rolling forecasting[2]).

Better allocation of resources. Allocating budgets on a quarter-by-quarter basis will mean that funding is adaptable to the changing conditions.

The finance team and budget holders are skilled staff that could be doing more meaningful activities.

Appropriate monthly targets. Setting monthly targets (budgets) a quarter ahead will make them more meaningful and improve the value of the variance commentary.

Better buy-in from budget holders. An adaptive quarterly rolling forecasting and planning process will have more buy-in, create less arguments, and greatly assist seeing the future clearer.

ANNUAL PLANNING IS A QUESTIONABLE ACTIVITY

Jeremy Hope was the world's foremost thought leader on corporate accounting issues. Sadly, he passed away in 2011. Hope had an uncanny ability to have a vision, at least five years ahead of time, about what better corporate accounting practices should look like. Hope has stated that not only is the budget process a time-consuming, costly exercise generating little value, but it also, and more importantly, a major limiting factor on how your organization can perform. He has many examples of how companies, following the philosophies he has expounded, have broken free and achieved success well beyond their expectations. Here are three quotes that challenge the very concept of budgeting.

> So long as the budget dominates business planning a self-motivated workforce is a fantasy, however many cutting-edge techniques a company embraces.
>
> Modern companies reject centralization, inflexible planning, and command and control. So why do they cling to a process that reinforces those things?
>
> The same companies that vow to respond quickly to market shifts cling to budgeting—a process that slows the response to market developments until it's too late.
>
> —*Jeremy Hope and Robin Fraser, Beyond Budgeting*[3]

Hope and Fraser in *Beyond Budgeting* pointed out that the annual budgeting process was doomed to fail. If you set an annual target during the planning process, typically 15 or so months before the last month of that year, you will never know if it was appropriate, given that the particular conditions of that year will never be guessed correctly.

A Burning Platform

The major problems that are associated with annual planning include:

- An annual funding regime where budget holders are encouraged to be dysfunctional building silos and barriers to success
- The monthly budgets set in the annual plan bearing no relation to reality
- Takes too long—often a three-month period where management is not particularly productive
- Using the annual plan as part of a bonus system
- Costs too much—annual planning costs in time alone runs into the millions each year for larger organizations
- Often needs to be updated during the year to reflect the dynamic and a rapidly changing environment we work in (see Exhibit 16.1)
- Is an "anti-lean" process

In a poll during webcasts to corporate accountants, I asked the attendees, "How long does your planning take each year? Around 80 percent were investing two months or more and 50 percent were taking three months or more.

In Chapter 9, the estimated cost for annual planning in a 500 FTE organization was stated as between $1.2 million and $1.7 million a year.

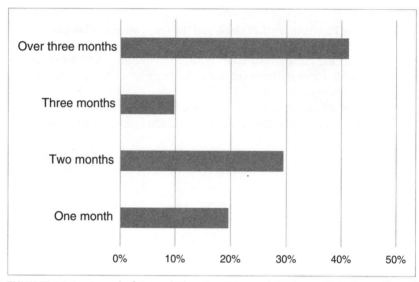

EXHIBIT 16.1 Speed of Annual Planning Waymark Webcast Polls Australia and NZ 2015, Popn: 95 entities

The only thing certain about an annual target is that it will be wrong; it will be either too soft or too hard for the operating conditions. The answer is to throw away the annual budget and its associated processes, as smart organizations do not do an annual planning process anymore. By 2020, very few progressive organizations will be doing annual planning as we know it today.

To find out the latest organizations that do not do annual planning, visit the Beyond Budgeting Roundtable (www.bbrt.org) that was co-founded by Jeremy Hope. You can access much valuable information including the Svenska Handelsbanken case study.

BEYOND BUDGETING IN NEW ZEALAND: A MAJOR ROAD CONTRACTING COMPANY

I was presenting Beyond Budgeting and key performance indicators (KPIs) in New Zealand and was introducing myself to the managing director of a large road contracting company. He politely informed me that he was mainly interested in hearing the KPI part of my presentation, as the beyond budgeting session was of little interest, as they were already doing it. In fact, the group had never had an annual planning process. He said, if the group could predict when it was going to sunny and when it was going to rain, annual planning would be useful.

The business encompasses concrete, transport (local and rural), fuel distribution, and roading. The group has around 1,000 staff members and a consistent profit growth, the envy of many larger organizations.

The growth path has been either to grow from scratch or buy existing family companies. As the CEO says, "Expansion is often driven by opportunity". It has 23 companies as well as a number of joint ventures.

The business has different performance tables depending on the size of operations, so the companies can compare with one another. Each table shows the ranking of the operations within that table with reference to some key ratios. The ratios they monitor include:

Return per km—revenue and cost per km
Margin per liter
Delivery cost per liter
Concrete cost per cubic meter
Cubic meter delivered by pay hour

Monthly reports are short and based on major cost categories (not at detail account code level). They do not waste time showing a consolidated result each month; this is done at year-end only. There is much delegation to the other offices, which manage staff levels within given limits, set staff salaries, and choose which suppliers to use (providing there is not a national contract in place).

 ## MYTHS AROUND ANNUAL PLANNING

There are many reasons why your annual planning in your organization is not working. One main factor is a lack of understanding of the myths surrounding annual planning.

Just like six centuries ago, we are blind to the realities that are there to see on closer observation. We have for centuries blindly applied old thinking to how we measure, monitor, and improve performance.

Myth 1: There Is a Need to Set Annual Targets

It is a myth that we know what good performance will look like before the year starts. Thus, it is a myth that we can set relevant annual targets. In reality, as former CEO of General Electric, Jack Welch says, "It leads to constraining initiative, stifling creative thought processes and promotes mediocrity rather than giant leaps in performance."[4] All forms of annual target are doomed to failure. Far too often, managers spend months arguing about what is a realistic target, when the only sure thing is that it will be wrong. It will be either too soft or too hard.

Jeremy Hope, and his co-author, Robin Fraser, were the first writers to clearly articulate that a fixed annual performance contract was doomed to fail. Far too frequently, organizations end up paying incentives to management when, in fact, they have lost market share. In other words, rising sales did not keep up with the growth rate in the marketplace. As Hope and Fraser point out, not setting an annual target beforehand is not a problem as long as staff members are given regular updates about how they are progressing against their peers and the rest of the market. Hope argues that if you do not know how hard you have to work to get a maximum bonus, you will work as hard as you can.

Just like a high jumper in the Olympics, in order to win, they have to jump the highest. Having a predetermined height set in their minds will only limit their performance.

Myth 2: We Could Set Monthly Targets from the Annual Plan

As accountants we like things to balance and our work to be neat and tidy. Thus, it appeared logical to break the annual plan down into 12 monthly breaks before the year had started. We could have been more flexible. Instead, we created a reporting yardstick that undermined our value to the organization. Every month we make management, all around the organization, write variance analysis that I could do just as well from my office in New Zealand. "It is a timing difference," "We were not expecting this to happen," "The market conditions have changed radically since the plan," and so on.

Myth 3: We Only Need to Forecast out to the Current Year-End

Typically, corporate accountants have reforecast the year-end numbers every month. This is flawed on a number of counts. Firstly, why should one bad month, one good month translate into a change of year-end position. We gain and lose major customers, key products rise and wane; this is the life cycle we have witnessed many times. Secondly, the forecast is a top-top forecast with little input and no buy-in from the budget holders. Thirdly, two months before year-end management appear to ignore the oncoming year. Fourthly management and the Board know whatever number you have told them is wrong. You will change it next month!

Myth 4: Giving Budget Holders an Annual Entitlement to Spend Made Sense

In Chapter 9, I explained the folly of giving budget holders an annual entitlement to funding. Just like the birthday-cake analogy from Chapter 9, we only need to fund them on a quarterly rolling funding regime. Please revisit Chapter 9 if this important point needs further clarification.

Myth 5: We Need to Budget at Account Code Level

What made accountants ever conceive that we needed to set targets at account code level? It was done by our forefathers so we duly followed in the well-trodden steps. It makes no sense.

Having budgets at account code level has encouraged budget holders to allocate expenditure to an account that that has room for it—thus, at a single stroke undermining the purpose of the G/L, which is to account for costs and revenue in the right areas.

Do you need a target or budget at account code level if you have good trend analysis captured in the reporting tool? I think not. We need to apply Pareto's 80/20 rule and establish a category heading, which includes a number of G/L codes.

Myth 6: An Annual Plan Requires Months of Work to Complete

The annual planning process is not adding value. Instead, it is undermining an efficient allocation of resources, encouraging dysfunctional budget holder behavior, negating the value of monthly variance reporting and consuming huge amounts of time from the board, senior management team, budget holders, their assistants and of course the finance team.

When was the last time you were thanked for the annual planning process? At best, you have a situation where budget holders have been antagonized; at worst, budget holders now flatly refuse to cooperate!

Like a laboratory rat, we go down the same pathway each year to find there is no cheese, no passing "Go" and no collecting $200 (Monopoly game), just mayhem. The annual planning process may have worked for Julius Caesar, for back then Caesar could predict success with almost certainty, it has not worked for centuries.

The nightmare of three to four months arguing over resource allocation when nobody knows the answer, the endless cut-back rounds, and the game playing, the spend–it-or-lose-it-mentality is not befitting the twenty-first century.

Myth 7: We Have to Plan Around Calendar Months

Julius Caesar gave us the calendar we use today. It is not a good business tool because it has divided up the year in uneven periods. With the week-days and number of weekend days, in any given month, being different to the next month, it is no wonder forecasting and reporting is unnecessarily compromised.

Even if we are stuck, in the short term with reporting results on calendar months we can and should base our forecasting models around a 4, 4, 5 weeks quarter—that is, there are two four week months and one five week month in a quarter (see Chapter 6). The model would then smooth back the numbers to the correct working days for monthly targets.

Myth 8: The Annual Planning Process Will Be Quicker This Year

Each year I was involved in the annual planning process, I thought I had dis-covered the secret to cut months out of the process. I even had budget holders on my side saying, "Yes, we agree that four months is ridiculous and we will cooperate." As you all know, the next annual plan will be as worse as the last one because once the annual planning process has begun budget holders com-mence their political gesturing. It is just like Pavlov and his dogs.

 QUARTERLY ROLLING FORECASTING AND PLANNING

The quarterly rolling forecasting (QRF) process is where management sets out the required revenue and expenditure for the next 18 months. Each quarter, before approving these estimates, management sees the bigger picture six quarters out. All subsequent forecasts, while firming up the short-term numbers for the next three months, also update the annual forecast. Budget holders are encouraged to spend half the time on getting the details of the next three months right, as these will become targets, on agreement, and the rest of the time on the next five quarters. The quarterly forecast is thus used to:

- Fund budget holders, on a quarterly rolling basis, once their forecast has been approved
- Set the monthly budgets to be used for month-end reporting (set only one quarter ahead)
- Update the annual forecast
- Give a view of the next financial year

Each quarter forecast is never a cold start, as budget holders have reviewed the forthcoming quarter a number of times. With the appropriate forecasting software, management can do their forecasts very quickly; one airline even does this in three days. The recommended elapsed time spent on the four quarterly forecasts during any given year is no more than five weeks.

Exhibit 16.2 shows how the quarterly rolling process works for a June year-end organization. The dark shaded zone is the forecast for the next quarter and the most important part to get right. The light shaded zone is the second quarter. Quarters one and two will be forecast monthly and quarters three to six are forecast in quarterly blocks as less detail is required.

As a guide, budget holders should spend 60 percent of their time on the first quarter because first quarter numbers will become targets, 20 percent on the second quarter and 20 percent on the remaining four quarters.

Most organizations can use the cycle set out in Exhibit 16.2 if their year-end falls on a calendar quarter end. Some organizations may wish to stagger the cycle say May, August, November, and February. An explanation of how each forecast works, using a June year-end organization, follows.

The Process Quarter by Quarter for June Year-End Organization

December update (takes one-week) In the second week of December, budget holders forecast to the end of the year, with monthly numbers, and the remaining period in quarterly breaks. Budget holders obtain approval to spend January-to-March numbers subject to their forecast, still going through the annual plan goalposts. The budget holders, at the same time, forecast next year's numbers for the first time. Budget holders are aware of the expected numbers, and the first cut is reasonably close. This is a precursor to the annual plan. This forecast is stored in the forecasting and reporting tool. This update process should take only one elapsed week.

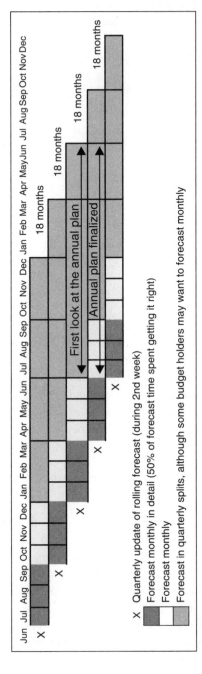

EXHIBIT 16.2 How the rolling forecast works for an organization (June year-end)

March update and annual plan (takes two weeks) In the second week of March, budget holders re-forecast to year-end in monthly numbers and we should be able to eliminate the frantic activity that is normally associated with the spend-it-or-lose-it mentality. They also forecast the first quarter of next year with monthly numbers, and the remaining periods in quarterly breaks. The budget holders at the same time revisit the December forecast (the previous forecast) of next year's numbers and fine-tune them for the annual plan. Budget holders know that they will not be getting an annual lump-sum funding for their annual plan. The number they supply for the annual plan is guidance only.

For the annual plan, budget holders will be forecasting their expense codes using an annual number and in quarterly lots for the significant accounts, such as personnel costs. Management reviews the annual plan for next year and ensures all numbers are broken down into quarterly lots. This is stored in a new field in the forecasting and reporting tool called "March ___ forecast" This is the second look at the next year, so the managers have a better understanding. On an ongoing basis, they would need only a two-week period to complete this process.

June update (takes one week) Budget holders also are now required to forecast the first six months of next year monthly and then on to December in the following year in quarterly numbers. Budget holders obtain approval to spend July-to-September numbers, provided their forecast once again passes through the annual goalposts. This is stored in a new field in the forecasting and reporting tool called "June ___ forecast." This updated process should take only one elapsed week.

September update (takes one week) Budget holders reforecast the next six months in monthly numbers, and quarterly to March 18 months forward. Budget holders obtain approval to spend October-to-December numbers. This is stored in a new field in the forecasting and reporting tool called "September ___ forecast." This updated process should take only one elapsed week.

You will find that the four cycles take about five weeks, once management is fully conversant with the new forecasting system and processes.

THE FOUNDATION STONES OF A ROLLING FORECASTING AND PLANNING PROCESS

In Chapter 9, on lean annual planning processes, I separated out the practices (foundation stones) that you have to adopt to progress forward, from those practices you can choose to adopt or not without adversely affecting the process.

This chapter needs to be read after you have absorbed Chapter 9 as some of the foundation stones are the same and thus are not repeated.

A number of QRF foundation stones need to be laid down and never undermined. You need to ensure the entire construction of the QRF model is undertaken on these foundation stones:

1. Abandoning processes that do not work
2. The QRF model should be built by in-house resources
3. Separation of targets from realistic forecasts (covered in Chapter 9)
4. A quarterly process using the wisdom of the crowd
5. Forecast beyond year-end (e.g., six quarters ahead)
6. The monthly targets are set, a quarter ahead, from the QRF
7. A quarter-by-quarter funding mechanism
8. The annual plan becomes a byproduct of the QRF
9. Forecasting at category level rather than account code level (covered in Chapter 9)
10. The QRF should be based around the key drivers
11. A fast light touch (completed in an elapsed week)
12. Built in a planning tool—not in a spreadsheet (covered in Chapter 4)
13. Design the planning tool with four and five week months
14. Invest in a comprehensive blueprint

Abandoning Processes That Do Not Work

Management guru Peter Drucker who I consider to be the Leonardo de Vinci of management, frequently used the word *abandonment*.[5] I think it is one of the top 10 gifts Drucker gave us all. He said,

"Don't tell me what you're doing, tell me what you've stopped doing."

He frequently said that abandonment is the key to innovation; in other words, the key to fast forecasting process. In planning, many of the processes are carried out, year-in year-out, because they were done last year. When staff question why we do this, the answer is, "There must be a reason."

All the previous givens with regards forecasting must be challenged and all the inefficient processes thrown out. Here is a list, by no means complete, of what needs to be abandoned.

Using Excel. Forecasting in Excel, just because we are good at it.

At account code level. Forecasting in detail, at account code level and to the dollar.

Only forecasting to year-end. Only forecasting to the current year-end as if next year did not exist.

An annual entitlement. Giving budget holders an annual entitlement, they have not got a clue as what the next year is really going to be, nor do we in finance.

Forcing numbers. Forcing the annual plan to be the same number that the board members want to see—we have just lied!

A three-month process. A three-month process when it can be done in two weeks—both will be wrong. You may as well be wrong quickly!

Setting the monthly targets. Setting the monthly targets from the annual plan—since we cannot see into the future, this breakdown of the annual plan has always been a stupid activity.

Written instructions. Annual plan written instructions—nobody reads them, and if they say they have, don't believe them.

Remember the advice of **Steve Jobs**

"Don't be trapped into living with the results of other people's thinking. Don't let the noise of other's opinions drown your own inner voice"

The QRF Model Should Be Built by In-House Resources

The project team must always design the model themselves. You need to use the planning tool consultants more as advisers and trainers and make sure you drive the mouse. The planning tools are relatively simple to use, providing the in-house staff have attended in-depth training.

If the model is built by the consultants, not only will the project cost more money, but you will have the added risk of bringing someone who may not fully understand your business and who will endeavor to build you a better annual planning model—the very thing you need to migrate away from.

The in-house team has a better chance of designing a model that fits your industry and your decision-making processes than an external consultant. Consultants, with the best will in the world, cannot help but design a model based on their prior experiences, which may be adrift of techniques described in this chapter.

In other words, it's just like learning to drive a car—the team will need a series of lessons and hopefully practice first on "quiet country roads" (pilot the model) before they drive on the highway (unleash the model to all budget holders).

Separation of Targets from Realistic Forecasts (Covered in Chapter 9)

Please review Chapter 9 to understand this important foundation stone.

A Quarterly Process Using the Wisdom of the Crowd

A forecasting and planning regime model should be designed with a view to involve budget holders in updates four times a year. The goal is for them to buy into the targets that they will report against and accept the new funding level.

Typically, management reforecasts the year-end numbers on a monthly basis. Why should one bad month, or one good month, translate into a change of the year-end position? We gain and lose major customers, key products rise and wane; this is the life cycle we have witnessed many times. Besides, if you change your forecast each month, it is too costly and the benefits are not worth the effort. Management and the board know whatever number you have told them is wrong—you will change it next month. As shown in Exhibit 16.3, we now have only four reforecasts a year, instead of the 12 updates.

Many forecasts have little input and no buy-in from the budget holders. Companies have, in order to save money, centralized data input within the finance function. I call these forecasts *a top-top forecast*, whereby finance team

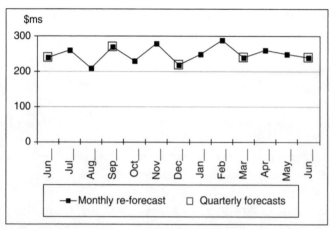

EXHIBIT 16.3 Reducing the number noise by quarterly re-forecasting

members talk amongst themselves and with senior management but believe they do not have time to involve budget holders. Such a centralized approach can slow down the forecasting process, limit the budget holders' buy-in to the planning tool, and not take advantage of collective knowledge of the wisdom of the crowd, as outlined in Chapter 9.

To achieve a bottom-up process, all budget holders should be able to enter their data. Training and adequate support from forecasters are needed, and you should have sufficient licenses to enable budget holders to enter data during the three day window for data entry.

Only businesses that are in a volatile sector would need to forecast monthly (e.g., the airline industry). Even for these organizations, you do not need to get all budget holders to participate in a monthly reforecast. You may be able to limit this extra work to sales and production, with the major all-embracing cycle still being quarterly.

Forecast Beyond Year-End (e.g., Six Quarters Ahead)

As mentioned, it is a myth to believe that you only need to forecast out to year-end. There are various options as to how far forward you go, including:

- Always forecast two years ahead — this is particularly relevant where the business is very seasonal and much activity happens in the last quarter.
- Forecast six quarters ahead.
- Use variations such as four or five quarters ahead.

I advocate the six-quarter-ahead (18-month) rolling forecast regime, as it has some substantial benefits, which include:

- You see the full next year halfway through the current year (e.g., the third-quarter forecast can set the goalposts for next year's annual plan).
- The QRF is consistent each time it is performed, as opposed to organizations that always look ahead for two financial years (the QRFs will vary between 15 to 24 months).
- Your annual plan is never set from a cold start, as you have seen the whole financial year in the previous quarter forecast.

Monthly Targets Are Set, a Quarter Ahead, from the QRF

As mentioned earlier it is a myth that we could set meaningful monthly targets from the annual plan.

We instead should report against more recent targets derived from the quarterly rolling forecasting process. This process will give us the monthly targets for the next quarter. It is important to realize that monthly targets are not set any farther out than the quarter ahead. In fact, information for quarters three, four, five, and six are set only quarterly. In other words, we patiently wait until the relevant quarter is upon us before putting the budget holders' estimates in the reporting tool.

This change has a major impact on reporting. We no longer will be reporting against a monthly budget that was set, in some cases, 15 months before the period being reviewed.

A Quarter-by-Quarter Funding Mechanism

As mentioned, it is a myth that we needed to give budget holders an annual entitlement to spend. The key to a better allocation of resources is to fund budget holders on a rolling quarter-by-quarter basis. In this process, management asks, "Yes, we know you need $1 million and we can fund it, but how much do you need in the next three months?" At first the budget holder will reply, "I need $ this quarter," The management team replies, "How is this? Your last five quarterly expenditures have ranged between $180,000 and $225,000. Pat, you are two team members short, and your recruiting is not yet underway; realistically, you will need only $225,000 tops."

It will come as no surprise that when a budget holder is funded only three months ahead, the funding estimates are much more precise and there is little room or nowhere to hide those slush funds.

This means that the approval process, through the senior management team (SMT), will be quicker as the SMT are approving only the annual number and can adjust the quarter-by-quarter allocations as the conditions and environment dictate.

By funding quarterly, and not yearly, the quarterly rolling forecasting and planning process thus highlights "free funds" that can be reallocated for new projects earlier in the financial year.

The released funds can provide for new initiatives that the budget holder could not have anticipated at the time of the budget round. This will get around the common budget holder dilemma, "We cannot undertake that initiative, although we should, as I did not include it in my budget." In the new regime the budget holder would say, "I will put it in my next update and if funds are available, I am sure I will get the go-ahead." This more flexible environment, as long as it is communicated clearly and frequently to budget holders, will have good buy-in.

The Annual Plan Becomes a Byproduct of the QRF

With quarterly rolling forecasting, one of the quarters also generates the annual plan. The QRF process will allow you to have a quick annual planning process, as:

- Budget holders will become more experienced at forecasting (they are doing it four times a year), and they have already looked at the next year a number of times.
- Politics is taken out of the annual planning cycle, as budget holders realize that they no longer obtain an annual entitlement. There is no use demanding more than you need, as the real funding is sorted out on a quarter-by-quarter basis, where slush funds cannot be hidden.
- The third-quarter forecast firms up both the fourth quarter funding and the annual plan numbers.
- The CEO supports the guillotined process.
- There is no point spending too much time, as the next quarter forecast is a more up-to-date view of the future.

Organizations that have truly adopted the Beyond Budgeting principles also will throw out the annual plan target. Why should one view of year-end be any better than a subsequent, more current view? The March quarter forecast is no longer called the annual plan—it simply is the March quarter forecast. The board will want to monitor the extent of forecast creep, and this can be easily shown in a graph.

Forecasting at Category Level Rather Than at Account Code Level

This was discussed in Chapter 9. Please reread this section, as it is an important foundation stone.

The QRF Should Be Based on the Main Events/Key Drivers

Forecasting needs to be based on the main events / key drivers, and thus the finance team should be able to quickly inform management of the impact should there be a major change with any of these drivers. In-depth interviews with the senior management team (SMT), coupled with some brainstorming, will quickly identify the main drivers, which may include:

- What if we contract in size (e.g., stop production of a major product line, sale of a business)?
- What if we grow through acquisition?
- What if we lose a major customer?
- What if there is a major change to key economic indicators (e.g., interest rates, inflation, and exchange rates)?
- What if a major overseas competitor sets up in our region?
- What are the plant capacity ramifications from gaining a large increase in business (e.g., collapse of a major local competitor)?

If you have second-guessed the likely SMT requests and have designed the model around them, you will have a planning tool that can quickly model the implications of such changes robustly.

American Express found that its forecast has principally based on two drivers—number of active card users and average customer expenditure.

A Fast Light Touch (Completed in an Elapsed Week)

QRFs should be performed within five working days (see Exhibit 16.4), with the one exception, that the fourth quarter forecast, which creates the annual plan (see Exhibit 16.5) will have one extra week for additional negotiations and quality assurance. QRFs can be quick because of these factors:

Reliability. Consolidation is instantaneous with a planning tool.

Pareto's 80/20. The model is based on Pareto's 80/20 and the "keep it simple stupid" (KISS) principle.

Process =>	Prior work		7 working days							
	Forecast pre work	Deliver forecast workshop	1	2	3	4	5	Weekend	6	7
Activities by team =>										
Strategic Planning		Attend				Review to ensure linkage to strategic plan - advise if any discrepancies			Attend	
Senior Management Team (SMT)	Set assumptions		BHs prepare and load their forecast		First look at numbers	Submissions by BHs to management board (for more funding or to justify unrealistic forecast)	Review submissions on an exceptions basis		Hear presentation and give instructions for final changes	
Finance Team	Prepare system, the presentation, overheads, personnel costs, travel standard costs etc	Give presentation to BHs		Help BHs with forecast (extended team)	First look at numbers / Quality assurance (QA) checks	Further QA and prepare presentation			Present forecast presentation	Finish off documentation
Budget Holders (BHs)		Attend	Prepare forecast			Present forecast and business plan where there is a major change			Present to SMT on an exceptions basis	Document and file all calculations

Additional Process-row items across working days: "First look at numbers" (day 3); "Re-run of forecast and give presentation to SMT" (day 6); "Final alterations and finishing off documentation" (day 7).

EXHIBIT 16.4 Seven-day reforecast process outline

14 working days

Process =>	Pre-work			1 2 3	4	5	Weekend	6 7 8	9	10
	Budget prework	Meeting with divisional heads (DHs)	Present budget workshop	Budget holders prepare and load their forecast	First look at numbers	Rework some budgets		Submissions by BHs to budget committee	Completion of final draft budget for board approval	Final alterations and finishing off documentation
Activities by team =>										
Strategic planning		Attend					Review to ensure linkage to plan, and advise on any discrepancies		Attend	
Senior management team (SMT)	Set assumptions	One-to-one with the finance team			First look at numbers			Budget committee review submissions in a "lock-up" session	Hear presentation and give instructions for final changes	
Finance team	Prepare system, the presentation, calculate known costs overheads, personnel costs etc.	One-to-one with DHs	Give presentation to BHs	Help BHs with budget plans (extended team)	Quality assurance	Help BHs		Further quality assurance	Complete preparation and deliver annual plan presentation	Complete documentation
Budget holders (BHs)			Attend	Prepare budget	Alter numbers after feedback	Rework numbers if necessary		Present plan to SMT when called	Attend or see presentation slides later	Document all calculations

EXHIBIT 16.5 Two-week fourth-quarter update that also generates the annual plan

Budget holders can enter numbers directly into the planning tool after training as the model is based around Pareto's 80/20 principle, focusing on the major items, events, drivers, and so on.

Because forecasting is at category level, only 12 to 15 categories are forecast by a budget holder.

You only need monthly data for the first two quarters.

Quarterly repetition. The quarterly repetition aids efficiency.

Prework. Repeat costs can all be standardized for the whole year (e.g., Dublin to London return flight $250, and overnight in London $280).

Extended support. There will be one-to-one support by expanding the budget team.

Exception based approval process. New funding requests or error-prone forecasts require an audience with the Forecast Approval Committee

Jeremy Hope sees no reason why the forecast process could not be done in a day in a financial services organization, where there is no physical supply chain and inventories to manage. For more complex businesses, Jeremy Hope believes that these forecasts can be done in several days.[6]

Built in a Planning Tool—Not in a Spreadsheet

As stated in Chapter 4, which covers the technologies you must have before you upgrade the G/L, I stated that there is no place for a spreadsheet in forecasting, budgeting and in any other core financial routine.

Acquiring a planning tool is the first main step forward, and one that needs to be pursued, not only for the organization's future, but also for the finance team members' future careers.

It has never been a better or easier time to do this. Planning tools are more affordable, many are cloud based, and can work with any general ledger. I consider it unprofessional for qualified staff to be working with spreadsheets over 100 rows. If not convinced, please reread the first section of Chapter 4.

Design the Planning Tool with Four- and Five-Week Months

As discussed in Chapter 6, the calendar we use today is a major hindrance to reporting and forecasting. With the weekdays and number of weekend days, in any given month, being different to the next month it is no wonder forecasting and reporting is unnecessarily compromised.

Forecasting models should be designed with months that consist of four or five weeks (e.g., based on a 4, 4, 5 quarter); that is, two four-week months and one five-week month are in each quarter, regardless of whether the monthly reporting has moved over to this regime. Calculating and forecasting the following items then becomes easier:

- Revenues. For retail, you either have four or five complete weekends (the high revenue days).
- Payroll. You either have four weeks of salary or five weeks of salary.
- Power, telecommunications, and property related costs. These can be automated and be much more accurate than a monthly allocation.
- Monthly targets. You can simply adjust back based on calendar or working days.

In any given year, between three and five months every year will end on a weekend, and finance teams often find that the month-end processes are smoother for these months. Why not close-off on the last or nearest Friday/Saturday of every month, like many US companies do? The benefits of this include precise four- or five-week months, which make comparisons more meaningful, and there is less impact on the working week as the systems are rolled over at the weekend.

Closing off at the weekend can be done for all sectors; some will require more liaison than others. It would also make a big difference in the public and not-for-profit sectors.

You need to choose if it is to be the last Saturday or the nearest Saturday, last Sunday or nearest Sunday to month-end, and so on. The last Saturday can have you closing six days before month-end, whereas the preferred option of nearest Saturday will only be a maximum of two working days out. See Exhibit 16.6 for a table.

Dates for a Friday close (nearest to calendar month-end) *					A/P close	A/R close	FA close	Stock close
	2016		2017					
	No. of week		No. of week					
May	4	Friday, May 27, 2016	4	Friday, May 26, 2017	Noon Fri	5 P.M.	Noon Fri	5 P.M. Fri
June	5	Friday, July 01, 2016	5	Friday, June 30, 2017	"_"	"_"	"_"	"_"
July	4	Friday, July 29, 2016	4	Friday, July 28, 2017	"_"	"_"	"_"	"_"
August	4	Friday, August 26, 2016	4	Friday, August 25, 2017	"_"	"_"	"_"	"_"
September	5	Friday, September 30, 2016	5	Friday, September 29, 2017	"_"	"_"	"_"	"_"

EXHIBIT 16.6 Closing month-end on the same day each month

Invest in a Comprehensive Blueprint

From a recent case study, I have learned how imperative it is to invest time in developing a robust blueprint that sets out the direction and the requirements.

In order to achieve this, you will need a series of lock-up workshops involving senior management, the organization's IT system experts, the staff involved in demand and production planning, the accountants, and a facilitator who has a broad experience in designing successful models in planning tools.

In the Ballance Nutrients Case study featured in Chapter 4, they had six weeks of workshops and this process led to a very successful implementation. So, if you decide to short circuit this process you have been warned.

EFFICIENT FORECASTING AND PLANNING PROCESSES

There are a number of better practices in QRF; some have been covered already in Chapter 9. I will discuss in detail all the new processes.

Linkage to Chapter 9 (A Lean Annual Planning Process)

If you have implemented the practices set out in Chapter 9, you are already part of the way to implementing the better practices for QRF. The following practices need to be adopted and have been covered in Chapter 9:

- Forecast demand by major customers by major products.
- Do required prework.
- Accurately forecast personnel costs.
- Automate the calculation for categories where trend data is the best predictor.
- Provide automated calculations for travel and accommodation.
- Have trend graphs for every category forecasted.
- Expand your team, as budget holders will need one-to-one support.
- Hold a briefing workshop for all budget holders.

Have One-Page Summary for Each Budget Holder

Design a simple one-page summary for the forecast of each budget holder and business. The consolidated summary will also be similar. See Exhibit 16.7 for a summary forecast update, which would be prepared each quarter.

Summary of Forecast Profit & Loss for the period ending _____

* includes estimate for December

$M	9 months to 31/12*	Quarter 1 Jan	Feb	Mar	Quarter 2 Apr	May	Jun	Y/E forecast	Quarter 3 Jul-Sept	Quarter 4 Oct-Dec	Quarter 5 Jan-Mar	Quarter 6 Apr-Jun
INCOME												
Income 1	56.5	6.5	6.5	7.0	6.5	6.0	6.5	76.5	18.5	18.5	18.5	18.0
Income 2	35.2	3.9	4.1	4.3	3.9	3.7	3.9	47.5	11.0	11.2	11.4	11.0
Income 3	22.7	2.5	2.7	2.9	2.5	2.3	2.5	30.8	6.8	7.0	7.2	6.8
Total Revenue	114.4	12.9	13.3	14.2	12.9	12.0	12.9	154.8	36.3	36.7	37.1	35.8
EXPENDITURE												
Cost category 1	35.4	4.6	4.7	4.6	4.8	4.9	4.8	49.3	12.4	14.4	14.6	12.0
Cost category 2	15.9	2.0	2.1	2.2	2.2	2.3	2.4	22.2	6.7	6.6	6.8	7.0
Cost category 3	9.5	1.1	1.2	1.1	1.3	1.4	1.3	12.9	4.0	3.9	4.1	3.6
Cost category 4	5.7	0.6	0.5	0.6	0.8	0.7	0.8	7.4	2.3	1.8	2.0	2.1
Cost category 5	4.3	0.5	0.6	0.5	0.7	0.8	0.7	5.9	2.2	2.1	2.3	1.8
Cost category 6	4.1	0.5	0.4	0.5	0.7	0.6	0.7	5.5	2.0	1.5	1.7	1.8
Other operational costs	8.1	0.9	1.0	0.9	1.1	1.2	1.1	10.9	3.4	3.3	3.5	3.0
Total Expenditure	83.0	10.2	10.5	10.4	11.6	11.9	11.8	114.1	33.0	33.6	35.0	31.3
Management overview								(0.7)				
Net Profit	31.4	2.7	2.8	3.8	1.3	0.1	1.1	40.0	3.3	3.1	2.1	4.5

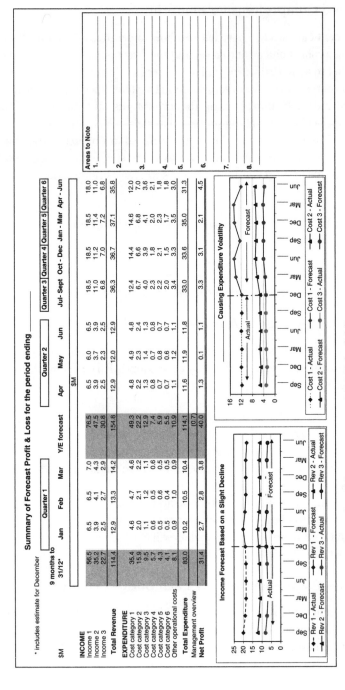

Income Forecast Based on a Slight Decline

— Rev 1 - Actual — Rev 1 - Forecast — Rev 2 - Actual
— Rev 2 - Forecast — Rev 3 - Actual — Rev 3 - Forecast

Causing Expenditure Volatility

— Cost 1 - Actual — Cost 1 - Forecast — Cost 2 - Actual
— Cost 2 - Forecast — Cost 3 - Actual — Cost 3 - Forecast

Areas to Note
1.
2.
3.
4.
5.
6.
7.
8.

EXHIBIT 16.7 Quarterly updated forecast on an A3 (US fanfold) page

Features of the forecast shown in Exhibit 16.7:

Rolling quarterly forecast showing year-end position and the remaining five
quarters of the 18 months forecast. Although Q2 is forecast monthly, it
may be shown as a quarterly number.

The expenditure graph looks at the main three expenditure lines and highlights
where BHs are playing the old game of locking in slack.

The revenue graph highlights the reasonableness of the sales teams' projections.

Also included is a management overview, which rounds the year-end number
to something more realistic.

Recognize that Quarterly Rolling Forecasts Involve All Budget Holders

Most forecasting models built in Excel tend to have restricted consultation
with budget holders and are carried out by staff members at headquarters
who are remote from the workforce. This is done for practical reasons; it would
be a disaster to unleash the Excel model once a quarter, as it takes weeks to
get completed even once a year. These forecasts do not have any buy-in from
budget holders, cannot be used to create meaningful targets for the months in
the next quarter, and are often a skewed view of the future business operations,
simply reiterating the misconceptions that head office management wishes
to believe.

Having all budget holders involved requires an investment in training and
good coordination. The benefits include buy-in to the numbers, a forecast that
more closely resembles reality, and a positive learning curve, as budget holders
get better at a repetitive task.

Quarterly Rolling Forecast Is a Quarterly Process

Only businesses that are in a very dynamic environment would need to forecast
monthly. One has to remember that for every event that goes your way, there
will be another event in the future negating the positive impact (e.g., it is not
worthwhile to change your year-end forecast due to the loss or gain of a large
customer). These changes are better picked up on a quarterly basis; this will
help ensure less oscillation of your year-end numbers.

For those organizations that are in a dynamic environment, you do not
need to get all budget holders to participate in a monthly reforecast; you may

be able to limit this monthly reforecast work to sales and production, with the major reforecast still being quarterly.

IMPLEMENTING A QUARTERLY ROLLING FORECASTING AND PLANNING PROCESS

The foundations stones and accompanying processes for QRF need to be understood, further developed and then implemented. A difficult but not impossible task. I will now outline the key implementation procedures. For further information, see the white paper "How to Implement Quarterly Rolling Forecasting and Quarterly Rolling Planning—and Get It Right First Time" on www.davidparmenter.com.

Overcoming the Implementation Barriers

Before you can make much progress, you need to understand the likely barriers and surmount them all. Exhibit 16.8 is a list, by no means complete, of some suggestions on how to overcome the common barriers accountants face in implementing QRF.

Hold a Focus Group Workshop

As explained in the section "The Power of the Focus Group" in Chapter 2, a focus group needs to be formed as part of the selling change process. We need the oracles in the business units to discuss what the forecasting regime default future looks like and agree that they do not want it. The focus group workshop, as set out in Exhibit 16.9, is important for a number of reasons:

- There are many pitfalls in such a project, and we need to ensure that all likely objections are aired in the focus group workshop.
- We need to reengineer the forecasting process using Post-it notes, as discussed in Chapter 10.
- The foundation stones for rolling forecasting and planning must be understood, agreed on, and put in place early on in the project.
- A green light from the focus group will help sell this concept to the SMT.
- The focus group will give valuable input as to how the implementation should best be done to maximize its impact.

EXHIBIT 16.8 Suggestions for Overcoming Barriers to QRF

Barriers	Suggested Actions
Lack of budget holder skills	▪ Find those staff who thrive with new technology and train them first. ▪ Set up the new forecasting regime in three units, a quarter ahead, to iron out the bugs and to promote the efficiencies. ▪ Train all significant budget holders, including one-to-one training. ▪ Set up from the outset a quarterly follow-up training course (as you should be using the model for forecasting)
Stop and start annual planning syndrome	▪ Big sell to management (historic evidence including costs, better practices, benefits to them). ▪ Get commitment for quick bottom-up forecasts. ▪ Work closely with the executive assistants regarding calendar bookings so SMT and budget holders are all present during the forecasting weeks. ▪ Maintain momentum with daily progress reports, flagging budget holders who are behind with their forecast (show on an intranet page).
Inaccurate and late data	▪ Provide more one-to-one support. ▪ Workshop the forecast process with all major budget holders. ▪ Provide incentives for prompt forecast returns (e.g., movie vouchers). ▪ Provide daily progress report to CEO of the late names. ▪ If still using Excel, have all returns go to the CEO's office first.
Lack of management ownership	▪ Take SMT to some better practice forecasting sites. ▪ Deliver more interesting information from the forecast process (e.g., trend graphs, key performance indicators). ▪ Market better practice stories constantly. ▪ Ensure budget holders are directly involved in the forecasting process (i.e., not delegating tasks).
Lack of faith in the reliability of the forecast	▪ Establish in-depth QA procedures. ▪ Have reliable working papers. ▪ Provide reasonability checks. ▪ Audit the forecast application prior to use. ▪ Migrate away from Excel to a planning tool.
Lack of understanding of the planning tool application	▪ Have forecasting/budget models reviewed and audited prior to use. ▪ More than one person involved in design of the QRF. ▪ Keep to Pareto's 80/20 (e.g., personnel costs should have much more detail). ▪ Key drivers should be easily identifiable.

(continued)

EXHIBIT 16.8 *(Continued)*

Barriers	Suggested Actions
Lack of linkage to strategic decisions	■ Brainstorm with SMT members regarding their likely scenarios. ■ Ensure you can accommodate key drivers in the model design.
Competency of the forecasting team	■ Select for: self-starter, innovator, excellent communicator, finisher, big picture thinker, team player, demonstrated that they are prepared to put long hours in when required. ■ Broad experience of organization. ■ Experience with problem solving, interviewing, process reengineering, forecasting. ■ Appoint an external facilitator to mentor the team.

Post-it Reengineering Forecasting Procedures

If you have not already Post-it reengineered the annual planning process, as discussed in Chapter 9, you will need to do it now; otherwise the four quarterly rolling forecast updates will take you all year.

To understand what is required to Post-it reengineer a process reread Chapter 10. The only difference is:

- The time scale is week −2, week −1 (last week before annual planning), week +1 (first week after year-end), week +2 instead of day −2, day −1, and so on.
- There will be different attendees to the workshop (e.g., forecasting team; budget holders, marketing team, SMT etc.).

Implementation Roadmap

The implementation plan shown in Exhibit 16.10 should help those about to start an implementation. One key feature is the time frame. A rolling forecast implementation is a five-to six-month process, including the acquisition of an appropriate planning tool.

See the PDF toolkit for a checklist on implementing a QRF. This checklist should be treated as an evolving tool and thus be tailored to better suit your needs. Using a checklist will help ensure that while you are juggling the balls, you do not drop the ones that matter.

EXHIBIT 16.9 Draft Agenda for a One-Day Focus Group Workshop

Date and Time: _____

Location: _____

Suggested attendees: Budget committee, selection of business unit heads, all management accountants, and a selection of budget holders involved in forecasting.

Learning Outcomes: Attendees after this workshop will be able to:

- Discuss and explain to management why _____ should adopt QRF.
- Use better practices to streamline current forecasting bottlenecks.
- Describe better practice forecasting and planning routines.
- Recall all agreements made at the workshop.

Prework: Teams to document forecasting procedures on Post-it notes. One procedure per Post-it. Each team to have a different color Post-it notes.

Requirements: event secretary, lap tops x2, data show, whiteboards x2

8:30 a.m.   Welcome by CFO, a summary of progress to date at _____, an outline of the issues and establishing the outcome for the workshop.

8.40   **Setting the scene:** Why smart organizations are not involved in the annual planning cycle—a review of better practices among public- and private-sector organizations. Topics covered include:

- Why annual planning is flawed, and the rise of the Beyond Budgeting movement
- Why quarterly rolling planning can and should work at _____
- Benefits of QRF to the board, SMT, finance team, and budget holders
- Better practice stories
- Current performance gap between _____ and better practice
- Foundation stones of quarterly rolling forecasting and planning
- Some of the foundation stones that are already in place at _____
- Some better practice features within _____'s forecasting process
- How the annual plan drops out of the bottom-up quarterly rolling forecasting regime
- Impact of assigning funds on a quarter-by-quarter basis
- Impact on monthly reporting
- How each subsequent forecast works
- Involvement of SMT in a forecasting process

This session would be attended by a wider audience. After the questions and answers, these people would leave.

(continued)

EXHIBIT 16.9 (*Continued*)

9:40	**Workshop One: Analyzing the Current Pitfalls of _____'s Forecasting.** Separate teams look at the key pitfalls and how they can be overcome.
10:15	Morning break.
10:30	**Workshop Two: Mechanics of Rolling Forecasting.** Workshop where separate teams look at the key components:

- Who should be involved in a bottom-up forecasting process?
- Potential pitfalls
- Reporting needs
- When can it be implemented?
- Training requirements
- What cost categories should be forecast? (higher than the general ledger account code level)
- Project structure

11:00	**Workshop Three: Workshop on "Post-it" Reengineering of the Annual Planning Process.** During the workshop, we analyze the bottlenecks of the forecasting process. In this workshop, we use sticky notes to schedule the steps (e.g., yellow—budget holder activities; red—forecasting team activities; blue—SMT activities during the forecast).
12:15 P.M.	Lunch at venue.
12:45	Feedback from work groups on both workshops and action plan agreed (Document deadline date and who is responsible).
	Individuals will be encouraged to take responsibility for implementing the steps.
1:15	Work groups are assigned to prepare a slide or two on a specified issue. They can also raise any issues they still have.
	The two individuals selected to summarize findings are allowed to roam around the group discussions.
1:45	Each work group presents its slide(s) and discussion held as what to accept or delete.
2:30	Two people are asked to present the initial thoughts of the whole focus group (up to 10 slides) to an invited audience covering the changes that the focus group would like to implement and when.
	Suggested audience: all those who attended the *setting the scene* morning session
3:00	Wrap up of workshop

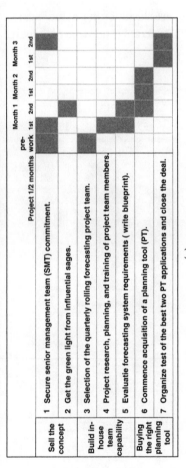

(a)

	pre-work	Month 1 1st	Month 1 2nd	Month 2 1st	Month 2 2nd	Month 3 1st	Month 3 2nd
Sell the concept 1 Secure senior management team (SMT) commitment.	▓						
2 Get the green light from influential sages.		▓					
Build in-house team capability 3 Selection of the quarterly rolling forecasting project team.		▓					
4 Project research, planning, and training of project team members.			▓				
5 Evaluatie forecasting system requirements (write blueprint).				▓			
Buying the right planning tool 6 Commence acquisition of a planning tool (PT).					▓		
7 Organize test of the best two PT applications and close the deal.							▓

(b)

	Month 4 1st	Month 4 2nd	Month 5 1st	Month 5 2nd	Month 6 1st	Month 6 2nd	Month 7 1st	Month 7 2nd	Month 8 1st	Month 8 2nd
Build and test model 8 Train in-house designated experts on the new application.	▓									
9 Build new model based on the blueprint.	▓	▓								
10 Pilot planning tool on three business units.			▓							
11 Roadshow of new rolling forecast process.					▓					
12 Roll out training of planning tool using in-house experts.						▓				
Rollout use 13 Complete quality assurance processes on the forecasting model in the PT.							▓			
14 Commence first quarterly rolling plan run.									▓	
15 Review process and ascertain lessons learnt.										▓

EXHIBIT 16.10 Timeline for implementing a QRF process example

Impact on Reporting

As already mentioned, a major mistake in all annual planning cycles has been the monthly apportionment of the plan. Leading to reporting against a monthly budget that was set, in some cases, over 15 months before the period being reviewed. If you report against more recent targets derived from the quarterly rolling forecasting process, it changes the report layout as shown in Exhibit 16.11.

The report format in Exhibit 16.11 compares last month's actual against the most recent forecast. The year to date (YTD) actual is no longer compared

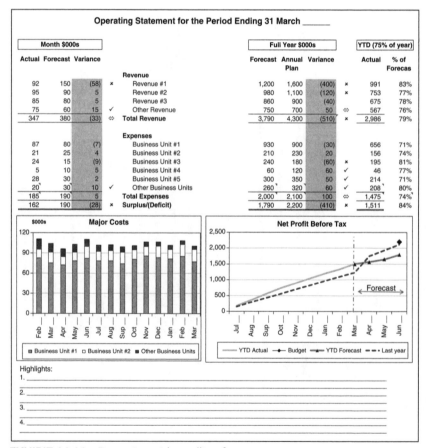

EXHIBIT 16.11 Reporting with a rolling forecast target

against a YTD budget. Instead, YTD progress is evaluated alongside progress against the year-end forecast and the accompanying trend graphs. Trend analysis now becomes much more the focus. The forecast year-end numbers are now more prominent and moved to where the YTD numbers traditionally are placed. Commentary is much more targeted, as there is no place for the explain-it-all-away "timing difference" comment as the forecast is updated quarterly.

PDF DOWNLOAD

To assist the finance team on the journey, templates and checklists have been provided. The reader can access, free of charge, a PDF of the suggested worksheets, checklists and templates from www.davidparmenter.com/The_ Financial_Controller_and_CFO's_Toolkit.

The PDF download for this chapter includes:

- Checklist to evaluate prospective project team members
- Implementing QRF regime checklist
- Performing a quarterly rolling forecast checklist
- The "planner tool supplier" evaluation checklist

NOTES

1. David Parmenter, "How To Implement Quarterly Rolling Forecasting And Quarterly Rolling Planning– And Get It Right First Time," www .davidparmenter.com, 2015.
2. *Rolling Forecasts Enable Accuracy and Agile Business Planning* (Aberdeen Group, 2013).

3. Jeremy Hope and Robin Fraser, *Beyond Budgeting: How Managers Can Break Free from the Annual Performance Trap* (Boston: Harvard Business Press, 2003).
4. Jack Welch and Suzy Welch, *Winning* (New York: HarperCollins, 2009).
5. To understand Peter Drucker's work, read Elizabeth Haas Edersheim, *The definitive Drucker: Challenges For Tomorrow's Executives—Final Advice From the Father of Modern Management* (New York: McGraw-Hill 2006).
6. Jeremy Hope, *Reinventing the CFO: How Financial Managers Can Transform Their Roles and Add Greater Value* (Boston: Harvard Business Press, 2006).

CHAPTER SEVENTEEN

Finding Your Organization's Operational Critical Success Factors

OVERVIEW

Critical success factors (CSFs) are operational issues or aspects that need to be done well day-in, day-out by the staff in the organization. This chapter looks at the alignment between CSFs and strategy. It highlights the importance of CSFs, identifying that this is a missing link in management theory. It is based on the assumption that an organization has typically five to eight CSFs, and that CSFs should be the source of all-important performance measures—the winning KPIs.

Many organizations fail to achieve their potential because they lack clarity regarding the more important things to do. This lack of clarity means that often staff members will schedule their work based around their team's priorities rather than the priorities of the organization,

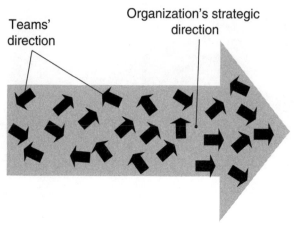

EXHIBIT 17.1 Discord with strategy   David Parmenter, *Key Performance Indicators: Developing, Implementing, and Using Winning KPIs, 3rd Edition,* copyright © 2015 John Wiley & Sons, Inc. Reprinted with permission of John Wiley & Sons, Inc.

that performance measures are often meaningless, and that many reports are prepared that serve no purpose. This chapter is an extract from my white paper, "Finding Your Organization's Critical Success Factors."[1]

As Exhibit 17.1 shows, even though an organization has a strategy, teams often are working in directions very different from the intended course.

This mayhem stems from a complete lack of understanding of their critical success factors (CSFs). While most organizations know their success factors, few organizations have:

- Worded their success factors appropriately
- Segregated out success factors from their strategic objectives
- Sifted through the success factors to find their critical success factors
- Communicated the CSFs to staff

If the CSFs of the organization are clarified and communicated, staff members will be able to align their daily activities closer to the strategic direction of the organization, as shown in Exhibit 17.2.

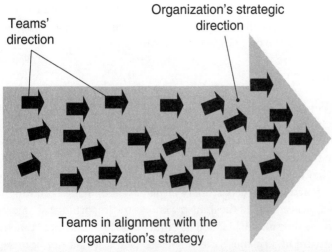

EXHIBIT 17.2   Alignment with strategy David Parmenter, *Key Performance Indicators: Developing, Implementing, and Using Winning KPIs, 3rd Edition*, copyright © 2015 John Wiley & Sons, Inc. Reprinted with permission of John Wiley & Sons, Inc.

BENEFITS OF UNDERSTANDING YOUR ORGANIZATION'S CRITICAL SUCCESS FACTORS

Knowing an organization's CSFs, communicating them to staff so they can better align their activities, and measuring teams' progress with the CSFs is the El Dorado (the goldmine) of management. There are some profound benefits of knowing your CSFs, including:

- It leads to the discovery of an organization's winning key performance indicators (KPIs).
- Measures that do not relate to your CSFs or impact them cannot, by definition, be important, and thus often can be eliminated.
- Staff members know what should be done as a priority, and thus their daily actions now are linked to the organization's strategies.
- The number of reports that are produced throughout the organization is reduced, as many reports will be clearly exposed as not important or irrelevant.

Reporting the progress the organization is making within each CSF gives the board and senior management a much clearer understanding about the current status of the organization's performance.

An Airline CSF

A good CSF story is about Lord John King, who set about turning British Airways around in the 1980s, reportedly by concentrating on one CSF and one KPI within it. Lord King appointed some consultants to investigate and report on the key measures he should concentrate on to turn around the ailing airline. They came back and told Lord King that he needed to focus on one CSF, the "timely arrival and departure of airplanes." I imagine Lord King was not impressed, as everyone in the industry knows the importance of timely planes. However, the consultants pointed out that while he knew that "timely arrival and departure of airplanes" was a success factor, it had not been separated out from all the other success factors, and thus staff members were trying to juggle too many things. The consultants' analysis proved that "timely arrival and departure of airplanes" was different from all the other success factors; it was in fact the most important one, as shown in Exhibit 17.3. With this

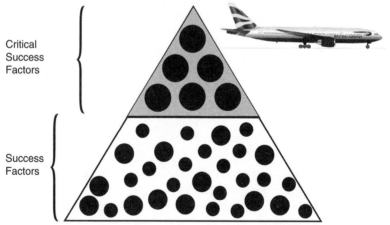

EXHIBIT 17.3 Hierarchy of success factors *Source:* David Parmenter, *Key Performance Indicators: Developing, Implementing, and Using Winning KPIs, 3rd Edition,* copyright © 2015 John Wiley & Sons, Inc. Reprinted with permission of John Wiley & Sons, Inc.

knowledge, it was a relatively short step to find the appropriate measure that would transform the organization. Was it timely planes or late planes? Analysis would have pointed them quickly to selecting late planes over a certain time. This late plane KPI is discussed in more detail in Chapter 18.

RELATIONSHIP AMONG CSFs, STRATEGY, AND KPIs

The relationship between CSFs (also sometimes incorrectly referred to as key result areas) and KPIs is vital, as illustrated in Exhibit 17.4. If you get the CSFs right, it is very easy to find your winning KPIs (e.g., once the "timely arrival and departure of airplanes" was identified as being the top CSF, it was relatively easy to find the KPI—"planes currently over__ hours late").

CSFs identify the issues that determine organizational health and vitality. When you first investigate CSFs, you may come up with 30 or so success factors that are important for the continued health of the organization. The second phase of thinning them down is crucial.

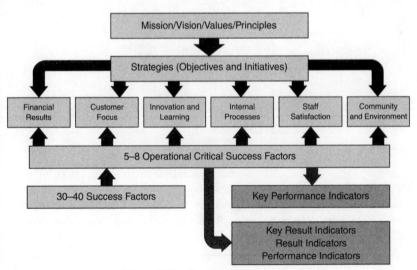

EXHIBIT 17.4 How CSFs and KPIs fit together and link to strategy

I recommend that operational CSFs should be limited to between five and eight, regardless of the organization' s size. However, for a conglomerate, the CSFs will be largely industry specific (e.g., the CSFs for an airline are different from those for a retail record chain store). Thus, there would be a collection of CSFs in the conglomerate greater than the suggested five to eight.

It is important to understand the relationship between CSFs and strategy. An organization's CSFs are impacted by a number of features. Most industries will have one or two generic CSFs (e.g., for the airline industry, "timely arrival and departure of airplanes"). However, each organization has some unique temporary conditions (e.g., a cash flow crisis), some CSFs specific to strategy, and other CSFs relating to normal business conditions (see Exhibit 17.5). The main impact of an organization's CSFs is on its business-as-usual activities. Strategic initiatives, if implemented successfully, will create new business ventures that then become managed through the CSFs (see Exhibit 17.6).

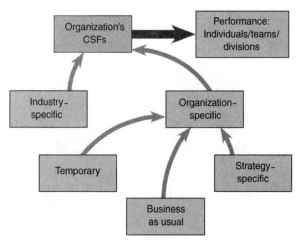

EXHIBIT 17.5 What impacts the CSFs David Parmenter, *Key Performance Indicators: Developing, Implementing, and Using Winning KPIs, 3rd Edition*, copyright © 2015 John Wiley & Sons, Inc. Reprinted with permission of John Wiley & Sons, Inc.

EXHIBIT 17.6 How strategy and the CSFs work together David Parmenter, *Key Performance Indicators: Developing, Implementing, and Using Winning KPIs, 3rd Edition,* copyright © 2015 John Wiley & Sons, Inc. Reprinted with permission of John Wiley & Sons, Inc.

OPERATIONAL CRITICAL SUCCESS FACTORS VERSUS EXTERNAL OUTCOMES

Recently, I have realized the importance of distinguishing between operational critical success factors and external outcomes. A member of the board of a charity rightly pointed out that the CSFs tabled (the operational CSFs) were too internally focused. They wanted to see, understandably, the external picture: the external outcomes. The board was naturally looking from the "outside-in" perspective. The board wanted to see the CSFs expressed as the outcomes and impacts they want to see. We want the organization to "deliver this," "deliver that," which will provide the evidence that there has been a successful implementation of the organization's strategy.

This recent clarification has fixed an issue I have noted in a number of in-house workshops I have run, where there was a mix of operational CSFs and externally focused outcomes. This distinction is important, and, while at first an added complication, it is worth the effort to understand and execute.

Stephen Covey pointed out in *First Things First*[2] the importance of understanding the order of things in achieving results. He talked about putting "rocks" in first every day. We can liken the operational CSFs to the rocks that the staff needs to attend to every day.

A philosophy professor is lecturing to his students. He brings out an empty jar and golf balls. Filling the jar with the golf balls, he asks if it is full. "Yes," they reply. Then he lifts a container of dried peas and pours them in. "Is it full?" "Yes," they reply. Then he lifts a container of sand and pours it in around the golf balls and peas. "Is it full?" "Yes, definitely," they reply. Then he pours in a cup of coffee. He explained, "Golf balls are the important things in your life—you must put them into your life first; otherwise, you can't fit them in. Dried peas are the next most important things. Next is sand—emails, meetings, daily chores." "So why the coffee?" a student asks. "To remind you to always have the time for a coffee with your friends, colleagues, or clients," the professor replied.

The CSFs are the rocks and should be priority, everyday, throughout the organization. Their role is to set direction to operational staff who meet current demand, current production, and, critically, deliver products and services on time. The critical success factor "delivery in full on time to key customers" is a mantra for staff meaning that major orders for our key customers, and often the difficult and complex orders, need to be tackled first. If left to handling deliveries as they saw fit, many staff would tackle the easy orders, putting the easy runs on the board and thus jeopardizing service to our most profitable customers.

External Outcomes Are Driven from the Organization's Strategy

External outcomes are driven from the organization's strategy and are the priority of a select few in senior management, such as the external outcome "developing and growing the new product __ (or market __)." This outcome is a result of many different activities happening, from secret alliance agreements being successfully signed to new operational capacity being organized in a new country. A new plant in a new country will, once operational, be guided by the operational CSFs already in existence elsewhere in the organization. To help further clarify, I have separated out the characteristics of external and operational critical success factors in Exhibit 17.7.

EXHIBIT 17.7 Characteristics of Operational Critical Success Factors and External Outcomes

Operational Vs Outcomes	Source for These Success Factors	Key Characteristics
Operational critical success factors— between five and eight	Can be found from discussions with the senior management team and the oracles residing in operations. Also will appear in strategic plans, induction training materials, and annual reports.	▪ 24/7 daily focus ▪ Involve most staff in operations. ▪ Also of concern to support staff. ▪ Need to be described as what staff should do. ▪ Describe an action or specific activities staff can focus on.
External outcomes —fewer than ten.	Often found in strategic plans. Also, gathered from discussions with directors and the strategy team.	▪ Success is a result of the operational CSFs—e.g., the outcome "retention of key customer" is a result getting daily activity such as the "delivery in full and on time to key customers." ▪ Involve senior staff often in negotiations. ▪ Need to be described as what success looks like. ▪ Describe an external result such as growth in a new market, an increased service level, etc.

I suggest that you will know when you have achieved some consensus of the CSFs when you have some sort of pictorial representation on office walls illustrating to staff what is important. If you cannot meaningfully explain what the staff need to do well day-in, day-out, you do not have a complete list of your organization's operational CSFs.

Operational Critical Success Factors—The Missing Link

I believe the main purpose of performance measures is to ensure that staff members spend their working hours focused primarily on the organization's critical success factors. You could be in your tenth year with a balanced scorecard and still not know your organization's critical success factors. It is like going to soccer's World Cup without a goalkeeper or, at best, an incompetent one. The term *critical success factors* does not appear to be addressed by some of the leading writers of the past 30 years. Peter Drucker, Jim Collins, Gary Hamel, Tom Peters, Robert Kaplan, and David Norton all appear to ignore the existence of critical success factors.

I argue that unless the operational CSFs are ascertained, managers, in their own empire, will have what is important to them embedded in the way things are done. Many counterproductive activities will occur based on this false premise. That is, what is important to me is important to the organization. For a chief executive officer to steer the ship, everybody needs to know the journey. The employees need to know what makes the ship sail well and what needs to be done in difficult weather. It can come as no surprise when I say that the term *critical success factors* could be a major missing link in the balanced-scorecard and other methodologies.

 ## FINDING YOUR ORGANIZATION'S CSFs

To help organizations around the world find their CSFs, I have developed a four-task process. This process is covered in Chapter 11 of my book *Key Performance Indicators, 3rd Edition.*[3] This chapter is part of the electronic media available to you in the PDF download. Other materials available are webcasts and a white paper on the topic,[4] which can be accessed at www .davidparmenter.com.

 ## PDF DOWNLOAD

To assist the finance team on the journey, templates and checklists have been provided. The reader can access, free of charge, a PDF of the suggested worksheets, checklists and templates from www.davidparmenter.com/The_Financial_Controller_and_CFO's_Toolkit.

The PDF download for this chapter includes:

- A copy of Chapter 11 from *Key Performance Indicators: Developing, Implementing, and Using Winning KPIs*, 3rd ed. (Hoboken, NJ: John Wiley & Sons, 2015).
- Common operational success factors

 ## NOTES

1. David Parmenter, *Finding Your Organization's Critical Success Factors*, www.davidparmenter.com, 2015.
2. Stephen Covey, A. Roger Merrill, and Rebecca R. Merrill, *First Things First: To Live, to Love, to Learn, to Leave a Legacy* (New York: Simon & Schuster, 1994).
3. David Parmenter, *Key Performance Indicators: Developing, Implementing, and Using Winning KPIs*, 3rd ed. (Hoboken, NJ: John Wiley & Sons, 2015).
4. David Parmenter, *Finding Your Organization's Critical Success Factors*, www.davidparmenter.com, 2015.

CHAPTER EIGHTEEN

Getting Your KPIs to Work

OVERVIEW

Many companies are working with the wrong measures, many of which are incorrectly termed key performance indicators (KPIs). It is a myth to consider all performance measures to be KPIs. This chapter explores how the four types of performance measures differ, with examples of each type. The seven characteristics of KPIs are defined. The confusion over whether measures are lead or lag indicators is addressed. The questions *How many measures should we have?* and How *many of each measure type?* are answered. The importance of timely measurement is also covered.

Performance measurement is failing organizations worldwide, whether they are multinationals, government departments, or not-for-profit agencies. Measures are often a random collection prepared with little expertise, signifying nothing. KPIs should be measures that link daily activities to the organization's critical success factors (CSFs), thereby supporting an alignment of effort within the organization, in the intended direction.

I see this alignment as one of the major goals of management. However, poorly defined KPIs can cost the organization dearly. Some examples are: measures gamed to benefit executives' pay, to the detriment of the organization; teams encouraged to perform tasks that are contrary to the organization's strategic direction; costly measurement and reporting regimes that lock up valuable employee time; and a six-figure balanced scorecard consultancy assignment resulting in a dysfunctional balanced scorecard.

KPI RESEARCH

A poll conducted during my webcasts came up with the following results, as shown in Exhibits 18.1 and 18.2. There is a move to limit the number of KPIs with just over 70 percent saying they have less than 20 KPIs, and to report them promptly with 45 percent reporting KPIs 24/7, daily or weekly. These trends are highly desirable as I will explain in this chapter.

THE MYTHS OF PERFORMANCE MEASURES

KPIs and balanced scorecards are also failing because management is not aware of the many myths surrounding performance measures and the balanced scorecard. Just like six centuries ago, when many thought the world

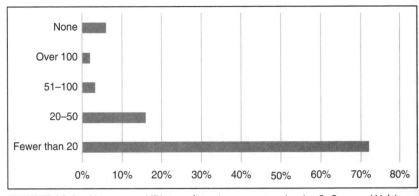

EXHIBIT 18.1 How many KPIs are there in your organization? *Source:* Webinars conducted by David Parmenter with feedback from approximately 300 attendees

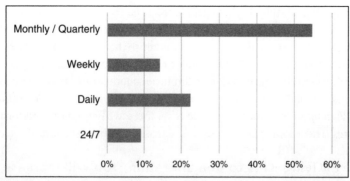

EXHIBIT 18.2 What is the most common time frame KPIs are reported within? *Source:* Webinars conducted by David Parmenter with feedback from approximately 300 attendees

was flat, mankind was blind to the realities that are there to see on closer observation. We are blindly applying old thinking on how we measure, monitor, and improve performance. Let us now look at some myths surrounding performance measures which I feature in my KPI book.[1]

Myth: Most Measures Lead to Better Performance

Every performance measure can have a dark side—a negative consequence or unintended action that leads to inferior performance. Well over half the measures in an organization may be encouraging unintended negative behavior. KPIs are like the moon; they have a dark side. It is imperative that before a measure is used, the measure is:

- Discussed with the relevant staff: "If we measure this, what will you do?"
- Piloted before it is rolled out.
- Abandoned if its dark side creates too much adverse performance. I expand on this dark side in the section on Unintended Consequences.

Myth: All Performance Measures Are KPIs

Throughout the world, organizations have been using the term *KPIs* to refer to all performance measures. No one seemed to worry that they have not agreed on a common definition of what a KPI actually is. Thus, measures that were key to the enterprise were being mixed with measures that were badly flawed.

Let's break the term down. *Key* means key to the organization. *Performance* means that the measure will assist in improving performance.

From research I have performed in diverse industries and as a byproduct of writing my book, *Key Performance Indicators—Developing, Implementing and Using Winning KPIs,*[2] I have concluded that there are four types of performance measures. These four types are discussed in a subsequent section.

Myth: By Tying KPIs to Remuneration, You Will Increase Performance

It is a myth that the primary driver for staff is money, and that an organization must provide financial incentives to achieve great performance. Recognition, respect, and self-actualization are more important drivers. In all types of organizations, there is a tendency to believe that the way to make KPIs work is to tie them to an individual's pay. But when KPIs are linked to pay, they can create key political indicators (not key performance indicators), which often leads to a manipulation of the measures to enhance the probability of a larger bonus.

KPIs should be used to align staff to the organization's critical success factors and show how teams are performing 24/7, daily or weekly. They are too important to allow them to be manipulated by individuals and teams to maximize bonuses. KPIs are so important to an organization that performance in this area is a given, or as Jack Welch says, "a ticket to the game."

Myth: Measuring Performance Is Relatively Simple and the Appropriate Measures Are Obvious

There will not be a reader of this book who has not, at some time in the past, been asked to come up with some measures with little or no guidance. Performance measurement has been an orphan of business theory and practice. While writers such as W. Edwards Deming, Wheatley and Kellner-Rogers, Gary Hamel, Jeremy Hope, and Dean Spitzer have been pointing out the dysfunctional nature of performance measurement for some time, it has not yet permutated into business practice.

Performance measurement is worthy of more intellectual rigor, in every organization, on the journey from average to good and then to great performance.

Myth: KPIs Are Financial and Nonfinancial Indicators

I firmly believe that there is not a financial KPI on this planet. Financial measures are a quantification of an activity that has taken place, and we have simply placed a value on the activity. Thus, behind every financial measure is an activity. I call financial measures *result indicators:* a summary measure. It is the activity that you will want more or less of. It is the activity that drives the dollars, pounds, and yen. Thus financial measures cannot possibly be KPIs.

Financial measures will always be used to measure the performance of a group of teams working together. However, they will never pinpoint the problem, or what went well, as they are a result indicator. When you have a pound or dollar sign in a measure, you can always dig deeper for the drivers of performance, the activities you want more or less of. Sales made yesterday will be a result of sales calls made previously to existing and prospective customers, advertising campaigns, product quality and reliability, amount of contact with the key customers, and so on. I group all sales indicators expressed in monetary terms as result indicators.

Myth: There Are Only Four Balanced Scorecard Perspectives

For over 20 years, the four perspectives listed in Kaplan and Norton's original work[3] (Financial, Customer, Internal Process, and Learning and Growth) have been consistently reiterated by them and their followers. I recommend that these four perspectives be increased by two more perspectives, and that the learning and growth perspective be reworded as "innovation and learning" (see Exhibit 18.3).

Myth: Indicators Are Either Lead (Performance Driver) or Lag (Outcome) Indicators

Regardless of where the lead/lag indicator labels came from, they have caused a lot of problems and are fundamentally flawed. Many management books that cover KPIs talk about lead and lag indicators; this merely clouds the KPI debate.

I believe we need to dispense with the terms *lag* (outcome) and *lead* (performance driver) indicators. At my seminars, when the audience is asked "Is the late-planes-in-the-air KPI a lead indicator or a lag indicator?" the vote count is always evenly split. The late plane in the sky is certainly both a lead and a lag indicator. It talks about the past, and it is about to create a future

FINANCIAL RESULTS Asset utilization, sales growth, risk management, optimization of working capital, cost reduction	CUSTOMER FOCUS Increase customer satisfaction, targeting customers who generate the most profit, getting close to noncustomers	ENVIRONMENT AND COMMUNITY Employer of first choice, linking with future employees, community leadership, collaboration
INTERNAL PROCESS Delivery in full on time, optimizing technology, effective relationships with key stakeholders	STAFF SATISFACTION Right people on the bus, empowerment, retention of key staff, candor, leadership, recognition	INNOVATION AND LEARNING Innovation, abandonment, increasing expertise and adaptability, learning environment

EXHIBIT 18.3 Suggested six perspectives of a balanced scorecard   *Source:* David Parmenter, *Key Performance Indicators: Developing, Implementing, and Using Winning KPIs, 3rd Edition,* copyright © 2015 John Wiley & Sons, Inc. Reprinted with permission of John Wiley & Sons, Inc.

problem when it lands. Surely this is enough proof that lead and lag labels are not a useful way of defining KPIs and should be counted among the myths of performance measurement.

Key result indicators replace outcome measures, which typically look at past activity over months or quarters. PIs and KPIs are now characterized as past, current, or future measures (see Exhibit 18.4).

Past measures are those that look at historic events—activity that took place last week, last month, last quarter, and so on. PIs and KPIs are now characterized as past-, current-, or future-focused measures. Current measures refer to those monitored 24/7 or daily (e.g., late/incomplete deliveries to key customers made yesterday). Future measures are the record of an agreed future commitment when an action is to take place (e.g., date of next meeting with key customer, date of next product launch, date of next social interaction with key customers). In your organization, you will find that your KPIs are either current- or future-oriented measures (see Exhibit 18.4).

KPIs are current- or future-oriented measures as opposed to past measures (e.g., number of key customer visits planned in the next month or a list by key customer of the dates of the next planned visits).

Most organizational measures are very much past indicators measuring events of the last month or quarter. These indicators cannot be and never were KPIs.

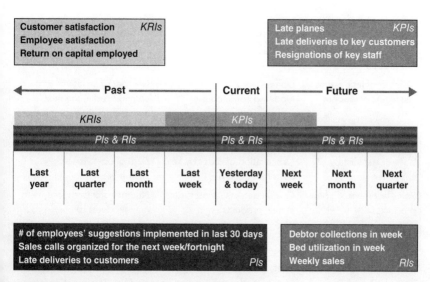

EXHIBIT 18.4 The four measures and their time zones

In workshops, I ask participants to write a couple of their major past measures in the worksheet shown in Exhibit 18.5 and then restate the measures as current and future measures. Try this exercise among a group of employees in your organization. Ask them to please take five minutes to restate three measures used in the organization.

The lead/lag division did not focus adequately enough on current or future-oriented measures. Most organizations that want to create alignment and change behavior need to be monitoring what corrective action is to take place in the future.

Monitoring the activity taken now about the organizing of future actions to occur will help focus staff on what is expected of them. Future measures are often the fence at the top of the cliff. They are in place so we do not have to report inferior performance (the body at the bottom of the cliff). In other words, future measures help make the right future happen. Here, in Exhibit 18.6, are some common future measures that will work in most organizations.

All these future measures would be reported in a weekly update given to the CEO. Although CEOs may let a couple of weeks pass with gaps appearing on these updates, they will soon start asking questions. Management would take action, prior to the next meeting, to start filling in the gaps to ensure they avoided further uncomfortable questioning. The differences in the four

Past measures	Current measures	Future measures
(Last week/fortnight/ month/quarter)	(24/7 and daily)	(Next day/week/month/ quarter)
Number of late planes last week/last month	planes over 2 hours late (updated continuously)	Number of initiatives to be commenced in the next month, months two and three to target areas which are causing late planes
Date of last visit by key customer	Cancellation of order by key customer (today)	Date of next visit to key customer
Sales last month in new products	Quality defects found today in new products	Number of improvements to new products to be implemented in next month, months two and three

EXHIBIT 18.5   Past, current, or future measures to replace lead/lag indicators
Source: David Parmenter, *Key Performance Indicators: Developing, Implementing, and Using Winning KPIs, 3rd Edition,* copyright © 2015 John Wiley & Sons, Inc. Reprinted with permission of John Wiley & Sons, Inc.

Future innovations	To be an innovative organization we need to measure the number of initiatives which are about to come online in the next week, two weeks, and month.
Future sales meetings	To increase sales we need to know the number of sales meetings which have already been organized/scheduled with our key customers in the next week, two weeks, and month.
Future key customer events	To maintain a close relationship with our key customers a list should be prepared with the next agreed social interaction (e.g., date agreed to attend a sports event, a meal, the opera, etc.).
Future PR events	To maintain the profile of our CEO we need to monitor the public relations events that have been organized in the next one to three, four to six, seven to nine months.
Future recognitions	To maintain staff recognition the CEO needs to monitor the formal recognitions planned next week/next two weeks by the CEO and SMT.
Key dates	Date of next product launch, date for signing key agreements.

EXHIBIT 18.6   Examples of future measures   *Source:* David Parmenter, *Key Performance Indicators: Developing, Implementing, and Using Winning KPIs, 3rd Edition,* copyright © 2015 John Wiley & Sons, Inc. Reprinted with permission of John Wiley & Sons, Inc.

measures and the past, current, and future time periods are further explained in Exhibit 18.4. KRIs are summaries of past performance, principally monthly trend analysis over 18 months. KPIs focus on activity in the past week, yesterday, and today, and that planned for the next week and the next two weeks. PIs and RIs will be heavily weighted to the past; however, we do need at least 20 percent of measures to be current- or future-focused.

They assume that a measure is either about the past or about the future. They ignore the fact that some measures, particularly KPIs, are about both the past and the future. I recommend that we dispense with the terms *lead* (performance driver) and *lag* (outcome) indicators. We should see measures as either past, current, or future. Current measures refer to those monitored 24/7 or daily. I also include yesterday's activities, as the data may not be available any earlier (e.g., late/incomplete deliveries to key customers made yesterday).

Future measures are the record of a future commitment when an action is to take place (e.g., date of next meeting with key customer, date of next product launch, date of next social interaction with key customers). In your own organization, you will find that your KPIs are either current- or future-oriented measures.

Myth: Measures Are Cascaded Down the Organization

This was probably the most damaging process used in the balanced scorecard approach. It assumed that by analyzing a measure such as "return on capital employed" you could break it down into myriad measures relevant to each team or division. It also assumed that each and every team leader, with minimal effort, would arrive at relevant performance measures. Kaplan and Norton ignored the crucial facts that team leaders and the senior management team need to know about the organization's critical success factors and the potential for the performance measure to have a "dark side," an unintended consequence.

I believe all measures are sourced from the organization's critical success factors and that it is better to find measures, from the ground up, at the team level within the operation, level 4 in Exhibit 18.7.

Other myths (discussed in my KPI book[4]) include:

- All measures can work successfully in any organization at any time.
- We can set relevant year-end targets.
- You can delegate a performance management project to a consulting firm.
- The balanced scorecard can report progress to both management and the board.

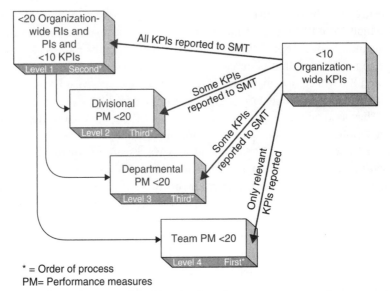

* = Order of process
PM= Performance measures

EXHIBIT 18.7 The interrelated levels of performance measures in an organization *Source:* David Parmenter, *Key Performance Indicators: Developing, Implementing, and Using Winning KPIs, 3rd Edition,* copyright © 2015 John Wiley & Sons, Inc. Reprinted with permission of John Wiley & Sons, Inc.

- Measures fit neatly into one balanced scorecard perspective.
- Strategy mapping is a vital requirement.
- Performance measures are mainly used to help manage implementation of strategic initiatives.

Unintended Consequences—The Dark Side of Performance Measures

Every performance measure has a dark side, an unintended negative consequence. The importance of understanding this dark side and the careful selection of measures should never be underestimated. Well over half the measures in an organization may be encouraging unintended behavior. The frequency with which performance measures are set to fail, is at best, naïve or, at worst, corrupt management. As Dean Spitzer says, "People will do what management inspects, not necessarily what management expects."[5] How performance measures can go wrong can be illustrated by two examples.

LATE TRAIN MEASURE BACKFIRES

A classic example is provided by a city train service that had an on-time measure with some draconian penalties targeted at the train drivers. The drivers who were behind schedule learned simply to stop at the top end of each station, triggering the green light at the other end of the platform, and then continue the journey without the delay of letting passengers on or off. After a few stations, a driver was back on time, but the customers, both on the train and on the platform, were not so happy.

Management needed to realize that late trains are not caused by train drivers, just as late planes are not caused by pilots. The only way these skilled people would cause a problem would be either arriving late for work or taking an extended lunch when they are meant to be on duty.

Lesson: Management should have been focusing on the controllable events that led to late trains, such as the timeliness of investigating signal faults reported by drivers or preventive maintenance on critical equipment that is running behind schedule.

TIMELINESS OF TREATMENT MEASURE FAILS IN ACCIDENT AND EMERGENCY DEPARTMENT

Managers at a hospital in the United Kingdom were concerned about the time it was taking to treat patients in the accident and emergency department. They decided to measure the time from patient registration to being seen by a house doctor. Staff realized that they could not stop patients registering with minor sports injuries but they could delay the registration of patients in ambulances as they were receiving good care from the paramedics.

The nursing staff thus began asking the paramedics to leave their patients in the ambulance until a house doctor was ready to see them, thus improving the "average" time it took to treat patients. Each day there would be a parking lot full of ambulances, with some even circling the hospital awaiting a parking spot.

Lesson: Management should have been focusing on the timeliness of treatment of critical patients. Thus, they only needed to measure the time from registration to consultation for these critical patients. Nurses would have treated patients in ambulances as a priority, the very thing they were doing before the measures came into being.

There needs to be a new approach to measurement—one that is done by trained staff, an approach that is consultative, promotes partnership between staff and management, and finally achieves alignment with the organization's critical success factors and strategic direction.

Dean Spitzer, an expert on performance measurement, has suggested the appointment of a chief measurement officer who would be part psychologist, part trainer, part change agent, and part project manager. The chief measurement officer would be responsible for setting all performance measures, assessing the potential dark side of a given measure, abandoning broken measures, and leading all balanced scorecard initiatives. I have included more information about this role in the attached PDF material to this chapter.

THE FOUR TYPES OF PERFORMANCE MEASURES

Over the last 25 years, I have come to the conclusion that there are four types of performance measures, which fall into two groups, as shown in Exhibit 18.8.

Key Result Indicators

The common characteristic of key result indicators (KRIs) is that they are the result of many actions. They give a clear picture of whether your organization is traveling in the right direction and at the right speed. They provide the board or

EXHIBIT 18.8   Four Types of Performance Measures

Two Groups of Measures	Two Types of Measures in Each Group
Result indicators reflect the fact that many measures are a summation of more than one team's input. These measures are useful in looking at the combined teamwork but do not help management fix a problem, as it is difficult to pinpoint which teams were responsible for the performance or nonperformance.	Result indicators (RIs) Key result indicators (KRIs)
Performance indicators are measures that can be tied to a team or a cluster of teams working closely together for a common purpose. Good or bad performance is now the responsibility of one team. These measures thus give clarity and ownership.	Performance indicators (PIs) Key performance indicators (KPIs)

governing body with a good overview of progress on the organization's strategy. These measures are easy to ascertain and are frequently reported already to the board or governing body.

The fact that key result indicators are called KPIs creates a problem that many organizations do not appreciate. They cannot understand why performance ebbs and flows and appears to be outside the control of the senior management team. Key result indicators that are reviewed typically on monthly or quarterly cycles will only tell you whether the horse has bolted and are thus of little use to management, as they are reported too late to change direction or shut the gate, so to speak. Nor do they tell you what you need to do to improve these results.

KRI measures that have often been mistaken for KPIs include:

- Customer satisfaction
- Employee satisfaction
- Return on capital employed

Separating KRIs from other measures has a profound impact on the way performance is reported. There is now a separation of performance measures into those impacting governance (up to 10 KRIs in a board dashboard, as shown in Chapter 8) and those RIs, PIs, and KPIs impacting management. Accordingly, an organization should have a governance report (ideally in dashboard format) consisting of up to 10 KRIs for the board, and a series of management progress reports at various intervals during the month, depending on the significance of the measure.

Result Indicators

The result indicators (RIs) summarize the activity of more than one team and they provide an overview of how teams are working together. The difference between a key result indicator and a result indicator is simply that the key result indicator is a more overall and more important summary of activities that have taken place.

As already mentioned, financial indicators are a result indicator as they are a result of activities often undertaken by a number of different teams. Financial indicators are useful, but they can mask the real drivers of the performance. To fully understand what to increase or decrease, we need to look at the activities that created the financial indicator.

Result indicators (RIs) could include:

- Number of employees' suggestions implemented in past 30 days
- Sales made yesterday
- Hotel bed utilization in a week

Performance Indicators

Performance indicators (PIs) are those indicators that are nonfinancial (otherwise they would be result indicators) that can be traced back to a team or teams working closely together, who share the same measures. The difference between performance indicators and KPIs is that the latter are deemed fundamental to the organization's well-being. Performance indicators, though important, are thus not crucial to the business. Performance indicators help teams align themselves with their organization's strategy. Performance indicators complement the KPIs; they are shown on the organization, division, department, and team scorecards.

Performance indicators (PIs) could include:

- Abandonment rate at call center (caller gives up waiting)
- Late deliveries
- Sales calls organized for the next week, two weeks, and so forth

Key Performance Indicators

What are KPIs? KPIs represent a set of measures focusing on those aspects of organizational performance that are the most critical for the current and future success of the organization. KPIs are rarely new to the organization. Either they have not been recognized or they were gathering dust somewhere.

HOW AN AIRLINE WAS TURNED AROUND BY ONE KPI

Let's return to the KPI story I introduced in Chapter 17 about a senior official who set about turning around British Airways (BA) in the 1980s, reportedly by concentrating on just one KPI.

The senior BA official employed some consultants to investigate and report on the key measures he should concentrate on to turn around the ailing airline. They came back and told the senior BA official that he needed to focus on one critical success factor (CSF), the timely arrival and departure of airplanes. The consultants must have gone through a sifting process sorting out the success factors which were critical from those that were less important. Ascertaining the five to eight CSFs is a vital step in any KPI exercise, and one seldom performed. In Exhibit 18.9, the CSFs are shown as the larger circles in the diagram.

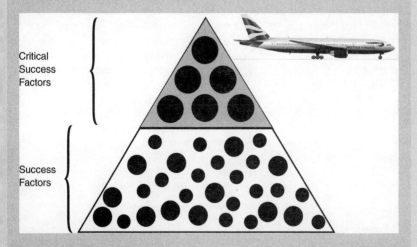

EXHIBIT 18.9   The importance of knowing your critical success factors
Source: David Parmenter, *Key Performance Indicators: Developing, Implementing, and Using Winning KPIs, 3rd Edition,* copyright © 2015 John Wiley & Sons, Inc. Reprinted with permission of John Wiley & Sons, Inc.

The senior BA official was not impressed, as everybody in the industry knows the importance of timely planes. However, the consultants then pointed out that this is where the KPIs lay and they proposed that he focus on a late plane KPI. He was notified, wherever he was in the world, if a BA plane was delayed over a certain time. The BA airport manager at the relevant airport knew that if a plane was delayed beyond a certain threshold, they would receive a personal phone call from the senior BA official (let's call him Sam). I imagine the conversation going like this:

"Pat, it's Sam. I am calling about BA135 that left Kennedy Airport over two and a quarter hours late. What happened?"

Pat replies, "The system will tell you that the plane was late leaving Hawaii. In fact it was one and three quarters hours late, and everything

(continued)

(continued)

was in order at our end except we lost an elderly passenger in duty-free shopping. We had to offload his bags and, as you can see, we did it in record time, only half an hour!"

"Pat, how long have you worked for British Airways?"

Pat, realizing this conversation was not going well, responded, "About 30 years, Sam."

"In fact, Pat, it is 32. In 32 years of experience with us, you are telling me that with six hours of advance notice the plane was already late, you and your team could do nothing to bring it forward, and instead you added half an hour. Quite frankly, Pat, I am disappointed, as you and your team are better than this!"

Pat and many others employed by the airline had the "not invented by us" syndrome. A late plane created by another BA team was their problem, not ours. Pat gathered the troops the next day and undertook many proactive steps to ensure they recaptured the lost time, no matter who had created the problem. Actions such as:

■ Doubling up the cleaning crew, even though there was an additional external cost to this.
■ Communicating to the refueling team which planes were a priority.
■ Providing the external caterers with late-plane updates so they could better manage re-equipping the late plane.
■ Staff on the check-in counters asked to watch for at-risk customers and chaperone them to the gate.
■ Not allowing business-class passengers to check in late, yet again, this time saying, "Sorry, Mr. Carruthers, we will need to reschedule you, as you are too late to risk your bags missing this plane. It is on a tight schedule. I am sure you are aware that the deadline for boarding passed over 30 minutes ago."

The late-planes KPI worked because it was linked to most of the critical success factors for the airline. It linked to the "delivery in full and on time" critical success factor, namely the "timely arrival and departure of airplanes," it linked to the "increase repeat business from key customers" critical success factor, and so on.

It is interesting that Ryanair, an Irish low-cost airline, has a sole focus on timeliness of planes. Ryanair knows that this is where it makes money, often getting an extra European flight each day out of a plane due to their swift turnaround and their uncompromising stand against late check-in. They simply do not allow customers to get in the way of their tight schedules.

The late-planes KPI affected many aspects of the business. Late planes:

- Increased costs, including additional airport surcharges and the cost of accommodating passengers overnight as a result of planes having a delayed departure due to late-night noise restrictions.
- Increased *customer dissatisfaction*, leading to passengers trying other airlines and changing over to their loyalty program preference.
- Alienated potential future customers as those relatives, friends, or work colleagues, inconvenienced by the late arrival of the passenger, avoided future flights with the airline.
- Had a negative impact on staff development, as they learned to replicate the bad habits that created late planes.
- Adversely affected supplier relationships and servicing schedules, resulting in poor service quality.
- Increased *employee dissatisfaction*, as they were constantly firefighting and dealing with frustrated customers.

The Seven Characteristics of Effective KPIs

From extensive analysis and discussions with over 3,000 participants in KPI workshops, covering most organization types in both public and private sectors, I have been able to define seven characteristics of effective KPIs (see Exhibit 18.10).

Nonfinancial. When you put a dollar sign on a measure, you have already converted it into a result indicator (e.g., daily sales are a result of activities that have taken place to create the sales). The KPI lies deeper down. It may be the number of visits to contacts with the key customers who make up most of the profitable business. As already mentioned, it is a myth of performance measurement that KPIs can be either financial or nonfinancial indicators. I am adamant that all KPIs are nonfinancial.

Timely. KPIs should be monitored 24/7, daily, or perhaps weekly for some. As stated above, it is a myth that monitoring *monthly* performance measures will improve performance. A monthly, quarterly, or annual measure cannot be a KPI, as it cannot be key to your business if you are monitoring it well after the horse has bolted.

CEO focus. All KPIs make a difference; they have the CEO's constant attention due to daily calls to the relevant staff. Having a career-limiting discussion with the CEO is not something staff members want to repeat, and in the

Nonfinancial	1.	Nonfinancial measures (not expressed in dollars, yen, pounds, euro, etc.).
Timely	2.	Measured frequently (e.g., 24 by 7, daily or weekly).
CEO focus	3.	Acted on by the CEO and senior management team.
Simple	4.	All staff understand the measure and what corrective action is required.
Team based	5.	Responsibility can be tied down to a team or a cluster of teams who work closely together.
Significant impact	6.	Major impact on the organization (e.g., it impacts more than one of the CSFs and more than one balanced scorecard perspective).
Limited dark side	7.	They encourage appropriate action (e.g., have been tested to ensure they have a positive impact on performance, whereas poorly thought through measures can lead to dysfunctional behavior).

EXHIBIT 18.10   Characteristics of KPIs   *Source:* David Parmenter, *Key Performance Indicators: Developing, Implementing, and Using Winning KPIs, 3rd Edition,* copyright © 2015 John Wiley & Sons, Inc. Reprinted with permission of John Wiley & Sons, Inc.

airline example above, innovative and productive processes were put in place to prevent a recurrence.

Simple. A KPI should tell you what action needs to be taken. The British Airways late-plane KPI communicated immediately to everyone the need for a focus on recovering lost time. Cleaners, caterers, baggage handlers, flight attendants, and front desk staff would all work to save a minute here and a minute there, while maintaining or improving service standards.

Team based. A KPI is deep enough in the organization that it can be tied to a team. In other words, the CEO can call someone and ask, "Why?" Return on capital employed has never been a KPI, because it cannot be tied to an individual manager—it is a result of many activities under different managers. Can you imagine the reaction if a GM was told one morning by the British Airways official, "Pat, I want you to increase the return on capital employed today."

Significant impact. A KPI will affect one or more critical success factors and more than one balanced-scorecard perspective. In other words, when the CEO, management, and staff focus on the KPI, the organization scores goals in all directions. In the airline example, the late-plane KPI affected all balanced-scorecard perspectives.

Limited dark side. Before becoming a KPI, a performance measure needs to be tested to ensure it produces the desired behavioral outcome (e.g., helping teams to align their behavior in a coherent way, to the benefit of the organization).

For the private sector, key performance indicators that fit the characteristics I have proposed could include:

- Number of CEO recognitions planned for next week or the next two weeks
- Staff in vital positions who have handed in their notice in the last hour—the CEO has the opportunity to try to persuade the staff member to stay
- Late deliveries to key customers
- Key position job offers issued to candidates that are more than three days outstanding—the CEO has the opportunity to try to persuade acceptance of offer
- List of late projects, by manager, reported weekly to the senior management team
- Number of vacant places at an important in-house course— reported daily to the CEO in the last three weeks before the course is due to run
- Number of initiatives implemented after the staff-satisfaction survey— monitored weekly for up to three months after survey
- List of level one and -two managers who do not have mentors, reported weekly to the CEO—this measure would only need to be operational for a short time on a weekly basis
- Number of innovations planned for implementation in the next 30, 60, or 90 days—reported weekly to the CEO
- Number of abandonments to be actioned in the next 30, 60, or 90 days— reported weekly to the CEO
- Major projects awaiting decisions that are now running behind schedule—reported weekly to CEO
- Complaints from our key customers that have not been resolved within two hours—report 24/7 to CEO and GMs
- Key customer enquiries that have not been responded to by the sales team for over 24 hours—report daily to the GM
- Date of next visit to major customers by customer name—report weekly to CEO and GMs

For government and nonprofit agencies, some additional key performance indicators could be:

- Emergency response time over a given duration—reported immediately to the CEO
- Number of confirmed volunteers to be street collectors for the annual street appeal—monitored daily in the four to six weeks before the appeal day
- Date of next new service initiative

My KPI book provides many examples of measures and illustrates the difference between these four measures.

 ## THE 10/80/10 RULE

How many measures should we have? How many of each measure type? What time frames are they measured in? To answer these questions, I devised, more than 10 years ago, the 10/80/10 rule.

I believe an organization with over 500 FTEs will have about 10 KRIs, up to 80 RIs and PIs, and 10 KPIs, and these are reported in different time intervals, as shown in Exhibit 18.11. These are the upper limits and in many cases fewer measures will suffice. For smaller organizations the major change would be a reduction in the number of RIs and PIs.

Reporting up to 10 KRIs to the board or governing body is entirely logical. We do not want to bury them in too much detail. A board dashboard can easily be designed to show these KRIs, along with summary financials all on one fanfold (A3) page, as shown in Chapter 8. For many organizations, 80 RIs and PIs will at first appear totally inadequate. Yet, on investigation, you will find that separate teams are actually working with variations of the same indicator, so it is better to standardize them (e.g., a "number of training days attended in the past month" performance measure should have the same definition and the same graph).

When we look at the characteristics of KPIs one will see that these measures are indeed rare and that many organizations will operate very successfully with no more than ten of them. Kaplan and Norton[6] recommend no more than 20 KPIs. Hope and Fraser[7] suggest fewer than 10 KPIs while many KPI project teams may at first feel that having only 10 KPIs is too restrictive and thus increase KPIs to 30 or so. With careful analysis, that number will

Types of performance measures	Characteristics	Frequency of measurement	Number of measures
1. **Key result indicators** (KRIs) give an overview on the organization's past performance and are ideal for the board as they communicate how management have performed (e.g., return on capital employed (%), employee satisfaction (%), net profit before tax and interest).	These measures **can be financial or nonfinancial.** Does not tell you what you need to do to more or less. A summary of the collective efforts of a wide number of teams.	Monthly, quarterly	**Up to 10**
2. **Result indicators** (RIs) give a summary of the collective efforts of a number of teams on a specific area (e.g., yesterday sales ($), complaints from key customers).		24/7, daily, weekly, fortnightly, monthly, quarterly	**80 or so.** If it gets over 150, you will begin to have serious problems.
3. **Performance indicators** (PIs) are targeted measures that tell staff and management what to do (e.g., number of sales visits organized with key customers next week/next two weeks, # of employees' suggestions implemented in last 30 days).	These measures are **only nonfinancial.** Staff know what to do to increase performance. Responsibility can be tied down to a team or a cluster of teams who work closely together.		
4. **Key performance indicators** (KPIs) tell staff and management what to do to increase performance dramatically (e.g., planes that are currently over two hours late, late deliveries to key customers).		24/7, daily, weekly	**Up to 10** (you may have considerably less)

EXHIBIT 18.11 The 10/80/10 rule *Source: David Parmenter, Key Performance Indicators: Developing, Implementing, and Using Winning KPIs, 3rd Edition, copyright © 2015 John Wiley & Sons, Inc. Reprinted with permission of John Wiley & Sons, Inc.*

soon be reduced to the 10 suggested, unless the organization is composed of many businesses from very different sectors. If that is the case, the 10/80/10 rule can apply to each diverse business, providing it is large enough to warrant its own KPI rollout.

It has no doubt been witnessed by many readers that too many measures will cloud issues. I believe the 10/80/10 rule is a good guide, as it appears to have withstood the test of time.

 ## PDF DOWNLOAD

To assist the finance team on the journey, templates and checklists have been provided. The reader can access, free of charge, a PDF of the suggested worksheets, checklists, and templates from www.davidparmenter.com/The_Financial_Controller_and_CFO's_Toolkit.

The PDF download for this chapter includes:

- The role of the chief measurement officer
- KPI articles

 ## NOTES

1. David Parmenter Key Performance Indicators — Developing, Implementing and Using Winning KPIs, (John Wiley & Sons Third Edition 2015)
2. Ibid.
3. Robert Kaplan and David Norton, The Balanced Scorecard: Translating Strategy into Action (Cambridge, MA: Harvard Business Press, 1996).

4. Parmenter, Key Performance Indicators.
5. Dean Spitzer, Transforming Performance Measurement: Rethinking the Way We Measure and Drive Organizational Success (New York: AMACOM, 2007).
6. Robert Kaplan and David Norton, The Balanced Scorecard: Translating Strategy into Action (Cambridge, MA: Harvard Business Press, 1996).
7. Jeremy Hope and Robin Fraser, Beyond Budgeting: How Managers Can Break Free from the Annual Performance Trap (Cambridge, MA: Harvard Business Press, 2003).

CHAPTER NINETEEN

Reporting Performance Measures

OVERVIEW

Reporting performance measures must be designed to accommodate the requirements of the different levels in the organization (board, senior management team, middle management, and the various teams). KPI reporting needs to be performed 24/7, daily or weekly, as appropriate to support timely decision making. Reporting other measures (result indicators and performance indicators) can happen less frequently. This chapter displays some better-practice formats that will help speed up this vital step.

There is a major problem with the reporting of performance measures. The report writers often do not understand enough about performance measures, report monthly, which is far too late for prompt action, and are often unaware of the science of data visualization.

I recommend the reader follow Stephen Few's work,[1] which can be accessed from his website (www.perpetualedge.com) and his three bestselling books on data visualization (see Chapter 7).

The reporting performance measures must reflect the four types of measures used (see Chapter 19) and accommodate the requirements of the board, senior management team, middle management, and the various teams.

REPORTING THE KPIS TO MANAGEMENT AND STAFF

Reporting measures to management needs to be timely. As mentioned previously, KPIs need to be reported 24/7, daily, or, at the outside, weekly; other performance measures can be reported less frequently (monthly and quarterly).

Intraday/Daily Reporting on KPIs

The main KPIs are reported 24/7 or daily. Exhibit 19.1 shows how KPIs should be reported on the intranet. Some form of table giving the contact details, the problem, and some history of performance is required. Another benefit of providing senior management with daily or weekly information on the key performance areas is that the month-end becomes less important. One government department had a 9 o'clock news report every morning covering the processing of benefit payments by each office around the country. Regional management teams were able to compare their service levels and achievements on a daily basis. In other words, if organizations report their KPIs on a 24/7 or daily basis, management knows intuitively whether the organization is having a good or bad month.

Intraday Exception Reporting to the Chief Executive Officer on Human Resources Issues

It is vital that key exceptions are reported to the chief executive officer (CEO) immediately when they occur. The following issues need to be addressed in private and public organizations:

- All job offers that are more than three days outstanding should be personally followed up by the CEO. The lack of acceptance means, in most cases, that the candidate is still looking around. A personal call from the CEO, saying, "I understand, Pat, that we have offered you the position of _____. I believe you will succeed well in this role and I will

Time: 4.30pm 12 Sept 201X

Planes more than two hours late

Flight number	Statistics of last stop			Region manager's name	Current time at location	Contact details			Number of planes over one hour late		
	Arrival late by	Departure late by	Time added			Work	Mobile	Home	Past 30 days	30-day average of past three months	30-day average of past six months
BA123	01:40	02:33	00:53	Pat Carruthers	18:45	xxxxx	xxxxx	xxxx	4	4	2
BA158	01:45	02:30	00:45	Basil John	10:48	xxxxx	xxxxx	xxxx	2	3	1
BA120	01:15	02:27	01:12	xxxxxxx	20:45	xxxxx	xxxxx	xxxx	4	4	7
BA146	01:25	02:24	00:59	xxxxxxx	21:45	xxxxx	xxxxx	xxxx	5	4	4
BA177	01:15	02:21	01:06	xxxxxxx	22:45	xxxxx	xxxxx	xxxx	1	4	2
BA 256	01:35	02:18	00:43	xxxxxxx	23:45	xxxxx	xxxxx	xxxx	5	4	5
BA124	01:45	02:15	00:30	xxxxxxx	00:45	xxxxx	xxxxx	xxxx	2	4	6
Total	7 planes										

EXHIBIT 19.1 Example of a daily KPI report *Source:* David Parmenter, *Key Performance Indicators: Developing, Implementing, and Using Winning KPIs, 3rd Edition,* copyright © 2015 John Wiley & Sons, Inc. Reprinted with permission of John Wiley & Sons, Inc.

take a personal interest in your career. What do we need to do to get your acceptance today?" could help convince the candidate to accept. This 10-minute call could well save over $20,000 of recruiting costs, a return of $120,000 per hour!

- Some in-house courses are poorly attended because staff members think that daily firefighting is more important. If this is the case, the CEO should phone the managers who have not registered staff in the workshop and make it clear that this is not good enough.
- Staff members who have been ill for over two weeks should have an activated back-to-work program—the CEO should phone the HR advisers responsible for setting up the back-to-work program, visits to the company doctor, and partial return planning (e.g., a couple of half days in the office each week).
- Most CEOs treat accidents or safety breaches seriously and, therefore, these are reported—an acceptable report-back time would be within an hour of the incident.
- It is imperative that the CEO follow up on all crucial staff members who have handed in their notice. This would be reported within an hour of resignation. A personal phone call might be enough to turn around the situation or, at the very least, open the door for a return in the future.

The aforementioned issues are set out in a suggested intranet-based report (see Exhibit 19.2). This report should be accessible by HR staff, the senior management team, and the CEO.

Weekly KPI Reporting to the CEO

Some KPIs need only be reported weekly. Exhibit 19.3 is an example of how they could be presented. Note that while all the KPIs will be graphed over time, at least 15 months, only the three KPIs showing a decline would be graphed. The other two KPI graphs would be maintained and used when necessary.

REPORTING OTHER PERFORMANCE MEASURES TO MANAGEMENT

Management will need some weekly reports covering result indicators and performance indicators. There thus will be a mix of financial and nonfinancial measures.

Position offers still outstanding	Candidate	Contact details		Details	
		Home	Mobile	Manager	Days outstanding
Financial controller	Pat Curruthers	XXXXX	XXXXX	Jim Curruthers	3
Stores manager, Brisbane	Basil John	XXXXX	XXXXX	Sally Smith	3

Teams not represented in the in-house courses due in next two weeks	Manager	Work	Mobile	Expected numbers from team	Average training days of team in past six months
Team xx	Jim Curruthers	XXXXX	XXXXX	3	1
Team yy	Sally Smith	XXXXX	XXXXX	4	1.25
Team zz	Jim Curruthers	XXXXX	XXXXX		1.5
Team ss	Ted Smith	XXXXX	XXXXX	1	0

Staff who have been ill for over two weeks	Manager	Work	Mobile	Length of illness	Back to work program started
xxxx xxx	Jim Curruthers	XXXXX	XXXXX	10	Yes
xxx xxxxxxxxxx	Sally Smith	XXXXX	XXXXX	15	Yes
xxxxx xxxxx	Ted Smith	XXXXX	XXXXX	25	No

EXHIBIT 19.2 Example of a daily HR exception report *Source:* David Parmenter, *Key Performance Indicators: Developing, Implementing, and Using Winning KPIs, 3rd Edition,* copyright © 2015 John Wiley & Sons, Inc. Reprinted with permission of John Wiley & Sons, Inc.

Accidents and breaches of safety	Manager	Work	Mobile	Remedial action
Pat Gow was in a car crash, unhurt but needs two weeks' recovery time	Jim Curruthers	xxxxx	xxxx	Increase participation in advanced driving courses paid by company

Staff who have handed in their notice today	Staff member	Work	Mobile	Length of service	Manager
Susan George	Tom Bent	xxxxx	xxxx	<1	John Bull
John Doe	Sally Shell	xxxxx	xxxx	<1	John Bull
Jenny Gilchrist	Ted Snell	xxxxx	xxxx	15	Sarah Marshall

EXHIBIT 19.2 (*Continued*)

Top Five KPIs
Weekly Report _____ 20 __

Top Five Weekly KPIs	Target	Result	Rating
_____ (see graph below)			X
_____ (see graph below)			X
_____			✓
_____ (see graph below)			X
_____			✓✓

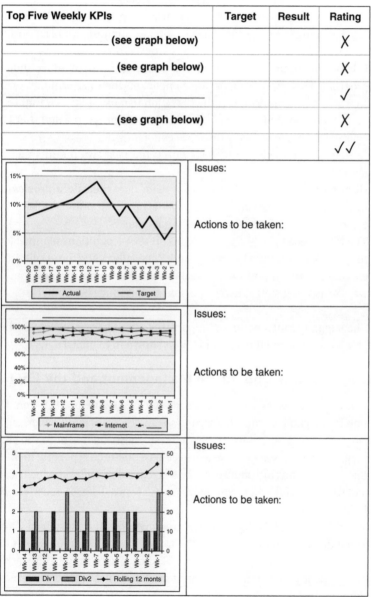

Issues:

Actions to be taken:

Issues:

Actions to be taken:

Issues:

Actions to be taken:

EXHIBIT 19.3 Example of a weekly KPI report *Source:* David Parmenter, *Key Performance Indicators: Developing, Implementing, and Using Winning KPIs, 3rd Edition,* copyright © 2015 John Wiley & Sons, Inc. Reprinted with permission of John Wiley & Sons, Inc.

Weekly Human Resources Update to CEO

There are some HR issues that the CEO needs to focus on weekly. They are not as critical as the intraday or daily HR exceptions, and thus are not considered KPIs. The following HR issues need to be addressed in most organizations:

- It is not uncommon for new staff to miss out on the planned induction program. This can have a negative impact on their performance over the short- to medium-term. It is the CEO's job to make it known that there is an expectation that staff will attend induction programs and that phone calls will be made to follow up on exceptions.
- In-house courses should be held within the next two months and highlighted weekly.
- Higher-than-average sick leave in a team may indicate a problem with leadership. It is important the CEO follow up on excessive sick leave when exploring inter-relationships within that team.
- The CEO needs to keep a weekly focus on the recognitions planned for the next week or two weeks. Peters and Waterman[2] and Jim Collins[3] have emphasized the importance of celebration as a communication tool and a way of inspiring staff to exceed normal performance benchmarks.

The suggested intranet-based report that should be accessible to the HR staff, senior management team, and CEO is shown in Exhibit 19.4.

Weekly/Monthly Updates to Management and the CEO

There are endless ways these can be shown (see Exhibits 19.5 and 19.6), through icons, gauges, traffic lights, and so on. There are many reporting tools available that are more robust than a basic spreadsheet. It is highly likely that your organization has the license to use at least one such reporting tool.

Stephen Few has introduced a new concept called *bullet graphs*. These are particularly powerful when combined with Edward Tufte's[4] *sparkline graphs* (see Exhibit 19.7).

A sparkline graph looks like a line graph without the axes. Even with this truncated diagram you can still see the trend. The bullet graph shows different details about current performance. The shades used range from dark gray (to indicate poor performance) to lightest gray (to indicate good performance). The dark vertical line indicates a comparative measure such as a target or last year's result.

New staff who have not attended an induction program

	Start Date	Name	Manager details		Staff turnover in past two years
			Office	Mobile	
Alan Bevin	12/12/xx	Pat Curruthers	xxxxx	xxx	30%
Carl Dodds	11/11/xx	Sam Smith	xxxxx	xxx	40%

In house training courses due in next two months

	Enrollments	Expected numbers	Date of course	Days left
First Aid	5	20	xxxxx	25
Supervisors Part 1	3	45	xxxxx	18
Leadership part 2	40	60	xxxxx	14
Presenting	6	20	xxxxx	15

Teams with above average sick leave

	Days lost		
	This month	Days per employee	Average per month for past three months
Team xx	5	1.5	4
Team yy	8	2	7

CEO recognitions planned for next week

	Manager	Date
Project ____	Jim Curruthers	xxxxx
Finance team	Sally Smith	xxxxx
	Ted Smith	xxxxx

EXHIBIT 19.4 Example of the weekly human resources report *Source: David Parmenter, Key Performance Indicators: Developing, Implementing, and Using Winning KPIs, 3rd Edition,* copyright © 2015 John Wiley & Sons, Inc. Reprinted with permission of John Wiley & Sons, Inc.

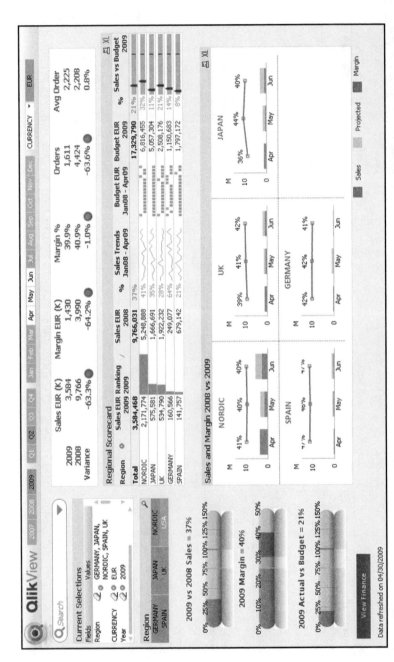

EXHIBIT 19.5 Example of a monthly report to management *Source:* Inside Info; see www.insideinfo.com.au

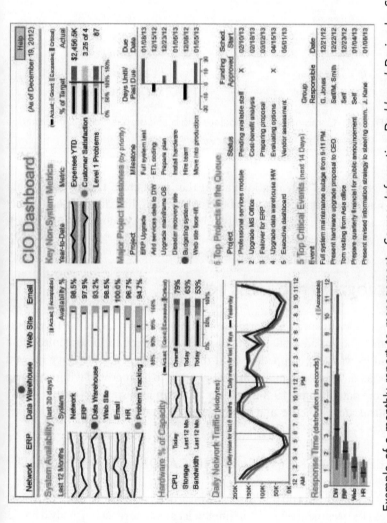

EXHIBIT 19.6 Example of a monthly report to management   *Source: Information Dashboard Design* by Stephen Few, www.perceptualedge.com.

Sales Dashboard

Key Metrics	Last 12 Months	Current	Variance from Plan
Sales		47.2M	
Expenses		33.4M	
Profit		13.8M	
Units Sold		165K	
● Market Share		13%	
Customer Sat.		84%	
			-15% 0% 15%

EXHIBIT 19.7   Combination of sparklines and bullet graphs *Source: Information Dashboard Design* by Stephen Few, www.perceptualedge.com.

Stephen Few is very cautious about the use of color. He points out that many readers will have some form of color blindness. In Exhibit 19.6, the only use of color would be red bullet points indicating the exceptions that need investigation and follow-up.

REPORTING PROGRESS TO STAFF

It is a good idea to have some form of monthly icon report for staff. If this report happens to be left on a bus, it would not be damaging to the organization if it found its way to a competitor. Icon reports are ideal because they tell you what is good, what is adequate, and what needs to be improved without giving away core data. Exhibit 19.8 is an example of an icon staff report that covers the critical success factors and reminds staff about the strategies.

REPORTING KEY RESULT INDICATORS TO THE BOARD

Entities in the private and public sectors need to report to a board, a council, or an elected government official. To simplify, let's call the reporting body a board.

In most organizations that have boards, there is a major conflict of interest over what information is appropriate for the board to receive. Because the board's role is clearly one of governance and not of management, it is totally

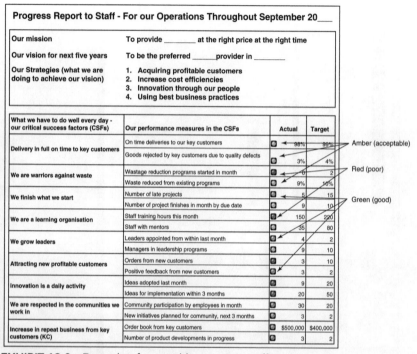

Progress Report to Staff - For our Operations Throughout September 20___

Our mission	To provide _____ at the right price at the right time
Our vision for next five years	To be the preferred _____provider in _____
Our Strategies (what we are doing to achieve our vision)	1. Acquiring profitable customers 2. Increase cost efficiencies 3. Innovation through our people 4. Using best business practices

What we have to do well every day - our critical success factors (CSFs)	Our performance measures in the CSFs	Actual	Target	
Delivery in full on time to key customers	On time deliveries to our key customers	98%	99%	Amber (acceptable)
	Goods rejected by key customers due to quality defects	3%	4%	
We are warriors against waste	Wastage reduction programs started in month	0	2	Red (poor)
	Waste reduced from existing programs	9%	10%	
We finish what we start	Number of late projects	5	15	Green (good)
	Number of project finishes in month by due date	9	10	
We are a learning organisation	Staff training hours this month	150	220	
	Staff with mentors	35	80	
We grow leaders	Leaders appointed from within last month	4	2	
	Managers in leadership programs	9	10	
Attracting new profitable customers	Orders from new customers	3	10	
	Positive feedback from new customers	3	2	
Innovation is a daily activity	Ideas adopted last month	9	20	
	Ideas for implementation within 3 months	20	50	
We are respected in the communities we work in	Community participation by employees in month	30	20	
	New initiatives planned for community, next 3 months	3	2	
Increase in repeat business from key customers (KC)	Order book from key customers	$500,000	$400,000	
	Number of product developments in progress	3	2	

EXHIBIT 19.8 Example of a monthly report to staff

inappropriate to be providing the board with KPIs. It should receive indicators of overall performance that need only be reviewed on a monthly or bimonthly basis. These measures need to tell the story about whether the organization is being steered in the right direction at the right speed, whether the customers and staff are happy, and whether we are acting in a responsible way by being environmentally friendly.

These measures are called key result indicators (KRIs). Typically, a board would need to see between 6 and 12 graphs covering the critical success factors and all six balanced scorecard perspectives. These measures work particularly well in helping the board focus on strategic, rather than management, issues, and they will support management in their thrust to move board meetings away from the monthly cycle. These KRIs are best reported in a board dashboard, which was discussed in Chapter 8 and is shown again in Exhibit 19.9.

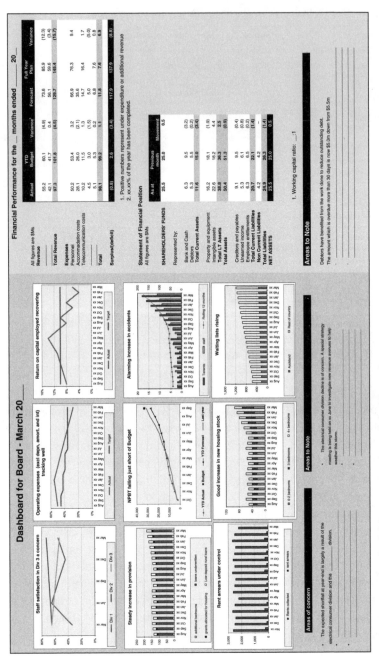

EXHIBIT 19.9 A3 (fanfold) one page board dashboard

REPORTING TEAM PERFORMANCE MEASURES

Exhibits 19.10 and 19.11 are examples of the weekly and monthly reporting a team would do to monitor its own performance.

The examples shown are in Excel, a useful template tool until a more robust and integrated solution is found. The weekly report tracks those measures too important to leave until the end of the month. Team reports should be communicated only to the team members until they are proud enough to report their performance to the rest of the organization on the intranet.

HOW THE REPORTING OF PERFORMANCE MEASURES FITS TOGETHER

Exhibit 19.12 shows how the reporting of performance measures should work in a private, public, or not-for-profit organization. The important reports are the daily and weekly reports shown in the left-hand column. These are seen by the senior management team and the relevant operational staff. Some of these would be intranet-based, being updated 24/7 (e.g., late planes in the sky). At month's end, summary information would be given to:

- The board, to help board members understand the operations and general progress within the critical success factors
- The staff, to give feedback on their efforts in progress with the critical success factors
- The management, summarizing progress in the critical success factors, which will have been monitored in the daily and weekly reports, and other success factors that are monitored only monthly

Weekly Progress Update During May			
	Week 1	Week 2	Target (month)
Proactive visits to in-house clients	0	1	6
Number of staff recognitions made	0	0	6
Projects in progress	7	7	<8
Reports/documents still in draft mode	12	15	<5
Initiatives underway based on satisfaction survey	0	0	5 by 30 June

EXHIBIT 19.10   Example of a weekly team-progress update

Informtion System's Scorecard

Customer Focus

Help desk	This month	Target
Programme visits to managers	4	6
Service requests out standing (faults, works requests) at month end	24	15
Service requests closed in month	45	55
% calls fixed by Help Desk from 1st call	55%	65%
Initiatives underway based on satisfaction survey	0	5 by 30 June

Services outages Vs SLA's	This month	Target
Average Mainframe Response Time	1 sec	<0.75 sec
Outage time per month / # of times	None	<1hr/mth

Information Systems Strategic Plan	This cycle	Target
Programme visits to managers	4	12
Presentations of ISSP to managers	2	6

Environment and Community

	This month	Target
Presentations given to third part organizations	1 in last 12 months	>3 in year
Number of Finance staff involved in community activities	10	>15

IS Team Satisfaction

	This month	target
No. of formal staff recognitions made in the month	1	>2
Date of next planned celebration	30-Jun	>1 per month
Number of abandonments made this month	5	>5 per month
Staff functions planned to occur in next three months	0	>2

Internal Process

Disaster recovery	This month	Target
Backup every night	100%	100%
Months since last back-up tested at remote site	3	<4
Rolling checks on C drives	25	40

Our ability to deliver	This month	Target
% of jobs completed on time on budget	44%	60%
% of time of developers spent on high priority / high value work	55%	65%
Staff trained to use _____ system	45	150

Completions	This month	Target
Projects in progress	7	<8
Reports/documents still in draft mode	15	<5

Innovation & Learning

Training needs outstanding	Next 3 months	Last 12 months
Chief information officer	0	2
Team _____	0	5
Team _____	0	2
Team _____	0	1
Team _____	0	1
Average for all IT staff	<0.1	2.5

Coaching sessions	This month	Last quarter
Number of staff who have had one-on-one coaching sessions	0	4

Innovations implemented	This month	Target
Number of staff innovations implemented	10	23

Projects Status

Percentage complete

■ Risk of non-completion　■ Behind　□ On-track　□ Done

Financial Results - Progress Against Plan

● Annual plan ── Forecast cumulative
──▲── Actual cumulative ── Last year

Findings:

Action to be taken:

EXHIBIT 19.11　Example of an is monthly team balanced scorecard

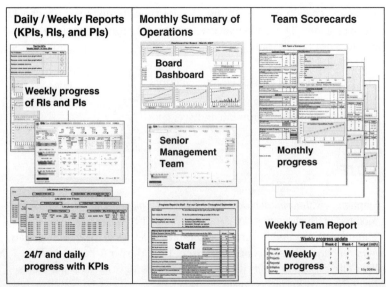

Daily / Weekly Reports (KPIs, RIs, and PIs)	Monthly Summary of Operations	Team Scorecards
Weekly progress of RIs and PIs	**Board Dashboard**	
	Senior Management Team	**Monthly progress**
		Weekly Team Report
24/7 and daily progress with KPIs	**Staff**	**Weekly progress**

EXHIBIT 19.12 Suggested performance reporting portfolio *Source:* David Parmenter, *Key Performance Indicators: Developing, Implementing, and Using Winning KPIs, 3rd Edition,* copyright © 2015 John Wiley & Sons, Inc. Reprinted with permission of John Wiley & Sons, Inc.

In the right-hand column of Exhibit 19.12, we show that teams will be monitoring performance through their scorecards. If a team is involved with a KPI, team members would also be monitoring the KPI reporting shown in the left-hand column of Exhibit 19.12.

PDF DOWNLOAD

To assist the finance team on the journey, templates and checklists have been provided. The reader can access, free of charge, a PDF of the suggested templates from www.davidparmenter.com/The_Financial_Controller_and_CFO's_Toolkit.

The PDF download for this chapter includes:

▪ The board dashboard template in Excel
▪ The reporting exhibits

 NOTES

1. Stephen Few, *Information Dashboard Design: Displaying Data for At-a-Glance Monitoring* (Burlingame, CA: Analytics Press, 2013).
2. Thomas J. Peters and Robert H. Waterman, *In Search of Excellence: Lessons from America's Best Run Companies* (New York: Harper & Row, 1982).
3. Jim Collins, *Good to Great: Why Some Companies Make the Leap and Others Don't* (New York: HarperBusiness, 2001).
4. Edward Tufte, *Beautiful Evidence* (Graphics Press, 2006).

PART SIX

VI

Areas where Costly Mistakes can be Made

CHAPTER TWENTY

Performance Bonus Schemes

OVERVIEW

Performance bonus schemes can be seen as an annual entitlement, be very costly, create endless arguments and not lead to notable improved performance. This chapter explores the foundation stones CFOs and controllers must be aware of if they are involved in designing or fixing a bonus scheme. It was first published in my book *The Leading Edge Manager's Guide to Success.*[1]

Performance bonus schemes have broken down across a wide range of organizations and they can be very costly without improving performance. This chapter is written for the CFO, or controller, who has been asked to design a performance bonus scheme based on better practice or to fix the current broken one. Jeremy Hope[2] summed up the situation in this quote:

> " ...But despite hundreds of research studies over 50 years that tell us that extrinsic motivation (carrot and stick financial targets and incentives) doesn't work, most leaders remain convinced that financial incentives are the key to better performance."

THE BILLION-DOLLAR GIVEAWAY

Performance bonuses give away billions of dollars each year based on methodologies where little thought has been applied. Who are the performance bonus experts? What qualifications do they possess to work in this important area, other than prior experience in creating the mayhem we currently have?

When one looks at their skill base, one wonders how they acquired the credibility in the first place. Which remuneration expert advised the hedge funds to pay a $1 billion bonus to one fund manager who created a paper gain that never eventuated into cash? These schemes were flawed from the start; "super" profits were being paid out, there was no allowance made for the cost of capital, and the bonus scheme was only "high side" focused. My recommendation to the reader is, do not seek so-called expert advice. Apply the following guidelines and some common sense.

FOUNDATION STONES OF PERFORMANCE BONUS SCHEMES

There are a number of foundation stones that need to be laid down and never undermined in order to build a performance-related pay scheme that makes sense and will move the organization in the right direction. The foundation stones include:

- Use relative measures instead of an annual target.
- Exclude super profits.
- Remove profit enhancing accounting adjustments.
- Apply the full cost of capital.
- Separate at-risk portion of salary from the scheme.
- Avoid any linkage to the share price or share options.
- Make bonuses team-based rather than individual-based.

- Avoid an annual entitlement.
- Link to a balanced performance.
- Exclude unrealized gains.
- Test scheme to minimize manipulation.
- Avoid linking to KPIs.
- Get the management and staff on side

Use Relative Measures Instead of an Annual Target

Most bonuses fail at the first hurdle, because they are based on annual targets. Jeremy Hope and Robin Fraser,[3] pioneers of the beyond budgeting methodology, have pointed out the trap of an annual fixed performance contract. If you set a target in the future, you will never know if it was appropriate, given the particular conditions of that time. You often end up paying incentives to management when, in fact, their performance was substandard. A good example of this would be in the private sector if rising sales did not keep up with the market growth rate.

Relative performance targets involve comparing performance to the marketplace. Thus, the financial institutions that are making super profits out of this artificially lower interest rate environment would have a higher benchmark set retrospectively, when the actual impact is known. As Jeremy Hope says, "Not setting a target beforehand is not a problem, as long as staff are given regular updates as to how they are progressing against the market." He argues that if you do not know how hard you have to work to get a maximum bonus, you will work as hard as you can.

Exclude Super Profits

Super profits should be excluded from schemes and retained to cover possible losses in the future. In boom times, schemes often give away too much. These *super-profit* years come around infrequently and are needed to finance the dark times of a recession. Yet, what do our remuneration experts advise? A package that includes a substantial slice of these super profits, but no sharing in any downside. This downside, of course, is borne solely by the shareholder.

There needs to be recognition that the performance in boom times has limited correlation to the efforts of teams and individuals. The organization was always going to achieve this, no matter who was working for the firm. As Exhibit 20.1 shows, if an organization is to survive, super profits need to be retained.

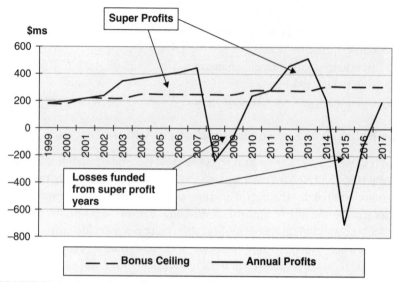

EXHIBIT 20.1   Retention of super profits   *Source:* David Parmenter, *The Leading-Edge Manager's Guide to Success: Strategies and Better Practices.* Copyright © 2011 by David Parmenter. Reprinted with permission of John Wiley & Sons, Inc.

This removal of super profits has a number of benefits:

- It is defensible and understandable to employees.
- It can be calculated by reference to the market conditions relevant in the year. When the market has become substantially larger, with all the main players reporting a great year, we can attribute a certain amount of period-end performance as super profits.
- These super profits can fund bonuses in loss-making years when staff are pulling the organization out of the fire.

The ceiling in Exhibit 20.1 is shown for illustration purposes only.

Remove Profit-Enhancing Accounting Adjustments

All profits included in a performance bonus scheme calculation should be free of all major "profit-enhancing" accounting adjustments. Many banks generated additional profits in 2010–2013 as the massive write-downs from the global financial crisis were written back when loans were recovered.

I remember a classic case in New Zealand where a CEO was rewarded solely on a successful sale of a publicly owned bank. The loan book was written down to such an extent that the purchasing bank reported a profit in the first year that equated to nearly the full purchase price. Most of the written-down loans had been repaid in full.

One simple step you can take is to eliminate all short-term accounting adjustments from the bonus scheme profit pool of senior management and the CEO. These eliminations should include:

- Recovery of written-off debt
- Profit on sale of assets

The aim is to avoid the situation where management, in a bad year, will take a massive hit to their loan book so they can feather their nest on the recovery. This type of activity is in active use around the globe.

Apply the Full Cost of Capital

The full cost of capital should be taken into account when calculating any bonus pool. Traders can only trade in the vast sums involved because they have a bank's balance sheet behind them. If this was not so, then the traders could operate at home and be among the many solo traders who also play in the market. These individuals cannot hope to make as much profit due to the much smaller positions their personal cash resources facilitate.

Each department in a bank should have a cost of capital, which takes into account the full risks involved. In today's unusual environment, the cost of capital should be based on a five-year average cost of debt and a risk weighting associated with the risks involved. With the losses that bank shareholders have had to tolerate, the cost of capital should be set in some higher-risk departments as high as 25 percent. With the current artificially low base rate, a fool could run a bank and make a huge bottom line. All banks should thus be adjusting their cost of capital based on a five-year average in their performance-related pay schemes.

Separate the At Risk Portion of Salary from the Scheme

Any at-risk portion of salary should be separate from the performance related pay scheme. The at-risk portion of the salary should be paid when the expected profits figure has been met (see Exhibit 20.2). Note that, as already mentioned,

	Remuneration		
	Mgr 1	Mgr 2	Mgr 3
Base salary, paid monthly	48,000	64,000	80,000
At-risk salary (bonus is paid separately)	12,000	16,000	20,000
Salary package	60,000	80,000	100,000
Relative measure, set retrospectively	not met	met	exceeded
Percentage of at-risk salary paid	40%	100%	100%
At-risk salary paid	4,800	16,000	20,000
Share of bonus pool	nil	5,000	10,000
Total period-end payout	4,800	21,000	30,000

EXHIBIT 20.2 At-risk component of salary   *Source:* David Parmenter, *The Leading-Edge Manager's Guide to Success: Strategies and Better Practices.* Copyright © 2011 by David Parmenter. Reprinted with permission of John Wiley & Sons, Inc.

this target will be set as a relative measure, set retrospectively, when actual information is known. When the relative target has been met or exceeded, the "at-risk" portion of the salary will be paid. The surplus over the relative measure will then create a bonus pool for a further payment, which will be calculated, taking into account the adjustments already discussed.

Avoid Any Linkage to the Share Price or Share Options

Bonus schemes should avoid any linkage to share price movements. No bonus should be pegged to the stock market price, as the stock market price does not reflect the contribution that staff, management, and the CEO have made.

Only a naive person believes that the current share price reflects the long-term value of an organization. Just because a buyer, often ill informed, wants to pay a certain sum for a "packet" of shares does not mean the total shareholding is worth that amount.

Providing share options is also giving away too much of shareholder's wealth in an often-disguised way. As strategy guru Henry Mintzberg has clearly stated, "Executive bonuses—especially in the form of stock and option grants—represent the most prominent form of legal corruption that has been undermining our large corporations and bringing down the global economy. Get rid of them and we will all be better off for it."

Jeremy Hope points out in his book *Reinventing the CEO*,[4] these incentives have been behind many corporate failures. Due to the pressure to manipulate the accounts, the share price is too great for the CEO and senior management to resist.

With share options, it is so easy to get it wrong, and in fact give away more wealth in a period than the actual net profits created. In other words, you have given away future profits that may never be generated, and often not by the executives in question.

There is another, more damaging issue in that these measures focus executives on manipulating the short term at the expense of innovation, where the costs are often front-loaded and the rewards back-loaded.

Make Bonuses Team-Based Rather Than Individual-Based

Basing accountability and rewards on teams, rather than individuals, has been talked about for years. It is much more closely linked to Douglas McGregor's *Theory Y* view that people are motivated by self-esteem and personal development, rather than by additional incentives (*Theory X*).[5] In Theory Y, organizations produce better results by encouraging their people to be creative, to work collaboratively, to improve their skills, and to derive satisfaction from their work. Only a simpleton would believe that you can separate out an individual's contribution to the bottom line. As Harvard professor of business administration Robert Simons asks, "How do we measure the contribution of a single violin player in relation to the successful season enjoyed by a symphony orchestra?"[6]

PROFIT SHARING PLAN AT SOUTHWEST AIRLINES

The profit sharing plan at Southwest started in 1973 and is at the heart of its compensation and benefits program. All employees qualify on January 1 following the commencement of their employment. Fifteen percent of pretax profits are paid into the profit-sharing pool, and this is shared across all employees according to base salary. The payments go into a retirement fund for individual employees. While employees are free to increase that amount, 25 percent of the profit-sharing fund is used to purchase Southwest shares. There are no incentive schemes based on achieving annual fixed targets.[7]

As Jeremy Hope points out: The profit-sharing system can only be understood in the context of its purpose. It is not intended to be an incentive for individuals to pursue financial targets; rather, it is intended as a reward for their collective efforts and competitive success.

Avoid the Annual Entitlement

The finance sector has a belief that the bonus is a right, and in many cases, it has already been spent. We need to move bonuses out of the annual cycle. Southwest does this very cleverly.

NO ANNUAL CASH PAYOUTS AT SOUTHWEST AIRLINES

Southwest doesn't make an annual cash payment; instead, they pay the bonus into an employee pension plan. This has the effect of minimizing any fallout from a poor year. In other words, employees are not planning to spend their bonus on "something special" and then become disappointed when it doesn't happen. The pension payment approach cushions poor years but also has the effect of relating performance to the share price (both pension schemes own a substantial element of company stock).[8]

Link to a Balanced Performance

Performance-related pay schemes should be linked to a "balanced" performance. The balanced scorecard has been used, I would argue, largely unsuccessfully, as a vehicle to pay performance. Schemes using a balanced scorecard are often flawed on a number of counts:

- The balanced scorecard is often based on only four perspectives, ignoring the important environment-and-community and staff-satisfaction perspectives.
- The measures chosen are open to debate and manipulation.
- There is seldom a link to progress in the organization's critical success factors.
- Weighting of measures leads to crazy performance agreements such as those shown in Exhibit 20.3.

Scorecard Perspective	Perspective Weighting	Performance Measure	Measure Weighting
Financial Results	60%	Economic value added	25%
		Unit's profitability	20%
		Market share growth	15%
Customer Focus	20%	Customer satisfaction survey	10%
		Dealer satisfaction survey	10%
Internal Process	10%	Ranking in external quality survey	5%
		Decrease in dealer delivery cycle time	5%
Innovation and Learning	10%	Employee suggestions implemented	5%
		Employee satisfaction survey	5%

EXHIBIT 20.3   Performance-related pay system that will never work   *Source:* David Parmenter, *The Leading-Edge Manager's Guide to Success: Strategies and Better Practices.* Copyright © 2011 by David Parmenter. Reprinted with permission of John Wiley & Sons, Inc.

An alternative would be to link the scheme to the organization's critical success factors. See an example of an airline scheme in Exhibit 20.4.

In this exhibit, all teams have the same weighting for the financial results. Some readers will feel that this is too low. However, when you do more research on the balanced-scorecard philosophy, you will understand that the greatest impact to the bottom line, over the medium and long-term, will be in the organization's critical success factors.

The operational team at one of the airports has a major focus on timely arrival and departure of planes. You could argue that this should have a higher weighting, such as 30 percent. However, this team does impact in many other critical success factors. This team clearly impacts the timely maintenance of planes by making them available on time; and impacts the satisfaction of our first class, business class, and gold-card-holder passengers. The public's perception of the airline is reflected in the interaction between staff and the public, along with press releases and the timeliness of planes.

Ensuring that staff members are listened to, are engaged successfully, and are constantly striving to do things better (Toyota's Kaizen) is reflected in the weighting of "stay, say, strive" as well as the catchphrase "encouraging innovation that matters." There is no weighting for "accurate timely information

	Operational Team	Public Relations Team	Maintenance Team	Finance	Team
Financial performance of team	30%	30%	30%	30%	—
Progress in the critical success factors (CSFs)					
Timely departure and arrival of planes	20%	0%	20%	0%	—
Timely maintenance of planes	10%	0%	30%	0%	—
Retention of key customers	10%	0%	0%	0%	—
Positive public perception of organization—being a preferred airline	10%	30%	0%	0%	—
"Stay, say, strive engagement with staff"	10%	20%	10%	20%	—
Encouraging innovation that matters	10%	20%	10%	20%	—
Accurate, timely information which helps decisions	0%	0%	0%	30%	—
	100%	100%	100%	100%	—

EXHIBIT 20.4 How the performance-related bonus would differ across teams (airline) *Source:* David Parmenter, *The Leading-Edge Manager's Guide to Success: Strategies and Better Practices.* Copyright © 2011 by David Parmenter. Reprinted with permission of John Wiley & Sons, Inc.

that helps decisions" because other teams such as IT and accounting are more responsible for this, and I want to avoid using precise percentages such as 7 percent or 8 percent, which tend to give the impression that a performance pay scheme can be a science-based instrument.

The public relations team has a major focus of creating positive spin for the public and for the staff. All great leaders focus in this area (a superb example is Sir Richard Branson). The weights for the public relations team will direct them in the key areas where they can contribute. By having innovation success stories and recognition celebrations, staff will want to focus in this important area of constant improvement, which has been demonstrated so well at Toyota over the past couple of decades.

The maintenance and accounting teams' focus is more concentrated. The accounting team has a higher weighting on "stay, say, strive" and "encouraging innovation that matters" to help converge their attention in these important areas. This will improve performance and benefit all the other teams they impact through their work.

Exclude Unrealized Gains

The treatment of unrealized gains is a sensitive issue. Some performance-related pay schemes include deferral provisions in an attempt to avoid paying out bonuses on unrealized gains that may never materialize. The question is whether the cure is worse than the ailment. The issue comes back to the impact on human behavior. Already, some financial institutions have adopted a deferral mechanism on unrealized gains to avoid situations like the $1 billion bonus to one fund manager who created a paper gain that never eventuated into cash as the global financial crisis wiped it all way.

Use history to work out the amount of deferral required and apply consistent rules. Where stocks have been volatile, history has shown the quicker they rise, the faster they fall. Use a table to establish how much of unrealized gain is held back (i.e., 20%, 40%, 60%). It is not recommended to hold back all unrealized profit, as there are some downsides that need to be mitigated:

- We do not want all stocks sold and bought back the next day as a window dressing exercise that dealers/brokers could easily arrange with each other.
- The financial sector is driven by individuals who worship the monetary unit, rather than any other more benevolent force—this is a fact of life. A deferral system will be very difficult for them to accept.

- Staff will worry about their share of the pool when they leave—the last thing you want is a team leaving so they can cash up their deferral pool while it is doing well.
- Underperforming staff may wish to hang around for future paydays out of their deferred bonus scheme.

It is my belief that while some sectors may be able to successfully establish deferral provisions, they will be fraught with difficulties in the financial sector. In some cases, it would be better to focus on the other foundation stones, especially the removal of super profits, and take into account the full cost of capital.

Test Scheme to Minimize Manipulation

All performance-related pay schemes should be tested to minimize the risk of being manipulated by participants in the scheme. All schemes in which money is at stake will be gamed. Staff will find ways to maximize the payment by undertaking actions that may well be not in the general interest of the organization. The testing of the new scheme should include:

- Reworking bonuses paid to about five individuals over the last five years to see what would have been paid under the new scheme and compare against actual payments made.
- Consulting with a cross section of staff and asking them, "What actions would you undertake if this scheme was in place?"
- Discussing effective best practices with your peers in other companies: this will help move the industry standard while avoiding the implementation of a scheme that failed elsewhere.

Performance-related pay schemes should be road tested on the last complete business cycle. When you think you have a good scheme, test it on the results of the last full business cycle, the period between the last two recessions. View the extent of the bonus on the net profit. You need to appraise the scheme with the same care and attention you would apply to making a major fixed asset investment.

In Exhibit 20.5, I have gone back 10 years, removed the impact of profit enhancing accounting adjustments (in this case, recovery of debt previously written off), deducted off the super profits (on the operations of last 10 years

	20	20	20	20	20	20	20	20	20	Last year
Annual profits (excluding all cost of capital charges)	(240)	(60)	290	310	460	520	210	(700)	(125)	200
Removal of profit enhancing adjustments			(20)		(30)	(20)				
Super profits clawback					(60)	(120)				
Adjusted profit	(240)	(60)	270	310	370	380	210	(700)	(125)	170
Expected profit using agreed benchmark ROCE			190	220	240	240	170			160
Adjusted profits for bonus pool calculation			80	90	130	140	40			10
Size of bonus pool if share is 25%	0	0	20	23	33	35	10	0	0	3
Size of bonus pool if share is 33%	0	0	26	30	43	46	13	0	0	3

EXHIBIT 20.5 Testing the performance scheme on past results

anything over $400 million deemed to be super profits) and removed the expected profit shareholders would see as a given using an agreed "return on equity" benchmark.

Avoid Linking to KPIs

Performance-related pay schemes should not be linked to KPIs. KPIs are a special performance tool, and it is imperative that these are not included in any performance-related pay discussions. KPIs, as defined in Chapter 18, are too important to be gamed by individuals and teams to maximize bonuses. Performance with KPIs should be considered a "ticket to the game."

Although KPIs will show how teams are performing 24/7, daily, or weekly, it is essential to leave the KPIs uncorrupted by performance-related pay. As mentioned in Chapter 18, it is a myth that by tying KPIs to pay, you will increase performance. You will merely increase the manipulation of these important measures, undermining them so much that they will become *key political indicators*.

Certainly most teams will have some useful monthly summary measures, which I call *results indicators*. These result indicators help teams track performance and are the basis of any performance-related pay scheme.

Get the Management and Staff On Side

Schemes need to be communicated to staff using public relations experts. All changes to such a fundamental issue as performance-related pay need to be sold through the emotional drivers of the audience. With a performance-related pay scheme, this will require different presentations when selling the change to the board, chief executive officer (CEO), senior management team, and management and staff. They all have different emotional drivers.

It is important to sell to management and staff why the existing scheme needs to change. As mentioned in Chapter 2, Leading and Selling Change, it is important to start the process off by getting management to see that the default future is not what they want. We need to sell the change using emotional drivers rather than selling by logic, as already discussed.

Many change initiatives fail at this hurdle because we attempt to change the culture by using logic, writing reports, and issuing commands via e-mail. It does not work. The new performance-related pay scheme needs a public relations machine behind it. In addition, you should road test the delivery of all of your presentations in front of the public relations expert before going live.

PDF DOWNLOAD

To assist the finance team on the journey, templates and checklists have been provided. The reader can access, free of charge, a PDF of the suggested templates, and a checklist from www.davidparmenter.com/The_Financial_Controller_and_CFO's_Toolkit.

The PDF download for this chapter includes:

- A checklist to ensure that you lay down these foundation stones carefully
- A printable version of the templates used in this chapter

NOTES

1. This chapter is adapted from David Parmenter, The Leading-Edge Manager's Guide to Success: Strategies and Better Practices (Hoboken, NJ: John Wiley & Sons, 2011).
2. Jeremy Hope, "How KPIs Can Help Motivate and Reward the Right Behavior," IBM white paper, 2010.
3. Jeremy Hope and Robin Fraser, Beyond Budgeting: How Managers Can Break Free from the Annual Performance Trap (New York: Harvard Business Review Press 2003).
4. Jeremy Hope, Reinventing the CFO: How Financial Managers Can Transform Their Roles and Add Greater Value (Boston: Harvard Business School Press, 2006).
5. Douglas McGregor, The Human Side of Enterprise (New York: McGraw-Hill, 1960).
6. Robert Simons, "Control in an Age of Empowerment," Harvard Business Review (March–April 1995): 80.
7. Hope, "How KPIs Can Help Motivate and Reward the Right Behavior."
8. Ibid.

2**1**

Takeovers and Mergers

OVERVIEW

The pursuit of growth through takeover or merger has made a small, select group very wealthy while diminishing the wealth of a vast number of shareholders. CFOs and controllers have a moral dilemma here and only they can decide what is appropriate. In many cases, the forces are huge to transact the takeover. This chapter explores why so many takeover and mergers, which have been based on perceived synergies and cost savings, fail, and if involved in one, why you need to move on before reality strikes.

It is often quoted, but even great leaders seem to forget, that "history has a habit of repeating itself." Company executives, directors, and the major institutional investors (whose support is often a prerequisite) need to learn the lessons and think more carefully before they commit to a takeover or merger (TOM).

REASONS FOR A TAKEOVER OR MERGER

To understand the forces at play, you need to look at the various reasons for a takeover or merger (TOM):

Purchasing future profits from either a related or diversified sector. Here the new subsidiary is left to grow in their own way. This method is characterized by successful investment companies like Berkshire Hathaway.

Purchasing to gain synergy. Here, the argument is $1 + 1 = 3$. These are the mergers/ takeovers typically targeted by investment banks and have a history of failure.

Purchasing for increased market share. Driven by aggressive executives, the cost frequently outweighing the structural costs that follow such a TOM. Also have a history of failure.

Purchasing to gain access to a new channels / new products. The Kraft Cadbury takeover was undertaken so Kraft could access rapidly developing economies such as India, Brazil, and Mexico where Cadbury was well entrenched.

Purchasing as a defensive move. Used to prevent another aggressive competitor gaining market share from a company that has become a soft takeover target. Often have duplication of assets that is both costly and time consuming to rationalize.

Preventing the newly acquired company to provide services to competitors. Volkswagen purchasing the car designer Italdesign Giugiaro.

Asset swaps. GSK-Novartis deal where each party swapped some operations.

 SOME BIG FAILURES

The landscape of mergers and acquisitions is littered with business flops, some catastrophic, highly visible disasters that were often hugely hyped before their eventual doom.

AOL and Time Warner

The media giants American Online (AOL) and Time Warner combined their businesses in what is usually described as the worst merger of all time. In 2001, Time Warner consolidated with AOL, the Internet and email provider, in a deal worth a staggering $110 billion. The merger was seen as a revolutionary partnership between a content owner and a company active in the brave new online world.

AOL and Time Warner parted company in December 2009, after almost nine years of nightmares. In less than a decade, the tie-up had destroyed close to $200 billion of shareholder wealth.

Vodafone/Mannesmann

Vodafone's takeover of German rival Mannesmann is difficult to beat for sheer shareholder value destruction. In February 2000, at the height of millennial dotcom madness, the agreed merger of Vodafone AirTouch and Mannesmann created a telecoms giant. The $160 billion all-share deal to acquire Mannesmann turned the merged group into the world's fourth-largest company, worth $330 billion.

In 2006, Vodafone plunged to massive losses after one-off costs of more than $35 billion connected to the Mannesmann deal.

Glaxo Wellcome/SmithKline Beecham

In December 2000, two of the United Kingdom's largest pharmaceutical companies, Glaxo Wellcome and SmithKline Beecham, came together to form global giant GlaxoSmithKline. At that time, GSK's share price was close to $30, valuing the firm at close to $160 billion and putting it in the top three of the FTSE 100.

Fast-forward 15 years, and GSK's share price is around $20, or about a third lower than at the time of the merger, destroying roughly $40 billion of shareholder wealth.

THE DRIVING FORCES BEHIND TOMS

I met an investment banker on a recent flight who told me about the takeover and merger game that is being played by large investment bankers around the world. It never made any sense to me, because only one in six mergers breaks even, and many have lost billions off the balance sheet.

The game is called *transactional fees* and involves the study, by the investment bankers, in minute detail of the motivational factors of the key

(continued)

(continued)

players. They end up knowing more about the private lives of the CFO, CEO, board members, and fund managers than they would like their partner to know. Investment bankers go to the CEO and CFO with a proposed merger and acquisition deal, and they often fail. The CFOs and CEOs know that these deals seldom work.

The investment bankers then go to the influential board members, and the CFO and CEO have to fight it out in the boardroom, which they typically will win. The investment bankers, who have now spent hundreds of thousands of dollars in research, are not finished. They go to the fund managers, who are the major shareholders, and say, "The board has lost the plot; they do not recognize the value in this deal!" The fund managers put pressure on the board, whose members, in turn, say to the CEO and CFO, "If we do not do this deal, the fund managers will change the board structure—but before that, we will see that you go first." The CEO says, "What the hell, we will do it." Here is the interesting part. The CEO is offered a big sum to go quietly, and this, along with the investment bankers' fees that are now amortized, through poorly thought out accounting principles, slowly kills the combined company for years to come.

 ## HOW TAKEOVERS OR MERGERS GO WRONG

There are many reasons why TOMs go wrong. Set out below are some of the common ones.

Synergy Calculations Are Totally Flawed

My interest in the failure rate of TOMs dates back to the *Economist*[1] series on six major takeovers or mergers (TOMs). In the articles, the writers commented that over half of TOMs had destroyed shareholder value, and a further third had made no discernible difference.

KPMG undertook a cutting-edge study[2] into TOMs and is a must read for CFOs and controllers involved in a TOM. The study found:

"Only 17% of deals had added value to the combined company, 30% produced no discernible difference, and as many as 53% actually destroyed value. **In other words, 83% of mergers were unsuccessful** in producing any business benefit as regards shareholder value."

TOM advisers and hungry executives are as accurate with potential cost savings estimates as they are with assessing the cost of their own home renovations (in other words, pretty hopeless). Press clippings are easily gathered with CEOs stating that the anticipated savings have taken longer to eventuate. The reason: It can take up to four years to merge the information technology platforms together, and even when this is achieved, many of the future efficiency and effectiveness initiatives have been put on the back burner.

CFOs and controllers, as the experts with the numbers, need to ensure that the CEO and the board are under no illusion about the extent of the cost savings synergies. You can put your last dollar on the fact that the investment bank behind the deal has well and truly overstated these benefits.

The synergy calculations never allow enough costs for the myriad of consultants who are in a feeding frenzy and largely left to their own devices, staff redundancies, loss of some key customers, productivity shortfalls due to uncertainty and the costs of recruiting for key positions, as talented staff decide to move to a less stressed organization.

CASE STUDY: THE MORRISONS TOMS GO ROTTEN

Morrisons, a relatively small but profitably supermarket based in the North of England, has made a number of failed takeovers.

It purchased Safeway for $3 billion, based on the following logic:

- Both businesses were supermarkets, so the merged company could apply greater pressure to suppliers.
- Back-office, distribution, and marketing costs could be cut because of economies of scale.
- Morrisons had a reputation for being very tightly run with good cost controls, and these skills could be applied to the much larger Safeway.

The merger went through in early 2004, and within the next 15 months, or so, Morrisons had to issue five profit warnings. In the year to the end of January 2006, the group made a pretax loss of around £300 million compared to combined profit of about £650 million before the merger. The mistakes made included:

- The 300 Safeway staff at their head office were alienated, severely damaging morale.

(continued)

(continued)

- Morrisons failed to persuade many key Safeway staff to move north to the group's headquarters.
- Morrisons did not protect the key Safeway IT staff who left leaving little knowledge of the Safeway IT system.
- Mixing the two brands, Safeway stores began stocking Morrisons-branded products, which were deemed inferior by Safeway customers.
- The companies underestimated the difficultly to integrate the two company's IT systems—a common mistake.

To prove the lessons had not been learned, in 2011 Morrison's made its first entry into online retailing by paying £70 million to acquire Kiddicare—a leading baby products retailer. The rationale was that the US online retailer would give it a cut-price entry into online retailing, even though the baby goods website had no grocery-related software.

Just three years later, Morrisons sold Kiddicare to a specialist private equity company (Endless) for just £2 million, with the grocery retailer also left with substantial ongoing liabilities for shop leases and other commitments it had made as it tried to grow the Kiddicare business under its control. The total cost of the disastrous takeover for Morrison's shareholders was in excess of £100 million.

Loss of Focus on Customers

There is no better way to lose sight of the ball than a merger. Merging the operations will distract management and staff from the basic task of making money. While meeting after meeting occurs at the office and sales staff focus on their futures (either applying for positions elsewhere or joining in the ugly scramble for the new positions), the customers are up for grabs. Researchers, sales staff, and marketers are all busy back at their desks trying to perform damage-control exercises as they either jockey for the lifeboats or stay on board to try to keep the ship afloat. It would be an interesting PhD thesis to assess the loss of customers due to merger activity.

Culture Clash

Managing the aftermath of a TOM is like herding wild cats. Where have readers seen cultures merged successfully? In reality, one culture takes over another. This is okay when one culture is fundamentally flawed. However, in many mergers, both entities have cultures that work. Now you have a problem. Many competent staff members may choose to leave rather than work in a culture that does not suit their working style.

There Is No Heart in a Merged Organization

How long does it take for a company to develop a heart? This is more than just the culture; it includes the lifeblood of the organization. I think it takes years, and some consistency among the management and staff. The merged organization thus cannot have a heart. The organization can be kept alive on life support, but just like a critical patient, it is effectively bedridden and will be in intensive care for some time.

Loss of Years of Intangibles

An organization is a collection of thousands of years of experience, knowledge, networking, research, projects, and methodologies. If a major blue-chip company said that it was going to disestablish all its staff and management, shareholder analysts would think management had simply lost control. The stock values would fall. This is exactly what a merger does. Research and development is another victim. How do you keep on projects and maintain the level of momentum with unhappy research staff? At worst, you will be moving one team to a new location, making redundant those whom you believe are making the least contribution, and hemorrhaging talent. Research basically gets decimated.

The Wrong Management Rises to the Top

I have a theory that the main beneficiaries of a merger are the piranhas, those managers who see burying a dagger in someone's back as a necessary occurrence. The result is quite interesting; the merged company very soon becomes dysfunctional as more and more of these caustic managers rise to the top.

The senior management meetings make the feeding frenzy over a carcass on the plains of Africa look orderly. These managers do not live and breathe the organization; the ones who did have long since left.

Salary Costs Escalate

There are many financial time bombs that impact shareholder value.

Severance packages can create further waste as staff members, especially the talented ones, leave before generous severance terms disappear. Thus, to retain such people, further salary incentives need to be made that create further pressure on the bottom line.

The TOM is often the time when the shareholders realize the dilution they have been a silent party to comes into full swing, the conversion of options. The surge of the share price as speculators play with the stock means that options can be exercised profitably by the executives who then leave the shareholders holding the rotten TOM.

Human Beings Find It Hard to Conceptualize the Intangibles

For many of us, conceptualizing the abstract is very difficult. A company is most definitely an abstract quantity. It is not a balance sheet; it is much more and much less. Executives in major corporations can write off the annual gross national product of a small country on a failed merger and still not lose sleep at night. The numbers are so large that they appear unbelievable, and the senior management team (SMT) seems to be able to pass them off as just poor management decisions. Yet they are a catastrophe for the investor whose savings are now reduced and the retiree who was relying on the dividends to cover yearly living expenses.

It is impossible for the average board and SMT to completely appreciate all the implications of a merger.

Mergers Are Seldom Done from a Position of Strength

Most mergers are defensive; management is on the back foot trying to make something happen. Defensive TOMs are not a great idea as the companies escaping from a threat often bring their problems into the marriage.

Alternatively, TOMs occur because management consider themselves invincible. They talk to the general public through the press, reveling in their moment in the limelight. Their brief track record of stellar growth is now extrapolated out of all proportion.

There Is Never Enough Time to Fully Evaluate the Target

A merger is like an auction. The buyer rarely has more than a cursory look at the goods before bidding. Management often does not want to find the dirty laundry as it would mean going back to square one again.

It is important not to limit due diligence in the haste to close the deal, as you tend to know less about each other than you think. The dirty laundry often takes years to discover and clean.

Avoiding a Lemon

Some companies are still making fictitious money like Enron did. They are shams, and we need to avoid purchasing a lemon. Companies that look successful, but in reality they grow through acquiring companies and the hype surrounding this activity clouds the real facts.

The Enron documentary should be a compulsory watch for all investors and employees with pensions invested in their companies. The lessons from Enron and other similar collapses provide a useful guide to predicting corporate collapses.

Takeover or Merger Scorecard

I have designed a scorecard covering the aspects executives need to know before boldly going where others have mistakenly gone before (five out of six TOMs fail to achieve the synergism planned). If the merger must go ahead, then please look at the TOM scorecard in the electronic media and get to it. I will not wish you good luck, as that would not be adequate enough.

The current talk is about getting the first 100 days right. Using the findings from Chapter 2, Selling and Leading Change, I would recommend that you master Kaffron and Logan's and John Kotter's work. Applying these learnings, I suggest following these guidelines:

Area	Guidelines
Select influential staff from each organization to be part of a Joint Council	Their role is to: ▪ Identify at-risk key staff. ▪ Identify the oracles that need to get behind the merger. ▪ Be full time on the project with a project office at both head offices. ▪ Communicate to staff across the organization what will happen. ▪ Develop strategies to capitalize on the synergies that are available.

Area	Guidelines
Communication of the merger	■ The communication should be frequent and comprehensive. ■ To staff: What teams are merging, what are not? What rhetoric in the lead to the merger needs to be dispelled / clarified? ■ To key customers (giving assurances about services and quality standards) ■ To key suppliers (likely impact on future ordering) ■ Select some PR consultants who know each organization and use them to draft all communications that will be delivered by respected and familiar faces. Remember the wise words of John Kotter, outlined in Chapter 2: You will undercommunicate by at least a factor of 10 and, at worse, a factor of 100.
Focus on the real synergies	Ignoring the TOM hype what are the real synergies available to the combined operation? Which ones offer the easiest goal and thus should be accessed first?
Maintain and protect the intellectual property	Both organizations will have IP that is under development. It is important that these are not slowed down or abandoned unintentionally.
Finalize the asset strategy	Which assets are duplicated and which ones should be sold? Take note that asset sales are off underpriced as executives are rewarded for achieving the disposals rather than achieving above average sale prices.
Information systems strategy	Which systems are to stay as they are, which systems need to be integrated, and which systems may get integrated? In today's world, having both entities using one system is not necessary. Systems can now convey information through the reporting tools that are now available. The costs of changing an accounting system are horrific in time taken and lost opportunities for the finance team. Leave them as they are. Should, at some later stage, the desired replacement GL be identical for both operations, then merge the accounting systems. This event, however, will be rarer than you think. Far better to use a consolidation and a forecasting and planning tool to coordinate forecasting and reporting.
Labor strategy	What staff reduction can be achieved via natural attrition, targeted early retirement, and finally redundancy? As discussed in Chapter 22 the cost of downsizing maybe greater than retaining the staff.

Although it is tempting, avoid bringing in outside consultants to run this transition process. Most of their previous assignments will have failed and they will have no credibility in-house. Far better to use takeover specialists as advisers to the joint committee.

ALTERNATIVES TO A ROTTEN TOM

Why is it then that senior management and boards rush like lemmings for this self-annihilation? It is understandable why the investment community and shareholders make the mistake; they are simply naive. Try to find an analyst who has been a successful manager in business. The individual's skill is in adding numbers up and the ability to write seemingly sensible evaluations based on little or no knowledge of why mergers cannot work. Shareholders usually have little time for research or are just plain greedy, looking for supernormal returns and believing all the promotional material that merely lifts share prices over the short term.

There are options other than a TOM. You can:

- Remain a boutique operator with strategic alliances. This may be better than risking the fate of many failed TOMs.
- Pay back shareholders the surplus reserves and let them reinvest elsewhere.
- Improve performance by focusing on underperforming assets (that is often the reason why the other company is interested in you in the first place).
- Look to grow the old-fashioned way by expanding from within.
- Invest as a silent partnership (Warren Buffett style) in small but fast-growing companies with complementary services and extract value by internationalizing their innovations.

PDF DOWNLOAD

To assist the finance team on the journey, templates and checklists have been provided. The reader can access, free of charge, a PDF of the suggested scorecard and checklist. www.davidparmenter.com/The_Financial_Controller_and_CFO's_Toolkit.

The PDF download for this chapter includes:

■ Takeover or Merger Scorecard
■ The Warning Signs of a Lemon Checklist

 NOTES

1. "How Mergers Go Wrong," The Economist , (July 22 – August 26, 2000).
2. KPMG Mergers & Acquisitions, A Global Research Report, 2000.

CHAPTER TWENTY-TWO

The Hidden Costs of Reorganizations and Downsizing

OVERVIEW

Far too often, the CFO and controller have been silent when a reorganization is muted. If anyone is to talk sense to the board and senior management team, it has to be the CFO. This chapter will hopefully make the reader aware as to why they need to be very vocal and take steps to prevent these costly mistakes.

A major reorganization is as complex as putting in a new runway at Heathrow Airport while keeping the airport operational. The steps, the consultation, the dynamics, and so forth are as difficult. Then, how is it that we are unable to fully understand the ramifications and costs of a reorganization? Why do organizations appear to have an addiction to reorganizations? This chapter, while not a cure for the addiction, may help management be more aware of the symptoms so that advice can be sought.

RAMIFICATIONS AND ASSOCIATED COSTS

The CFO has historically been far too silent about the associated costs when a reorganization is muted. If anyone is to talk sense to the board and senior management team, it has to be the CFO. The CFO needs to ascertain the costs of such an exercise. To assist, I set out what typically happens in a reorganization.

Loss of key staff in the third- and fourth-tier management ranks. There is a period of chaos, where staff members are disillusioned and many key staff in the third- and fourth-tier management ranks walk out the door with a golden parachute and straight into employment elsewhere.

Dysfunctional management teams. A reorganization can leave you with the also-rans, and the vultures (those nasty individuals busily burying hatchets in all those around).

Higher costs as ex-employees come back as contractors. The bedding-in process starts to kick in somewhere between the seventh and twelfth months. The completion of all the redundancies takes longer than expected and, yes, more than a few will come back as contractors at a higher cost. These costs must not be ignored

Consultants' fees. Costs begin to escalate, especially consultants' fees. You will need help with the culture change and communication.

Designing a new logo, letterhead, signage, and stationery. Look back to the last time these were done for a reasonable estimate.

Recruiting assistance required. As all staff affected will need to reapply for their position, additional HR resources will be required.

Property leases. Unwinding of the property leases that may become surplus can take up to 24 to 36 months until the organization is released from its prior commitment.

About 24 months after the reorganization was announced, productivity is back to normal; thus, for the duration you effectively have been going backward. In the 24- to 36-month period advantages may kick in provided that the reorganization has been successful. It is useful to remember that only one out of seven takeovers or mergers actually works. While reorganizations may have a greater success rate than this, it may well be less than 50 percent.

AN ADDICTION TO REORGANIZATIONS

CEOs seem to think restructuring operations are good for efficiency, improving service, and, of course, their future aspirations. In some sectors, it is an addiction. Government agencies are forever splitting up and then amalgamating. The only purpose I see is to distribute some of the public purse to the private sector advisers, consultants, and contractors (some of whom were previous employees).

As Francis Urquhart, a fictional character in the BBC's 'House of Cards'[1] might say, "Some of you may think that restructuring a department frees the newly formed teams to deliver, others may think that the confusion, miscommunication that often goes with a reorganization undermines people's confidence in what they do and in their team, giving rise to a period of stagnation. You may think that, but I cannot possibly comment."

TYPICAL REASONS FOR A REORGANIZATION

Let us analyze four typical reasons for a reorganization. None of these reasons, in my opinion, really warrants a reorganization.

Reorganizing to Remove Certain Staff

In government and nonprofit agencies, it is not uncommon for a reorganization to occur in order to remove one or two senior managers. It is quite remarkable how much will be done to conceal this real intention. This not only is weak management, it is also stupid.

As Jack Welch[2] points out you need to apply candor and allow these senior managers to move on. In many cases, it is to the benefit of both parties.

Reorganizing to Improve Efficiency

Merging two units/teams together or splitting teams up and re-forming into new teams certainly does create a climate change. The question is whether it leads to efficiency. In order to become more efficient, there needs to be a behavioral and procedural change. Staff members need to change work habits so that logical efficiencies can be introduced.

One energy sector company has made much progress with continuous improvement programs. Senior managers are heavily involved in the change management, and now this is part of the culture. The company has workshops to identify areas where change needs to occur, and people at the meetings agree to take on the process of change. They have had a number of successful projects.

One finance company has had a number of successes with business reengineering. It has made significant inroads by using preferred suppliers and eliminating paperwork or passing over the paperwork to suppliers. Continuous improvement is now part of company culture. There is an ongoing requirement for staff members to keep up in their field, bonuses are paid if you pass a tertiary exam, and so forth.

The interesting point about these two stories is that they arose from business reengineering as opposed to business reorganization. Any efficiencies that reorganizations achieve are simply those that are associated with reengineering the processes. Thus, one can surmise it would have been better to have performed a reengineering exercise in the first place.

One mistake that the uninitiated often make is assuming that large savings are available when merging corporate service functions, such as merging two accounting functions together. In many cases, the costs of changing systems far outweigh the savings from eliminating any duplication of labor costs.

Reorganizing to Improve Service

As stated earlier, a reorganization or merger is like putting in a new runway at Heathrow Airport. Surely, you might think, simply laying down foundations, concrete, and a bit of infrastructure is not that hard. You try telling that to the management at Heathrow Airport.

Likewise, a reorganization is a lot more complex than your planning will have indicated. Day-to-day routines are disrupted with meetings to discuss the new organization, staff members applying for new positions, staff members searching the papers and recruitment agencies for alternative jobs—need I go on? Service does not improve, not in the first two years anyway.

For service to improve, you need a behavioral change. Staff members need to buy into becoming more customer oriented, measuring their performance in a balanced way. You have only to see the quotes on the wall in any Tony's Tire Service (a tire company in New Zealand) customer waiting room to understand that staff members live and breathe service.

Every job is a *self-portrait* of those who did it. Autograph your work with quality. Quality only happens when you care enough to do your best.

A positive behavioral change does not often occur with a reorganization; in fact, quite the reverse occurs in the first two years. So if you are looking for better service, maybe a service program is what is needed rather than a reorganization.

Reorganizing to Show There Is a New CEO

Many CEOs like to stamp their authority by throwing out systems they do not understand and reorganizing the business to fit a model they are more familiar with. They like to show there is a new broom in the organization. This is typical of a CEO with an ego problem. Many reorganizations occur within the first 6 to 12 months of a new CEO arriving, and often these CEOs are making decisions without full knowledge of the business. The cost to the enterprise is huge. In fact, as part of the recruitment process, one should evaluate the reorganizations the CEO has done.

 ## ALTERNATIVES TO A MAJOR REORGANIZATION

Many reorganizations are totally unnecessary. Here are alternatives to a major reorganization that are worth considering.

Remove the Targeted Staff

Instead of putting everybody through a lot of pain, be direct and open and face the issues. Simply remove the one or two senior managers causing the problems. Jack Welch in his book *Winning* offers very sound advice on candor.[3]

Appoint a CEO Who Is a Successful Change Agent

I believe an inspirational CEO will create more value than any reorganization ever will. In fact it would be worthwhile looking to see if inspirational leaders ever fall back on reorganization to solve a problem. I can recall the early days of George Hickton, an eminent New Zealand CEO, taking over the reins of a newly formed government department. Very soon, with a combination of new blood and inspirational leadership, the government department was revolutionized. I believe it was one of the most impressive organizations I have had the pleasure of working for.

I can recall the time when George Hickton was presenting at the Institute of Chartered Accountants conference where the front row was taken up by his direct reports who were both interested and passionate about what the CEO was talking about. This was a rare sight, and I expected David Attenborough, safari shorts and all, to come through the curtains at any moment saying, "You are witnessing an event which is rarely caught on camera."

Move Buildings

A few years ago, a major oil company had a top-heavy head office. The new CEO realized that the best way to change was to sell the large and spacious head office and acquire a smaller head office building, about one third of the size of the original building. He called the business leaders in and said, "Fit in that building, and the staff with members who cannot make it will be made redundant." It transpired, after the move, that there were layers of management whose sole purpose was to attend meetings. Surprisingly enough, when these managers and meetings ceased to exist, the oil company found that operations were unaffected.

Rotate Offices

Arthur Andersen & Co's office in Manchester, UK had another solution. Each year, the senior management team (i.e., the partners) were instructed to move offices. This had the desired effect of energizing and giving the partners a chance to get on top of the paper war. The partners agreed that even though physically moving offices was an inconvenience at the time, the outcome was largely a positive experience.

Improve the Leadership from Within

A reorganization may be an attempt to get around the problem that is created by inadequate or ineffective leadership from the senior management team and the management tier that reports just below that. One way of improving the issue is to undertake a leadership survey, which is a more in-depth look at leadership than a 360-degree feedback process will achieve.

You are then able to support these leaders with mentors and follow with an up-skilling leadership program. Seek mentors who have the X factor. Many would welcome the chance to pass on their knowledge and experience. I guess that if half the people who masterminded a reorganization had talked it through with their mentor, if they had one, many reorganizations would have stayed on the drawing board.

A CHECKLIST TO PUT YOU OFF A REORGANIZATION

Before you look at a reorganization, complete the checklist in the electronic media.

HIDDEN COSTS OF DOWNSIZING

As a CFO, you should never underestimate the long-term impact of downsizing staff. Wherever possible, I believe the CFO should argue that it is better to fund the shortfall out of retained earnings. The cost of firing and rehiring, when added to the public relations disaster it creates, often is much higher than holding onto the staff.

By my calculations (see Exhibit 22.1), an organization with 500 full-time employees that is contemplating dismissing between 50 and 70 staff members would be no worse off if the staff members were kept on and redeployed, where possible, for up to two years.

When faced with a situation where the business is contracting, you can explore a number of options:

- Discuss the issues with the affected operational units and ask them to find new initiatives that can help part fund their salaries. Often, there are a number of income generating possibilities that have not been explored.
- Can you redeploy the staff and buy some time so staff members have time to seek further employment while employed? This is a managed staff reduction process and will save a huge amount of money on redundancies while at the same time giving your staff an opportunity to find employment. This option is unlikely to be available in a major recession.
- Working with the human resources team, formally establish a voluntary redundancy program. This has some downsides, as you can't directly target staff members with lesser skill sets.
- Undertake a reorganization and have everybody reapply for their jobs. This is not a course I would recommend, for reasons stated above.

Based on 500 FTE organization

	General Managers' Time	Managers' Time	Staff to Stay On	Staff Laid Off
Staff involved	4 to 6	90 to 100	340 to 350	50 to 70
		Number of weeks worked		
Unproductive time due to uncertainty	6 to 8	2 to 3	4 to 5	4 to 5
Time spent re-applying for own job	n/a	1 to 2	1 to 2	1 to 2
Interview time	2 to 3	2 to 3	0.5	0.5
Weeks paid as redundancy settlement	n/a	n/a	n/a	10 to 16
Number of weeks worked per person	8 to 11	5 to 8	5.5 to 7.5	15.5 to 23.5
Total weeks for category	32 to 66	450 to 800	1870 to 2625	775 to 1645

Total salary cost (time, redundancy payments) $4.8m to 7.8m

Redundancy support

Cost of rehiring $1.7 to 2.8m

Cost of training

Unproductive time (new staff)

Total cost $6.5m to 10.6m

The downsizing costs would fund between 2.2 and 2.5 years of the laid-off workers' salary and even longer if they could develop some other income.

EXHIBIT 22.1   Hidden Costs of Dismissing Staff

The experts in this area are the human resource team; never make decisions or move to the next stage without full consultation with them. I hope you are never involved in a massive downsizing, but if you are, prepare for it very carefully. Ensure that you have been as innovative with your solutions as possible. If done well, it could create an achievement that lasts for a career.

PDF DOWNLOAD

To assist the finance team on the journey a checklist has been provided which the reader can access, free of charge, from www.davidparmenter.com/ The_Financial_Controller_and_CFO's_Toolkit.

- The reorganization checklist

NOTES

1. House of Cards, 1990 BBC mini-series, which was centered on the scheming politician Francis Urquhart. This series has now been replicated in the highly successful Netflix production, where U.S. Rep. Francis Underwood of South Carolina, a ruthless politician is portrayed so brilliantly by Kevin Spacey.
2. Jack Welch and Suzy Welch, *Winning* (New York: HarperCollins, 2009).
3. Ibid.

Useful Letters and Memos

Email from accounts payable sent to new budget holders

Date _____

Dear _____

Welcome from the accounts payable team

The accounts payable team is committed to adopting and implementing best practices. To this end, we need to work in an effective partnership with all budget holders.

Practices in our organization may differ significantly from those you are used to.

We would like to meet with you for 20 minutes or so to go through our procedures, which will help you in your role as a budget holder. We have a short 20-minute PowerPoint presentation, which we will present on a laptop at your desk. Please advise us of a suitable time within the next few weeks.

In the meantime, you might like to visit our intranet page on _____. We look forward to offering you a seamless service.

Kind regards,

Accounts Payable Team Leader

Memo from CEO sent to all budget holders re attending general ledger (G/L) training

Date _____

Dear _____

Attending G/L training

Please be aware that we have decided to implement a new accounting package. According to research, these implementations are prone to failure without adequate training.

The general ledger licenses and associated costs will be over $_____. Thus, it is imperative that we make this project a success and get it right the first time!

We are also using this implementation to radically alter the way we process accounting transactions. This means that you should be able to spend fewer nights and weekends working on administrative matters.

You will need to attend in person. Please select one course and email back today. I will be taking a personal interest in this and will be monitoring course attendance and no-shows.

If you are unable to attend at any of the scheduled times, please contact me so we can discuss the reasons and possible alternative training times.

Kind regards,

CEO

Memo from CEO inviting all budget holders to attend fast month-end training

Date _____

Dear _____

Attending fast month-end workshop

Please be aware that we have decided to radically change the way we prepare our monthly accounts. Our aim is to free both you and the accounting team from many routines that do not add value.

It is my firm belief that, after this workshop, we will be able to spend more time working in our critical success factors and spend fewer evenings and weekends working on administrative matters.

You will need to attend in person. Please select one course and email back today. I will be taking a personal interest in this and will be monitoring course attendance and no-shows.

If you are unable to attend any of the scheduled workshops, please contact me so we can discuss the reasons and possible alternative times.

Kind regards,

CEO

Memo from CEO inviting selected individuals to attend a quick month-end Post-it reengineering workshop

Date _____

Dear _____

Attending quick month-end workshop—target by 3 working days or less

Sounds impossible, doesn't it, when you consider that we spend __ days on each month-end producing numbers well after the horse has bolted. We have been investing many long evenings and weekends away from our home carrying out a task that is not adding value.

The finance team is proposing a radical change based on best practices. The board and I are convinced it will work. It is estimated to save us over $_____ in time and much more when adding in the full opportunity cost.

It is my firm belief that, after this workshop, we will be able to spend more time working in our critical success factors and spending fewer evenings and weekends working on administrative matters.

I am inviting you, as I value your contribution. You will need to attend in person. Please leave your schedule free during this time so you can attend. I will be attending the first session and I look forward to seeing you there. Should you feel that you are unable to attend, please first contact me so we can discuss the reasons.

Kind regards,

CEO

Memo from CEO sent to all budget holders re compulsory attending of a fast annual planning workshop

Date _____

Dear _____

A two-week annual planning process—workshops on _____ and _____

Sounds impossible, doesn't it, when you consider the four months of pain last year, involving endless discussion, argument, and many long evenings and weekends away from our home.

The finance team is proposing a radical change based on the world's best practices. The board and I are convinced it will work. It is estimated to save us over $_____ in time and much more when adding in the full opportunity cost.

An important part of the process is holding a workshop where the oracles in the business are being asked for their view. We want to use every brain in the game.

You will need to attend in person. Please select one workshop and email back today. I will be taking a personal interest in this and will be monitoring course attendance and no-shows.

Should you feel that you are unable or do not need to attend, please contact me so we can discuss the reasons.

Kind regards,

CEO

Memo from CEO sent to all subsidiary companies re new month-end processes

Date _____

Dear _____

A "nonevent month-end"—no more month-end intercompany disputes

You are no doubt aware that at month-end, we have numerous intercompany disagreements. This delays month-end reporting and means excessive time is spent delivering news well after the horse has bolted.

Modern organizations in the twenty-first-century do not have this problem, and I want our organization to replicate their better practices.

To this end we will be investing in an intercompany application that means one party, the seller, will update both general ledgers simultaneously. I will advise when this occurs.

As from today, the new intercompany rules are as follows:

- The party making the sale will close the ledger off on day−2; all sales on the last day will be treated as next month's transactions and processed then.
- The balance on the accounts payable ledger is to be emailed to the intercompany debtor, who has to process an adjustment to agree.
- All disputes are to occur after month-end.

I will be taking a personal interest in this area and will be monitoring all major intercompany adjustments.

Should you not understand these rules, please first contact the CFO.

Kind regards,

CEO

Letter from accounts payable team leader to suppliers

Date _____

Dear _____

We have thrown away the checkbook and are at a loss as to how to pay you

We are a modern company and have now thrown away the checkbook, which is a technology from Charles Dickens's time. In fact, the last check is mounted in a frame in the CEO's office. Other than trying to recycle that mounted check—of which there is little chance, as the CEO is proud of its symbolic meaning—we have no means of paying you. You should be aware that we have sent you a number of direct credit forms for completion. One solution is that you complete this direct credit form today and email us

(Continued)

at accountspayable@_____; another solution is that you direct debit us; alternatively, we could start a barter system. (I am joking!)

We value the relationship we have with your company and are looking at ways we can link our IT systems with yours so that we process a transaction between us only once. Our IT experts will be in contact with your IT experts sometime in the future. Let's move into the twenty-first-century together!

Kind regards,

AP Team Leader

Memo from CEO to invite selected staff to attend a focus group workshop (needed for quarterly rolling planning and KPIs projects)

Date _____

Invitation to attend a one-day focus group to look at _____

It is important that we have a focus group workshop to kickstart this assignment as:

- There are many pitfalls in such a project, and many projects have failed to deliver in other companies.
- A wide ownership is required, and a focus group can have a huge impact on the selling process.
- The foundation stones need to be understood and put in place early on in the project.
- A focus group will give valuable input on how the implementation should best be done to maximize its impact.

We are seeking a focus group selected from experienced staff members covering the regions, branches, and head office and the different roles, from administrators to the senior management team. I believe you would offer much to this exercise and request that you set aside the time to assist. I welcome your support on this important project. The project team of _____, _____, _____, and _____ will need and appreciate your support.

Please confirm availability to attend this focus group workshop after having discussed it with your manager. I look forward to meeting you at the workshop.

Kind regards,

CEO

Memo to a member of the team for going the extra mile

Date _____

Dear _____

Re: Completing project _____

I would like to comment on the exceptional skills you demonstrated in completing the _____ project on time and within budget. You managed all this while maintaining the routine day-to-day tasks! Please accept this voucher as a small token of the organization's appreciation. I have discussed the recognition with the CEO, who also would like to show her appreciation in person. I have arranged a morning coffee at the CEO's office next Tuesday at 10:30 a.m.

Kind regards,

_____

Letter to a supplier who has gone the extra mile

Date _____

Dear _____

Re: Breathtaking improvement

I would like to acknowledge the exceptional skill your staff and your contractors have demonstrated in the recent installation of XX. The finished product has exceeded my expectations and has been well worth the wait. Should you need a reference, please feel free to give potential customers my number.

Kind regards,

CFO

Letter to the auditors to organize a quick sign-off of year-end accounts

Date _____

Dear _____

Re: Year-end audited accounts

Over the past few years, our year-end has been very costly in lost opportunities. Management and staff have spent far too much time in this exercise.

We wish to adopt world's best practice and complete our accounts within 5 working days, and achieve a sign-off within 15 working days post year-end. As auditors, your firm will be aware of the better practices we wish to adopt.

We would like to hold a meeting within two weeks to ascertain your commitment and agreement on the better practices that need to be adopted.

The outcome should be beneficial to both parties, as we will be much better prepared for your visits, will appoint an audit coordinator role, and so forth.

The agenda of this meeting will cover:

a. Status of prior-year significant audit findings
b. Unresolved internal control and accounting issues
c. The quick year-end better practices
d. Content of audit checklist
e. Proposed deadlines
f. Discussions of new accounting standards and policies
g. Procedures to alert each other to any potential issues
h. Role of internal audit team
i. Content of an "information needs" list

We request that the audit partner, audit manager, and audit senior attend this meeting. We will have a representative from the audit committee, the CFO, and financial controller attending.

Kind regards,

CFO

Letter to the auditors who signed off quickly

Date_____

Dear_____

Re: Year-end sign-off

I would like to acknowledge the exceptional skill your staff has demonstrated during the audit. Your cooperation in a swift audit has been most beneficial and has freed up time to focus on making this year a good year.

I would also like to thank you for your balanced management letter, which celebrated the areas where we have improved and commented on areas for improvement. We can report that we have already made good progress in the suggested areas.

Should you need a reference, please feel free to give potential clients my number.

Kind regards,

CFO

Letter to a mentor

Date _____

Dear _____

Re: Seeking guidance

For a long time now, I have treasured the times I have spent with you. Your wise counsel has been most beneficial.

I would very much like to meet with you periodically to seek your guidance on matters such as career progression, training I should take to fill in experience and skill gaps, and industry issues, as well as advice on problems.

I thought we could hold these meetings over lunch, at my expense, at your convenience.

Kind regards,

_____

Rules for a Bulletproof Presentation

D elivering compelling, bulletproof presentations is a skill you need to acquire for implementing change, so it is best to start learning now. I will assume that you have attended a presentation skills course, which is a prerequisite to bulletproof PowerPoint presentations. The speed of delivery, voice levels, using silence, and getting the audience to participate are all techniques that you need to be familiar with and comfortable using.

To assist you I have prepared a list of 25 rules for a good presentation as shown in Exhibit B.1.

EXHIBIT B.1   Preparing and Delivering a Compelling Presentation Checklist

Prepare a paper to go with the presentation	1. Always prepare a paper for the audience covering detailed numbers and so forth so that you do not have to show detail in the slides (see rule 2).
	2. Understand that the PowerPoint slide is not meant to be a document; if you have more than 35 words per slide, you are creating a report, not a presentation. Each point should be relatively cryptic and be understood only by those who have attended your presentation.

(continued)

EXHIBIT B.1 *(continued)*

| Presentation planning | 3. Last-minute slide presentations are a career-limiting activity. You would not hang your dirty washing in front of a hundred people, so why would you want to show your audience sloppy slides? Only say yes to a presentation if you have the time, resources, and enthusiasm to do the job properly.

4. Create time so that you can be in a "thinking space" (e.g., work at home, go to the library, etc.).

5. Map the subject area out in a mind map and then do a mind dump on Post-it stickers covering all the points, diagrams, pictures you want to cover. Have one sticker for each point. Then place your stickers where they fit best. Using stickers makes it easy to reorganize them. This will lead to a better presentation.

| Presentation content | 6. At least 10% to 20% of your slides should be high-quality photographs, some of which will not even require a caption.

7. A picture can replace many words; to understand this point you need to read *Presentation Zen: Simple Ideas on Presentation Design and Delivery* by Garr Reynolds,[1] and *Slide:ology: The Art and Science of Creating Great Presentations* by Nancy Duarte.[2]

8. Understand what is considered good use of color, photographs, and the "rule of thirds."

9. For key points, do not go less than 30-pt-size font. As Nancy Duarte says, "Look at the slides in the slide sorter view at 66% size. If you can read it on your computer, it is a good chance your audience can read it on the screen."

---

[1] Garr Reynolds, *Presentation Zen: Simple Ideas on Presentation Design and Delivery*, New Riders, 2008.
[2] Nancy Duarte, *Slide:ology: The Art and Science of Creating Great Presentations*, O'Riley, 2008.

EXHIBIT B.1　*(continued)*

	10. Limit animation; it is far better that the audience is able to read all the points on the slide quickly rather than holding them back.
	11. Use Guy Kawasaki's "10/20/30 rule." A sales-pitch PowerPoint presentation should have 10 slides, last no more than 20 minutes, and contain no font smaller than 30 pt.
	12. Be aware of being too cute and clever with your slides. The move to creating a lot of whitespace is all very well, provided your labels on the diagram do not have to be very small.
	13. Never show numbers to a decimal place or to the dollar if the number is greater than 10,000. If sales are $9,668,943.22, surely it is better to say, "approx. $10 million" or "$9.6 million." The precise number can be in the written document if it is deemed worthwhile.
	14. Never use clipart; it sends shivers down the spine of the audience and you may lose them before you have a chance to present.
Use technology	15. Where possible, if you are going to present on a regular basis, make sure you have a Tablet PC, which gives you the ability to draw when you are making points. This makes the presentation more interesting, no matter how bad you are at drawing.
	16. Have a simple remote mouse so that you can move the slides along independently of your computer.
Practice, practice, practice	17. Practice your delivery. The shorter the presentation, the more you need to practice. For my father's eulogy, I must have read it through 20 to 30 times. It still remains today the best speech I have ever delivered and the one I prepared the most for.
Presentation itself	18. Bring theatrics into your presentation. Be active as a presenter, walking up the aisle so that those in the back see you close up, vary your voice, get down on one knee to emphasize an important point. Have a bit of fun and your audience will, too. Very few things are unacceptable as a presenter.
	19. Always tell stories to relate to the audience, bringing in humor that is relevant to them. A good presenter should be able to find plenty of humor in the subject without having to resort to telling jokes. No doubt, some of the audience have heard the jokes and would rather hear them from a professional comedian.

(continued)

EXHIBIT B.1 *(continued)*

20. Make sure your opening words grab the audience's attention.

21. Understand Stephen Few's work on dashboard design if you are using graphs.

22. Always remember that the audience does not know the whole content of your speech, particularly if you keep the details off the slides; if you do leave some point out, don't worry about it—they don't know or would not realize the error.

23. If there has been some issue relating to transportation, technology, and so forth that has delayed the start, avoid starting off with an apology. You can refer to this later on. Your first five minutes is the most important for the whole presentation and must therefore be strictly on the topic matter.

24. Greet as many members of the audience as you can before the presentation, as it will help calm your nerves, and it will also give you the opportunity to clarify their knowledge and ask for their participation, such as at question time. The other benefit is that it confirms that nobody in the audience would rather be doing your role, so why should you be nervous?

25. If you are delivering a workshop at the end, shake hands with as many of the audience as possible by positioning yourself by the door when the audience leaves. This develops further rapport between presenter and audience.

In addition, I have included a checklist for preparing and delivering a presentation; see Exhibit B.2.

EXHIBIT B.2 PowerPoint Presentations Checklist

Planning

Develop a purpose of the presentation.	☐ Yes	☐ No
Have a goal for the number of slides you will need.	☐ Yes	☐ No
Perform a research of the subject.	☐ Yes	☐ No
Do you know your audience?	☐ Yes	☐ No
Do you know what they are like?	☐ Yes	☐ No
Do you know why they are coming to the presentation?	☐ Yes	☐ No
Do you know what their emotional drivers, points of pain are?	☐ Yes	☐ No

EXHIBIT B.2   *(continued)*

Planning		
Can you solve any of their problems?	☐ Yes	☐ No
Have you thought about solutions that they can work with immediately?	☐ Yes	☐ No
Have you thought of what handouts you can provide electronically to help them with the next steps?	☐ Yes	☐ No
Have you thought about why they might resist your suggestions?	☐ Yes	☐ No
The creative phase		
While you are creating, avoid editing as you are going along. As stated above, map the subject area out in a mind map and then do a mind dump on Post-it stickers covering all the points, diagrams, pictures you want to cover.	☐ Yes	☐ No
Review recent articles or recent seminars you have attended for clever and concise diagrams.	☐ Yes	☐ No
Find some diagrams that tell a story.	☐ Yes	☐ No
The editing phase		
The person preparing the slides needs to have attended a course on PowerPoint.	☐ Yes	☐ No
Are you using the whole slide? (Avoid using the portrait option for slides.)	☐ Yes	☐ No
Do you create a progress icon to show the audience the progress through a presentation?	☐ Yes	☐ No
Portrait pictures can be moved to one side and the title and text to the other.	☐ Yes	☐ No
Are all detailed pictures expanded to the whole slide? (Ignore the need for a heading.)	☐ Yes	☐ No
Any typeface in a picture smaller than 24 point will need to be enlarged.	☐ Yes	☐ No
Limit bullet points to 5 to 6 separate points per slide.	☐ Yes	☐ No
Repeat a good diagram if you are talking about a section of it at a time.	☐ Yes	☐ No
Have slides read through by someone who has good editing skills.	☐ Yes	☐ No
If you have pictures of people, do you ensure that they are looking toward the slide content?	☐ Yes	☐ No

(continued)

EXHIBIT B.2 *(continued)*

First run through of the presentation		
Once the slides have been edited, go straight into a full practice run with one or two of your peers in attendance.	☐ Yes	☐ No
Time the length and avoid any interruptions; the practice audience should note improvements as they are spotted.	☐ Yes	☐ No
Now repeat this process twice more; if it is a short, 15- to 20-minute presentation, up to five full practices will be necessary. The shorter a presentation is the more practice sessions will be required.	☐ Yes	☐ No
Prepare the master copy of the slides so you can check all is clear, and courier to seminar organizer.	☐ Yes	☐ No
If workshop exercises are to be included, read through these carefully and get them checked for clarity by an independent person.	☐ Yes	☐ No
Print slides 3 to a page except for complex slides that should be shown on their own.	☐ Yes	☐ No
Test your laptop on at least two data shows, as some custom settings that maximize your network can prevent your laptop linking to the projector.	☐ Yes	☐ No
Night before		
Avoid late changes. Nothing annoys the audience more than the presentation being in a different order to the presentation handout. You will make a rod for your own back when you get requests for the missing slides!	☐ Yes	☐ No
Always test the data show projector the night before if you are required to run it (you may find a missing cable).	☐ Yes	☐ No
Carry with you a spare power extension lead and the standard laptop to data show cable.	☐ Yes	☐ No
Travel the night before (plane travel deadens the senses, it can affect hearing, and you cannot trust the schedules).	☐ Yes	☐ No
If possible, bring a spare projector with you for extra protection.	☐ Yes	☐ No
Avoid alcohol the night before, as it will reduce the quality of your performance the next morning.	☐ Yes	☐ No
Bring your own laptop to the presentation.	☐ Yes	☐ No
Practice the night before, especially the first 5 minutes (you will need two stories in the first 5 minutes).	☐ Yes	☐ No

EXHIBIT B.2 *(continued)*

On the day		
Do a brief run through the first 5 minutes at the proper speed before breakfast.	☐ Yes	☐ No
Light exercise is a great idea to freshen the mind (I usually go for a swim before I speak).	☐ Yes	☐ No
Tell stories instead of jokes unless you are very good at it (joke telling requires excellent timing).	☐ Yes	☐ No
Greet as many members of the audience as you can before the presentation. It will help calm your nerves and give you the opportunity to clarify their knowledge and ask for their participation, such as at question time.	☐ Yes	☐ No
At the first break, meet with a sample of the audience and enquire about whether the material is of interest and about the pace of delivery. This may pick up any problems and thus helps improve the assessment ratings.	☐ Yes	☐ No
Never apologize to the audience; simply state the facts if there is a difficulty of some kind.	☐ Yes	☐ No
Run through an example of the workshop exercise to ensure every workshop group has the correct idea of what is required.	☐ Yes	☐ No
Recap what has been covered to date and ask for questions.	☐ Yes	☐ No
At the end of the presentation, shake hands with as many of the audience as possible by positioning yourself by the door when the audience leaves. This develops further rapport between presenter and audience.	☐ Yes	☐ No
Celebrate—you have done your best.	☐ Yes	☐ No

Satisfaction Survey for a Finance Team

nitially, once a year and then twice a year, run a statistically based sample survey on your in-house customers. Send them the survey set out in this appendix. The key features are:

- Ask two open-ended questions that will generate most of the benefit for the survey: "What are the three things we do well?" and "What are the three things we can improve on?" Never ask about the problems, as half of them will not be fixable.
- Categorize all responses to these questions in a database and sort out by positive comments and suggestions for improvement.
- Use a five-point scale.
- Separate out accounting system dramas from the services your team provides by asking a series of system-related questions.
- Send them by email or use a web-based survey package as sourced from www.SurveyMonkey.com.
- Never ask questions you will not act on.
- Make the questionnaire simple and able to be completed in 10 minutes.

FINANCE TEAM USER SATISFACTION QUESTIONNAIRE

The purpose of the user satisfaction survey is to aid the finance team to deliver a quality service. In this questionnaire we are seeking to investigate your satisfaction with your relationship with the **finance team since** _____. Your response will help us make sure we deliver a quality service.

Your response (in the shaded areas) will help us make sure we deliver a quality service. The comment fields are a very helpful part of a feedback to the finance team. Please invest time in making the comments as specific as possible and give examples where this is appropriate. Your ratings and your comments are totally confidential. _____ (the company conducting the survey) will prepare the statistical data and display comments so as to conceal the identities of respondents. Please return no later than _____ by e-mail to _____ @ _____ .

How satisfied are you with the finance team's systems in the following areas? Please use the rating scale for the survey.

Rating 5 = Very satisfied, 4 = Satisfied, 3 = Neither satisfied nor dissatisfied, 2 = Dissatisfied, 1 = Very dissatisfied, X = cannot rate						
Finance System	Cannot Rate	Ease of Use	Ease of Accessing Data You Need	Adequacy of Reporting	Usefulness of System's Reference Guide	Adequacy of Help Desk Support
Purchase order system						
Accounts payable system						
Expense claim system						
Purchasing card system						
Accounts receivable system						
General ledger/ Reporting system						
Payroll system						
Forecasting system						

How satisfied are you with the following finance team's activities? Please use the rating scale for the survey.

Rating

5 = Very satisfied, 4 = Satisfied, 3 = Neither satisfied nor dissatisfied, 2 = Dissatisfied, 1 = Very dissatisfied, X = Not applicable, cannot rate

How satisfied are you with the:	Cannot Rate	Timeliness	Accuracy (Quality Assurance)	Proactive/ Responsiveness	Expertise of Staff	Output (Fit for Purpose)
Processing of sales invoices?						
Processing of purchase invoices?						
Fixed assets processing/ reporting?						
Payment of expenses?						
Coordination and support of budget process?						
Coordination of reforecasting?						
Advice to business units? (on variance analysis, planning, financial implications of policy, etc.)						
Monthly financial information?						
One-to-one training?						
_____ (please specify)						
_____ (please specify)						

Please rate your satisfaction with the finance team's working style (only those teams you have contact with).

Rating 5 = Very satisfied, 4 = Satisfied, 3 = Neither satisfied nor dissatisfied, 2 = Dissatisfied, 1 = Very dissatisfied, x = Not applicable, cannot rate					
How satisfied are you with the:	Accounts Payable	Accounts Receivable	Management Accounting	Payroll	Systems Accountants
Team's accessibility and promptness in replying to your queries?					
Willingness to take ownership of issues (including responding constructively to criticism)?					
Proactive role of the team in anticipating issues?					
Team's understanding of issues from your perspective?					
Team's service ethic (approachability, positive attitude, supportiveness, commitment to continuous improvement)?					
Degree of respect the team demonstrates toward you (e.g., arriving on time for meetings, delivering to deadlines, honoring promises, responding to e-mails)?					
Team's follow through/ability to close issues?					

Please rate your satisfaction with the finance team's communication (only those teams you have contact with).

Rating
5 = Very satisfied, 4 = Satisfied, 3 = Neither satisfied nor dissatisfied, 2 = Dissatisfied, 1 = Very dissatisfied, x = Not applicable, cannot rate

How satisfied are you with the:	Accounts Payable	Accounts Receivable	Management Accounting	Payroll	Systems Accountants
Frequency of face-to-face communication (e.g., not hiding behind emails)?					
Way we communicate operational/routine issues?					
Way we communicate complex issues?					
Overall effectiveness of our communication?					
Meetings that we host (keeping the meeting on track and on time)?					
Contribution we make to meetings you host (being prepared, our level of participation, and the follow-up action we undertake)?					
Presentations we deliver?					
Content of the finance team's intranet pages?					
Reporting we give you?					

What do you consider to be the three main strengths of this service? (If you have used any "5" ratings, please give examples).

What do you consider are three main areas for this service to develop? (If you have used any "1" ratings, please give examples. Please also give suggestions of specific changes you would like.)

Please insert your name. Your name will only be used for administrative purposes.	
If the findings of this survey were to be presented, would you be interested in attending the presentation?	Yes / No *(Circle as appropriate)*

Thank you for participating.

Index

Abandonment
  annual reporting processes 231–232
  preached by Peter Drucker 11–13
Accounts payable,
  early closing 36–37
  "shame and name" lists 87
  ban payment by check 84
  buyer-created invoices 89
  changes in the balance of work
    (exhibit) 78
  electronic ordering 80
  frequent direct credit payment runs 85
  improving budget holder cooperation 85
  paperless 79–80
  purchasing card 81–83
  self-generated invoices 89
  the accounts payable network 79
  timing of payment runs 85
  welcome letter to new budget holders 86
  working with the main suppliers 88
Accounts payable systems,
  payables automation (exhibit) 60
  providers and their applications
    (exhibit) 62
  technology to use (exhibit) 60
Accounts receivable,
  aged debtors graph (exhibit) 247
  debtors' collection 248
  direct debiting 248
  early closing 38
  month-end bottlenecks 247
Accruals
  early closing 36–37
  setting materiality 37
Activity based costing
  Why you should avoid it 275–276
Agile techniques 211
Annual planning
  a burning platform 283
  questionable activity 282–285

see budgeting and planning
  speed of (exhibit) 284
Annual reporting
  audit coordinator 236
  case studies 242–243
  collaborative disclosure software
    235–236
  consolidation software 235
  controlling the last mile 240–242
  costing the process 227–228
  costing the process (exhibit) 228
  data capture 241
  draft agenda for the quick annual
    reporting workshop (exhibit) 233
  fixed assets verification 238–239
  get organized 229–234
  hard close month 10 or 11 231
  help get the auditors organized 230
  intercompany software 235
  internal auditors 239
  management letter 239–240
  minimize year-end stress 236–240
  overs and unders schedule 237
  post-it re-engineering 232
  quality assurance 242
  renegotiate the auditor's deadline
    230–231
  scrum meetings 232
  selling the need for change
    226–229
  stocktakes 237–238
  the five stages 226
  time frames (exhibit) 229
  use technology 235–236
  work in progress valuation 238
  year-end rules 229–230

Baggaley, Bruce 266
Balanced scorecard,
  six not four perspectives 332

Balanced scorecard,
  six perspectives (exhibit) 332
Benchmarks
  finance team bad habits (table) 5–6
  finance team benchmarks 7
Beyond budgeting 150, 284
Board dashboard
  key result indicators 362–364
Board papers software
  features 67
  some providers and their applications
    (exhibit) 67
Board reporting
  avoiding the rewrites 138
  better practices 136
  costing the preparation 136–137
  costing the preparation (exhibit) 137
  examples of key result indicators for a
    board dashboard (exhibit) 144–147
  one-page board dashboard A3 / fanfold
    (exhibit) 143
  paperless board meeting 139
  scheduling more timely meetings 139
  scoping the information requests 138
  top mistakes 140–141
Budgeting and planning 4 or 5 week
    months 163–164
  account codes 159–160
  annual targets 285–286
  avoid monthly phasing of the annual
    budget 154, 156
  better practices 152–164
  birthday cake analogy (exhibit) 158
  budgeting at category level rather than
    account code level 159–160
  built in a planning tool (exhibit) 163
  consolidating account codes
    (exhibit) 161
  costing template (exhibit) 152
  costing the process 151–152
  costing the process (exhibit) 152
  counting the trees analogy (exhibit) 159
  draft agenda for a focus group
    (exhibit) 165
Budgeting and planning,
  draft agenda for the briefing workshop
    (exhibit) 174
Budgeting and planning, efficient processes
  hold a focus group workshop

  forecasting demand by major customers
    by major products
  required pre-work
  accurately forecasting personnel costs
  automate the calculation for some
    expense categories
  provide automated calculations for travel
    and accommodation
  prepare a simple reporting template for
    the annual plan
  have trend graphs for every category
    forecasted
  if using a spreadsheet simplify the model
    to make it more robust
  expand your team as budget holders will
    need one-to-one support
  hold a briefing workshop for all budget
    holders 164–174
  expenditure trend graph (exhibit) 172
  focus group workshop 164–166
  forecasting demand by major customers
    by major products 166–168
  forecasting demand by major customers
    (exhibit) 167
Budgeting and planning,
  the foundation stones,
  separation of targets from
    the annual plan.
  bolt down your strategy beforehand.
  avoid monthly phasing of the annual
    budget
  the annual plan does not give an annual
    entitlement to spend.
  budget committee commit to a lock - up
  budgeting at category level rather than
    account code level
  getting it wrong quicker
  built in a planning tool –not
    in spreadsheets 153–164
  one-page annual plan (exhibit) 157
  payroll calculation worksheet
    (exhibit) 163
  questionable activity 282–285
  revenue forecasting 166–168
  travel and accommodation calculator
    (exhibit) 171
  two-week timetable (exhibit) 162
  wisdom of the crowd 167
Budgeting and planning myths
  annual targets 285–286

plan around calendar months 288
requires months of work 287–288
annual entitlement 287
budget at account code level 287
forecast out only to the current year-end
284–287
monthly targets 286
quicker this year 288
Budgeting software
see planning and forecasting tools

Candour 203
Case studies
a major road contracting company
284–285
Ballance Agri-Nuturients 54–56, 303
British Airways CSF 318–319
Johnson & Johnson 96–98
Motorola 98–99
Cash flow report,
longer range (exhibit) 115
shorter range (exhibit) 114
Celebrate 212 ,214
Change, leading and selling,
annual budgeting and planning
150–152
burning platform 4
burning platform presentation 20,
23–24
default future 18
elevator speech 20,
emotional drivers 22, 24, 150–151
invented future 18, 21
John Kotter's eight stage process 20–21
power of the focus group 24–25
Self-persuasion (exhibit) 19
Chart of accounts
limiting to 60 P/L account codes
266–267
rules 267
subsidiaries' chart of accounts 267
Churchill, Sir Winston 18
Collaborative disclosure management
background 65–66
some providers and their applications
(exhibit) 66
Collins, Jim 21, 200, 202, 250, 358
Consolidation software
background 64–65
some providers and their applications
(exhibit) 65

Cost apportionment 267–268
Covey, Stephen 322
Critical success factors
alignment with strategy (exhibit) 317
benefits 317–319
British Airways CSF (case study)
318–319
characteristics (list) 323
differences from external outcomes
321–324
external outcomes 322
first things first (analogy) 322
hierarchy of success factors (exhibit) 318
how CSFs and KPIs fit together
(exhibit) 319
how strategy and the CSFs work together
(exhibit) 321
linkage to strategy (exhibit) 319
operational in nature 321–322,
323–324
the missing link 323–324
what impacts the CSFs (exhibit) 320
relationship among CSFs strategy
and KPIs 319–321
Cunningham, Jean 8, 277

Dashboards
common problems with dashboards
128–129
Data visualisation
better practices 130–133
combination of "sparklines" and "bullet"
graphs (exhibit) 362
common problems with dashboards
128–129
Downsizing
hidden costs 405–407
hidden costs (exhibit) 406
other options 403–405
Drucker, Peter 12, 204, 206, 292
Duarte, Nancy 24, 219

Email handling
golden rules 193–196
Enneagram 200–201

Few, Stephen 102, 113, 125, 128, 358,
361–362
Fiume, Orest j. 266
Ford, Dr. Richard 255

Forecasting,
a fast light touch (completed in an
elapsed week) 298–301
a quarter-by-quarter funding
mechanism 296–297
a quarterly process using the wisdom
of the crowd 294–295
abandonments (list) 293
Ballance Nutrients (case study) 303
built in a planning tool –not
in a spreadsheet 301
checklists 313
comprehensive blueprint 303
draft agenda for a focus group
workshop 309
efficient processes 303–306
emotional drivers 282
fast because of (list) 298–301
forecast beyond year-end (e.g. six
quarters ahead) 295–296
forecasting at category level rather than
account code level 298
forecasting on a 445 basis exhibit 302
foundation stones 291–303
how the rolling forecast works for an
organization (exhibit) 290
implementation barriers (list) 307
invest in a comprehensive
blueprint 303
involve all budget holders 305
one-page summary 303–304
planning tool with four and five week
months 301–302
post-it reengineering 308
quarterly process 294–295, 305–306
quarterly updated forecast
(exhibit) 304
quarterly updated forecast, fourth
quarter (exhibit) 300
reporting template (exhibit) 312
separation of targets from realistic
forecasts 294
seven-day reforecast process timetable
(exhibit) 299
templates 313
the annual plan becomes a by-product
of the QRF 297
the monthly targets are set a quarter
ahead from the QRF 296
the QRF model should be built
by in-house resources 294

the QRF should be based around the key
drivers 298
wisdom of the crowd 294–295
Forecasting software
see planning and forecasting tools
Fraser, Robin 346

Gallo, Carmine 24, 219
General ledger
avoiding the hard sell to upgrade your
G/L 68–69
delay changing your G/L 95
front-end tools (exhibit) 63
maximize the use of the existing G/L 68
Graphics
better practices 130–133
Gunnarsson, Jan 202

Haas Edersheim, Elizabeth 13
Hermann's thinking preferences 201
Hope, Jeremy 7, 95, 150, 275, 282, 283,
286, 301, 372, 373, 301, 377, 378
Hope, Jeremy's quotes 51, 150, 283,
372, 373
Hostmanship 202

IBM
whitepaper library 53
global c-suite study 5
Implementing a new system
"planner tool provider" evaluation
checklist (exhibit) 71
appraising the options 69–70
best three applications 70–72
have three pilots 72–73
the key steps 70, 72
Integrity 202–203
Intercompany software
some providers and their applications
(exhibit) 65

Jobs, Steve 13–14

Kanban board
exhibit 188–189
Kaplan, Robert 331, 335, 346,
Kawasaki, guy 218
Kennedy, Frances 8, 106, 269
Kotter, John 20–21

KPI myths
  all performance measures are KPIs
    329–330
  by tying KPIs to remuneration you will
    increase performance 330
  indicators are either lead or lag indicators
    331–335
  KPIs are financial and nonfinancial
    indicators 331
  measures are cascaded down the
    organization 335–336
  measuring performance is relatively
    simple 330
  most measures lead to better
    performance 329
  there are only four balanced scorecard
    perspectives 331
KPIs
  10/80/10 rule 346–348
  10/80/10 rule (exhibit) 347–348
  A3 (fanfold) one-page board dashboard
    (exhibit) 364
  British Airways KPI story 318–319
  daily human resources (exhibit) 355
  daily KPI report (exhibit) 353
  daily reporting 352
  examples 345–346
  financial and nonfinancial indicators 331
  financial measures 354
  future measures (exhibit) 334
  human resources 352–354
  information systems monthly team
    balanced scorecard (exhibit) 366
  key performance indicators 340–343
  key result indicators 338–339
  KPI myths 328–338
  monthly report to management
    (exhibit) 360
  nonfinancial measures 354
  past current or future measures 334
  performance indicator 340
  reporting progress to staff (exhibit) 363
  reporting to management and staff
    352–354
  research 328
  result indicators 339–340
  seven characteristics 343–345
  suggested performance reporting
    portfolio (exhibit) 367
  the dark side 336–338

  the four measures (exhibit) 338
  the four types of performance measures
    338–346
  the four types of performance measures
    (exhibit) 338
  unintended consequences 336–338
  unintended consequences accident and
    emergency department
    (case study) 337
  unintended consequences late train
    measure backfires (case study) 337
  weekly human resources report
    (exhibit) 359
  weekly KPI report (exhibit) 357
  weekly team-progress update
    (exhibit) 365

Lead / lag indicators 331–335
Leadership foundation stones
  minimize personal baggage
  "love thy neighbor as thyself"
  mastery of communication and public
    relations
  have a cluster of mentors and a safe
    haven
  fearless in pursuit of legacy
  be a follower of the paradigm shifters
    200–207
Leading change, see change, leading and
    selling
Lean management techniques 208–211
Lean accounting
  costing of a product 274–275
  impact on profitability 271–274
  one-off deals 275
  rate of flow (exhibit) 274
Lean movement
  background 7–11
  eight types of waste (table) 9–10
  Toyota 14 lean management principles
    10–11
Liker, Jeffrey 119
Logan, Dave 18, 20–21
Lorber, Robert 205

Marketing the finance team,
  celebrate 212, 214
  in-house customer survey 220–222
  networking 215, 217
  putting the finance team on the map
    215–222

Marketing the finance team (*Continued*)
  relationships with budget holders 220
  walkabout 204–205
Maskell, Brian 8, 105–106, 269
Mcgregor, Douglas 377
Mcintosh, David 210
Meetings
  action meetings 210–211
Mentors, the four types 205–206
Mills, Harry 19, 21, 255
Mintzberg, Henry 376
Month-end reporting
  accruals 37
  adjustments 34–35, 41–42
  avoiding rewriting 92–93
  benefits of quick reporting (table) 31
  changing the focus of the finance team's
    work (exhibit) 32
  day one reporting 96
  early closing of capital expenditure 38
  establishing reporting rules 33–34
  flash report 39–40
  flash report to CEO at end of day
    one exhibit 39
  four or five week months 93–94
  implementing four or five week months
    93–94
  intercompany adjustments 37–38
  inventory 38–39
  key activities of a day three month-end
    (exhibit) 44
  major steps you can do before next
    month-end 33–41
  materiality 33–35, 37, 39, 41–42
  overs and unders schedule 34–35
  quality assurance 41–43
  speed of month-end reporting ranking
    exhibit 30
  timing of time sheets 92
  virtual closing 99

Neuro-linguistic programming 201
Norton, David 331, 335, 346

One-on-one progress meetings 214–215
Osborne, Mike 210

Performance bonus schemes,
  apply the full cost of capital 375
  avoid an annual entitlement 378
  avoid any linkage to the share price
    or share options 376–377
  avoid linking to KPIs 384
  checklist (pdf toolkit) 385
  communication 384
  exclude super profits 373–374
  exclude unrealized gains 381–382
  foundation schemes 372–384
  get the management and staff
    on side 384
  link to a balanced performance 378–381
  make bonuses team based rather than
    individual based 377–378
  NZ bank (case study) 375
  remove "profit enhancing" accounting
    adjustments 374–375
  retention of super profits (benefits) 374
  retention of super profits (exhibit) 374
  separate at-risk portion of salary from
    the scheme 375–376
  southwest airlines (case study) 377–378
  test scheme to minimize manipulation
    382–384
  test scheme to minimize manipulation
    382–384
  testing the performance scheme on past
    results (exhibit) 383
  the billion-dollar giveaway 372
  theory x theory y 377
  use relative measures instead of an
    annual target 373
Performance management
  finance team performance gaps
    (exhibit) 5
Peters, tom 358
Planning and forecasting tools 53–59
  Ballance Agri-Nuturients case study
    54–56
  some providers and their applications
    (exhibit) 57–59
Planning tools 301–302
Presenting
  deliver killer presentations 219–220
Procurement system
  see accounts payable
Project accounting 267
Public relations 203–205
Purchasing card 81–83
  a free accounts payable system 81
  better practices 83

example of a purchasing card (exhibit) 82
how the purchasing card works 82–83
what it is targeting (exhibit) 81

Quality assurance
error free reporting 125–127
month-end reporting 41–43
text- to- voice 127
two gremlin rule 127
two-person read-through 126–127
Quarterly rolling forecasting, see forecasting

Recognition 212, 214, 219
Recruiting
advert 254
assessment centers 258
Cathay Pacific recruitment (case study)
255–256
ever-present danger 250–251
final check against requirements
(exhibit) 261
finance team involvement 260
first round 255
fourth round 258–260
general motors (case study) 250
human resources team 257
induction 260–262
look for values and fit 252–253
need to up-skill 251
never give a new job to a new person 253
paint the picture first 253
promote your finance team to the outside
world 252
psychometric testing 257–258
recruiting agencies 254
reference checks 258–260
second round 256
seek internal referrals 254
simulation exercises 257–258
the marathon 252–260
third round 256–258
Recruiting, Peter Drucker's advice
paint the picture first
never give a new job to a new person
focus on interviewee's strengths
minimum of three candidates for shortlist
previous boss check 253, 256, 259
Re-engineering
annual planning 185
annual reporting 185

instructions (exhibit) 179
post-it reengineering month-end routines
178–185
post-it sticker 178–185
post-it sticker case studies 184–185
workshop agenda (exhibit) 181
Reorganizations
alternatives to a major reorganization
403–405
an addiction to reorganizations 401
checklist to put you off
a reorganization 405
ramifications 400
typical reasons for a reorganization
401–403
some providers and their applications
(exhibit) 63
Report templates
balance sheet (exhibit 110
business unit's report (exhibit) 104
capex approval report (exhibit) 118
capital expenditure proposal
(exhibit) 120
cash flow reporting (exhibits) 114–115
Report templates,
CEO's finance report A3 /fanfold
(exhibit) 109
consolidated profit and loss (exhibit) 107
daily sales report(exhibit) 121
late projects (exhibit) 123
late reports (exhibit) 124
one page board dashboard A3 / fanfold
(exhibit) 143
rolling forecasting (exhibit) 111
simple capex slippage report (exhibit) 117
smart phone report (exhibit) 125
sparkline and bullet graphs (exhibit) 116
value stream reporting (exhibit) 105
weekly sales report (exhibit) 122
Reporting using value streams, exhibit 270
Reporting, foundation stones 102
Reynolds, Garr 24, 219
Rolling forecasting
see forecasting

Scrum meetings
annual reporting 232
the daily scrum / fortnightly sprint
(exhibit) 187
the process 185–188

Selling change,
  implementing rolling forecasting 282
  Board reporting 136–137
Selling change, see change, leading
  and selling
Simons, Robert 377
Spitzer, Dean 336, 338
Spreadsheets
  ban spreadsheets from core finance
    routines 50–52
  career limiting 52
  common problems with spreadsheets
    50–51
  new CFO finds an error (case study)
    51–52
  removing from the month - end routines
    95–96
  rule of 100 rows 51
Strategy
  a strategy slide deck (exhibit)155
  external outcomes 322–323
  on slides on in a report 155
  relationship between strategy and CSFs
    319–320
Surowiecki, James 167
Svenska Handelsbanken,
  case study 284

Takeover and merger
  AOL and Time Warner (case study)
    388–389
  big failures 388–390
  culture clash 392–393
  Glaxo Wellcome / Smithkline Beecham
    (case study) 389
  hard to conceptualize the intangibles 394
  how they go wrong 390–397
  investment banker reveals driving forces
    389–390
  KPMG study 390
  Kraft Cadbury takeover (case study) 388
  loss of focus on customers 392
  loss of years of intangibles 393
  mergers are seldom done from a position
    of strength 394
  Morrisons (case study) 391–392
  no heart in merged organization 393
  reasons for a takeover or merger 388
  salary costs escalation 393–394
  synergy calculations 390–391

takeover and merger scorecard 395–397
the wrong management rises to the top
  393
there is never enough time to fully
  evaluate the target 394–395
Vodafone / Mannesmann
  (case study) 389
Team building,
  in-house training 214
  lessons from a world - class coach 207
  making the finance team a great place to
    work 207–215
  offsite team meeting (agenda) 213
  outdoor adventure learning 207–208
Technology
  seven technologies to understand
    and evaluate 53
Time sheets
  timing of 92
Toyota
  Toyota's 14 management principles
    189–193
Toyota management principles
  become a learning organization through
    relentless reflection and continuous
    improvement 192–193
  build a culture of stopping to fix problems
    to get quality right the first time 191
  help your extended network of partners
    and suppliers to improve 192
  help your extended network of partners
    and suppliers to improve 192
  level out the workload (Heijunka) 190
  make decisions slowly by consensus
    and then implement the decisions
    rapidly 192
  use visual control so no problems are
    hidden 191–192
Tufte, Edward 358

Ukleja, Mick 205

Value stream accounting 268–275

Walkabout 204–205
Waterman, Robert 358
Welch, Jack 154–155, 200, 203, 205, 214,
  257, 259

Zaffron, Steve 18, 20–21